ENVIRONMENT AND HUMAN RESPONSE
(Selected essays in geography)

Prof. (Mrs.) V.A. Janaki felicitation volume

ENVIRONMENT
AND
HUMAN RESPONSE

(Selected Essays in Geography)

Edited by

RAM NANDAN P. SINHA

CONCEPT PUBLISHING COMPANY, NEW DELHI-110059

ISBN-81-7022-243-5

First Published 1990

Published and Printed by
Ashok Kumar Mittal
Concept Publishing Company
A/15-16, Commercial Block, Mohan Garden,
NEW DELHI-110059 (India)

***Phones*: 25351460, 25351794**
***Fax*: 091-11-25357103**
***E-mail*: publishing@conceptpub.com**

V.A. JANAKI
(Born : 25 March, 1918)

Contents

List of Contributors xi
Preface xv
V.A. Janaki: a sketch xvii
Introduction xxi

PART I – **Environment**

1. An Appraisal of Urban Environment and Suggestions for Improvement of Kanpur Region : A Case Study
–*S.L. Kayastha* and *V.K. Kumra* 3

PART II – **Urban Geography**

2. Urban Systems and Urban Regions in Libya
–*Abdalla Misallati, Wilford A. Bladen* and *P.P. Karan* 27

3. Changes and Trends in the Urban Systems of Maharashtra : 1971-81
–*P.T. Malshe* 43

4. Population Density Changes in Dual City: Ankara, from 1961 to 1977.
–*John R. Clark* 65

5. Urban Sprawl: A Problem in Regional Development
–*A. Kumar* and *U.P. Singh* 83

6. Evolution of Ranchi City
–*R.N.P. Sharma* and *D.N. Singh* 95

PART III – **Population and Settlement Geography**

7. Process of Population Diffusion in Rural Areas and the Phenomenon of Hamletisation (with Reference to Maharashtra)
–Jaymala Diddee and *V.S. Datye* 105

8. Geographical Factors in the Location and Growth of Settlements in Rajasthan
–Arun Kaul 123

9. Impact of Out-Migration on Population Characteristics of South Konkan
–S.B. Sawant and *A.S. Bhole* 131

PART IV – **Marketing Geography**

10. Planning and Retailing in South Delhi: A Personal Appraisal
–Howard F. Hirt 151

11. Periodic Markets and Intra-Urban Mobility: A Case Study of Kanpur Metropolis
–R.C. Srivastava 157

PART V – **Economic Geography**

12. Road Pattern in Akola District, (Maharashtra)
–N.G. Jain 187

13. Industry and Segregation: A Case Study of Gaya (Bihar)
–Suman Kumar 199

PART VI – **Cultural Geography**

14. Religious Diversity Patterns: Rajasthan and India
–Ashok K. Dutt and *Allen G. Noble* 207

15. Geography of Crimes: A Study of Ahmedabad City
–K.M. Kulkarni 221

PART VII – **Historical Geography**

16. The Sources of Jadeite in Middle American Cultural Artifacts: A Geographical Approach
–*Paul B. Wilson* and *Darshan S. Kang* 235

17. Origin and Evolution of Urban Central Places in Uttar Pradesh
–*O.P. Singh* 251

18. Ports and Harbours of Shivaji's Kingdom
–*B.G. Tamaskar* 277

19. Geographical Boundary of Bharatvarsha in the Ramayan and the Mahabharata
–*Bhagwansingh Suryavanshi* 293

PART VIII – **Political Geography**

20. Mountain Boundaries: A Case Study of China-Pakistan Boundary
–*Sudeepta Adhikari* 303

21. Tribal Boundary Concepts: A Case Study in a Garo Village (India)
–*Ram Nandan P. Sinha* 315

PART IX – **Cartography**

22. Rural Settlement Mapping in India.
–*S.P. Das Gupta* 329

Research Publications of Prof. (Mrs.) V.A. Janaki 333
Index 335

List of Contributors

1. Dr. Abdulla Misallati,
   University of Elfatah, Tripoli (Libya).

2. Dr. Allen G. Noble,
   Professor and Head, Department of Geography,
   University of Akron, Ohio (U.S.A.)

3. Dr. Anil Kumar, Professor,
   P.G. Dept. of Geography, Bhagalpur University,
   Bhagalpur (Bihar)

4. Shri Arun Kaul,
   P.G. Dept. of Geography, Madhav College,
   Vikaram University, Ujjain (M.P.)

5. Shri A.S. Bhole,
   Lecturer in Geography, University of Poona,
   Pune, (Maharashtra)

6. Dr. Ashok K. Dutt,
   Prof. of Geography and Urban Studies,
   University of Akron, Ohio (U.S.A.)

7. Dr. Bhagawansinh Suryawanshi, Retd. Professor,
   Dept. of Ancient History and Archaeology,
   M.S. University, Baroda (Gujarat).

8. Dr. B.G. Tamaskar,
Retired Professor, Post-Graduate College,
Amravati (Maharashtra)

9. Dr. D.P. Singh,
Reader in Geography, Magadh University,
Bodh Gaya (Bihar)

10. Dr. Darshan S. Kang,
Asst. Professor, University of Montana,
Missoula, Montana (U.S.A.).

11. Dr. Howard S. Hirt
Professor of Geography, Framingham State College,
Framingham , Mass; (U.S.A.)

12. Dr. (Mrs.) Jayamala Diddee,
Reader in Geography,
University of Poona, Pune, (Maharashtra)

13. Dr. John R. Clark
Coordinator of Operation Research,
Graduate School of Arts and Sciences,
University of Harward,
Cambridge, Mass (U.S.A.)

14. Dr. K.M. Kulkarni, Reader,
Department of Geography,
School of Sciences, Gujarat University,
Ahmedabad (Gujarat)

15. Dr. N.G. Jain, Head,
P.G. Dept. of Geography, Nagpur Mahavidyalay,
Nagpur (Maharashtra)

16. Dr. O.P. Singh, Reader and Head,
Dept. of Geography,
Kumaun University, Nainital (U.P.)

17. Dr. Paul B. Wilson,
Dept. of Geography, University of Montana,
Missoula, Montana (U.S.A.)

18. Dr. Pradyumna P. Karan,
Professor of Geography, University of Kentucky,
Lexington, Ky (U.S.A.)

19. Dr. P.T. Malshe,
Reader in Geography,
University of Poona, Pune (Maharashtra).

20. Dr. R.C. Srivastava, Reader,
P.P.A. Post-graduate College,
Kanpur (U.P.)

21. Dr. Ram Nandan P. Sinha
Professor, Dept. of Geography,
M.S. University, Baroda (Gujarat),

22. Dr. R.N.P. Sharma, Professor of Geography
Magadh University,
Bodh Gaya (Bihar).

23. Dr. S.B. Sawant, Reader in Geography,
University of Poona,
Pune (Maharashtra).

24. Sri S.P. Das Gupta,
Ex. Director, National Atlas and
Thematic Mapping Organisation,
Calcutta (W.B.)

25. Dr. S.L. Kayastha, Retired Prof. of Geography,
Banaras, Hindu University,
Varanasi (U.P.)

26. Dr. Sudeepta Adhikari, Professor and Head,
Dept. of Geography,B. N. College, Patna University,
Patna (Bihar).

27. Sri Suman Kumar,
U. G. C. Research Fellow, Dept. of Geography,
Magadh University, Bodh-Gaya (Bihar)

28. Dr. U. P. Singh, Reader,
P. G. Dept. of Geography,
Bhagalpur University (Bihar)

29. Dr. V. K. Kumra, Lecturer,
Dept. of Geography, Banaras Hindu University,
Varanasi (U. P.)

30. Sri. V. S. Datye, Lecturer in Geography,
University of Poona,
Pune (Maharashtra)

31. Dr. Wilford A. Bladen, Professor of Geography
University of Kentucky, Lexington,
Kentucky (U. S. A.).

Preface

THIS volume presents a series of essays on varied sub-fields of geography through which runs a common thread of eternal geographic concern - human response to environment. This is in keeping with the varied interest of Mrs. V.A. Janaki, in whose felicitation this volume is being brought out. Being aware of the full breadth of the field of geography, she moved her pen with utmost ease from one sub-field to another, whether it be historical geography or political geography, economic geography or social geography, land use or urban geography, population geography or settlement geography. The quality and quantity of her publications listed in the pages following carry the justification for the publication of this sort of a collection.

This volume made possible by the contributions of eminent Indian and foreign geographers is offered with confidence that it will be welcomed by many as a very useful addition to the realm of geographical thought and practice – a compendium of geographic material of enduring significance.

While the intent is as much to honour a geographer as to serve the field of geography, publication of this collection is one of the means by which his colleagues in the Department of Geography of the Maharaja Sayajirao University of Baroda, Vadodara (Gujarat, India) wish to recognise Mrs. Janaki for her twenty-six years of service as the founder and builder, and twenty-one years as the Head of the Department.

Baroda, R. N. P. SINHA

V. A. Janaki : A Sketch

DEPARTMENT of Geography, Maharaja Sayajirao University of Baroda. 11.30 a.m. A chauffeur-driven white Fiat stops near the staircase. Out comes an elegant looking lady, clad in spotless white saree and blouse, a sleek wallet in her left hand, grave round face, penetrating scholarly eyes; negotiates the stairs with graceful medium pace steps and heads towards her chamber on the first floor of the three-storey building. This is Mrs. Vengalil Achyutha Menon Janaki, the Head of the Department. She sits in her chamber guiding both teachers and students in their research; engaging herself in her own scholarly research and publication; promoting geographic education; and disseminating geographic knowledge, helping scholars from sister disciplines. At 4.30 p.m. her chauffeur knocks at the door. She folds her papers, comes out of her chamber, descends the stairs in measured paces, steps into the car which heads towards Pro-Vice-Chancellor's bungalow situated in Chameli Baug, for she resided there with her husband Prof. Suresh Sethna, the P. V. C. of the University. This familiar scene I had been witnessing being repeated every working day with such a clock-like precision for three years from August 1980 to March 1983, that sometimes I feel the same car will stop and she will come out to carry on her usual academic pursuits. But no, she no longer comes to the Department, no longer resides in the Chameli Baug bungalow, for her husband, Prof. Sethna, retired from service and after some time abandoned his mortal coil to attend to his assignment in the World Eternal. She now resides in her bungalow at New Sama Road which has turned into a pilgrimage for geographers coming to Baroda from India and abroad. She is leading the life of a modernised hermit sitting alone amidst her life-long companion : books and magazines; reading, recollecting, contemplating, the serenity interrupted only by occasional visitors friends, admirers, seekers of knowledge.

Looking back over the records of Indian geography, during the years in which she involved herself in the profession, I am struck by the number of different aspects in which Mrs. Janaki has made outstanding contribution to the field. All the varied works are recorded in the list of her publications. For Mrs. Janaki has been a prolific writer, recognising that what is taught in the class or presented orally at a meeting but remains unpublished will in a very short time perish. That the publications vary greatly in level of consideration is a reflection of the variety of professional purposes she aimed at. From this point of view she stands apart as a collossus, head and shoulders above any lady, and many other, geographers of India.

Mrs. Janaki's career as a teacher of undergraduate students began thirty-three years ago in 1952 when she joined M. S. University as a founder lecturer in geography. Prior to that she had received her M. A. degree from Madras University in 1941, where she did further P. G. Courses till 1943. She went to Oxford to get her B. Litt. degree in 1950, whereafter she did some courses at Cambridge for two years from 1950 to 1952. She took to teaching in the University immediately after her return from abroad. She started post-graduate classes in the department in 1957, was promoted to the rank of Reader the same year and became Professor in 1963. She put in twenty-six years of dedicated and distinguished service in the department retiring on 31st March, 1978. But she continued to serve the department till 31st March 1983 under the U. G. C. Retired Teachers' Scheme during which period she authored Economic Geography, a text book for P.G. students.

Prof. Janaki has been very shy of any sort of publicity. She believes in quiet work and selfless service. Though she has been a member of the Indian National Committee on Geography and has served as the paper setter and examiner of the Union Public Service Examinations for several terms, hardly anybody knows about it. She started the Geography Department in Baroda which was the first in Gujarat. She, and through her the Geography Department of M. S. U., Baroda, served as the fountainhead of inspiration of geography teaching and research in the State and whatever has been achieved in the field of geography in the State owes to her groundwork and planning.

Lest I am accused of bias in my assessment of the qualities of her head and heart, I could do no better than place here verbatim the full text of a letter received from Madam Maria Renee Cura, a leading geographer of Argentina.

V. A. JANAKI : A GREAT FRIEND

November 1968. In India was held the XXI International Geographical Congress and in Baroda the Symposium on *Rural Settlements*. It was, also, my first trip to India.

For me, to know India in her geographical aspects have been to know V. A. Janaki in the Department of Geography of M. S. University of Baroda. From the very beginning of our first meeting I found in V. A. Janaki all the characteristics of a very good geographer and almost at the same time I felt she would be a great friend.

After the Symposium her letters to my country, the so far away Argentina, and also some of her publications about the Historical Geography of India have been very useful for me in my lectures at the University. Because, they are very good researches and also because they bring to us, the Latin Americans, a new point of view about the History and the Geography of India, new and different from the Western point of view of the Western historians.

Four years later I came back to India and almost directly to Baroda. The purpose was to study the rural development, especially in the villages near Baroda city. The teacher : V. A. Janaki. With her I went to the villages all the days during more than one month. With her I have shared very good moments and I have learned many things – many important things-about India. All the professors from the Department of Geography, the cartographers and the driver (the same driver I met 8 years later) and the same professors – we have seen and learned with V. A. Janaki in the villages, and also during those wonderful trips to Rajkot, Jamnagar, Baroch. Always learning. Always sharing.

I could say and write much more if I could do it in Spanish, my mother tongue. But I think that the most important here is to let a warrant of the personality of V. A. Janaki : a great person, a great friend.

Buenos Aires, Argentina MARIA RENEE CURA

Introduction

In the opening article "An appraisal of urban environment and suggestions for improvement of Kanpur Region : a case study", Prof. S. L. Kayastha and Dr. V. K. Kumra deal with one of the most absorbing probelms of our time, environmental pollution. They have studied the causes and the present status of the environmental pollution in Kanpur city and suggested remedial and precautionary measures in the wider context of comprehensive integrated planning of the Kanpur Region as a whole.

The next Chapter on Urban Geography consists of five articles : two on urban systems, two on urban population and one on evolution of an urban centre. In the article "Urban systems and urban regions in Libya" Dr. Misallati, Dr. Balden and Dr. Karan, after reviewing the evolution of urbanisation in Libya, study the contemporary pattern and analyse the distribution of cities in the light of Jefferson's "Law of the Primate City' and Zipf's rank-size rule. Finally, on the basis of dependency relationships of urban places in Libya, they have delimited the hinterland of Tripoli Region. In the next article "Changes and trends in the urban systems of Maharashtra" Dr. Malshe, analyses the structural changes in the urban systems of Maharashtra that have occurred during the decade 1971-1981, in relation to the relevant physical and cultural factors. The article by Dr. Clark traces the spatial extension of Ankara's population between 1961 and 1977 particularly in relation to two goals : reduction in the number of people living in substandard housing, and the distribution of population more evenly by distance from the centre. The degree of success in the second goal has been measured with density gradient model. Compared to this, the next article by Dr. Kumar and Singh examines and analyses the urban sprawl in the Bokaro Coalfields taking the urban centre of Kuzu as an example. They have highlighted the problems the urban sprawl has created in the of regional planning and have suggested some measures to integrated the urban sprawls into the planning format of the region. In the last article of this Chapter, Dr. Sharma and Dr. Singh have traced the evolution of Ranchi city, its morphological and functional structure, in the light of the relative influence of the different factors–physical, economic and cultural.

The third Chapter on Population and Settlement Geography contains three articles. The first, "Process of Population Diffusion in Rural Areas and the Phenomenon of Hamletisation" concerns, as the title suggests, both population and settlements, in which Dr. (Mrs.) Jayamata Diddee and Shri V. S. Datye have tried to find a correlation between growth of population in the villages and its diffusion on the one hand and formation of satellite rural settlements on the other. They investigated, in the district of Poona in Maharashtra State, the proces of hamlet formation on a broader frame and have taken a close-up view of a village for in depth study and verification of their observations. The second article deals with settlements only. In this Shri Arun Kaul and urban settlements in the State of Rajasthan. The third article by Dr. Sawant and Dr. Bhole is concerned only with population in which the authors have studied the impact of out-migration on the population characteristics of the villages of South Konkan. They have taken sex-composition to represent the conditions created by sustained and large scale out-migration. Different factors contributing towards the disturbed sex-composition have been analysed with the help of a correlation matrix.

The fourth Chapter on Marketing Geography consists of two articles: one dealing with retailing in South Delhi and the other with periodic markets in Kanpur city. Dr. Hirt in his article "Planning and retailing in South Delhi : a personal appraisal" tries to spell out the economic, administrative, conceptual and cultural factors that have led to the proliferation of "informal" or "unorganised" sector in retailing business in the city and wishes to develop a technique for optimising the numbers, types and location of shops in the lowest level of the retail hierarchy. Dr. Srivastava, on the other hand, aims in his article, "Periodic markets and intra-urban mobility", to recognise the importance of periodic market trader and consumer movements as a part of intra-urban mobility in Kanpur metropolis. He analyses in detail the role of travel patterns of the consumers and traders, identifies the factors affecting their travel decisions and examines the relative degree of interdependence between such markets and the existing business structure of the city.

In Chapter five there are two articles on Economic Geography. Dr. Jain in his article "Road Pattern in Akola District, Maharashtra" determines the path orders with the help of Strahler's method of stream order and correlates the path orders with the levels of economic development of the micro-regions of the district. In the other article, "Industry and Segregation : a case study of Gaya, Bihar", Shri Kumar measures degree of segregation of industries of Gaya town on the basis of plant ownership and input and after correlating this with profitability finds that there is a negative relationship between the two.

Chapter six carries two articles pertaining to cultural geography. One by Dr. Dutt and Dr. Noble studies the religious diversity patterns of Rajasthan using the Index of Diversity employed by Shortridge, and after relating it to all-India pattern confirms the observation of Brush and Davis that peripheral areas demonstrate greater diversity, whereas centralised location illustrate greater unity or homogeneity. In the next article Dr. Kulkarni aims to understand the spatial pattern of crime in Ahmedabad city in the background of its socio-economic environment and confirms the generaly held belief that the high incidence of crimes is related to religious diversity, high population density, substandard housing, high dependency ratio and high proportion of females.

The seventh Chapter contains four articles falling within the field of Historical Geography. In the first article Dr. Wilson and Dr. Kang have tried to trace the possible sources of the Jadeite variety of the gem stone, jade, which is found widely scattered as artifact in Middle America. After investigating various historical, geological and mineralogical evidences the authors have come to the conclusion that their possible sources are the Orient (Burma and China), California and Middle America, the last being the most likely source. In the second article Dr. O. P. Singh analyses the evolutional characteristics of urban central places of Uttar Pradesh in the context of the prevailing historical circumstances in the three major historical periods, Ancient, Medieval and Modern. He has summarised his findings in the form of a model showing the influence of prominent factors in the process of their origin and growth. In the third article Prof. Tamaskar locates, studies and classifies the ports and harbours of Shivaji's kingdom and assesses the relative significance of his maritime activities and maritime policy. In the fourth article, Dr. Suryawanshi goes still further behind time to probe into the obscure recessses of the past and tries of fix the boundaries of ancient India as evidenced in the texts of Valmiki's Ramayan and Mahabharat.

The eighth Chater contains two politico-geographical papers dealing with boundaries. The one by Dr. Adhikari discusses the characteristics of mountain boundaries and examines in this context in detail the evolution and characteristics of the China-Pakistan boundary in north-western Kashmir. The other deals with the concept of linear boundary prevalent among the Garos of Meghalaya. In this paper Dr. Sinha has tried by his investigation to correct the assumption of Western Political Geographers, the primitive societies under their 'tribal' political systems have no concept of linear boundaries; but only of boundary zones or frontiers.

The concluding Chapter on Cartography has one article in which Sri Das Gupta explains the technique of mapping the rural settlements in India adopted by the National Atlas and Thematic Mapping Organisationn, Calcutta. This technique is suited to the special Indian environmental conditions.

PART – I

ENVIRONMENT

ONE

S.L. Kayastha and **V.K. Kumra**

An Appraisal of Urban Environment and Suggestions for Improvement of Kanpur Region: A Case Study

Introduction

AN explosive increase in population growth and rapid industrialization have together caused havoc in the human adjustment to urban as well as rural environment. This has been reflected in two forms in the social context: more people are ill-housed, mal-nourished and under-privileged than ever before; and a continuous degradation of environment has taken place. The urban dwellers, especially those in the middle and lower income-groups, are increasingly found living in wretchedly over-crowded and polluted areas of cities, which have rightly been called "Miseropolis".[1] Such an emerging Miseropolis is Kanpur, in Kanpur region. With the premise that the urban environment may continue to deteriorate even beyond the permissible limit, an appraisal of environment of Kanpur region, especially of the Kanpur city, becomes essential.

The Region

The Kanpur region, extends from 25°3′N to 27°37′N latitude and 79°E to 81°15′E longitude. It comprises all of the Kanpur, Farrukhabad, Etawah, Jalaun, and Hamirpur districts excluding Khaga tehsil, Banda district excluding Mau and Karwi tehsils and a narrow stretch of land lying to the south of Unnao and Hardoi road of Hardoi district (Fig. 1.1). Physically, the region can be divided into two major regions, the Ganga plain, and the northern fringe of Vindhyan plateau.

FIG. 1.1:

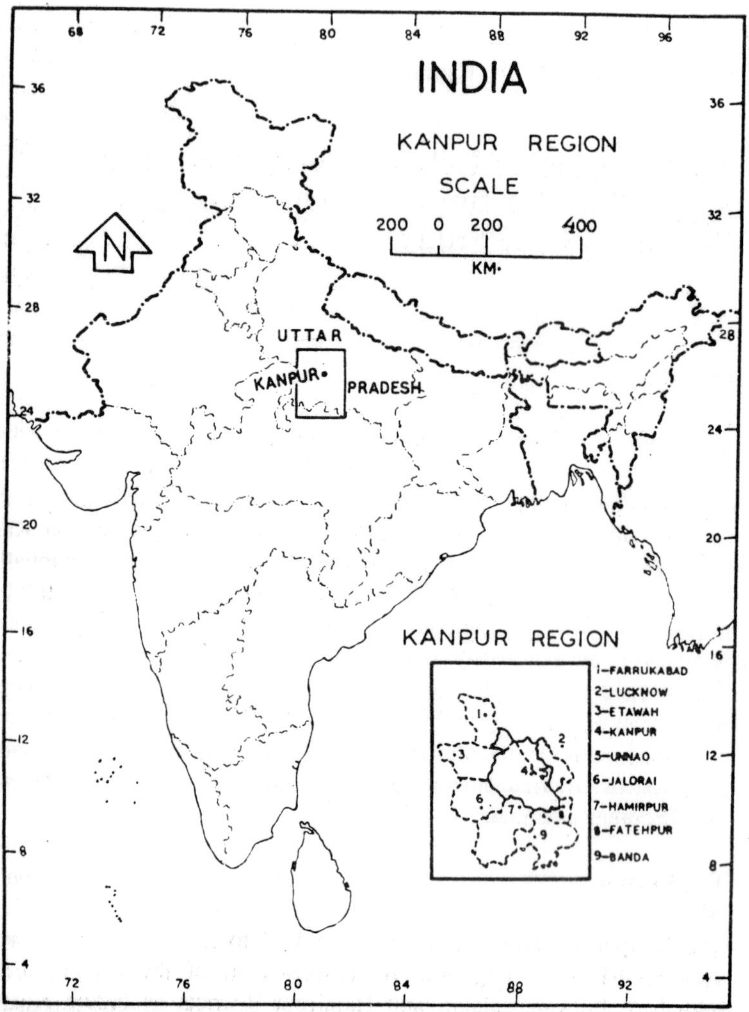

The area lying to the north of River Jamuna is a part of monotonous Ganga plain, which is the result of detritus brought by the River Ganga and Jamuna from the Himalayas. The area lying to the south of Jamuna in a part of transition zone between the Ganga plain and Peninsular India and shares the characteristics of both.

This region does not possess any significant mineral resource and is primarily agricultural. The soil, the climate, and the potential availability of water promise a considerable increase in agricultural productivity, provided proper inputs are available. Thus the new industrialisation has to be based on sound agricultural prosperity. Mainly three types of industries appear to have considerable prospect of growth in the region; (i) industries supplying inputs required for raising agricultural productivity; (ii) industries for processing agricultural produce; and (iii) industries catering to the final consumer demands of a prospering agrarian community. In the light of these prospects, the areal delimitation should take into account not only the existing ties between Kanpur and rural population of the surrounding region, but also the role of Kanpur as a positive factor in the progress of the region, and all possible increase in agricultural productivity.

In terms of population, only 16.24% is urban, which, however, is higher than the 13.0% for the whole of U.P. Almost all of this urban population is concentrated in the Kanpur city (1.27 million in 1971), although there are in addition to this, other small urban centres in the region. Among all the districts, which come under Kanpur region, Kanpur district has maximum urban population (42.79%). Occupationally, the region is rural with 88% of the labour force engaged in agriculture. Only 5.94% of the total workers are engaged in household industry, while 5.02% are engaged in manufacturing activities. Kanpur district has maximum working force with 14.12% of the total workers engaged in manufacturing activities.

Kanpur is the most congested urban centre in the Kanpur region. As the premier service centre, it provides services to the markets and population living in the surrounding rural part of the region. In addition to this, due to its industrial character, it has also attracted population from rural areas of the region. About 36.96% of the total population of Kanpur city comprises of migrants mainly from different parts of the region, as well as some from other parts of the country. This rapid migration to urban centre of Kanpur has in turn created several urban problems such as insanitary conditions, haphazard and wasteful use of land, over-crowding and unemployment which all too frequently characterise major urban centres of the developing world. Above all, this unhealthy urban development in Kanpur city, the centre for the services to whole region, has contributed to the environmental pollution of the surrounding areas. This is mainly because of industrialisation and migration in only Kanpur city and not so in other towns of the region, though the region has potential for agro-based industries.

To analyse the problem of urban environment, geographical analysis of various attributes such as population, air, water and solid-wastes has been made. For this purpose Kanpur city has been taken as the specific area in this region and a scientific study has been made.

Kanpur: The City

Kanpur is the largest city of Uttar Pradesh, located on the right bank of River Ganga. Its population in 1971 was about 1.5 million which was 9,71,062 in 1961 and by 2001 A.D. it will be about 3 million.[2] The central part of the city is very much congested with a population density of more than 35,000 persons per sq. km, while the outskirts, covering mostly agricultural land have below 5000 persons per sq. km.. There are about 600 small and heavy industries. Among different types of industries located in and around the city are: 48 tanneries, one fertiliser industry, 10 textile mills, 2 jute mills, 3 woollen mills, 25 chemical and pharmaceutical factories and several other small-scale industries such as flour and oil mills. It is estimated that about 1.25 million tonnes of coal along with huge amount of gasoline are consumed annually for various industrial purposes, causing severe environmental pollution in the city. Ganga and Pandu rivers are the main sources of water for the city as well as other parts of the regions. Due to high consumption of water for domestic and industrial purposes, these rivers receive huge amounts of waste water every day, contributing several toxic pollutants to river water. As it is the main service centre for the region, traffic flow is very high in certain parts of the city causing air and noise pollution. In addition to this, huge amounts of garbage is disposed of every day in the streets of the city which not only create nuisance but also cause severe health problems. It has been attempted to evaluate some of the environmental problems separately in detail.

Air Pollution

The main sources of air pollution in the city are power plants, industries and automobiles. In addition to this, burning of fuel and garbage serve as secondary sources. These sources emit huge amounts of sulphurdioxide, oxides of nitrogen, carbon monoxide, hydrocarbons, dust particles and aldehydes. The main source of carbonmonoxide, oxides of nitrogen and hydrocarbons are automobiles which are the main transportation system of the city. The city is well connected with the surrounding parts of the region by roads, which causes high traffic density varying from 500 vehicles per hour at I.I.T. Crossing located in the outermost part of the city, to 2500 vehicles per hour at Parade Crossing, the most congested part of the city.

FIG. 1.2:

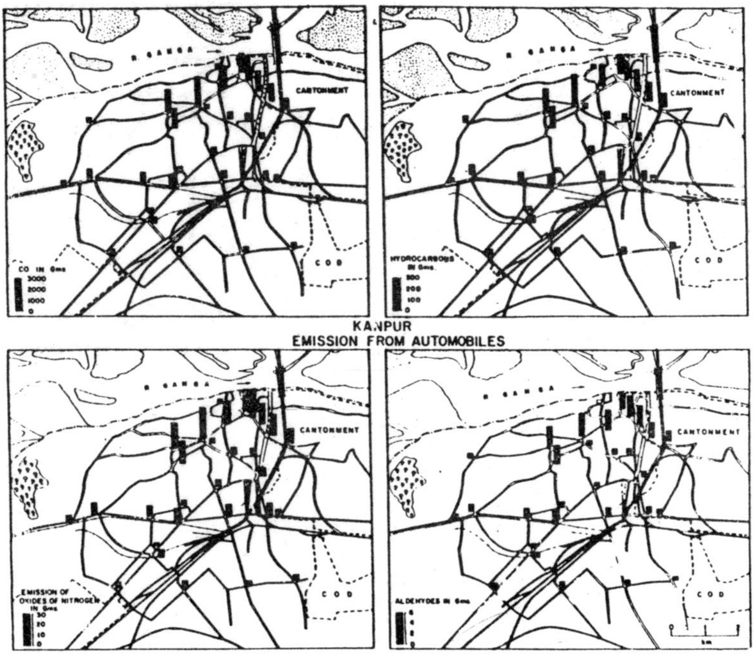

Due to variation in traffic density, the emission of exhaust gases also varies from one crossing to another. Fig. 1.2 shows the total emission of exhaust gases at various crossings of the city, calculated on the basis of standards prescribed by National Environmental Engineering Research Institute, Nagpur, considering the traffic density. Total emission of CO varies from 250.56 gm at Parachute Crossing to 2404.32 gm at Parade Crossing. Similarly total emission of hydrocarbons varies

FIG. 1.3:

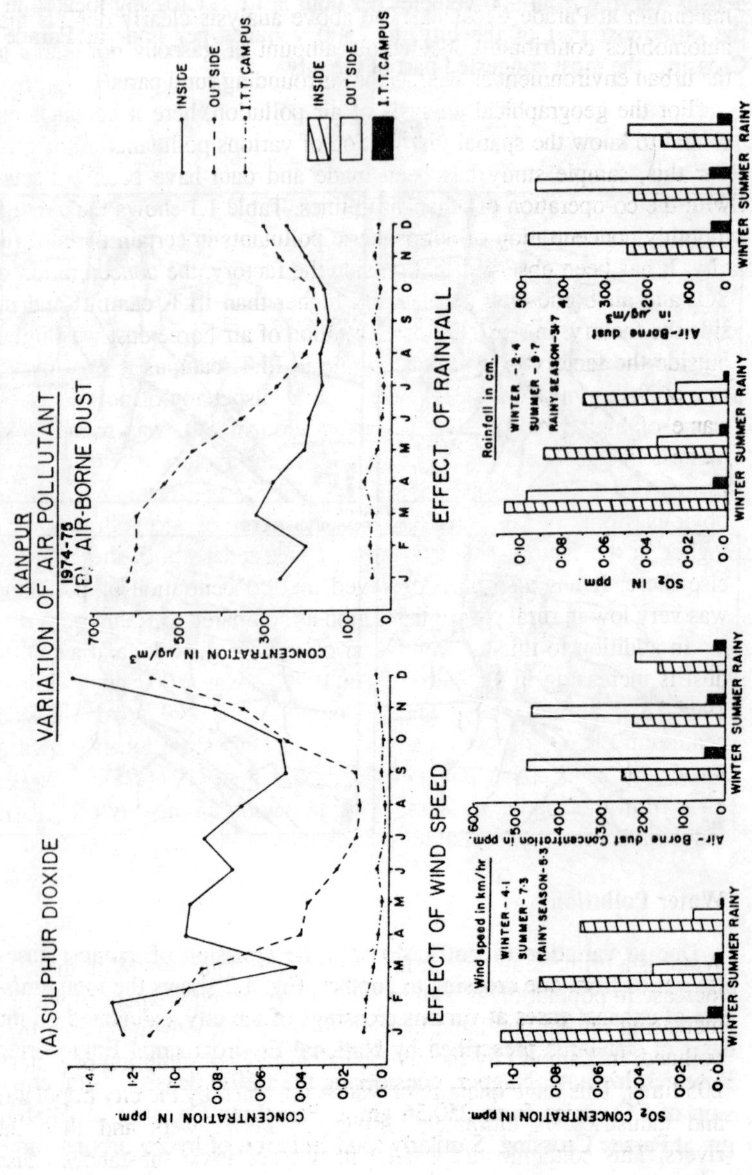
KANPUR
VARIATION OF AIR POLLUTANT
1974-75
(A) SULPHUR DIOXIDE
(B) AIR-BORNE DUST
INSIDE
OUT SIDE
I.T.T. CAMPUS
CONCENTRATION IN ppm.
CONCENTRATION IN µg/m³
J F M A M J J A S O N D
EFFECT OF WIND SPEED
EFFECT OF RAINFALL
Wind speed in km/hr
WINTER - 4·1
SUMMER - 7·3
RAINY SEASON - 5·3
Rainfall in cm.
WINTER - 2·4
SUMMER - 9·7
RAINY SEASON - 31·7
SO2 CONCENTRATION IN ppm.
Air - Borne dust Concentration in ppm
SO2 IN ppm
Air-Borne dust in µg/m³
WINTER SUMMER RAINY

from crossing to crossing. It was found to be maximum (258.72 gm) at Parade while minimum at Parachute Crossing. It is evident from the Fig. 1.2 that the level of pollution due to automobiles was found to be maximum at Parade Crossing. The above analysis clearly depicts that automobiles contribute considerable amount of gaseous pollutants to the urban environment as well as the surrounding rural parts.

For the geographical analysis of air pollution, here it becomes essential to know the spatial distribution of various pollutants in the city. For this, sample study has been made and data have been collected with the co-operation of other disciplines. Table 1.1 shows the average monthly concentration of atmospheric pollutants in certain parts of the city. It has been observed that outside the factory, the concentration of SO_2 and air-borne dust is relatively higher than I.I.T. campus and inside the factory. In April the concentration of air-borne dust was higher outside the factory (536 $\mu g/m^3$), while in I.I.T. campus it was lowest, i.e., 66.96 $\mu g/m^3$ (Fig. 1.3). This is due to dispersion of pollutants because of high wind velocity. Concentration of SO_2 was found to be highest in the month of December inside the factory (0.149 ppm) in comparison to other zones (0.113 ppm outside the factory). Thus it is obvious from the analysis that concentration of air pollutants was higher in the factory area as well as congested parts of the city than elsewhere. It has also been observed that concentration of pollutants was very low in rural part of the region as compared to Kanpur city.

In addition to this, concentration of sulphur dioxide, and air-borne dust is increasing in Kanpur city. In 1971, it was 0.007 ppm while in 1974-75 it became 0.010 ppm in purely residential area. The concentration of SO_2 has also increased in the industrial locality such as Fazalganj from 0.055 ppm (1971) to 0.074 ppm (1974-75). Thus it is clear from the spatial variation of air pollutants in the city that due to industrialization the level of air pollution has considerably increased.

Water Pollution

Water is a prime requirement for every living organism. With the rapid increase in population as well as industries, the requirement of water is increasing on the one hand; and on the other, it is being increasingly polluted. In Kanpur city the per capita per day consumption of water is 205 litres. This huge quantity of water consumed by the city population and industries, is ultimately discharged into sewers and then into rivers. This contaminated water with various toxic substances causes pollution of river water, which affects mostly the population living along River Ganga in the downstream, and this part of Kanpur region suffers from river water pollution.

TABLE 1.1: Monthly Average Concentration of SO_2 and Air-borne Dust in the Ambient Air

Months	Atmospheric Pollutants					
	Inside the factory		Outside the factory		I.I.T. Kanpur campus	
	SO_2 (ppm)	Air borne dust ($\mu g/m^3$)	SO_2 (ppm)	Air borne dust ($\mu g/m^3$)	SO_2 (ppm)	Air-borne dust ($\mu g/m^3$)
January	0.125	261.49	0.112	619.17	0.011	44.81
February	0.130	197.54	0.099	601.36	0.010	49.58
March	0.044	322.48	0.088	601.00	0.007	44.85
April	0.096	283.44	0.041	536.00	0.005	66.96
May	0.094	203.29	0.038	469.21	0.003	36.26
June	0.074	194.65	0.025	359.70	0.006	25.55
July	0.088	163.04	0.016	273.01	0.002	23.74
August	0.070	176.29	0.014	205.41	0.001	36.21
September	0.049	149.97	0.016	176.59	0.004	42.85
October	0.051	158.24	0.048	189.81	0.003	28.06
November	0.083	205.77	0.069	269.79	0.005	43.50
December	0.149	249.88	0.113	302.10	0.006	38.11

Source: Department of Social and Preventive Medicine, Medical College, Kanpur, 1974-75.

It has been estimated that at present about 40 million gallons of waste water per day is discharged into River Ganga which was only 30 million gallons per day in 1964-65. This is due to the growth of urbanization and industrialization mainly in past four decades in Kanpur city. At the same time owing to the maximum use of river water upstream for irrigating fields, flow of water has declined so much that the river front near the city has remained grossly polluted for years, thereby causing deterioration in the quality of water downstream.

To know the characteristics of Ganga water as it is the main source of water supply of the city, and parts of the region, data have been collected. Table 1.2 shows that pH of river water fluctuated within the narrow range of 7.20 to 7.65. It was 7.5 at Jajmau where the main sewage outfall joins the river. It is evident from the table that mean value of BOD was lowest (2.86 mg/l) at Bithoorghat while maximum (30.33 mg/l) at Bengalighat. In addition to this, it has been also observed that level of pollution has been increasing during the past 10 years. Fig. 1.4 shows that concentration of toxic pollutants is not more population combined with the far reaching effects of a rapid rise in national, as well as individual wealth, are expected to maintain high rate of natural growth over the next two decades. This growth is currently estimated at 3.9 percent per year. Adding to this growth will be worker immigration to meet Libya's manpower needs. As a result the total population is expected to reach 6 million before the year 2000. The proportion of Libya's population residing in towns with 20,000 or more people is expected to rise to about 76 percent by 2000. If such a projection proves valid, it will result in a major increase of Libya's population over the next twenty years.

FIG. 2.2:

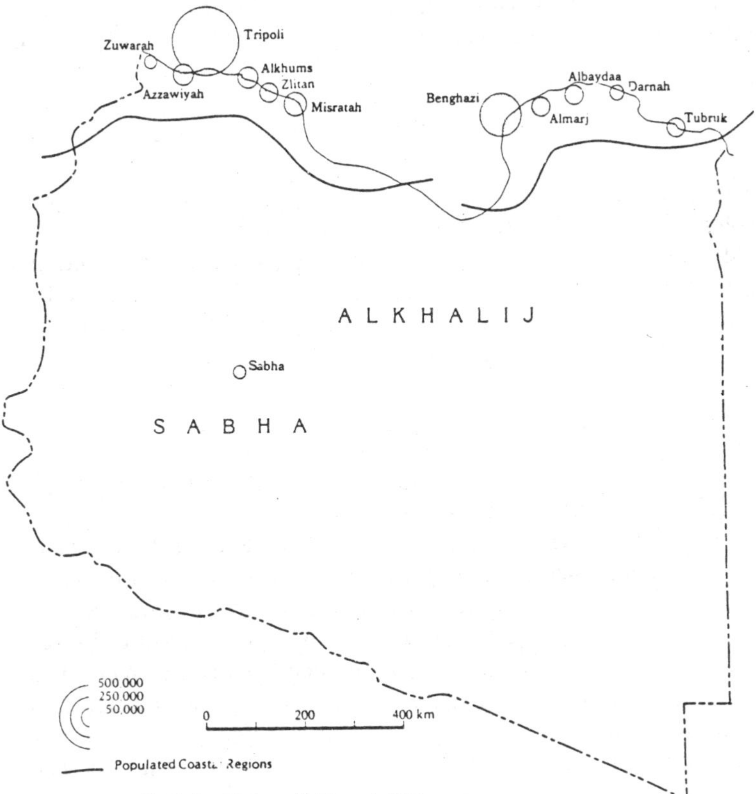

The Regional Pattern of Settlements, 1979

The levels of urban and economic development in Libya show extreme spatial and regional imbalances. The two coastal regions of Tripoli and Benghazi, with less than 10 percent of the total areas of the nation, accounted in 1973 for over 90 percent of the total population, and fourteen of the fifteen towns with 10,000 population size or over (Tables 2.1 and 2.2).[10] Here also was 85 percent of the nations's agricultural production; 96 percent of all livestock; and 95 percent of all electric power production.[11] Most of Libya's little urbanized and less developed areas are located in areas to the south. (Fig. 2.2)

Among the two macro-regions, the Tripoli region dominates the country in terms of urban and economic development. The Benghazi region is smaller in its agricultural base, although numbers of livestock are large. The Sabha region lacks a well developed industrial infrastructure, while Al Khalij is poorly developed in all aspects of infrastructural developments, particularly in terms of water, electric supply and adequacy of roads.

Within the Tripoli region, spatial development is characterized by the extreme dominance of Tripoli; pronounced spatial differentiation in development levels, and specialization among subregions. All of these are signs of a higher degree of spatial interaction and hierarchical integration. Tripoli's population increased from 130,000 in 1954 to 550,438 in 1973. A number of other growing urban centres within 50 to 60 kilometres of Tripoli reflect the enormous social and economic importance of the Tripoli region. They are emerging around Tripoli whose attraction is already powerful and gaining momentum.

The Distribution of Cities by Sizes

One way of investigating the process of urban growth and development in a country is to examine the system of cities in terms of their size and distribution. This analysis may shed light on questions about the nature of the historical process of urbanization and development. It can certainly be used to identify specific growth points within the urban hierarchy. In this case, it may be a fruitful way to examine Tripoli in the context of the regional system of cities and assess its role in urban development. Figures 2.3 and 2.4 illustrate the size of urban population of 1973 in the western and eastern parts of the nation.

The whose idea of city-size distribution is an exceedingly complex one. Many of the issues and questions relating to "primary"[12] and "rank-size" as concepts for describing systems of cities within a given country continue to be unresolved.

than the tolerance limit except at Bengali and Jajmaughats. To know the degree of pollution, composite deviation index has been calculated from deviation indices for selected parameters for every ghat. Fig. 1.4 shows that the degree of pollution at Jajmaughat is highest (1.169), and lowest at Bithoorghat (0.710). The analysis reveals that there is low level of water pollution at Bithoorghat and medium level of pollution at Bhairon, Ganga, Guptar, and Kanjara Kabilaghats, while it is medium high at Jajmau and Bengali ghats. No ghat represents high degree of pollution. Therefore, over all characteristics of River Ganga water showed that if the rate of pollution continues, the region has to face a very acute problem.

FIG. 1.4:

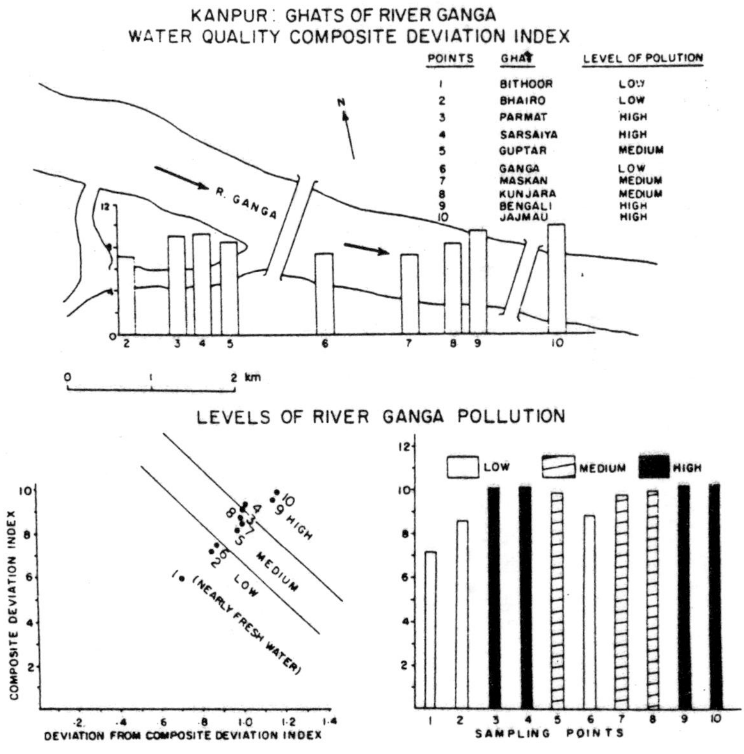

FIG. 1.5:

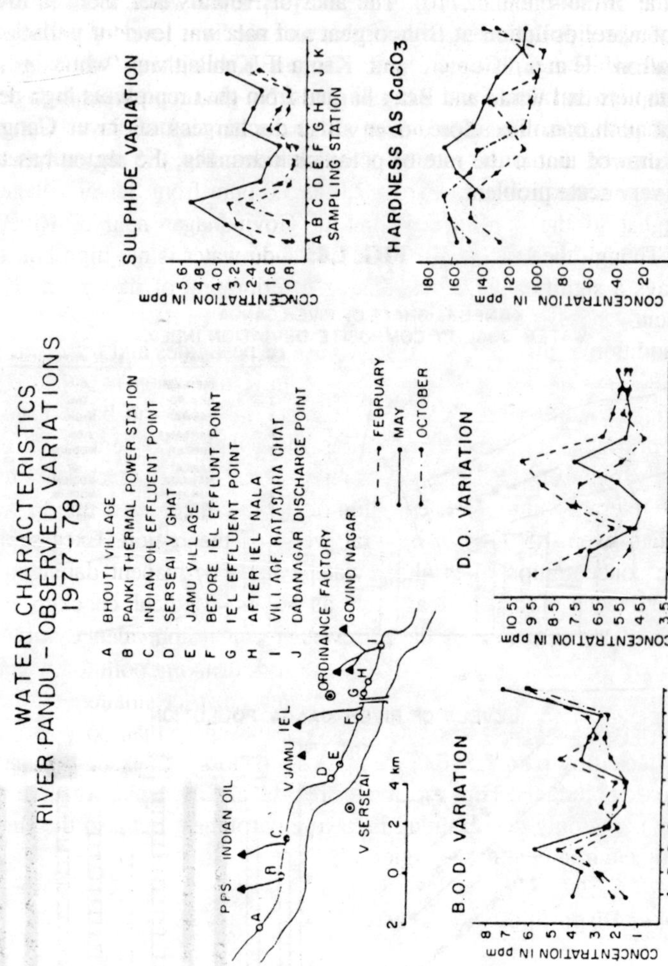

WATER CHARACTERISTICS
RIVER PANDU - OBSERVED VARIATIONS
1977 - 78
A BHOUTI VILLAGE
B PANKI THERMAL POWER STATION
C INDIAN OIL EFFLUENT POINT
D SERSEAI V GHAT
E JAMU VILLAGE
F BEFORE IEL EFFLUNT POINT
G IEL EFFLUENT POINT
H AFTER IEL NALA
I VILLAGE RATASARA GHAT
J DADANAGAR DISCHARGE POINT
ORDINANCE FACTORY
GOVIND NAGAR
FEBRUARY
MAY
OCTOBER
P.P.S. INDIAN OIL
V JAMU IEL
V SERSEAI
0 2 4 km
SULPHIDE VARIATION
HARDNESS AS $CaCO_3$
D.O. VARIATION
B.O.D. VARIATION
CONCENTRATION IN ppm
SAMPLING STATION

As River Pandu also receives huge amounts of waste water from Indian Explosives Limited and domestic waste water from Govindnagar and other localities of the city, it becomes necessary to evaluate physio-chemical characteristics of Pandu water. Fig. 1.5 shows the physio-chemical characteristics of Pandu water. Concentration of total solids upstream of confluence of nala was found to be only 0.22 mg/l, while at a distance of 1 km from IEL nala it was 0.407 mg/l, which depicts that waste water discharged from the urea plant has high contamination of solids. The industry also discharges urea in its water in the form of ammonia, nitrates and sulphides. Fig. 1.5 depicts that sulphide concentration varies from 2.0 to 5.0 ppm from Sersai village bathingghat to the confluence point of Govindnagar nala of River Pandu. Though the level of pollution of Pandu water is not high but it also plays a significant role in causing deterioration of the urban environment.

In addition to this, due to excessive use of pesticides and fertilizers, ground water sources, mainly well water, have also been found to be contaminated with pollutants like alkalinity, fluorides and bacteria. A survey of well-water of a few villages showed that concentration of chloride varies from 62.25 to 256.00 mg/l in well-water, which is more than the tolerance limit. Concentration of fluoride has been found to be more than even 1.5 mg/l in several wells of the region. Excess of flouride concentration in drinking water causes permanent damaging effect on teeth of children as well as adults. Medical checkup of children of a few sample villages revealed that its prevalence varies from 40 to 75%.[3] Along with this, the effect of drinking polluted water has also been observed in a village of Unnao district situated on the bank of River Ganga. It has been observed that more than 55 persons were affected by paralysis due to high concentration of sulphides and other toxic pollutants. Thus the above analysis clearly depicts that Kanpur city is not only deteriorating its own environment but also the surrounding environment of the region.

Improper Disposal of Solid Waste

Solid waste disposal is a pressing problem now-a-days not only in Kanpur city but also in Kanpur region. Here attention has been paid towards the problem of disposal of solid wastes in the Kanpur city. It has been observed that improper disposal of garbage in the city has created unpleasant look and bad odour. About 2,28,830 tonnes of

TABLE 1.2: Showing Characteristics of River Ganga Water at Kanpur City

Parameter	Bithoorghat	Bhaironghat	Parmatghat	Sarsaiyaghat	Guptarghat	Gangaghat	Maskarghat	Kunjara Kabila ghat	Bengali ghat	Jajmau ghat
TemperaturełC	24.0	24.8	25.6	25.7	24.5	21.8	22.71	23.0	22.5	22.5
pH	7.50	7.23	7.57	7.50	7.65	7.40	7.58	7.48	7.56	7.5
Odour	Odourless	Odourless	Musty	Musty	Unpleasant	Unpleasant	Unpleasant	Fishy	Musty	Fishy
Turbidity (mg/l)	33.16	58.66	181.25	179.14	140.5	89.66	64.28	107.66	279.60	205.54
Total solids (mg/l)	66.66	76.66	154.75	144.70	137.5	118.33	160.00	170.00	173.30	154.33
Hardness (mg/l)	115.33	126.60	130.00	140.20	137.12	118.33	156.85	130.83	151.30	160.30
Nitrate Nitrogen (mg/l)	Nil	0.004	0.118	0.027	0.13	0.005	0.016	0.13	0.818	0.013
Chloride (mg/l)	9.33	9.83	15.5	15.57	17.37	13.00	13.42	13.16	13.16	13.88
D.O. (mg/l)	5.5	4.96	3.73	4.34	3.05	5.2	4.74	4.70	4.98	5.66
B.O.D. (mg/l)	2.86	27.63	29.25	27.34	29.1	17.0	29.70	26.6	30.33	21.06
C.O.D. (mg/l)	0.66	14.0	76.75	89.14	32.12	12.0	22.85	19.5	69.1	17.85
Sulphate (mg/l)	21.66	38.33	151.2	74.28	142.5	55.0	91.42	70.0	106.66	233.33
Chromium (mg/l)	Nil	Nil	Nil	Nil	Nil	Nil	Nil	Nil	Nil	Absent
Total Colifurm Bacteria (MPN)	80	506.80	1112.5	1171.42	1396.87	105.2	839.00	845.8	966.61	800.
Distance in km	0	11.0	13.0	14.0	15.0	15.5	17.5	19.0	20.0	21.0
Outfall	—	Outfall between site & 2 & 3	Outfall between 3 & 4	—	Lower Ganges Canal between 5 & 6	Outfall between 6 & 7	Outfall between site 7 & 8	Tannery waste outfall between 8 & 9	Tannery out all	

Source: Department of Social and preventive Medicine, Medicine, Medical College, Kanpur.

FIG. 1.6.A:

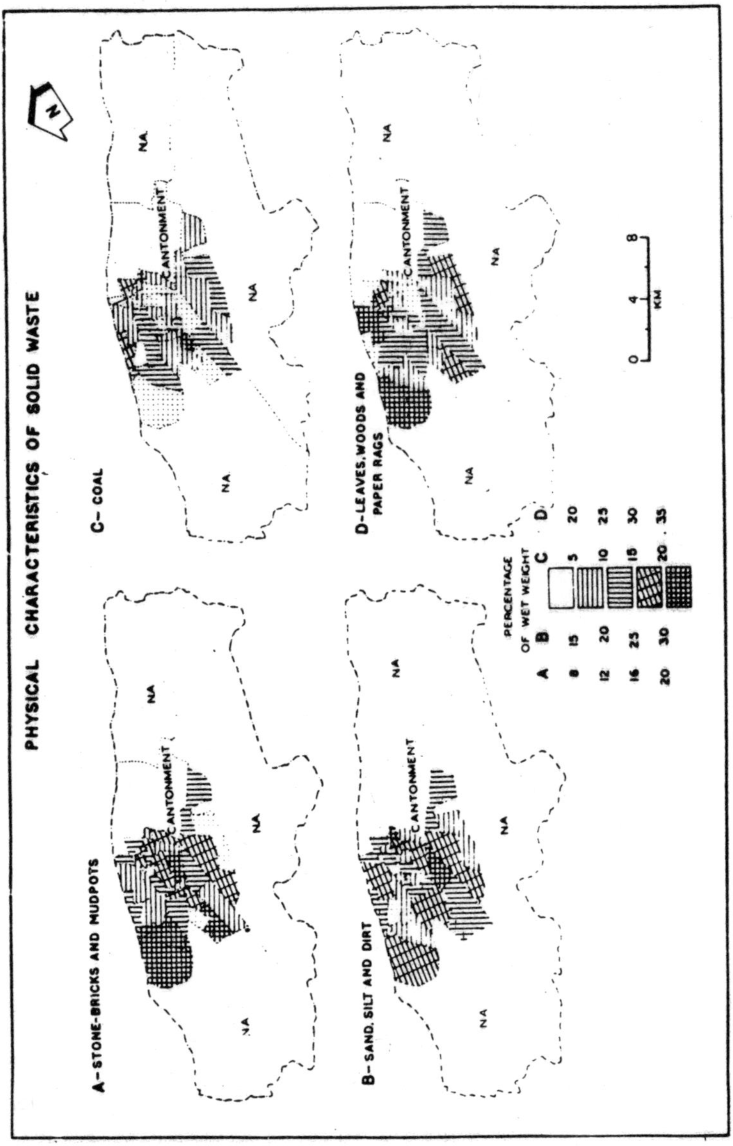
PHYSICAL CHARACTERISTICS OF SOLID WASTE
A–STONE-BRICKS AND MUDPOTS
B–SAND, SILT AND DIRT
C–COAL
D–LEAVES, WOODS AND PAPER RAGS
CANTONMENT
NA
PERCENTAGE OF WET WEIGHT
KM

FIG. 1.6:B:

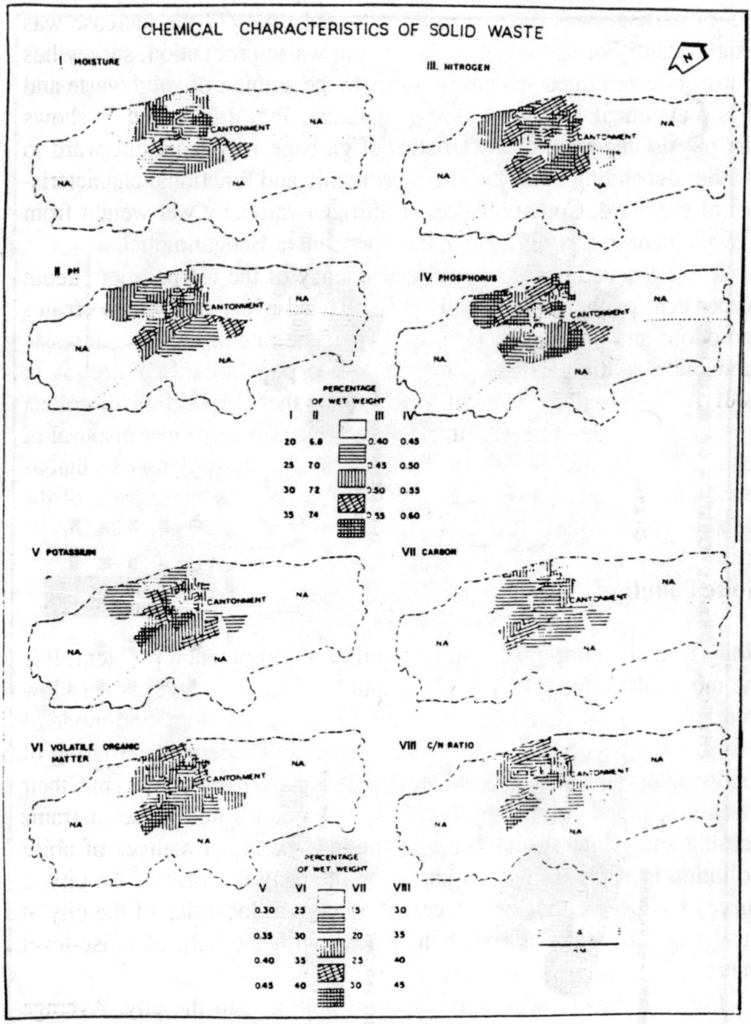
CHEMICAL CHARACTERISTICS OF SOLID WASTE
I MOISTURE
II PH
III. NITROGEN
IV. PHOSPHORUS
V POTASSIUM
VI VOLATILE ORGANIC MATTER
VII CARBON
VIII C/N RATIO
CANTONMENT
NA
N
PERCENTAGE OF WET WEIGHT
I II III IV
20 6.8 0.40 0.45
25 7.0 0.45 0.50
30 7.2 0.50 0.55
35 7.4 0.55 0.60
PERCENTAGE OF WET WEIGHT
V VI VII VIII
0.30 25 15 30
0.35 30 20 35
0.40 35 25 40
0.45 40 30 45
KM

garbage was collected in 1971, which increased to 2,51,137 tonnes in 1976. Kalyanpur, Panki and Jajmau, the rural areas, are the main disposal sites of Kanpur. During 1970-71, the per capita per day production of garbage was 0.49 kg in the city and till 1977 the increase was insignificant. For spatial analysis of solid waste production, survey has been conducted in each ward to estimate the amount of solid waste and physio-chemical characteristics of garbage. Fig. 1.6 A and B shows that physio-chemical characteristics of garbage vary from one ward to another depending upon the socio-economic and functional characteristics of the ward. Contamination of nitrogen varies by wet weight from 0.39 per cent in Laxmipurwa to 0.67 per cent at Bengalimohal.

It is estimated that owing to inefficiency of the Corporation, about 20 per cent of the city refuse is not collected every day which creates bad odour and unclean look to the city. If the rate of increase in waste production continues to be the same with a population of 3 million in 2001 A.D., it will be a great problem for the Corporation to collect waste and dispose it of at suitable sites. Thus, the improper disposal of garbage badly affects the whole region. This case study reveals that as in Kanpur city it is becoming a serious problem in other parts of the Kanpur region also.

Noise Pollution

Noise is also an important aspect of urban environmental problem. It is the most subjective pollutant in Kanpur city while its level is very low in urban areas of the region. With developing technology and mode of living it has penetrated almost every aspect of modern life. Blaring of loudspeakers at all hours, intolerable sound from industries and their machines, noise emitted by horns of automobiles and noise of trains coming and going at odd hours are among the major sources of noise pollution in Kanpur city. To know the intensity of noise in the city, a survey has been conducted in certain important localities of the city at busy road crossings and near industries, with the help of noise-level metre.

Fig. 1.7 shows the pattern of noise pollution in the city. Average noise level varies from 40 decibels at H.B.T.I., West Campus to 89 decibels at Parade Crossing. It has been observed that noise levels at Moolganj, Barachauraha, Meston Road, and Medical College Crossing are considerably high. The outer zone of the city covering I.I.T., Kidwainagar, Nawabganj, and Cantonment, come under the

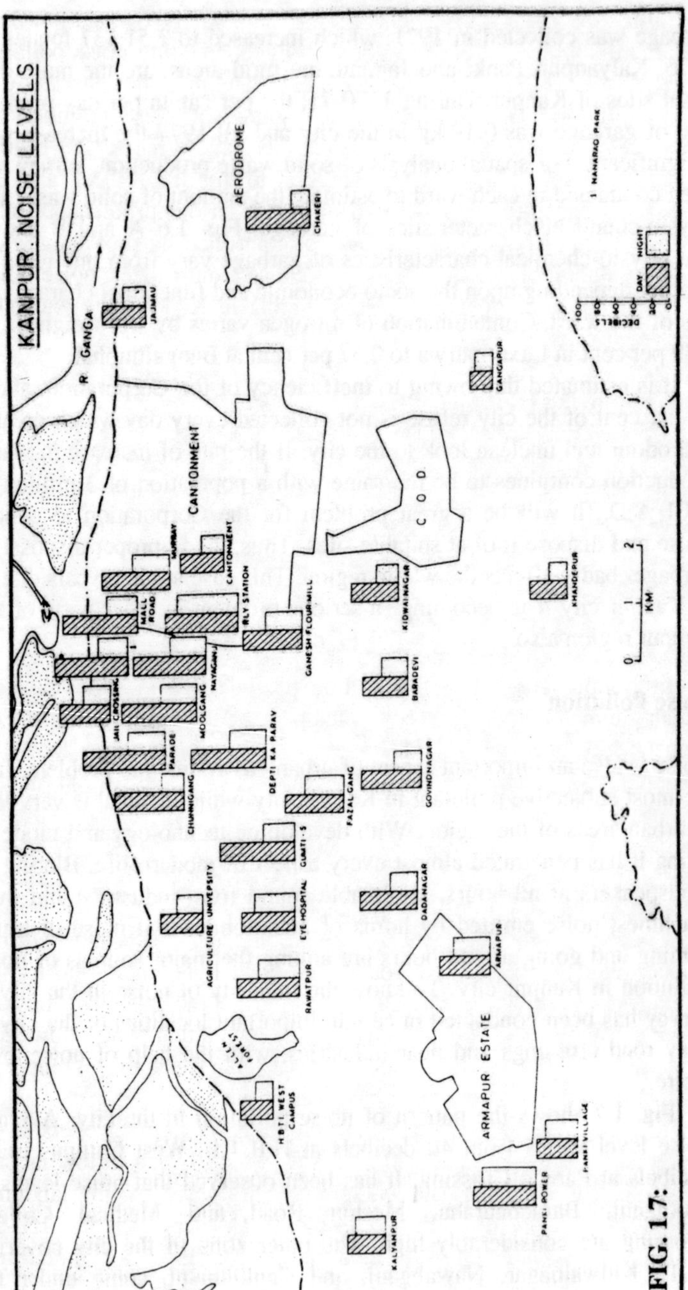

FIG. 1.7: KANPUR: NOISE LEVELS

least-noisy zone. At Chakeri airport, the main source of loud noise are the aircrafts which have a few limited flights, creating noise pollution problem at only the time of take-off and landing. Thus the study of noise pollution reveals that the main source of noise pollution are automobiles in the city. High noise levels have affected the hearing capacity of several persons. In addition to this it has been also observed that except in Kanpur city, it is not a serious problem for other areas of Kanpur region. But if it is not controlled by providing wider roads to automobiles and introducing Noise Control Act, noise pollution may become intolerable and damaging in Kanpur city and other urban centres of the region.

Slums Showing Housing Problem

Over industrialisation and related migration towards Kanpur city, mainly from rural areas of Kanpur region has resulted in housing problem, and ultimately creation of slum localities in the city. The main cause of rural-urban migration is least opportunity of employment in rural areas of Kanpur city. Due to the more industrial establishments in the city, demand for workers is increasing and growth of slums along roads and the railway line has developed recently.

In Kanpur city about 0.5 million persons live in slum localities which are mostly located in congested parts of the city and near the old industrial establishments. There are three types of slum localities: 'ahatas', newer slums and temporary hutments, among which 'ahatas' are most frequently observed in the city. At present there are 835 ahatas accommodating 2,59,552 persons in the city. It is evident from Fig. 1.8 that population residing in these 'ahatas' has been increasing during the past two decades. About 60% of the industrial workers reside in these 'ahatas'. Lack of separate kitchens, water taps, latrines, underground sewers, proper roads and street lights make the locality filthy and unsuitable for human living. Fig. 1.8 indicates that 'bustees' (poor-colonies) also accommodate a huge population of slum dwellers. Examples of 'bustees' can be observed in Kakadev, Babupurwa, Jazipurwa and Harzendranagar localities of the city.

It has been observed that the condition of slum dwellers is the worst as regards their standard of living, which is due to low income. Most of them are industrial workers or daily wage-earning labourers. About 24 per cent of slum dwellers have an income of Rs. 150-200 which is not sufficient to fulfil their daily needs (Fig. 1.8). Therefore, it

FIG. 1.8:

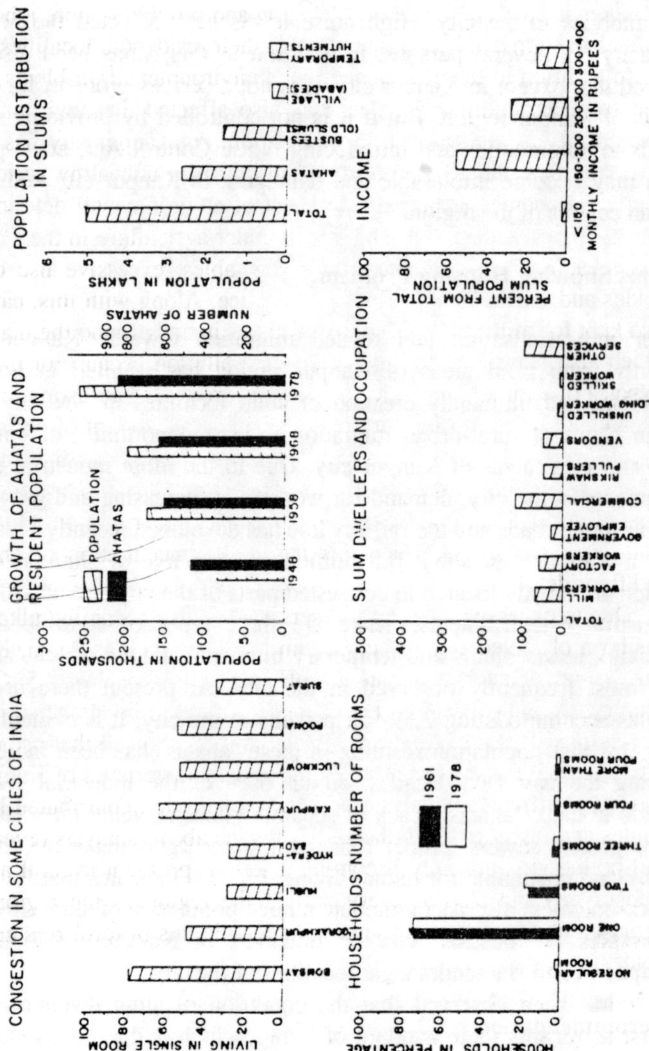
KANPUR
CHARACTERISTICS OF SLUMS
CONGESTION IN SOME CITIES OF INDIA
PERCENTAGE OF POPULATION LIVING IN SINGLE ROOM
BOMBAY
GORAKHPUR
HUBLI
HYDERABAD
KANPUR
LUCKNOW
POONA
SURAT
GROWTH OF AHATAS AND RESIDENT POPULATION
POPULATION
AHATAS
POPULATION IN THOUSANDS
NUMBER OF AHATAS
1948
1958
1968
1978
POPULATION DISTRIBUTION IN SLUMS
POPULATION IN LAKHS
TOTAL
AHATAS
BUSTEES (OLD SLUMS)
VILLAGE (ABADIES)
TEMPORARY HUTMENTS
HOUSEHOLDS NUMBER OF ROOMS
HOUSEHOLDS IN PERCENTAGE
1961
1978
NO REGULAR ROOM
ONE ROOM
TWO ROOMS
THREE ROOMS
FOUR ROOMS
MORE THAN FOUR ROOMS
SLUM DWELLERS AND OCCUPATION
TOTAL
MILL WORKERS
FACTORY WORKERS
GOVERNMENT EMPLOYEE
COMMERCIAL
RIKSHAW PULLERS
VENDORS
UNSKILLED BUILDING WORKER
SKILLED WORKER
OTHER SERVICES
INCOME
PERCENT FROM TOTAL SLUM POPULATION
MONTHLY INCOME IN RUPEES
<150
150-200
200-300
300-400

has been concluded that the establishment of slum localities in the heart of the city not only gives a bad look to the city but also contributes to deterioration of urban environment and resulting health hazards. Increasing slums can be stopped by providing more housing localities in satellite towns of the region and providing more job opportunities to slum dwellers at the place of their residential localities.

In addition to the above-mentioned environmental problems, pollution from agricultural practices has also affected the environment of Kanpur city as well as the Kanpur region. As Kanpur city has a considerable area under agriculture, pollution from unhealthy agricultural practices becomes an important aspect of environmental deterioration. About 16,500 hectares of land is still under agriculture in the Corporation area. For growing crops and vegetables, excessive use of pesticides and fertilizers is a common practice. Along with this, cattle are also kept for milk and other dairy products in and around the main city, which also contribute to environmental pollution because of improper disposal of their excreta. Along with this, growing, harvesting, processing and storing of crops contribute considerable amount of agricultural waste products in the natural environment.[4] Chemicals mixed with irrigated water flow into rivers, ponds, as well as into ground-water storage through soil, and cause water quality deterioration. Quality of well-water has shown that water has high concentration of chlorides and fluorides.

Due to excessive use of fertilisers, soil is also becoming alkaline. It has been observed that soil of certain localities such as Panki, Kalyanpur, Ahirawan and Gangapur has pH value of more than 8.5. Content of nitrogen and organic carbon was also found to be less than its content before 10 years. Analysis of soil samples showed that use of pesticides and fertilizers has affected the soil characteristics of Kanpur but it is very difficult to analyse the level of pollution contributed by pesticides and insecticides in the soil. Thus the above analysis reveals that soil pollution is not only becoming a serious problem in rural areas of Kanpur city but also in every part of the region as the region is an agricultural area and is consuming large amounts of fertilizers and pesticides.

Recommendation

The study of Kanpur city demonstrates that its environment is deteriorating day by day. Only a healthy organism can contribute towards a healthy environmental development and an unhealthy organism needs remedial measures before it can act as a healthy growth pole for regional development. In this context measures have been suggested for improving its environment with a view to making it a healthy centre for imparting stimulating impulses to its region and for its own well-being. To clean the city and making its environment healthy for human living following suggestions have been made:

(i) It is estimated that the population of the city will be 3 million in 2001 A.D., which will become a problem if remedial measures to check the increase of population in Kanpur are not taken in time. To provide more and better facilities, satellite towns around the city should be developed. These towns will include Bhanpur, Bithoor, Bindki, Kannauj, Hamirpur and Akbarpur. The size of these towns should range between 50,000 to 1,00,000 persons. These towns should be well-linked with the surrounding villages. Then only the goal to bring industrial, rural and urban integration will be achieved for the overall development of Kanpur region.

(ii) To avoid industrial pollution, large-scale factories should not be permitted in future inside the city. Further, in the proximity of the industrial estates of the city, regulation must be imposed on the new industrial growth as well as construction of new houses, except for the workers. The big industries should be developed in some satellite towns or in the rural areas in the metropolitan region of Kanpur. The small-scale industries and the cottage industries should be developed in the villages where transport facilities and electric power and manpower are available. An advantageous site for the location of large-scale industries has been suggested along the Kanpur-Lucknow highway, across the River Ganga between Unnao and Gangapur.

(iii) To save River Ganga from pollution, capacity of Jajmau sewage treatment plant should be increased because, at present, it treats very limited amount of sewage due to old machines and pumps. One more sewage treatment plant should be set up where waste water from Govind Nagar and Gumti No. 5 joins River Pandu. This will reduce the quantity of pollutants discharged in River Pandu and make the water suitable for aquatic life.

(iv) To control air pollution from industries and domestic sources, plantation of trees, establishment of parks on available land and along roads have been suggested. Agricultural land should be maintained as green belts around Kanpur city as well as the other towns in the Kanpur region. Air pollution control equipments must be used by large-scale industries and thermal power plants qcto save the deterioration of the city environment.

(v) Efficiency of Kanpur corporation should be increased so that proper disposal and management of garbage may be done. Garbage should not be dumped near the rural settlements and cultivable land as it is a common practice in Kanpur. This should be done at only selected sites. This will not only reduce the level of odour from garbage but also make the city and surrounding rural areas clean and healthy.

(vi) Provisions should be made to regulate the discharge of industrial-urban waste water into bodies of water by establishing control measures in the context of overall water management policy, taking into account both qualitative and quantitative requirements. As the city discharges its waste-water into River Ganga, which serves most of the Kanpur region, there is urgent need to control practices that cause water pollution.

(vii) As the outer traffic mixes with the city traffic, off and on, creating problem of traffic congestion and noise, especially at busy road crossings, control of traffic is very essential. With a view to avoiding the congestion caused by traffic, some suitable bypasses and overbridges at rail crossings are suggested. Kanpur city being the main service centre for the whole region, must be connected by metalled roads from every town and service centre of the region. This will help in overall industrial-economical development of the region.

(viii) To avoid pollution from fertilisers and pesticides, only recommended doses should be used by cultivators. Soil samples and well water samples should be periodically tested, so that future effects of pollutants can be evaluated earlier.

(ix) A pressing problem which should be solved by the Corporation of Kanpur is the provision of housing accommodation for the low-income workers. Therefore, it is essential to have a target for providing housing facility for the workers as well as slum dwellers at low cost with all essential facilities. Slums which are located in the heart of the city, must be cleared and dwellers rehabilitated suitably at other sites. Satellite towns may be also developed so that people may get employment and can settle there in a healthy environment. Rural migration towards the city must be regulated as not to tax the Corporation beyond its capacity to provide employment and civic amenities. Protected water supply should be made available in every village near the city, and in phases, to whole of the Kanpur region, as it is the most important requirement for the health of the population.

It is obvious that environmental planning although desirable in itself, is not sufficient to deal with the urban problems of Kanpur. If the surrounding region can be developed to a point where substantial employment opportunities exist, rapid migration towards Kanpur could be reduced. The overall development of the Kanpur region may solve the problem of Kanpur city and this aim may be achieved only by comprehensive integrated planning of the region. In addition, to the abovementioned suggestions, public education and interest is also necessary for maintaining the environment of Kanpur and its region, clean and healthy.

REFERENCES

1. Penalosa, E. "Habitat : The Problems of Human Settlements", *The Draper World Population Report* No. 2 (1976) p. 3.
2. Kanpur Development Authority Information (1975).
3. Department of Social and Preventive Medicine, Medical College, Kanpur.
4. Christman, R.F. *et al.* "The Natural Environment" *Waste and Control, Waste Production of Civilization*, Good Year Publishers (1973) p. 59.

PART -- II

URBAN GEOGRAPHY

TWO

Abdalla Misallati, Wilford A. Bladen and **P.P. Karan**

Urban Systems and Urban Regions in Libya

Urbanization

Ancient Period

LIBYA has ancient traditions dating back to 800 B.C. when the Carthaginians took over a number of Phoenician trading stations along the Mediterranean Coast and the requirements of defence and commerce stimulated the growth of the urban centres (Fig. 2.1).[1] After the Sixth Century B. C. Tripoli became an important city, but the total number of towns remained comparatively few. Both the Phoenicians and the Carthaginians made some attempt to develop the area architecturally and agriculturally.

The Romans destroyed Carthage in 146 B. C. and controlled an extensive network of coastal towns in Tripolitania section of Libya and elsewhere in North Africa. Extensive Roman urbanization occurred along the North African Coast. Ports, route centres and fortified frontier towns were established by the Romans, usually on the site of Carthaginian settlements. A large number of Roman settlements were subsequently abandoned including rich and magnificent cities such as Leptis Magna, Sabratah and Oea, the ancient name for Tripoli (see Fig. 2.1 for location of old urban centres). During most of Roman rule more attention was paid to Leptis Magna and Sabratah than the city of Tripoli. When Septimus Severus took over he realized the importance of Tripoli and transferred the capital from Leptis Magna to Tripoli. From that time the name of the city was changed to Tripolis meaning the three cities. This transfer gave Tripoli as well as the Tripolitania region considerable importance. The most important remaining Roman ruins in Tripoli is the Arch of Marcus Aurelius facing the port of Bab El-

Baher.

In Cyrenaica section of Libya, the Greeks began their settlements in the Seventh Century B. C. The Greeks founded the city of Cyrene which became a major centre for them. Within two hundred years of Cyrene's foundation, four other Greek cities were established in the eastern part of Libya, Almarj, Benghazi, Tukrah, and Susah. All of these along with Cyrene were known as the Pentapolis – five cities. From Cyrene, the major city and the foremost of the five, the overall name of Cyrenaica for the region was derived.[2]

Tripolitania and Cyrenaica both became prosperous Roman provinces between 86 B. C. to A. D. 450. Throughout the period of Greek colonization, the area of Fezzan in the south was dominated by the Garaments, a tribal people who entered the region sometime before 1000 B. C. In southern Libya they established an important centre, Germah; from there the Garaments controlled the trans Saharan caravan trade, from Ghadamis south to the Niger River, eastward to Egypt, and west to Mauritania. The trade routes between the southern areas and the Mediterranean coast were connected through Germah.[3] Many of Graeco-Roman towns in Libya declined in importance or were abandoned in later centuries or raiders destroyed the elaborate aqueducts and tunnels on which the water supply of the ancient towns depended. In addition the sporadic raids of desert nomads from the south disrupted communications, destroyed effective administration and ruined settlements.

Arab Towns: Seventh to Nineteenth Centuries

The great Arab/Islamic conquests of North Africa following the death of Mohammed in 632 A. D. further stimulated changes in the pattern of urbanization in Libya. Some cities declined rapidly as political and economic situations changed. New towns were established which took over the roles of more ancient towns or regional centres. The Arab Empire was essentially land based, and all the new centres of power–Zuwaylah, Murzug–were at inland locations (Fig. 2.1). The period of Arab/Islamic domination was marked by urban revival as the religious precepts of Islam encouraged the close association of believers and favoured an urban-oriented society.[4] A large number of existing urban centres in Libya were favourably located to participate in the resurgence of trade with followed the spread of Islam. Many Libyan towns such as Ghadamis, Germah and Zuwaylah located on the trans-Saharan caravan routes developed considerable transit trade. The towns which developed during the Arab/Islamic period exhibit striking affinities in morphology.

FIG. 2.1:

Arab/Islamic urban development reached its peak in the eleventh century in Libya. A period of stagnation then set in which continued until the end of the nineteenth century. Precise figures are not available, but urban decline is supported by evidence from several sources.[5] Some towns, such as Mespite, Thenadassa Borevm, Cerkar, and Digdiga, disappeared altogether. Others, such as Zuwaylah, Ghadamis, and

Germah dwindled in size and importance (Fig. 2.1). The period between the fifteenth and eighteenth centuries was marked by succession of wars and political convulsions. During the sixteenth and seventeenth centuries the Ottoman Turks conquered Libya. A succession of long, exhausting wars left most of the urban centres in a state of decline.[6] The Ottomans failed to revive handicrafts, agriculture and trade. They imposed crippling taxation and arbitrary levies on merchants in the towns, which inhibited development. During the Ottoman rule the amount of cultivated area under irrigation contracted. The quality of urban life also deteriorated with the exception of Tripoli. The wealth of the extensive Ottoman empire flowed through the port of Tripoli. A distinct hierarchy of settlements, consisting of ports, regional centres, market cities, villages, and nomad groups, developed during the era of Ottoman domination. This hierarchy was based both on the functional differentiation of cities and on the relation between the cities and their hinterlands.

Contemporary Patterns of Urbanization and Spatial Development

The beginning of modern economic activity associated with European colonization, created new urban forms, changed the functions of many old towns, and stimulated the process of urbanization which has accelerated markedly in recent years. During the Italian rule some urban settlements, especially Tripoli, evolved from Arab towns into modern cities with well built streets and residential quarters. Large residential villas were introduced into cities.[7] The Italians achieved their aims by building new areas based on urban master planning. The core area of Tripoli emerged as the central business district for the first time in the history of the city. During British occupation, 1945-1951, there were no significant changes in Libya's urban system.

High rates of natural increase and migration to towns have resulted in accelerating rates of urban growth in Libya since the early sixties. Urban population, which accounted for 18 percent of Libya's population in 1955, increased to 25 percent in 1965.[8] In 1973, half of Libya's total population of two and a quarter million lived in settlements with 20,000 population size or over. While national population increased at an average annual rate of 4.2 percent between 1964 and 1973, the urban population grew at an average rate of over 20 percent.[9] The high rates of growth are expected to continue in the future. The government's policy of encouraging the growth of its relatively small

FIG. 2.3:

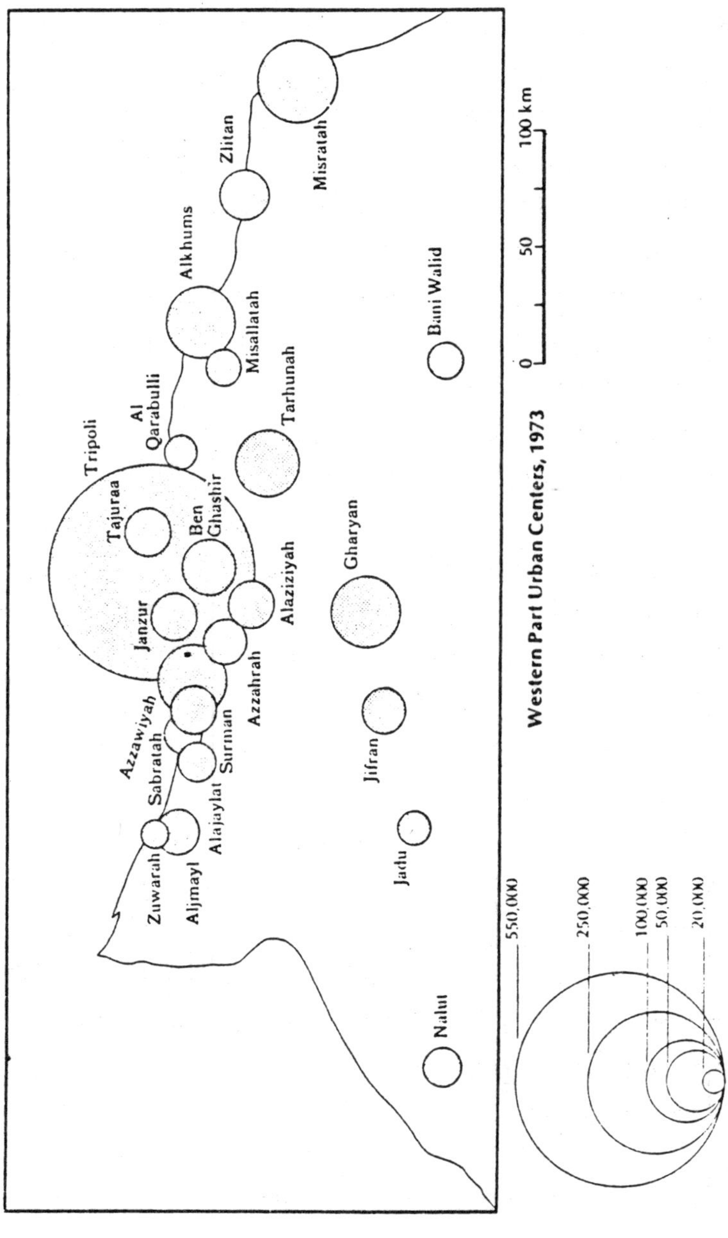

Western Part Urban Centers, 1973

FIG. 2.4:

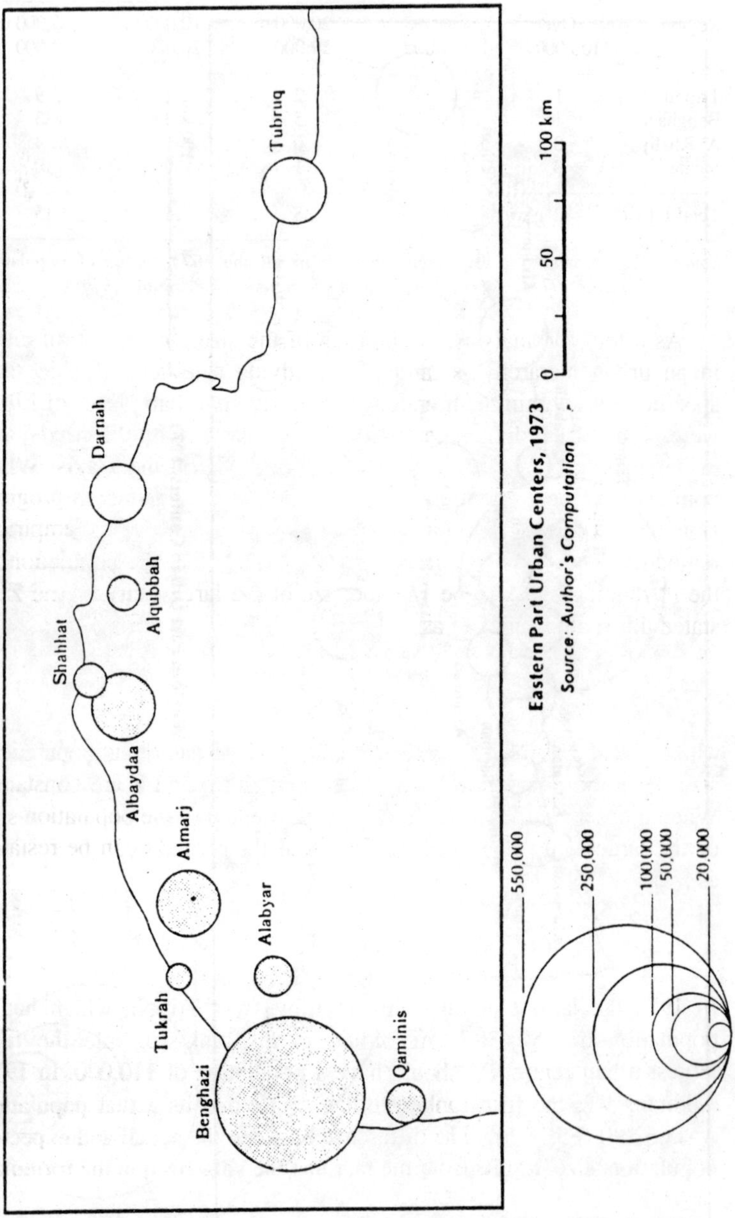

Eastern Part Urban Centers, 1973

Source: Author's Computation

TABLE 2.1: Regional Distribution of Settlements (1973)

Region	Number of Settlements by Population Size				
	Over 100,000	50,000 to 100,000	20,000 to 50,000	10,000 to 20,000	5,000 to 10,000
Tripoli	1	2	2	11	9
Benghazi	1	0	5	3	3
Al Khalij	0	0	0	1	3
Sabha	0	0	1	0	0
Total Libya	2	2	8	15	15

Source: Government of Libya preliminary return of the 1973 census of population (Tripoli, 1974). Also personal contacts Secretariat of Planning, 1979.

As a tool for analysis, the plotting of the size distribution of cities in an urban hierarchy is unique in studying a system of cities and specific cities within the hierarchy. The forty-six urban places of Libya were plotted according to their 1973 population size on the y-axis, and in descending order by their rank in population on the x-axis. When both axes on the graph are scaled the result was not a smooth progression approximating straight line but a curved line. This empirical regularity, known as "the rank-size rule," states that the population of the rth ranking city will be $1/r^{th}$ the size of the largest city.[13] And Zipf stated this mathematically as:

$$r \xi p_r q = k$$

where r is the rank of a particular city on the basis of its population size; P_r is the population size of that city, and q and k are constants. When q has a value of 1.0, the value of k is equal to the population size of the largest city (P_1) in the system, and the formula can be restated as :

$$r \xi P_r = P_1$$

In 1973 the largest urban centre in Libya was Tripoli, which had a population of 550,438.[14] According to the rank-size rule the fifth largest urban centre, P_5, should have a population of 110,000. In 1973 Alkhums was the fifth ranking urban centre and its actual population was 66,890 (Fig. 2.5). The difference between the actual and expected population size results from the fact that the value of q in the formula,

TABLE 2.2: Population of Baladiah (1963-73)

Rank	Name of Baladiah	Population size 1973	% to Largest Settlement	Population size 1963	% to Largest Settlement	Growth rate Percentage
1.	Tripoli	550,438	100.00	270,500	100.00	103.5
2.	Benghazi	286,943	52.2	192,000	71.0	49.4
3.	Misratah	102,439	18.6	68,000	25.1	50.6
4.	Azzawiyah	72,092	13.1	59,000	21.8	22.2
5.	Alkhums	66,890	12.1	47,602	17.6	40.5
6.	Gharyan	65,224	11.8	58,401	21.6	11.7
7.	Albaydaa	59,765	10.9	29,818	10.0	100.4
8.	Zlitan	58,981	10.7	45,112	16.7	30.7
9.	Tubruq	58,384	10.6	32,825	12.1	77.9
10.	Almarj	55,444	10.1	43,824	16.2	26.5
11.	Ajdabiyah	53,170	9.7	37,643	13.9	41.2
12.	Tarhunah	52,657	9.6	50,554	18.7	4.1
13.	Darnah	44,145	8.0	27,383	10.1	61.2
14.	Ben Ghashir	43,676	7.9	36,359	13.4	20.1
15.	Sabha	35,879	6.5	15,526	5.7	131.0
16.	Tajuraa	34,521	6.3	19,976	7.4	72.8
17.	Surman	34,180	6.2	20,964	7.7	63.0
18.	Alaziziyal	34,077	6.2	25,000	9.2	36.3
19.	Aljmayl	32,730	5.9	24,351	9.0	34.4
20.	Azzahrah	32,158	5.8	23,152	8.5	38.9
21.	Sabratah	30,836	5.6	19,193	7.1	60.7
22.	Yifran	30,821	5.6	22,349	8.3	37.9
23.	Janzur	30,202	5.5	20,964	7.7	44.0
24.	Alajaylat	27,382	5.0	22,043	8.1	24.2
25.	Ashshati	27,183	4.9	23,874	8.8	13.9
26.	Nalut	23,535	4.3	20,717	7.6	13.6
27.	Sirt	22,797	4.1	18,123	6.7	25.8
28.	Misallatah	22,222	4.0	21,224	7.8	4.7
29.	Murzug	22,185	4.0	16,023	5.9	38.4
30.	Alqubbah	20,455	3.7	17,136	6.3	19.4
31.	Awbari	19,132	3.5	12,767	4.7	49.8
32.	Baniwalid	19,113	3.5	17,500	6.5	9.2
33.	Alabyar	17,683	3.2	14,200	5.2	24.5
34.	Shahhat	17,167	3.1	13,683	5.0	25.5
35.	Jadu	17,073	3.1	14,955	5.5	14.1
36.	Qaminis	16,991	3.1	13,500	5.0	25.8
37.	Aljufrah	16,709	3.0	12,421	4.6	24.5
38.	Zuwarah	15,078	2.7	13,834	5.1	9.0
39.	Al-Qarabulli	14,524	2.6	10,270	3.8	4.0
40.	Alkufrah	12,466	2.3	7,300	2.7	70.8
41.	Mizdah	11,472	2.1	6,213	2.3	84.6
42.	Tukrah	10,714	1.9	7,000	2.6	53.0
43.	Benjawwad	8,584	1.6	7,360	2.7	16.6
44.	Jalu	8,032	1.5	5,890	2.1	36.4
45.	Ghat	6,924	1.2	4,800	1.8	44.2
46.	Ghadamis	6,172	1.1	5,500	2.0	12.2

Source: Government of Libya, preliminary return of 1963 and 1973 Census of population (Tripoli, 1964-74)

FIG. 2.5:

DISTRIBUTION OF LIBYAN URBAN CENTERS

RANK SIZE OF URBAN POPULATION OF LIBYA

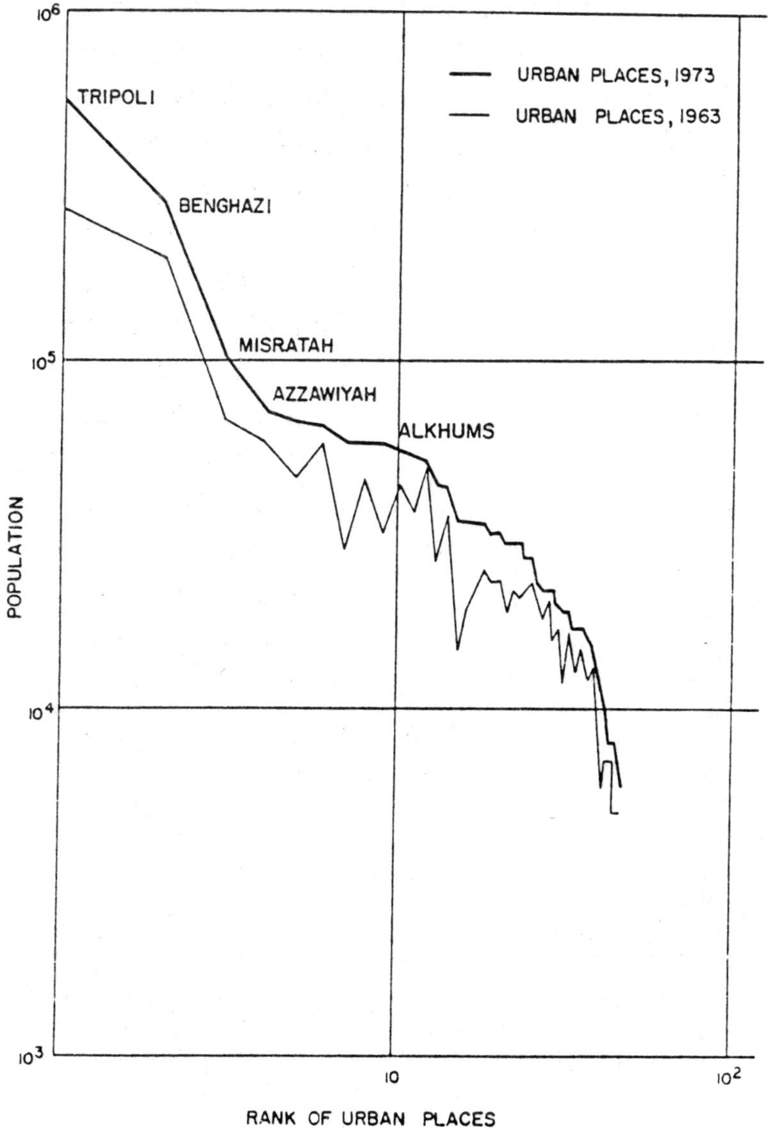

which is the slope of the line in the graph, does not equal 1.0. Thus although the rank size distribution of urban places may approximate a straight line for many nations, and at times for some smaller areas, there is normally some variation from the rigid relationship postulated by the rank-size rule. In a modern society the size of urban settlements depends upon the range of goods, the distance people travel to secure a particular service or good, and the threshold or the minimum sales that an establishment must secure in order to survive. These variables give the ability of such a settlement to maintain a specific range of goods and any sales threshold depends upon its size. For any given region in Libya there will be a primate city and all other city sizes will be related to the size of this primate city. In this relationship the second city in a given region should be half the population size of the first; the third city one-third of its size, and the fifth city a fifth of its size and so on.

In Libya, the size distributions of urban settlements in 1963 and 1973 are characterised with a high degree of primary reflecting the extreme spatial development disparities discussed earlier. There is a dual nature to the spatial development of Libya, with its two almost isolated western and eastern spatial systems centered around Tripoli and Benghazi. Primary measures in this dual system would be meaningful only within each of the two sub-systems, where such values became considerably higher. Below the population levels of Tripoli and Benghazi, the rest of the city-size distribution is separated by a wide gap. In fact, if Tripoli and Benghazi were removed from the city-size distribution analysis, Libya's pattern of settlements would show hierarchical qualities close to those of Zipf's rank-size rule. The large shares of Tripoli and Benghazi, not only of settlement populations but also of the total population, is the primary contributor to the skewed nature of the rank-size distribution curve. The rank-size distribution characteristics for the system of settlements between 1963-1973 shows a tendency towards a more primate pattern or a greater degree of concentration of population in larger cities, particularly in Tripoli. A hierarchical grouping of clustering of settlements by size into four distinct levels can be distinguished. The first level consists of Tripoli; the second level consists of Benghazi; which at the third and fourth levels there are several settlements such as Misratah, and Azzawiyah. There has been a tendency towards equalisation within the third cluster between 1963 and 1973. The relative differences in size between settlements in this cluster have significantly decreased over the ten-year period.

The rank-order of cities indicates that over a period of ten years

(1963-1973) the system of cities and towns in Libya was trending gradually from a more primate to a more rank-size or log normal ranking of cities by size [a straight line when graphed on log normal cumulative probability paper]. Such a finding would appear to support Berry's contention that over time a city system in a developing economy such as Libya's tends to move toward entropy or a steady state in terms of the city-size distribution found within the city system.[15] Undoubtedly there are many variables in this equation, and Libya is but one example, but the chronological progression of the city-size distribution bears a strong resemblance to the stages proposed in Berry's idealized set of city-size distribution in a developing economy. This is in contrast to the evolution of an "S" shaped skewed distribution of cities by size suggested by Stewart.

The more balanced city-system which is beginning to evolve in Libya is in part attributable to government efforts at locating major industrial developments and demonstrates the government's commitment to spread the development and growth over a based area. This is viewed as a positive good even though the causal link between balanced growth in a system of cities and economic growth has not been established.[16] Moreover, as Ginsburg has pointed out, in most developed countries with balanced hierarchies, the small and medium-sized cities are declining in relative importance, while there is continued growth in the larger cities and great metropolises.[17] Ginsburg attributes this shift to changes in technology and suggests that changes in transportation and marketing technology in developing countries may well render small and medium-sized cities obsolete as far as their traditional roles in national and regional development are concerned. Thus, the construction of a super-highway along Libya's coastal corridor will undoubtedly have dramatic effects on the growth and size of the hierarchy of cities and their adjacent hinterlands. This development may lead to a re-arrangement of that hierarchy that is less rank-size and more primate. At least it may be skewed at the upper end as fewer, but larger, centres dominate the hierarchy at the expense of the number and size of smaller places.

Tripoli Region

Up to now, Tripoli and other Libyan cities and towns have been considered within the hierarchy of Libyan cities. This implies differences in growth rates and changes in the hierarchy of cities which in turn

FIG. 2.6:

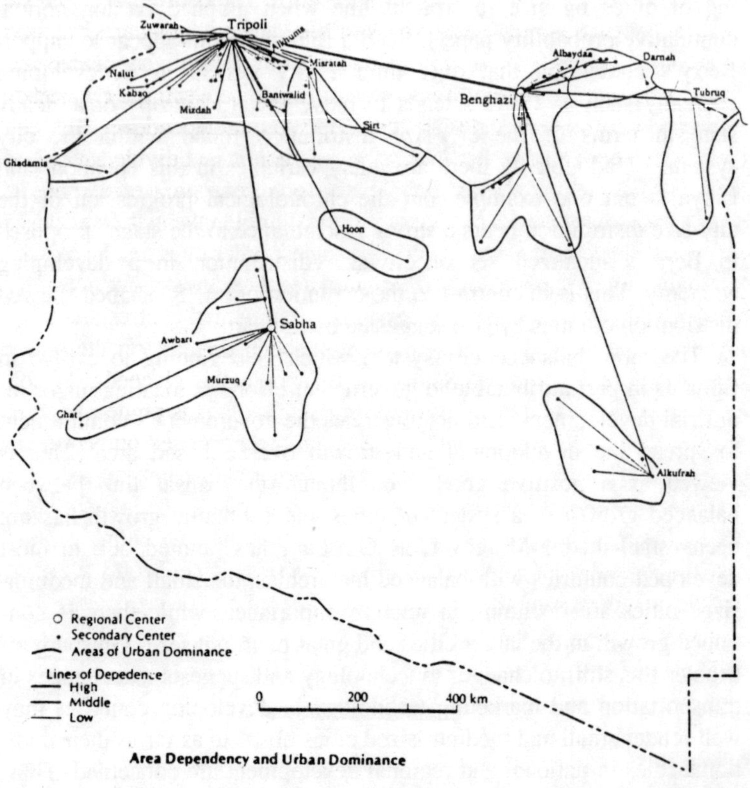

have locational significance for regional development within the nationwide space economy/polity. One way to approach the question of locational aspects of regional development is to consider Tripoli in its regional setting: to attempt to establish interrelations between city and region; to determine the extent of Tripoli's field of urban dominance; and to delimit its hinterland. To accomplish these tasks, highway and airline flow data and data on marketing fields were collected for Tripoli. Inter-urban and inter-regional flow data for people, goods, and services were used to determine zones of urban dominance. Fig. 2.6 shows the dependency relationships of urban places in Libya. The dependency relationships indicated by the lines on the map are based on flow data as well as on information collected from field interviews at Tripoli, Benghazi, Sabha, and Kufra.[18]

Just how large is Tripoli's hinterland? Tripoli's hinterland extends over the western half of the country (Fig. 2.6). The configuration of the road and air line network made Tripoli one of the major transportation nodes in Libya.[19] The heavy line connecting Tripoli and Benghazi reflects the high volume of air passenger traffic between the two cities. In terms of commerce and trade there is little interdependence between Cyrenaica and Tripolitania. In general, the country is divided into two major economically independent areas : one consisting of Cyrenaica and Al Khalij, the second composed of Tripolitania and Fezzan. In mediate order settlements between the lowest order ones and Benghazi, the main city of the region. Tripolitania and Fezzan are hierarchically less developed, many of the intermediate commercial centres are missing, and most of the small settlements depend directly on the major settlements of Tripoli and Sabha for their commercial needs. Tripoli commands the western part of the country. Benghazi is predominant in eastern Libya. The hinterlands described above are based on economic and commodity data.[20] In other words, administrative interdependence does not follow the functional relationship of settlements. For example, Tripoli is the national capital and to that extent has the entire country as its hinterland for administrative functions. Yet commercially, Tripoli has the dominance only over the western part of the country.

REFERENCES

1. D. B. Harden, *The Phoenicians*, New York : Praeger, 1962.
2. H. D. Nelson, *Area Handbook Series : Libya a Country Study*. Washington, D. C. : U. S. Government Printing Office, 1979, pp. 5-12.
3. C. Daniels, *Garaments of Southern Libya*, Stoughton, Wis. : Oleander Press, 1972.
4. Philip K. Hitti, *Islam : A Way of Life*, Minneapolis : University of Minnesota Press, 1970; and W. J. Fischel, "The City of Islam", *Middle Eastern Affairs*, No. 7, 1956, p. 227.
5. James Wellard, "Lost Cities of the Libyan Sahara : A Ghost of Ancient Prosperity in the Desert," *Geographical Magazine*, Vol. 37, 1964, London, pp. 602-615.
6. Anthony J. Cachia, *Libya Under the Second Ottoman Occupation*, 1835-1911. Tripoli : Government Press, 1945.
7. Geoffrey, Furlonge, *The Lands of Barbary*, London : John Murray, 1966, pp. 40-43.
8. Abdu A. Elkholy, "Modernization and Social Changes in the Libyan Arab Republic". Paper prepared for presentation of American Sociological Association, Annual Meeting, San Francisco, 1975, pp. 1-15.

9. United Nations, *Demographic Yearbook, 1973,* New York : United Nations Publications, 1973, pp. 82-85; and Libyan Arab Republic, 1973 Population Census Preliminary Results, Tripoli : Ministry of Planning and Scientific Research, Census and Statistical Department, 1973, pp. 1-15.
10. S. El-Shakhs, "Spatial Development and Future System of Settlements, Libya," Ital. Consult, Rome, Italy, 1974.
11. Government of Libya Preliminary Return of the 1973 Census of Population, Tripoli, 1974; also personal contacts Secretariat of Planning, 1979.
12. *Ibid.*, 1963-1973; and author computation.
13. The Concept of Primary and the Primate City was first introduced by geographer Mark Jefferson who was interested in explaining patterns of urbanization on a worldwide basis. See Mark Jefferson, "The Law of the primate City," *Geographical Review,* Vol. 29, No. 2, April 1939, pp. 226-32.
14. The rank-size association among cities is a mathematical regularity which Zipf discussed in detail. See G. K. Zipf, *National Unity and Disunity*. Bloomington, Ind., Principia Press, 1941.
15. Government of Libya, *op. cit.*, 1973.
16. For an explanation, see B. J. L. Berry and W. L. Garrison. "Alternate Explanations of the Urban Rank-Size Relationship", *Annals of the Association of American Geographers,* Vol. 48, No. 1 March 1958, pp. 83-91. Stewart presents a contrasting point of view, in Charles T. Stewart, "The Size and Spacing of Cities", *Geographical Review,* Vol. 48, No. 2 April 1958, pp. 222-45.
17. Brian J. L. Berry, "City-Size Distribution and Economic Development," *Economic Development and Cultural Change,* Vol. 9 Jul. 1961, pp. 573-88.
18. Norton Ginsburg, "Planning the Future of Asian City", *The City as a Centre of Change in Asia,* edited by D. J. Dwyer, (Hong Kong : Hong Kong University Press, 1972), and M. Murphey "The City as a Centre of Change : Western Europe and China," *Annals Association of American Geographers,* Vol. 44, 1954, pp. 349-362.
19. Commodity and passenger flow data for Tripoli and other major urban centres were obtained from official sources in November, 1979.
20. The data were obtained during field studies in Libya in November 1979. For more explanation on zones of urban dominance, see Buhdan Gruchman, "Growth Poles in the Spatial Structure of Libyan Economy", pp. 195-205, in *Growth Poles and Growth Centres in Regional Planning,* edited by Antoni Kuklinski, Paris, Mouton Co., 1972.

THREE

P.T. Malshe

Changes and Trends in the Urban Systems of Maharashtra: 1971-81

Introduction

THE urban system of Maharashtra is well-defined and firmly oriented towards Bombay, the capital of the State, as well as the economic capital of the country. As is well-known, the modern era of industrialisation commenced a little before dawn of the present century at Bombay and the industrial growth has diffused inland along the arteries of communication by and by, since then. Modern industrial centres, thus, occur in the umland of Gt. Bombay, mainly along principal highways and railways. The net result of this process is the emergence of: (a) A well-defined national urban system converging on Bombay. The Bombay-Ahmedabad-Delhi, Bombay- Nagpur-Calcutta and Bombay-Pune-Solapur-Hyderabad railway routes and/or highways support the developing national urban system.[1] (b) Some regional urban systems are developing along Pune-Bangalore highway through Satara and Kolhapur; and Manmad-Nanded and Manmad-Dhond systems are developing along railways. (c) Nagpur-Chandrapur and Bombay-Goa urban systems are likely to develop depending upon several factors like encouragement to industrialisation of Wardha, Yeotmal and Chandrapur districts and completion of the Konkan railway project etc., in future.

Factors: Physical and Cultural

The aspects of examination of urban growth behaviour[2] and the analysis of the settlement system of Maharashtra[3] have been accomplished earlier by the author and the present attempt thus, concerns itself with the structural changes that have occurred during the preceding decade, only. The structure of an urban system can be succinctly displayed in terms of a few indices viz. degree of urban population concentration, number, size, distribution and growth behaviour of urban settlements etc. These facts would be better understood on the background of the following information pertaining to the physical and cultural aspects of Maharashtra. The urban systems of Maharashtra are conditioned by some significant physical factors, mentioned below:

(i) The Western Ghat and its spurs form water divides between several river vallyes in Western Maharashtra. The Satpuras in the north constitute an effective barrier between the Narmada and the Tapti river valleys. The modern transportation systems of these regions are considerably governed by these natural features.

(ii) The longitudinally oriented semi-famine zone occurring in the rain-shadow of the Western Ghat, is a distinct climatic zone to be reckoned in the context of urban growth. The contrast between the irrigated and non-irrigated tracts, so far as growth rates of towns and cities are concerned, is striking.

The principal cultural factors that have been instrumental in guiding the growth of the urban systems are as follows:

(a) The first urban settlements dawned in the upland district of Western Maharashtra in the Pravara-Godavari valley over three thousand years ago, as an extension of the Indus valley culture in the Deccan.

(b) The establishment of various kingdoms during the following long period of history by Hindu and Muslim rulers gave rise to new urban centres at nodal points i.e. at cross-roads, confluences of rivers, commanding locations controlling routes through saddles in the mountains and sea ports along the Arabian sea littoral. Thus, Dhule, Nagpur, Pune, Junnar, Kolhapur, Nasik, Aurangabad, Ahmednagar, Nanded and the port towns of Sopara, Bassein, Thane, Kalyan, Chiplun, Rajapur and Malwan etc. were born to serve some discrete purpose during historical times.

(c) The medieval urban system sustained a jolt with the introduction of the modern highway and railway systems under the British rule. Several former trading towns on the plateau viz. Balapur, Junnar, Jejuri and Dharangaon etc., as well as, sea ports as Dasgaon, Bassein, Rajapur, Chiplun, Jaigarh etc. lost their trading importance and fell into decay. New centres, however, rose into prominence along the new systems of highways and railways during the past one hundred years or so. The British rulers developed Bombay as a port city and made it a focus of highway and railway systems of the country. These advantages helped it to grow fast as a multi-functional urban magnet along the west coast. In fact, not unlike several modern coastal metropolises in the world, the diffusion of modern industries has occurred from Bombay inland.

Processes of Change

The principal processes that are responsible for infusing change in the urban systems are as under:

1. The industrialisation of Pune, Thane and Nasik occurred due to congestion of industries at Bombay. In fact, Pune and Nasik are outposts of Bombay and commuting between these centres is ever on the increase. Presently, industries are diffusing in the rural areas occurring in the umlands of these centres following highways and railways due to congestion of industrial units at these cities. Several erstwhile rural settlements in Thane, Raigad (Kolaba) and Pune districts have been upgraded as urban in the census of 1981, as a result of this process. Pune's industrial belt is expanding towards Saswad.
2. The process of induction of industries from Bombay inland continues unabated. The development of industries at Dhule, Jalgaon, Aurangabad, Satara, Ahmednagar etc., during recent times is a result of it.
3. The recent discovery of oil-bearing structures of the coast of Bassein, Bombay and Ratnagiri in the sea have opened up a new vista of developing Petro-Chemical industries all along the Konkan coast. Though, presently they are located only in

Bombay, more new units will come up along the sea coast as the production of crude starts from off-shore areas, in the near future.

4. The two-fold efforts of the State Government in triggering growth of modern industries in relatively backward areas as south and central Konkan, Marathwada and eastern Vidarbha etc., by offering incentives to private agencies, as well as, by developing new Industrial Estates through Government Department are also significant factors to note in this respect. The concept of industrial estates has been adopted throughout the world in recent decades, firstly in the industrialised countries and subsequently by the Third World nations.[4] The industrial estate concept now generally provides an important initial stage in the existing structural and spatial development of industry. Kudal, Ratnagiri and Roha in Konkan and several centres on the plateau as Dhule, Jalgaon, Aurangabad etc. are examples of this sort.
5. Several rural pockets in Nasik, Ahmednagar, Pune, Satara, Sangli, Kolhapur and Solapur districts, where facilities of irrigation have been provided during the past thirty years or so, are experiencing relative economic prosperity and faster urban growth that is attributed mainly to the success of sugarcane culture and the consequent rise of industries and commerce etc. in those areas.

The profile of processes operating in Maharashtra presented above provides the necessary background for understanding the nature of changes in the urban systems, discussed below.

Nature of Change

Masharashtra countinues to enjoy first position in percentage of urbanisation according to 1981 census.[5] The percentage has gone up from 31.17 in 1971 to 35.03 in 1981 for Maharashtra whereas, for India it has improved from 19.90% in 1971 to 23.73% in 1981. The first five highest urbanised States in the country are Maharashtra (35.03%), Tamilnadu (32.98%), Gujarat (31.08%), Karnataka (28.92%) and Punjab (27.72 %). West Bengal has now lost its position amongst the first five leading States in the country. Consideration of absolute density, followed by that of variation in percentage of urbanisation and changes in the settlement systems reveals the structure of Maharashtra's urban systems. It also provides an explanation to its continued position as the leading urbanised-industrialised State in the country.

Fig. 3.1 throws light upon the changes in the absolute density values, according to districts. Greater Bombay's density value (number of persons per sq. km.) has tremendously gone-up from 9,901 in 1971 to 13,644 in 1981, whereas in Thane district it has increased from 239 to 349, i.e. a net increase by 110. Pune district has registered a growth by 63 (203 to 266), Kolhapur district by 57 (254 to 311) and Nagpur district by 64 (196 to 260). All these figures suggest ever-increasing concentration of population in the Greater Bombay district, followed by Pune and others noted above, due mainly to industrial and commercial development during the period under review. Lowest value of absolute increase in density is 9 for Ratnagiri district. It is significant, however, to note that Raigad (Kolaba) district, that is juxtaposed with the fast developing twin-Bombay, has registered a higher value of 33. Nasik and Jalgaon districts enjoy efficient railway and road links with Bombay and have registered absolute increase in population density values by 40 and 43, respectively.

Figs. 3.2 and 3.3 are concerning urbanisation. The spatial distribution of urban population in Maharashtra is extremely unbalanced. 38 percent of the State's total urban population was concentrated in Greater Bombay according to 1971 census. The same figure obtains for 1981. If Greater Bombay, Thane and Pune, the three contiguous industrialised-urbanised districts, are considered together it is found that their combined share in the State's total urban population has increased from 51.72 percent in 1971 to 53.17 percent in 1981. It indicates that the trend of concentration of industries and commerce at increasing rate continued in the Bombay-Pune, tract during the decade under review. One should bear in mind, however, that most of this development occurred along the main arteries of communication, only. The eleven districts viz. Greater Bombay, Thane, Nasik, Jalgaon, Buldhana, Akola, Amravati, Wardha, Nagpur, Pune and Solapur constituting the two segments of the developing national urban corridors shared 77.41 percent of the State's total urban population in 1971 (Fig. 3.7). This figure holds true for 1981, too. Evidently, it is due to the fact that most of the development was concentrated in these two tracts only, with the exception of some isolated pockets in Kolhapur, Sangli, Osmanabad, Parbhani, Chandrapur and Bhandara districts. The remaining fifteen districts are, thus, still relatively backward.

A perusal of Fig. 3.2 reveals that values of urbanisation exceeding 30 percent according to 1981 census occur in Greater Bombay, Thane, Pune and Nasik districts towards West and Nagpur in the east. Fig. 3.3 showing variation in percentage of urbanisation during 1971-81, brings out that significant variations have occurred in relatively developed areas, only. A remarkable as well as welcome feature is the diffusion of urbanisation towards south in Raigad (Kolaba) district due to proximity to Bombay and towards east in Aurangabad district due to induction of industries from Bombay. The emergence of a belt, occurring towards south-east of the more developed area, extending from Kolhapur in the south-west to Nanded in north-east, with trend of increasing urbanisation consequent upon rural development, is a very important development.

FIG. 3.1:

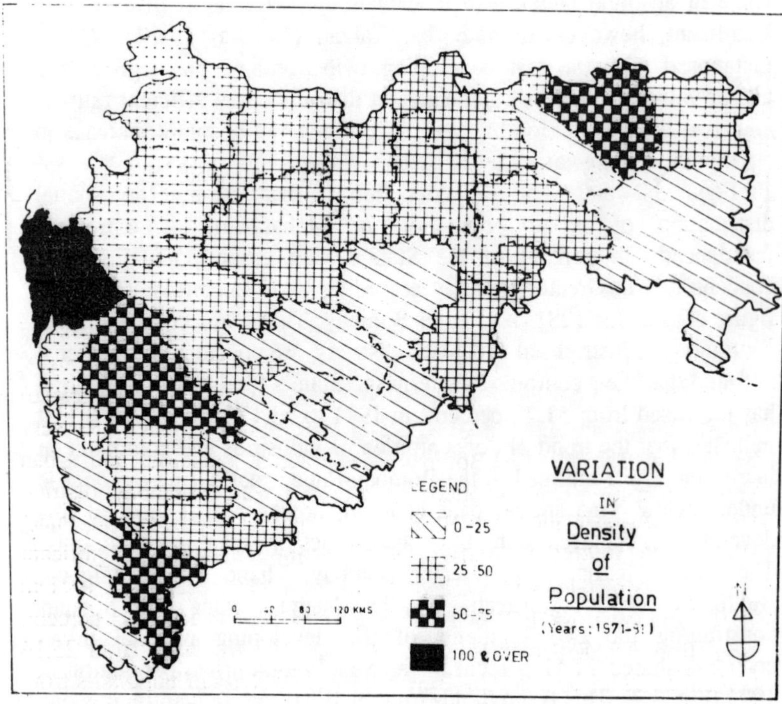

FIG. 3.2:

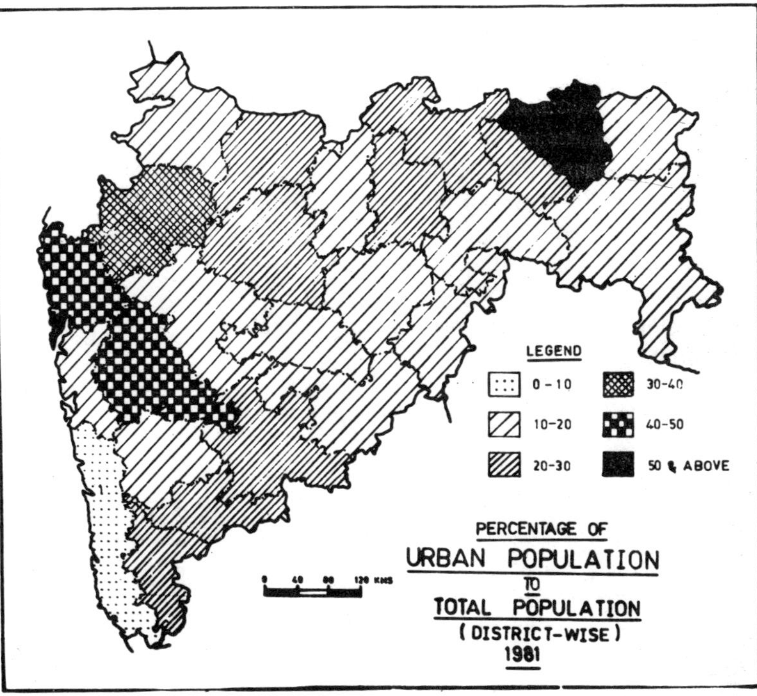

It actually hints at the current trend of diffusion of industries in the umland of class I cities following communication links.

The Fig. 3.4, showing the percentage of urbanisation (Tahsilwise) in the relatively more developed districts of the State, are very interesting. The existing Bombay-Pune tract of industrial and urban growth can be clearly noticed on them. Greater Bombay district, Thane, Kalyan, Ulhasnagar, Bhiwandi, Karjat, Khalapur, Maval, Pune, Haveli and Daund (Dhond) tahsils constitute this belt. Significant variations have occurred in Thane tahsil from 65.62 percent in 1971 to 72.90 percent in 1981, Bhiwandi from 32.34 percent to 43.03 percent, Uran from 17.68 percent to 24.53 percent and Khalapur from 25.14 percent to 32.75 percent etc. Haveli, Maval and Purandhar tahsils from Pune district deserve mention in this regard. Particularly, the expansion of the industrial belt southwards of Pune through Purandhar tahsil is a new feature to note.

FIG. 3.3:

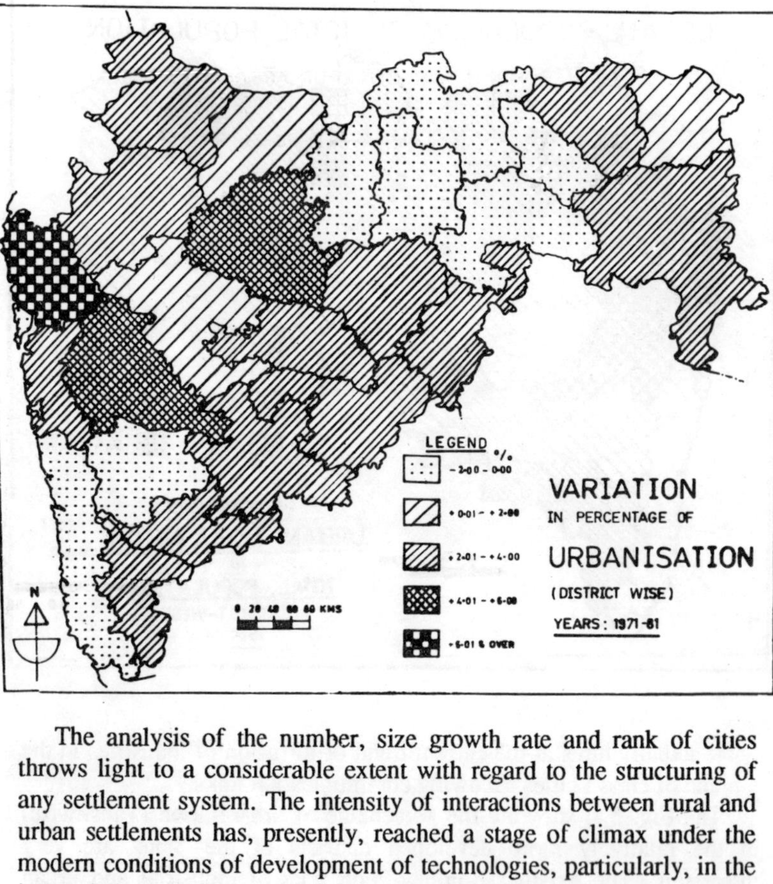

The analysis of the number, size growth rate and rank of cities throws light to a considerable extent with regard to the structuring of any settlement system. The intensity of interactions between rural and urban settlements has, presently, reached a stage of climax under the modern conditions of development of technologies, particularly, in the industrially developed areas. The villages from remote areas are also, these days, dependent upon cities to varying degrees, in a variety of ways. Thus, the consideration of the above noted aspects of towns and cities reveal the structure and state of a settlement system.

The total number of urban centres in Maharashtra has increased from 257 in 1971 to 276 in 1981 registering a net increase by 19. A break-up of this number reveals that, as much as ten of them occur in Thane district, and three each in Pune, Nasik and Nagpur districts. Thus, an overwhelming number of sixteen occurs in the immediate umland of Bombay alone.

FIG. 3.4:

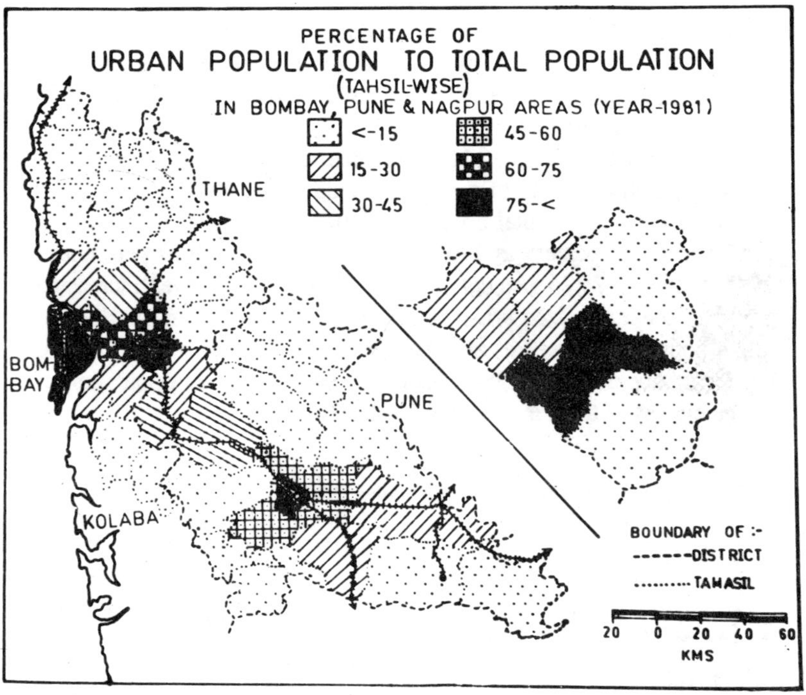

TABLE 3.1: Number and Class-wise Distribution of Urban Centres

Class	Year 1971	Year 1981
I	17	25
II	17	20
III	61	81
IV	90	91
V	58	43
VI	14	16
Total	257	276

The structural changes in the classes of towns are clearly noticeable from Table 3.1 and Tables 3.3 and 3.4. The number of class I cities (urban settlements with population of 1 lakh or more) was 3 in 1901, 4 in 1921, and also in 1941 and 13 in 1961. It increased to 17 in 1971 and according to 1981 census it is 25. This increase has occurred at the cost of lower order settlements due to escalation. A decline in the number of class V towns, that are mainly rural service centres, is an adverse feature. Secondly, most of these class I centres occur along main arteries of communication.

An examination of the class-wise distribution of the State's total urban population points to a specific trend. The class I cities shared 34.40 per cent of the total urban population in 1901, 40.34 percent in 1931 and 65.91 percent in 1961. The figure rose to 70.79 per cent in 1971 and it is 75.24 percent in 1981. The trend of ever increasing power of the large-sized urban centres both in number and the share of urban population, deserves attention of experts as it is just opposite of the ideal. According to 1981 census, the share of urban population of all the classes of town is shown in Table 3.2.

TABLE 3.2: Towns' Share of Urban Population (1981)

		Percent
(A)		
Large Towns	Class I centres	75.24
(B		
Medium Towns	Class II centres	05.95
	Class III centres	10.88
(C)		
Small Towns	Class IV centres	06.10
	Class V centres	01.58
	Class VI centres	00.25
	Total	100.00

These values speak for themselves.

FIG. 3.5:

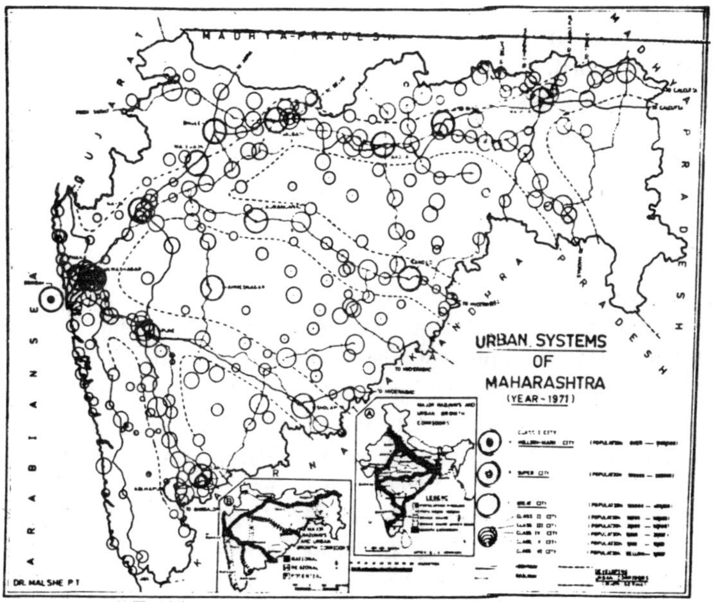

Fig. 3.5 displays the spatial distribution of urban centres in Maharashtra as in 1971. The inset map 'A' shows major railways and urban growth corridors in India and the inset map 'B' shows the national, regional and potential urban growth corridors of Maharashtra. The developing urban corridors of 50 kms. width occur along railways and highways, as mentioned earlier. Significantly, out of 17 class I cities all except two, viz. Dhule and Ahmednagar, occur in these corridors. This map reveals several characteristic features as: (a) The convergence of urbanized-industrialized belts on Bombay, (b) the dense cluster of urban settlements around Bombay-Thane-Ulhasnagar, (c) relatively vacant areas in Konkan, Western Ghats, drier tract around Ahmednagar and a large part of Bhandara and Chandrapur districts.

Fig. 3.6 reveals clearly the conditions prevailing in 1981. Out of a total of 25 class I cities all except three, viz., Dhule, Ahmednagar and Latur, occur in the urban corridors. The regional distribution of the new eight class I cities is as follows:

(a) Khandesh	1
(b) Vidarbha	2
(c) Marathwada	3
(d) Western districts	2
Total	8

It supports the previous observation that the recent industrial growth in Khandesh, Marathwada and south Maharashtra has been instrumental in the growth of urbanisation during the decade.

The map further features the increased clustering of urban centres at Bombay-Thane-Ulhasnagar, Pune-Chinchwad, Kolhapur- Sangli, Jalgaon-Bhusawal, Nasik and Nagpur. The relatively vacant areas mentioned above, continue to remain as they were a decade ago. The two inset maps at the right hand bottom of Fig. 3.6 furnish the details of the first two clusters. Note the linear development on either side of Pune, however, with a more pronounced development in the direction of Bombay. A sizable portion of Bombay's industrial-urban growth occurs in the area contained by Bassein, Bhiwandi, Ambarnath and Bombay. New expansions are occurring presently on mainland around Uran, Panvel, and Khopoli.

The foregoing discussion clearly shows, that modern industrialisation commenced from Bombay and that it has been diffusing from the sea coast to inland stations, as observed with respect to several leading coastal metropolises in the world, e.g. Scottish port cities.[6]

Entire Maharashtra, Goa and Gujarat, portions of M.P., Rajasthan, A.P. and Karnataka constitute the umland of Bombay. Generally speaking (a) The Bombay's urban district occurs within a radius of 50 km. with the centre of the semi-circle located in the centre of Greater Bombay district. It is characterised by occurrence of a large number of secondary industrial nodes, industries of various sorts, slums, problems of pollution and traffic, etc. that constitute modern chronic urban syndrome. (b) The immediate umland occurs within a radius of 150 km. from Bombay inland extending upto Mahabaleshwar, the celebrated hill resort, Pune, Nasik and Bulsar (Gujarat). It is characterised by intensive industrial growth at the two important outposts viz. Pune and Nasik and their environs. These are also the farthest points from where commuters consisting of trading and workers communities perform journey to various places in Bombay's urban district. (c) The meso-umland of Bombay occurs within a radius of 400 km. reaching up to Panjim (Goa), Bijapur (Karnataka), Parbhani, Malkapur, Khargone (M.P.), and Anand (Gujarat). The meso-umland is characterised by growth of modern industries at various centres within it during comparatively recent times, as evidenced through the preceding discussion. (d) The farther umland occurs within a radius of 700 km. extending upto Mangalore (Karnataka), Hyderabad (A.P.), Nagpur, Bhopal (M.P.) and Kota (Rajasthan). The farther umland is characterised by mainly trading and

FIG. 3.6

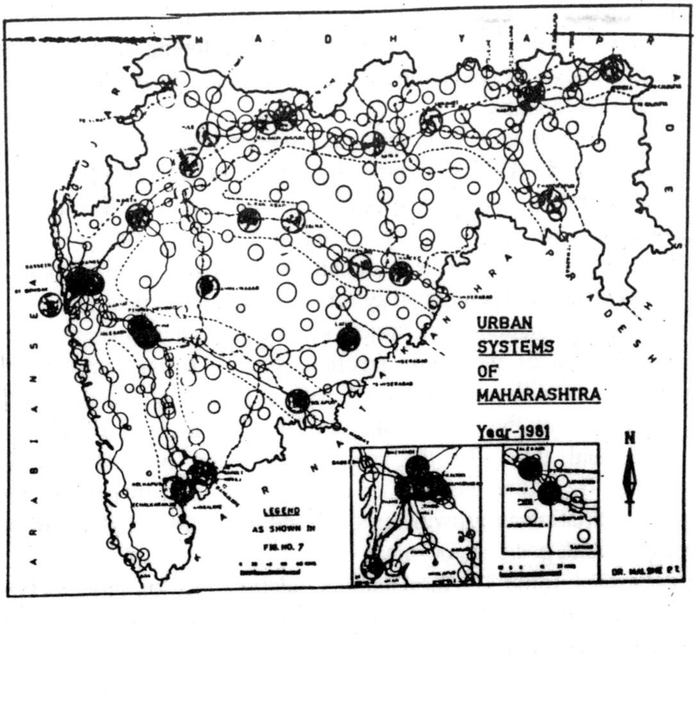

export-import dependence on Bombay. Areas even beyond this limit look to Bombay for these facilities owing to obvious reasons. Bombay's influence extends eastwards a little beyond Gondiya City, only.

Instability in the System

The consideration of the state of a settlement system involves time factor. The values of variables chosen for identifying the state of the system are taken at a particular point in time and, therefore, the "state" is a temporary aspect of a system. It may be transient or in a state of equilibrium. For measuring this aspect of the system a variety of variables could be used, such as, population growth rates, migration levels, growth rates of higher order central places etc., individually or jointly, according to suitable spatial units (districts or cultural regions). A fruitful comparison of values for the various spatial units throws considerable light upon the relative stability or instability of the settlement system bringing out its existing condition. Such an analysis is extremely useful in an economically fast developing country from the point-of-view of planning for urbanisation, a facet, hitherto neglected in our country.

The variable used below for analysing relative stability of the settlement system of Maharashtra, is growth behaviour of Class I cities/agglomerations, over a period of last eight decades. The choice of growth rate of city for measuring instability is of particular importance to Maharashtra as it directly reflects the socio-economic changes occurring in a settlement system of developing countries.

Detailed examination of the trajectories of individual cities in terms of population size and rank position show varying amount of turbulence or instability in the growth process. A stable growth pattern could be defined as the one in which (a) all cities grow at exactly the same rate, and thus, (b) the rank-size position of each city is unchanged.[7] The more unstable or turbulent the growth pattern, the greater the variation in growth rates of individual cities and the more switching of rank positions occurs.

A perusal of Table 3.3, furnishing population data for various class I cities from 1901 to 1981 reveals that the growth of population in various cities has occurred at varying paces.

TABLE 3.3: Growth of Class I Cities in Maharashtra (1901 - 1981)

Year	Gt. Bombay City	Pune Agglo.	Nagpur Agglo.	Ulhasnagar Agglo.	Solapur City	Nasik Agglo.	Thane Agglo.	Kolhapur Agglo.	Aurangabad Agglo.	Sangli Agglo.	Amravati City	Malegaon City	Akola City
	1	2	3	4	5	6	7	8	9	10	11	12	13
						(Population Data in '000) (↑ij)							
1901	**812**	**164**	**166**	11	75	24	16	54	37	35	39	19	29
1911	**1018**	**172**	**118**	12	61	32	15	42	35	37	41	19	26
1921	**1245**	**198**	**165**	8	**119**	57	22	52	37	41	45	23	38
1931	**1268**	**250**	**241**	26	**145**	57	21	67	37	53	57	29	48
1941	**1686**	**324**	**328**	31	**213**	74	29	93	51	67	74	36	62
1951	**2966**	**605**	**485**	**169**	**277**	**157**	67	**137**	67	90	**102**	55	89
1961	**4152**	**790**	**690**	**247**	**337**	**215**	**109**	**193**	98	**127**	**138**	**121**	**116**
1971	**5970**	**1135**	**930**	**396**	**398**	**271**	**207**	**267**	**165**	**201**	**194**	**191**	**198**
1981	**8202**	**1685**	**1298**	**631**	**514**	**429**	**389**	**351**	**316**	**269**	**261**	**245**	**225**

Year	Dhule City	Nanded City	Ahmednagar Agglo	Jalgaon City	Ichalkaranji City	Bhusawal Agglo.	Jalna City	Chandrapur City	Bhiwandi City	Latur City	Parbhani City	Gondia City
	14	15	16	17	18	19	20	21	22	23	24	25
1901	25	14	36	16	13	16	20	18	10	10	10	—
1911	30	18	34	17	10	15	19	20	13	8	9	6
1921	29	21	50	23	10	25	17	23	12	16	15	11
1931	39	27	57	34	12	28	22	28	16	31	17	15
1941	53	37	70	48	19	36	38	36	19	25	22	20
1951	77	65	**105**	68	27	54	58	41	26	35	33	37
1961	99	81	**119**	80	51	79	67	51	48	41	37	56
1971	**137**	**126**	**148**	**106**	88	**105**	91	75	80	70	62	78
1981	**211**	**191**	**181**	**145**	**134**	**132**	**122**	**115**	**115**	**112**	**109**	**100**

(Class I City = Population 1,00,000 or more: in black face

(i) Between 1901-71 the population of class I cities of Konkan, viz. Ulhasnagar, Thane, Bombay and Bhiwandi, grew by approximately 36, 13, 7 and 8 times, respectively. The population of Ulhasnagar grew at a phenomenally high rate due to the influx of refugees from Pakistan, as well as, the growth of industries. It has again almost doubled itself during the past decade. Thana was a residential suburb of Bombay for quite some time and, therefore, the population did not grow much upto 1941. However, with growth of industries during the past thirty years or so, the population of the city grew tremendously. It has almost doubled itself during the past decade. The rate of growth of population of Bombay is also quite fast. Bombay's population grew by 76 percent between 1941 and 51, by 40 percent between 1951 and 61, 43 percent between 1961 and 71 and by 38 percent between 1971 and 81; pretty high for a mommoth city.

(ii) The population of class I cities of upland districts of western Maharashtra seems to have increased at modest rates between 1901 and 1971: Nasik (11), Malegaon (10), Pune (7), Sangli (6), Solapur (5), Kolhapur (5), Ichalkaranji (6), and Ahmednagar (4), times approximately. Pune, Nasik and Malegaon have witnessed industrial growth during the past two/three decades due to excessive concentration of industrial activities and the resultant degeneration of conditions in Greater Bombay. This factor resulted into excessive population growth during this period at these three places. These cities maintained their tempo of growth during the past decade.

(iii) During 1901-71 the population of class I cities of Khandesh, Marathwada and Vidarbha grew on the whole at modest paces viz. Dhule (5), Bhusawal (6), Jalgaon (6), Aurangabad (5), Latur (7), Parbhani (6), Jalna (4.5), Nanded (9), Akola (6), Amravati (5), Nagpur (6) Chandrapur (4) and Gondia (12) times with the exception of Nanded and Gondia, the regional centres occurring in the midst of fertile tracts. The growth at Aurangabad between 1971-81 has been tremendous, whereas, it slowed down at Akola.

Conclusion

The preceding discussion clearly indicates that the growth behaviour of cities was turbulent in north Konkan and those not far away from

Bombay, whereas it was modest in remote areas either in the south or in the east. Ulhasnagar ascended from seventeenth position to fifth, Thane progressed from fifteenth to eighth, whereas, Greater Bombay retained its first position par excellence, throughout the period of seven decades from 1970-71. Ulhasnagar ascended to fourth and Thane to seventh position by 1981. Such class I cities nearer to Bombay as Nasik, Pune and Malegaon, have also progressed in rank positions. The remaining cities have either lost their higher positions in the hierarchical order or just managed to retain their earlier ranks. Aurangabad has ascended from thirteenth to ninth position in 1981. The decline in the ranks of Ahmednagar, and Amravati is really spectacular.

FIG. 3.7:

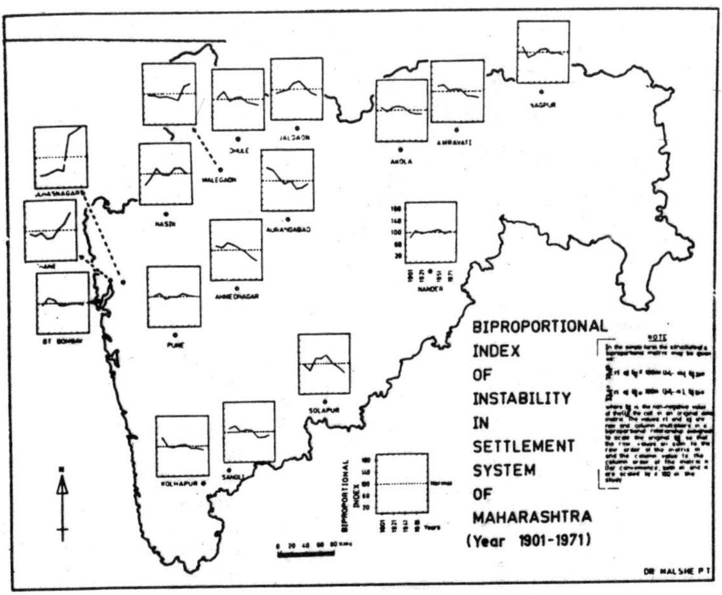

To facilitate more precise understanding of relative growth of class I cities in the settlement system, the biproportional index method has been applied (see Table 3.2). The biproportional matrix of the table shows the changing fortunes of the twenty-five areas in an index standardized so that row totals equal 2500 and column totals 900. Cell values = 100 indicate that a city in that time period has changed in phase with change in the whose set of cities. Values above 100 indicate faster than system growth and vice versa. In other words, the variance of lijs allows an overall estimate of the instability of growth paths to be gauged. Note the accelerated growth of Ulhasnagar, Thane, Nanded and Nasik, the relative stagnation of Pune, Greater Bombay and Nagpur and decline of Solapur and Ahmednagar between 1901 and 1971 (Fig. 3.7). The growth rates of primate cities such as Solapur, Sangli, Amravati, Akola, Ahmednagar, Dhule and Aurangabad, etc.,

FIG. 3.8:

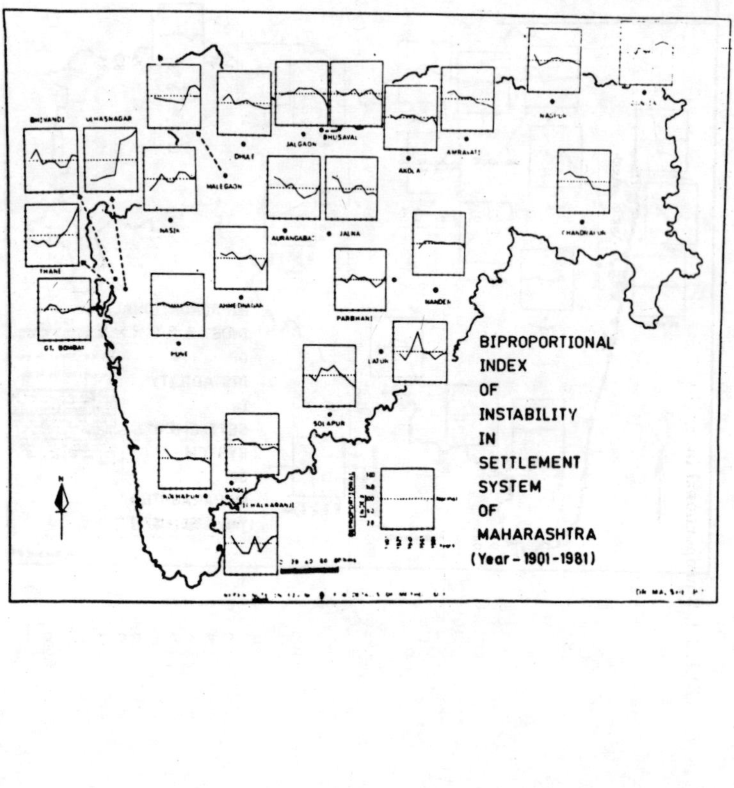

TABLE 3.4: Biproportional Index (Ij)

Year	Gt. Bombay	Pune Agglo.	Nagpur Agglo.	Ulhasnagar Agglo.	Solapur	Nasik Agglo.	Thane Agglo.	Kolhapur Agglo.	Aurangabad Agglo.	Sangli Agglo.	Amravati	Malegaon	Akola
	1	2	3	4	5	6	7	8	9	10	11	12	13
1901	96	102	121	34	102	64	81	129	135	115	119	95	109
1911	117	106	84	37	81	84	72	102	125	119	124	92	96
1921	111	95	91	45	123	117	82	98	104	104	106	86	110
1931	89	93	104	47	117	92	63	97	114	104	105	86	107
1941	94	94	110	49	133	91	65	104	85	104	107	82	108
1951	100	109	101	157	108	121	96	97	70	87	91	79	96
1961	102	103	106	167	94	121	112	99	75	88	88	129	90
1971	99	99	94	172	76	101	145	92	84	94	83	134	104
1981	92	99	89	**192**	66	**109**	**184**	82	**108**	85	77	**117**	80
Total	900	900	900	900	900	900	900	900	900	900	900	900	900

Year	Dhule	Nanded	Ahmednagar	Jalgaon	Ichalkaranji	Bhusawal	Jalna	Chandrapur	Bhiwandi	Latur	Parbhani	Gondia	Total
	14	15	16	17	18	19	20	21	22	23	24	25	
1901	110	85	114	97	126	109	136	122	104	91	104	—	2500
1911	129	108	107	101	92	99	127	132	135	72	91	68	2500
1921	98	107	118	104	70	100	87	112	88	111	117	116	2500
1931	103	101	99	118	68	116	87	114	98	167	105	106	2500
1941	110	105	100	115	123	90	107	114	94	101	109	106	2500
1951	96	100	109	116	74	107	109	79	77	94	100	127	2500
1961	90	102	91	106	101	112	82	76	78	75	78	135	2500
1971	84	104	63	86	121	85	85	72	115	90	89	129	2500
1981	80	88	99	57	**125**	82	80	79	**111**	99	**107**	**113**	2500
Total	900	900	900	900	900	900	900	900	900	900	900	900	22500

all located on the plateau, were faster than system growth before 1951. However, since 1951 onwards the main vista of economic growth seems to have shifted from the plateau to centres in north Konkan and centres nearer to them. The primate cities of the plateau away from Bombay, are generally speaking, experiencing a hard time on this account. Thus, a shift in system growth is perceived from the plateau to Bombay-Pune tract.

Fig. 3.8 however, reveals that some cities of Marathwada viz. Aurangabad, Parbhani and Latur; Gondia from Vidarbha and Ahmednagar from Western Maharashtra have registered relatively faster rates of growth, recently. The graphs for all 25 class I cities furnish a view for the total period from 1901-81.

If a balanced growth of urbanisation has to be achieved in the State, alongwith arresting further migration of population to Bombay-Pune tract, then a policy of dissemination of urban growth should be encouraged to offset the current trend indicated above. The role played by Maharashtra Industrial Development Corporation (M.I.D.C.) in this direction is quite commendable. However, more bold and timely steps are required to be taken by the concerned agencies/authorities to restore balance to the settlement system, especially when according to experts, the percentage of urbanisation in the State is likely to rise upto 45 by the end of current century. Thus, very great and sincere efforts are urgently needed, firstly, to arrest the current trend and then, secondly, to reverse it, if possible. But, is it possible to do so under modern conditions of technology and economy? Thirdly, therefore, is there any positive answer to such question as, can Bombay be saved?[8]

REFERENCES

1. Johnson, B.L.C. *Indian-Resources & Development,* Arnold-Heinemann, London, (1980). Refer Fig. 12.6, p. 171.
2. Malshe, P.T. "An Analysis of Urban Growth behaviour in Maharashtra and the Role of Urban Planning", *Journal of the Indian Town & Country Planning Asso.*, Bombay. Vol. XV, No. 1, (1977) , pp 6-18.
3. Malshe, P.T. "Settlement System of Maharashtra", Paper contributed to the National Seminar on Settlement Systems of India, Hyderabad, (1980).
4. Haas, H.D. "The Effectiveness of the Industrial Estate Concept in Developing Nations, Taking the Caribbean Countries as an Example", *Applied Grography and Development,* Vol. 17, (1981), pp. 17-28.
5. *Census of India*, 1981, Series 12-Maharashtra, Paper 1 of 1981- Supplement, Provisional Population Totals.
6. O'Dell, A.C. "Port Facilities and the Dispersal of Industry: The Problem in Scotland"; *Geographical Journal*, London, Vol. 97, No. 2 (1941).

7. Haggett, P. "Measuring Instability in the Growth of Urban Systems: A Biproportional Index", *General Problems of Geography & Geosystems Modelling*, I.G. Congress, Moscow, Vol. 11, (1976), pp. 116-117.
8. "Can Bombay be Saved?", *Business India*, No. 95, (1981), pp 42-60.

FOUR

Join R. Clark

Population Density Changes in a Dual City: Ankara from 1961 to 1977

Introduction

THE rapid growth of cities in developing countries is one of the most important demographic events in the period since World War II. Although some of the growth is the result of natural increase within cities, the bulk is caused by in-migration of large numbers of people from rural areas. No city has escaped this growth, even when there have been substantial efforts to prevent it. The greatest of these efforts have been made in the new capital cities of some developing countries, which are intended to be modern showcases that reflect an attempt to recast national images in the European mould often admired by local elites.

Such showcase cities are often showcases of traits often considered less desirable by forward-looking national leaders. One of these traits is the dual economy, which is the result of a modern industrial style economy being superimposed upon a traditional agricultural one. This may have been caused by a history of colonial domination, as is the case in most of Africa and South Asia, or be the results of local independent leaders' efforts to modernise, as is the case in Turkey or Iran. Many large cities in developing countries show the existence of the dual economy: they have split personalities. A large part of the city will have the trappings of a western metropolis and house the well-to-do, while an even larger and more densely populated portion is the home of the city's traditional working masses, many of whom are recent arrivals from rural areas.

John Brush has investigated[1] this phenomenon in a number of Indian cities, where the legacy of British Colonial rule was still visible in the urban landscape in the 1960's. Considering the frequency of this phenomenon, it is surprising how little of the work on population density distribution within third-world cities has taken any cognizance of the issue at all. Brush is the only scholar to have produced separate population density gradients for the two types of urban area. Comparative studies are needed, and the present paper is an effort to produce such a work.

Ankara, the capital of Turkey since 1923, is an early case of the "new capital" phenomenon. Intended by Ataturk, the revolutionary founder of the Turkish Republic, and its President from 1923 to 1938, to symbolize the transformation of Turkey from a medieval theocratic empire to a modern republic of European style, Ankara was planned as small city of spacious boulevards and public places, equipped with all modern amenities including comfortable, healthful dwellings. The Jansen plan of 1932 projected a population of 300,000 by 1985.[2] Ankara was planned to be a city representing the modern side of the dual economy, although of course, in the 1930's no one was thinking in those terms. However, it should be stated at the outset, that the practice of planning in most developing countries has been heavily biased towards the interests and values of the modernizing elite, and has thus tended to encourage the modern, or foreign, side of the dual economy.

Several things have happened to thwart Jansen's plan. First, in the 1930's no one imagined that such rapid population growth was to occur in the coming decades.[3] At the end of World War II, Turkish officials were still concerned with how to cause population growth[4] rather than prevent it. Also, at that time, no country outside the industrial world had had much experience with the rapid urbanization that accompanies industrial development. Thirdly, the development of the countryside through farm mechanization and the extension of a road network gave peasants both a reason for leaving the country (unemployment) and a means to do it (transport). Lastly, the development of migrant settlements at the city margins removed many of the psychological and material barriers to migration, for migrants now had a large number of friends or relatives already there. Thus, once migration streams had begun to flow, the process fed on itself and accelerated rapidly. As a result, in 1975 Ankara's population numbered 1.7 million, wit 3 million projected for 1985.

This development has caused a number of problems, for the migrants have settled in a series of squatter areas (*gecekondu*) that cover approximately 69% of the land developed for urban uses[5] since 1945. This has severely restricted planned development and has forced large expenditures on development of urban infrastructure, money that might have been better spent on other kinds of development. From the migrant's point of view, given the facts of the demographic and mobility (Zelinsky's term[6]), transitions that have accompanied industrial development everywhere, it is hard to imagine what else they might have done, but in the eyes of the established urban elites, the whole process has seemed threatening, if not catastrophic.

Purpose

The purpose of this paper is to trace the spatial extension of Ankara's population between 1961 and 1977, particularly in relation to two planning goals: reduction of the number of people living in sub-standard housing in both the old city (settled before 1923) and squatter areas, and the distribution of population more evenly by distance from the centre than would otherwise occur in a free market economy. The development of 19th Century Western cities was usually characterised by the existence of crowded slums near the city centre that were both unsightly and unhealthy. Turkish planners have tried to avoid this through the control of building density. In terms of the first goal, their success can be measured by counting the number of people in each type of housing. This is relatively easy to do for they cluster in distinct neighbourhoods.[7] As for the second goal, their success in regulating the spatial structure of population density, can be measured with density gradients. These are curves fitted to population density data by least squares methods that summarize the pattern of population density at varying distances from the city's centre.

Method – The Density Gradient Model

Colin Clark[8] noticed that for a larger number of European and American cities the equation:

$$Dx = Do^{-ebx} \qquad (1)$$

where:

Dx = the population density at distance x from the

centre of the city;

Do = the hypothetical density at the city's centre;

e = the base of the natural logarithms;

b = the population density gradient; and

x = the distance from the centre of the city,

described the pattern of population density with considerable accuracy.

The equation represents a pattern of great density at the centre that declines toward the city's edge. It becomes linear when the densities are transformed to logarithms, which makes for easy calculation of the parameters (Do and b) by least square regression, in the form:

$$\ln Dx = \ln Do - bx \qquad (2)$$

Clark also noticed that the steepness of the gradient (b) declined with time. This, as observed by both Clark and Berry *et al.*,[9] was the result of transportation improvements that allowed more people to live further from the centre of an expanding city.

In the logarithmic equation, the gradient is assumed to be linear, with the greatest density at the centre (Do), but in fact, the residential densities of the city's commercial core are usually not as high as those in the residential areas near the centre. To accommodate this curve, a second degree term has been added to the equation, producing:

$$\ln Dx = \ln Do + bx - cx^2 \quad (3)$$

In equations (3) and (4) (below), c and d are parameters similar to b, that determine the form of the curve that describes the density distribution. Polynomial curve fitting by regression requires some caution for it is always possible to keep adding terms that will always improve the fit, while not necessarily adding anything to the theoretical or practical understanding of urban processes. Another problem is that while things like a central depression in the population density curve may be visible in the raw data, this effect might not be seen in the equation fitted to them if the effect is relatively weak and thus overwhelmed by the overall downward trend of the gradient.[10] However, the addition of further terms could be useful, for they could make the method more sensitive to variations that are present in the data. Addition of a third-degree term results in:

$$\ln Dx = \ln Do - bx - cx^2 + dx^3 \quad (4)$$

which generates the "S" curve that appears both in Newling's[11] hypothetical diagrams of density gradients and Rees's[12] data-based diagrams of Chicago. A third-degree equation has already been used by Lentz[13] to describe the density gradients of Warsaw.

Three important density parameters can be derived from these equations: the central, maximum, and critical densities. In any rapidly growing city, the central density (Do) should decline as housing in the central area is replaced by service and transport facilities. Under the same conditions, the maximum density (the highest point on the curve) should move downward and outward with time. This has been shown by Newling[14] for London and by Latham and Yeates[15] for Toronto. The critical density, defined by Newling[16] as the density that, if exceeded, will lead to a decline in density, but below which increases will occur, should also move downward and outward with time. The critical density is defined operationally as the point where two temporally successive density gradient regression lines cross. Thus in each time period, the crossing points of the successive gradient lines should be at lower densities and further from the city centre.

In terms of planning goals, the planned areas should show flatter density gradients with lower maximum and critical densities. They should also have more success in maintaining housing stocks near the centre and therefore have a relatively slow decline of the central density. By contrast the *laissez faire* economy of the unplanned city should produce conditions like those in U.S. cities with rapidly declining central densities, relatively high maximum densities and a steep gradient outward from the point of maximum density.

Data

Density gradient analysis requires data on the population densities of small subdivisions of the city studied. There are no published census figures for Turkish cities that correspond to the census tracts of U.S. cities, but the Ankara Master Plan Bureau (AMPB) has obtained unofficial figures by *mahalle* (neighbourhood) from the 1965 and 1970 censuses[(see 17, 18 for what is published)]. I know of no *mahalle* figures for other census years. However, there are published voter registration figures for the national elections of 1961, 1965, 1969, 1973, and 1977[19, 20, 21, 22, 23]. In Turkey, neighbourhoods are canvassed and all adults (over 21) are registered. These figures are published by *mahalle* and ballot box, and while there are some discrepancies between these and the census figures, in the main they correspond to the latter, but before they are usable they require some adjustments.

The need for the first of these adjustments stems from the fact that the ratio of registered voters to resident population has not remained constant. Populations for the four subprovincial (kaza) units in Ankara[24] were estimated by geometric interpolation (Table 4.1 A) for the months that the elections took place (October for every year except 1977, when it was in June) and divided into the voter totals (Table 4.1 B) to get a proportion of participation for each kaza and year (Table 4.1 C). An adjustment factor (Q) was derived for each election year by taking each year's proportion of participation and dividing it into the 1965 proportion (Table 4.1 D). Since the 1965 election and census occurred within two weeks of one another, their figures can be considered equivalent and are thus useful as a base line.

The transformation of the registration data into populations was done differently for each election year. The 1965 election was the simplest, for its census figures were taken as the populations. For 1961 I assumed that the *mahalle* by *mahalle* proportions of voters to total population was the same as 1965 and calculated their populations as:

$$P61 = V61 \times (P65/V65) \times Q61 \qquad (5)$$

where:

V61, V65 = the 1961 and 1965 registration figures for a *mahalle*,

P65 = its 1965 census population, and

Q61 = the adjustment factor for the proportion of the population that was registered in 1961 (Table 4.1 D).

TABLE 4.1: Calculation of Q

Year	1961	1965	1969	1973	1977
Kaza: A. *Estimated Populations:*					
Merkez	121242	121680	115835	102312	89243
Altindağ	151285	206109	304056	432345	590313
Cankaya	298235	422849	598856	789110	994027
Yenimahalle	71001	86220	122209	169370	226865
Ankara	641763	836858	1140956	1493137	1900448
B. Voter Totals:					
Merkez	57033	52027	47226	43175	53515
Altindağ	65389	81688	118595	176962	277730
Cankaya	139902	180728	255144	331836	452088
Yenimahalle	27756	31289	45985	71888	116780
Ankara	290080	345372	466950	623861	900113
C. Voter Totals / Estimated Populations:					
Merkez	0.4704	0.4276	0.4077	0.4220	0.5997
Altindağ	0.4322	0.3963	0.3900	0.4093	0.4705
Cankaya	0.4691	0.4274	0.4261	0.4205	0.4548
Yenimahalle	0.3909	0.3629	0.3763	0.4244	0.5148
Ankara	0.4520	0.4127	0.4093	0.4178	0.4736
D.Q.:					
Merkez	0.9090	1.0000	1.0488	1.0133	0.7131
Altindağ	0.9169	1.0000	1.0160	0.9682	0.8423
Cankaya	0.9111	1.0000	1.0032	1.0163	0.9397
Yenimahalle	0.9283	1.0000	0.9644	0.8550	0.7050
Ankara	0.9130	1.0000	1.0084	0.9877	0.8714

Estimation of the population for 1969 requires two interpolations because the elections and censuses did not fall in the same years. First the ratio of voter to population (R 70) was interpolated by:

$$R70 = \{(V69 + (V73 - V69)/4)\}/P70 \quad (6)$$

where:

V69, V73 = the number of voters in a *mahalle* in 1969 and 1973, and

P70 = the census population of the same *mahalle* in 1970.

The ratio for 1969 (R69) can then be estimated by:

$$R69 = .2 \times (V65/P65) + .8 \times R70 \quad (7)$$

where V65 and P65 are the numbers of voters and the populations in each *mahalle* in 1965. Linear interpolations were used because *mahalle* by *mahalle* growth patterns were very irregular, so assuming that they were geometric seemed inappropriate. A simple linear interpolation appeared to cover the largest number of cases adequately. The ratio for 1969 was then used to estimate *mahalle* populations for that year by:

$$P69 = V69 \times R69 \times Q69 \quad (8)$$

Since 1970 was the most recent census year, the proportion of registered voters in each *mahalle's* population for 1973 and 1977 were based on the 1970 ratio (R70). The populations for 1973 and 1977 were thus:

$$P73 = V73 \times R70 \times Q73 \quad (9)$$
$$P77 = V77 \times R70 \times Q77 \quad (10)$$

The areas of the *mahalles* and their distances from the Peak Value Intersection (PVI)[24] were measured with an electronic digitizer coupled to a computer from maps of the 1965, 1970 and 1977 *mahalle* boundaries supplied by the AMPB. Many *mahalles*, particularly at the city margins, were divided into smaller *mahalles* at various times. Changes were traced through each election year on the basis of the *mahalle* lists published in the election returns.[25]

Population of Unplanned, Mixed and Planned Areas

The population in each type of area (Table 4.2 A) grew rapidly during the study period, and shows the effects of the workings of the dual economy quite clearly. Examination of the percentage of Ankara's population in each type (Table 4.2 B) shows a relative gain for the planned areas from 1961 to 1969, in accordance with planning goals. The ground gained by the modern economy during the 1960's was lost during the 1970's. In 1977 the proportion living in unplanned areas was slightly higher than it had been in 1961 and the proportion in planned areas was substantially lower.

TABLE 4.2: Population by Year and Neighbourhood Type.

Year:	1961	1965	1969	1973	1977
A. By population:					
Neighbourhood type:					
Unplanned	320449	399901	539924	714838	956160
Mixed	100242	143409	185623	287056	348728
Planned	221072	293548	415409	491243	595560
Total	641763	836858	1140956	1493137	1900448
B. By percent:					
Unplanned	49.9	47.8	47.3	47.9	50.3
Mixed	15.6	17.1	16.3	19.2	18.4
Planned	34.5	35.1	36.4	32.9	31.3
Total	100.0	100.0	100.0	100.0	100.0

The cause of these shifts is certainly economic, for during the 1960's there was substantial industrial growth in Turkey and they also were successful at exporting surplus labour to Europe. The families of the "European" workers more often than not stayed in their rural places of origin where living costs were low. When the demand for Turkish labour in Europe dried up, workers that would have gone there and families that would have remained in the country converged on Turkey's cities, increasing pressures on their resources of employment and housing. At the same time there has been a serious recession in Turkey (virtually no industrial growth since 1974) so the economic gains that might have countered the stress induced by the increased number of migrants and provided them with more planned housing, simply were not there.

Density Gradients

Third-degree equations in the form of equation (4), were derived from the data for unplanned, mixed planned, and all neighbourhoods for

FIG. 4.1:

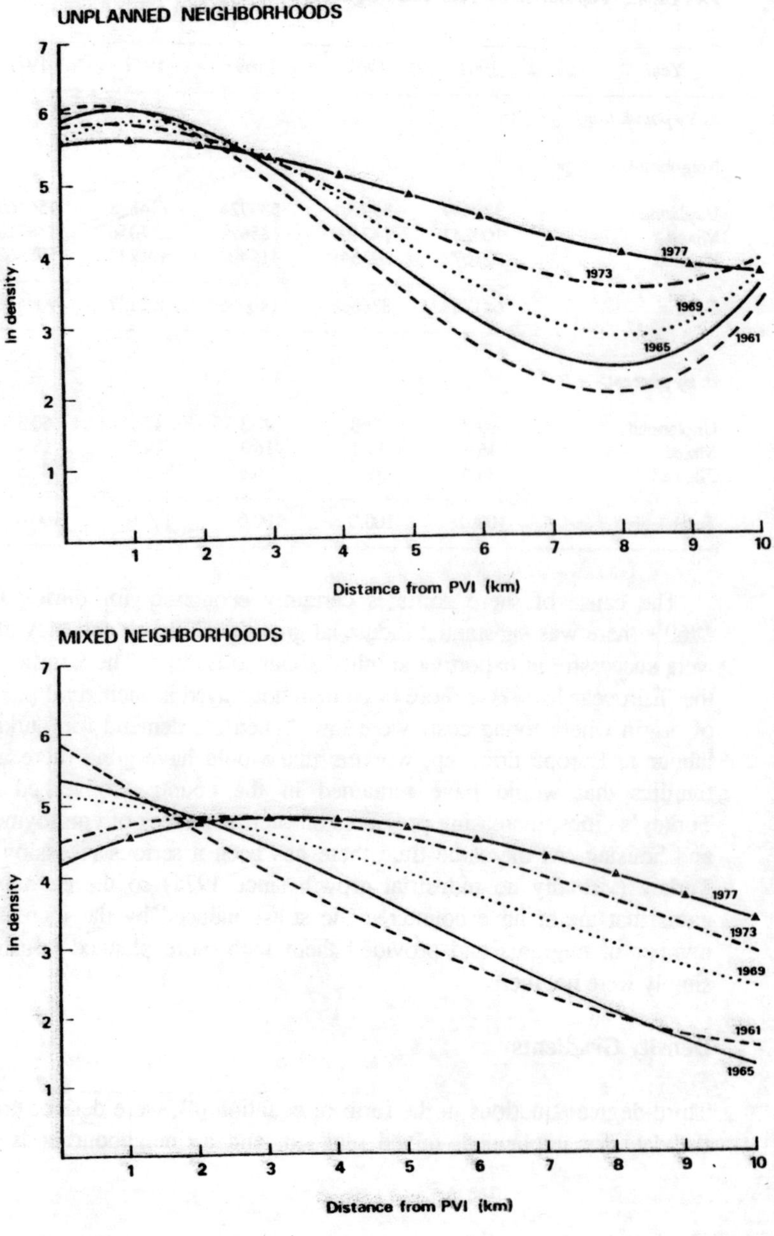
UNPLANNED NEIGHBORHOODS
ln density
Distance from PVI (km)
1977
1973
1969
1965
1961
MIXED NEIGHBORHOODS
ln density
Distance from PVI (km)
1977
1973
1969
1961
1965

PLANNED NEIGHBORHOODS

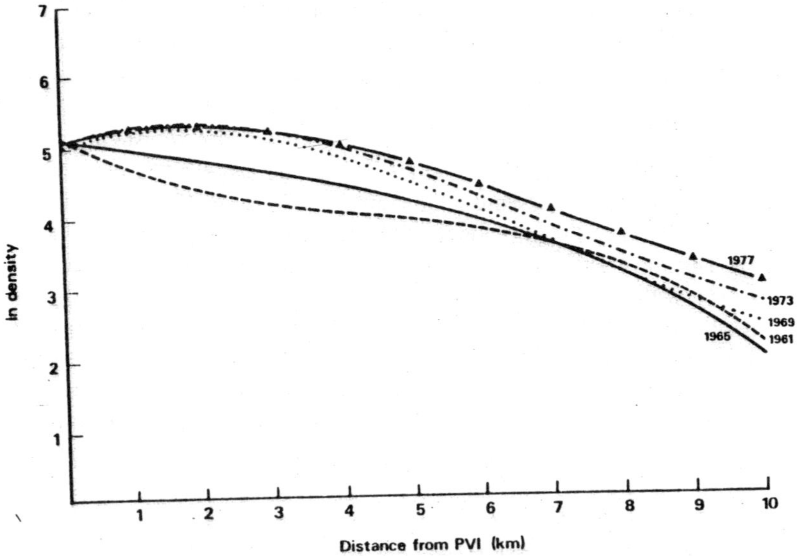

ALL NEIGHBORHOODS

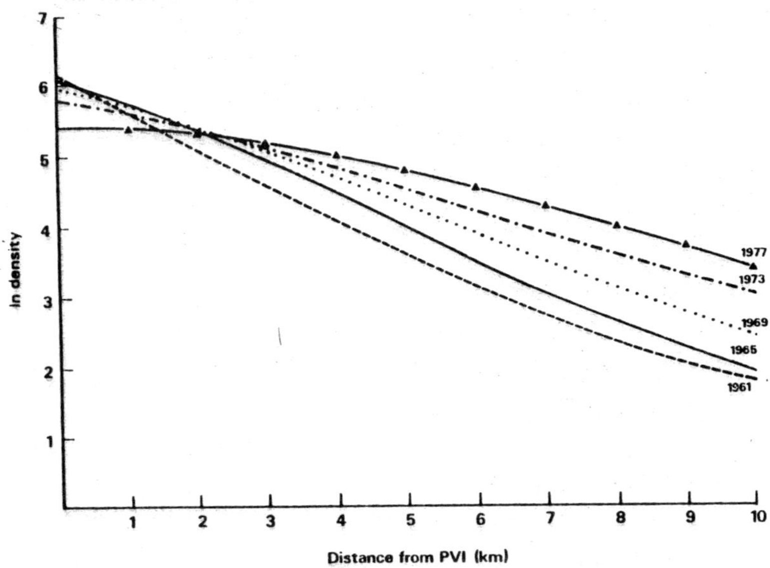

each of the five years studied (Table 4.3, Figure 4.1). These resemble, in a rough way, the density curves illustrated by rush for "two centered" (Group III) cities in India.[26] Brush's diagrams do not show the difference in gradient seen for the earlier years in Ankara, but they do show the absolute difference in levels of density, those of the former colonial districts being lighter. The unplanned city of Ankara most resembles Brush's Group II cities, which are large cities of a traditional kind, but possessing a large commercial core. This of course, is essentially what the traditional, unplanned sections of Ankara are.

The most striking feature of the Ankara diagrams is the convergence of the curves for the planned and unplanned cities. In 1961, the unplanned city had an interior depression and a steep overall density gradient beyond about 1 km. from the city centre. This is consistent with the behaviour of cities in a *laissez faire* market economy. The unplanned city was compact, the centre densely populated and the effective margin (where the curve begins to sweep upward again) was between 7 and 8 km. from the centre. The planned equation for 1961 is quite different. The signs are reversed, meaning that there was no marked central depression and the general slope of the gradient is much more gentle. In accordance with planning goals, excessive central densities, characteristic of the unplanned city, were avoided: population in the planned city was much more evenly distributed by distance from the PVI. Beyond about 4 km. from the centre, the density of the planned neighbourhoods was generally higher than the unplanned ones. This also underlines the fact, consistent with Alonso's[27] theory, that the more affluent inhabitants of the planned areas were less sensitive to commuting costs than the poorer people in the unplanned settlements. This indicates that the modern side of the dual economy had succeeded to some degree in creating at least part of a city tailored to modern tastes.

Thus, until 1961, the planning process appears to have been successful. However, as time passed, the density parameters (Tables 4.3 and 4.4) of the planned city came to resemble those of a "free market" city, while the unplanned city underwent an evolution (decrease in the steepness of the gradient and lowering of central density) characteristic of unplanned western cities. This evolution probably reflects the abandonment of unattractive overcrowded central neighbourhoods and increased access to motor transport, resulting in suburbanization. That the residents of the older (pre-1923) districts of Ankara wished to move elsewhere was amply demonstrated by Keles,[28] and that transportation has materialized through an explosion of the *dolmus* (shared taxi and jitney) population is impossible to ignore.[29]

TABLE 3: Third Degree Equations

Neighbourhood Type:	ln Do	b	c	d	R2
	A. 1961				
Unplanned	6.084	.203	–.251	.0203	.694
Mixed	5.835	–.661	.0198	.000321	.722
Planned	5.115	–.513	.0876	–.00661	.096
All	6.121	–.495	–.00808	.00147	.418
	B. 1965				
Unplanned	5.928	.359	–.260	.0200	.687
Mixed	5.321	–.183	–.0557	.00334	.550
Planned	5.128	–.166	.00618	–.00207	.148
All	6.005	–.284	–.0392	.00268	.439
	C. 1969				
Unplanned	5.612	.506	–.254	.0184	.609
Mixed	5.116	–.0920	–.0364	.00183	.467
Planned	5.014	.281	–.105	.00512	.284
All	5.906	–.203	–.0349	.00204	.462
	D. 1973				
Unplanned	5.804	.156	–.140	.0105	.547
Mixed	4.480	.304	–.0763	.00305	.364
Planned	5.108	.281	–.0996	.00478	.268
All	5.779	–.152	–.0273	.00152	.423
	E. 1977				
Unplanned	5.571	.107	–.0753	.00459	.409
Mixed	4.203	.425	–.0805	.00296	.248
Planned	5.111	.251	–.0848	.00389	.153
All	5.414	.0414	–.0424	.00181	.297

The trend towards a "free market" evolution of the planned city has several causes. One is certainly that the government now has less power to enforce its desire than it once did. Urbanization practices of a more traditional or freewheeling capitalistic kind have taken over. Thus land speculation and violation of zoning regulations have become routine. The effects of governmental impotence were not limited to the planned city, for the same climate that encouraged speculation there also permitted the allocation of large tracts to unplanned development. Between 1961 and 1977, the settled area (*mahalles* with more than 20 persons/ha.) of planned neighbourhood roughly doubled (Table 4.6) while that of unplanned neighbourhoods more than trebled. By 1977 the unplanned areas nearly surrounded the city, leaving little conveniently located land for planners to work with. The ability of the builders of unplanned housing to pre-empt land has led to the spreading of these districts and a general lowering of their densities, while the densities in planned areas have risen. In a sense, the traditional side of the economy has taken over the developable land of the city.

TABLE 4.4: Natural Logarithms of the Maximum Densities

Neighbourhood type:	1961	1965	1969	1973	1977
Unplanned	6.1	6.0	5.9	5.9	5.6
Mixed	5.8	5.3	5.1	4.7	4.7
Planned	5.1	5.1	5.2	5.3	5.3
All	6.1	6.0	6.0	5.8	5.4

TABLE 4.5: Natural Logarithms of the Critical Densities

Neighbourhood type	1961-65	1965-69	1969-73	1973-77
Unplanned	6.0	5.8	5.3	5.4
Mixed	5.0	4.8	4.8	4.8
Planned	5.1	5.1	none	5.2
All	6.0	5.8	5.3	5.3

TABLE 4.6: Areas (in hectares) of *Mahalles* with more than 20 Persons/sq. ha. by Neighbourhood Type 1961

Neighbourhood type	Planned	Mixed	Unplanned
1961	2669.2	1664.3	2918.4
1977	5290.7	4929.1	10648.2
1977/1961	1.982	2.962	3.649

There have been three responses to this lack of land for planned development. The most significant has been the redevelopment of existing neighbourhoods at higher densities. One *mahalle*, Bahcelievler, ("Garden Houses") was originally developed in the 1940's and 50's as detached or semi-detached houses. Starting in 1965, however, the entire *mahalle* was redeveloped into four and five storey apartments. The population density went from 84/ha. in 1961 to 542/ha. in 1977. Similar, if less spectacular, changes have occurred in most planned areas of Ankara. A second response has been the development of housing that resembles that of planned areas, only it is developed in an unplanned way. The result is a neighbourhood (Demetevler - "Bouquet Houses") of 8 to 12 storey apartment houses with only six-foot spaces between buildings. Demetevler is a planner's nightmare: the buildings are tall and close together, cutting out light; the densities are so high that both sewers and streets (many not paved) are woefully inadequate. There is no planned open space. Most of the apartments are held as condominiums, which means that it will be nearly impossible to dispose of the fragmented property when the buildings come down, as they inevitably must, whether through human agency or the action of natural forces. Land fragmentation, usually seen as a rural problem, will increasingly become an urban one also. There will probably be more construction of this type: demand is high, the construction cheap and profit to the builders great. According to the AMPB, the government's ability to prevent its proliferation was nil in 1978.

The third and numerically least significant response is the creation of apartment developments far from the city, "leapfrogging" the ring of unplanned housing. These advertise their clean air (an important advantage, considering Ankara's winter air pollution) and modernity. Thus far they are available only to the very well-to-do, for they are only practically accessible by car – still a luxury in Turkey. The municipality of Ankara has felt obliged to provide these places with bus service, but the routes are long, serve little else and doubtless represent a considerable subsidy by the city government. Given the worldwide oil shortage and the concomitant expense of automobile commuting, these developments will probably not represent a housing solution for Ankara's middle class. However, it does represent an escape for the westernized elite from a rapidly traditionalizing city, one which they own less than they once did.

Conclusions

In both its residential and population density structures, Ankara has reflected the larger history of Turkey over the past two decades. During the 1960's progress was being made; in the middle of the decade industrial production was growing at 12% per year and large numbers of workers were going abroad, both increasing Turkey's foreign exchange earnings and relieving some of the migration pressure on her cities. In Ankara this development was reflected in the more rapid growth of the planned parts of the city. With the economic crises of the 1970's, Turkey's situation has steadily worsened and much of the progress of the 1960's was undone. In Ankara the planned city lost ground to the unplanned and the planned area's population density structure increasingly resembled that of unplanned development. This is both the result of Turkey's larger troubles and part of the background to what appears in the press about Turkey: outbursts of violence and rapid inflation, both of which are particularly hard on urban dwellers. As long as both the world's economic difficulties and Turkey's high rates of population growth and urbanisation continue, there will probably be no change in this declining trend. Two things might have any effect at all: a declining birth rate and the continued effects of inflation. Turkey's birth rate has begun to decline: from 39/1000 in 1967 to 30/1000 in 1973,[30, 31] but the effects of this on urbanization will only be felt after fifteen or twenty years. Inflation's effect on urbanization might be seen more quickly, for in recent years it has had a greater adverse effect in the cities than in the countryside. While the productivity of urban activities (services and manufacturing) has risen slowly, if at all, the productivity of farming has increased substantially through the introduction of green revolution technology. As an example, average wheat production for 1975-7 was 23.6 million tons per year[32], 47% greater than the 1965-7 average of 16.1 million tons per year. During the period from 1965 to 1975, village population grew by about 13.5%[33, 34], which means that productivity per worker increased by about one-third during the decade. Added to this is the recent tendency of the prices of primary (including agricultural) products to rise faster than those of manufactured ones. Thus many rural areas have made real economic progress in the 1970's while the real wages of urban workers have tended to decline. This should make city life seem less attractive to prospective migrants. Perhaps inflation is an unusual tool to use to slow runaway urban growth, certainly it would never be adopted as a conscious policy, but this situation possibly shows that not every consequences of unwanted events is undesirable.*

* Research for this paper was supported by the National Geographic Society, Washington, D.C.

REFERENCES

1. Brush, John E., "Spatial Patterns of Population in Indian Cities", ***Geographical Review***, V. 58 (1968), pp. 362-391.
2. Imar ve Iskân Bakanliği, *Urban Development Strategy: Ankara* 1970-1990, Ankara, Yuksek Teknik Ogretmen Okulu Matbaasi Atolyesi, (1978). p. 3.
3. Levine, Ned and Sunday, Uner, *Population Policy Formation and Implementation in Turkey*, Ankara, Hacettepe University pub. # D-24 (1978).
4. Yucelug, Ratip, *Savas, Sonu Nufus Meseleleri*, Ankara, Basveskalet Istatistik Umum Mudurlugu yay. # 230, 1944.
5. Imar Ve Iskan Bakanligi, *op. cit*., p.73.
6. Zelinsky, Wilbur, *A Prologue to Population Geography*, Englewood Cliffs, N.J., Prentice-Hall, 1966.
7. Akcura Tugrul, *Ankara: Turkiye Cumhuriyeti'nin Baskenti Hakkinda Monografik bir Arastirma*, Ankara, Orta Dogu Teknik Universitesi Mimarlik Fak. yay. # 16 (1971) pp. 86 - 89.
8. Clark, Colin, "Urban Population Densities," *Journal of the Royal Statistical Society*, Series A, V. 114 (1951), pp. 490-496.
9. Berry, Brian J.L., Simmons, James W. and Tennant, Robert J., "Urban Population Densities: Structure and Change," *Geographical Review*, V. 53 (1963), pp. 389-405.
10. Compare Casetti's results to the data presented in Blumenfeld. Blumenfeld, H., "The Tidal Wave of Metropolitan Expansion," *Journal of the American Institute of Planners*, V. 20 (1954), pp. 3-14.
11. Newling, Bruce E., "Spatial Variation of Urban Population Densities," *Geographical Review*, V. 59 (1969), pp. 242-252.
12. Rees, Philip H., "The Urban Envelope: Patterns and Dynamics of Population Density," In: *Geographic Perspectives on Urban Systems*, edited by Brian J.L. Berry and Frank E. Horton, Englewood Cliffs, N.J., Prentice-Hall, (1970) pp. 276-305.
13. Lentz, Peggy A., "A Model of Residential Structure in a Socialist City: A Case Study of Warsaw," *Geographia Polonica* V. 31 (1975), pp. 65-97
14. Newling, Bruce E, *op. cit*., p. 251.
15. Latham, R.F. and Yeates, M.H., "Population Density Growth in Metropolitan Toronto," *Geographical Analysis*, V. 2 (1970), pp. 177-185.
16. Newling, Bruce E., "Urban Growth and Spatial Structure: Mathematical Models and Empirical Evidence," *Geographical Review*, V. 56 (1966), pp. 213-225.
17. Devlet Istatistik Enstitusu, *Census of Population by Administrative Division, 24/10/1965*, Ankara, D.I.E. yay. # 537, (1968).
18. Devlet Istatistik Enstitusu, *Census of Population by Administrative Division, 25/10/1970*, Ankara, D.I.E. yay. # 672, (1973).
19. Devlet Istatistik Enstitusu, *Census of Population by Administrative Division, 26/10/1975*, Ankara, D.I.E. yay. # 813, (1977).
20. Devlet Istatistik Enstitusu, *15/10/1961 Milletvekili ve Senato Uyesi Secimi Sonuclari*, Ankara, D.I.E. yay. # 463, (1964)
21. Devlet Istatistik Enstitusu, *1950-1965 Milletvekili ve 1961, 1964 Cumhuriyet Senatosu Uyesi Secimleri Sonuclari*, Ankara, D.I.E. yay. # 513, (1966).
22. Devlet Istatistik Enstitusu, *12/10/1969 Milletvekili Secimi Sonuclari*, Ankara, D.I.E. yay. # 610, (1970).
23. Devlet Istatistik Enstitusu, *Milletvekili Secimi Sonuclari 14/10/1973*, Ankara, D.I.E. yay. # 702, (1974).

24. Clark, John R., "The Growth of Ankara 1961-1969," *Review of the Geographical Institute of the University of Istanbul*, V. 13 (1971), pp. 119-139 Clark, John R., "Comparison of the Population Density Gradients of the Planned and Unplanned Sections of Ankara," in: *Population and Migration Trends in Eastern Europe*, edited by H.L. Kostanick, Boulder, Colo., Westview Press, (1977), pp. 135-156).
25. See references 20, 21, 22, 23, see also Devlet Istatistik Enstitusu, *Mületvekili Secimi Sonuclari*, 5/6/1977, Ankara, D.I.E. yay. # 836, (1978).
26. Brush, John, E., *op. cit*. p. 373.
27. Alonso, William, "A Theory of the Urban Land Market," *Papers and Proceedings of the Regional Science Association*, V. 6 (1960), pp. 149-158.
28. Keleş, Rusen *Eski Ankara' da bir Sehir Tipolijisi*, Ankara, Universitesi S.B.F. yay. # 314, Ankara, Sevinc Matbaasi, (1971) pp. 61-68.
29. Tekeli, Ilhan, Guloksuz, Yigit and Okyayi, Tarik, *Gecekondulu, Dolmuslu, Isportali Sehir* Istanbul, Cem Yayinevi, (1076).
30. Turkish Demographic Survey, *Vital Statistics: 1966-1967*, Ankara, Hacettepe Basimevi, (1970), p. 37.
31. Toros, Aykut, : 1973 Arastirmasi Dogurganlik" in: *Turkiye'de Nufus Yapisi ve Nufus Sorunlari: 1973 Arastirmasi*, Ankara, Hacet epe Universitesi yay. # D-25 (1978); p. 70.
32. Devlet Istatistik Enstitusu, *Summary of Agricultural Statistics: 1977*, Ankara, D.I.E. yay. # 846, (1978) p. 9.
33. Devlet Istatistik Institusu, Census of Population by Administrative Division 24/10/1965, *op. cit*., p. XIII.
34. *Ibid*, 24/10/1965 and 26/10/1975, p. XIV.

FIVE

A. Kumar and U.P. Singh

Urban Sprawl: A Problem in Regional Development

Introduction

A planned obsolescence programme has created rather than solved the problems of regional development in the coal belts of Bihar. The process of development which initiated the inland occupancy in the region involving the conversion of rural lands to non-agrarian purposes as housing, commerce and industry took an insidious attitude. Problems in form of derelict lands around mining and industrial centres and urban sprawl along transport routes, spread as 'greed belt' through gobbling up countryside. The haphazard and random growth of urban sprawl, showing disregard for ecological setting, is responsible for new emerging development problems.

Coal mining and industries make a great and growing contribution to our national wealth. The process of mining and industrial growth in the Damodar Valley has also created unusual stress on the natural landscape through land-use degradation in process of industrialisation and urbanisation. In absence of any comprehensive planning and landscape management, land deterioration during haphazard development became more insidious in the form of urban sprawl and derelict lands. The problems related to the regional transformation have become alarmingly magnified in the eastern Damodar Valley industrial region, while degradation of regional terrain at various stages of deterioration can be observed in the mining areas of the western coal fields. The purpose of this paper is to examine and analyse urban sprawl which has intruded into the regional scene, taking *KUJU* located in the Bokaro coalfield, as a case study. A full awareness of the necessity for a balanced regional development can only be consummated through an integrative approach.

Urban Sprawl: Characteristics

The urban sprawls are contiguous areas of unmeasured forces and agglomeration of units of all sizes and descriptions built in unincorporated countryside. It is the rapid expansion of suburban development without complete planning for the optimum control and utilisation of land resources.[1] Urban sprawl is invariably haphazard and random without concerted concern or attempt at regional development with zoning ordinances that consider natural processes. Commonly, urban sprawl consumes seven times the area of land compared to planned communities.[2] A distinction is made here between slums, squatter colonies and urban sprawl. Slums are high density living parts of towns or cities owned by the residents and grown as an integral part of locality. They reveal homogeneity within a pocket in terms of caste/religion/language, and develop in traditional domestic architecture with frequent adoption of its parts to various uses under expendiency for space.[3] Squatters with their colonies of easily perishable material or semi-durable constructions in and along peripheral areas of the cities are illegal occupants of land belonging to the poorest workers serving that area. Urban sprawl is even different from suburb which forms the outer continuation of towns into rural areas. Slums, squatter colonies and suburbs are the concern of the government and the planners, as they add to the deterioration of the little environmental quality, which economically better-off residents try to maintain. These are also secondary or tertiary phenomenon of the city. But urban sprawls are mostly the primary phenomenon of urbanisation of the countryside and exist independent of a town or city.

The growth of urban sprawl in the obscured pattern is dependent upon the economic exploitation of natural resources, associated activities and transportation facilities. It functions as service centre and dormitory of the nearby mining and industrial centres, and its growth of population is rapid in comparison with the surrounding countryside. The inhabitants are mostly urban migrants belonging to varied community, religion, caste and economic levels. The chief explanation for their existence relates to the economic exploitation of the region and their obligation lies with the profit and share of economic booty, with total disregard to the rural community and local environment. Urban sprawls are prelude to new towns.

Case Study

Many areas, in the Bokaro Coalfields, both mining and industrial, could be taken as examples of urban sprawl, but the spread of urban sprawl in various stages of growth occurs in the area only along the Hazaribagh-Ramgarh and Ramgarh-Chas roads. Though the Raniganj-Jharia coal belts provide classical case of urban sprawl, it is difficult to distinguish them from suburbs. Along the Hazaribagh-Ramgarh road a number of villages previously used to provide services to traffic and transports. Soon after the fuller exploitation of Bokaro and Ramgarh Coalfields, road traffic became the chief source of coal transportation from the region. Attracted to this, various types of enterprises were started at the villages located along the main traffic routes. The gradual spread of unplanned 'highway strip service centres' gradually brought changes in the rural landscape. The functional and cultural transformation of the chaotic and undisciplined community is responsible for social disorder and development problems in the tribal green belt of the coal-fields. The former villages of Charhi, Kuju, Patratu, Barlong, Chitarpur etc. are at present neither villages nor towns. The represent strip of haphazardly built-up areas in transition from one state to another, providing minimum environmental amenities to the community but consuming greater amount of open space with crazy patchwork of houses, business establishments, shops, repair shops, garages, restaurants, jhuggi hotels, transport offices etc. The utter disregard for the economic and cultural setting is responsible for numerous problems. As far as two decades back the seriousness of the situation was perceived by the Regional Diagnostic Survey of Damodar Valley (Patna Unit,).[4] It observed that sanitation and congestion were the main problems of these centres, this prompted it to recommend for proper planning and control at the very beginning to prevent their being transformed into slums.

Kuju, located mid-way between Mandu and Ramgarh on Hazaribagh-Ranchi Road (Fig. 5.1), has been serving the surrounding tribal areas as a place of weekly market (Sunday and Thursday). The coal mining around Kuju, Mandu and Ramgarh provided new impetus to the settlement. Gradually motor repair workshops and jhuggi hotels were established along the road to provide facilities to the road traffic. The process intensified since sixties with the working of new coal mines and gradually the village transformed into a kilometre long highway string urban sprawl. The settlement is less than 500 metres wide all along its length and rarely 3 houses deep each side of road.

FIG. 5.1:

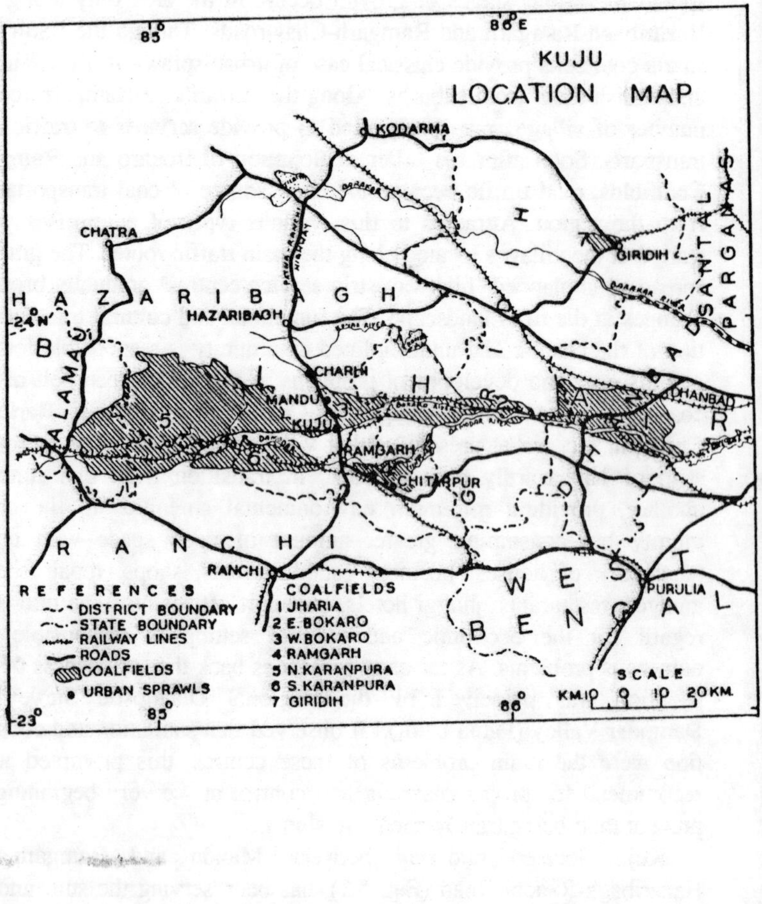

Kuju provides services to the Kuju, Ara, Sarubera, Relligada, Giddi, Sirka, Topa and Pendra coal fields located within a radius of 12 km. from it. Its importance has been enhanced after the opening of the headquarters of Central Coalfields Ltd. All the financial transactions and sales contracts of coal are executed at Kuju and almost 100 odd transport agencies located here provide the transportation facilities to the purchasers. There are mediators who act as guide to the purchasers; they guide them to the correct coal mine and help in loading of coal. The State Bank of India, Bank of India, Hazaribagh Co-operative Bank and Industrial Investment Co. have opened their respective branches at Kuju.

The scatterisation of establishments as a natural growth is not uniform along the highway. The area north of Kuju Chawk is economically better off than the area south of the chawk. Northern section is the chief business section of the settlement while southern section is more residential.

All the Banks, Transport agencies, Auto-electric workshops, Service Centres, most of the hotels and restaurants and wine shops are located in the north. Survey conducted in Kuju reveals that the northern business section is responsible for daily transaction of about 10 lakhs of rupees. But the flexibility in economic achievement is apparent in the morphology of Kuju. Only 29 pucca houses are located in the north of chawk of which only 6 are used for residential purposes while there are 52 pucca residential houses located south of the chawk (Fig. 5.2). The rich northern section is dominated by bricks and tiles, and bricks and asbestos houses. Even temporary sheds are more common in the north. The need for offices and business establishments near the banks and agencies has resulted in quickly constructed rental houses.

TABLE 5.1: House Types North and South of the Chawk

House type	North of Chawk	South of Chawk
Pucca house	29	52
Brick wall and tiles	56	76
Brick wall and asbestos	73	1
Mud wall and Tiles	0	5
Sheds	17	8

Source; Personal Survey.

FIG. 5.2:

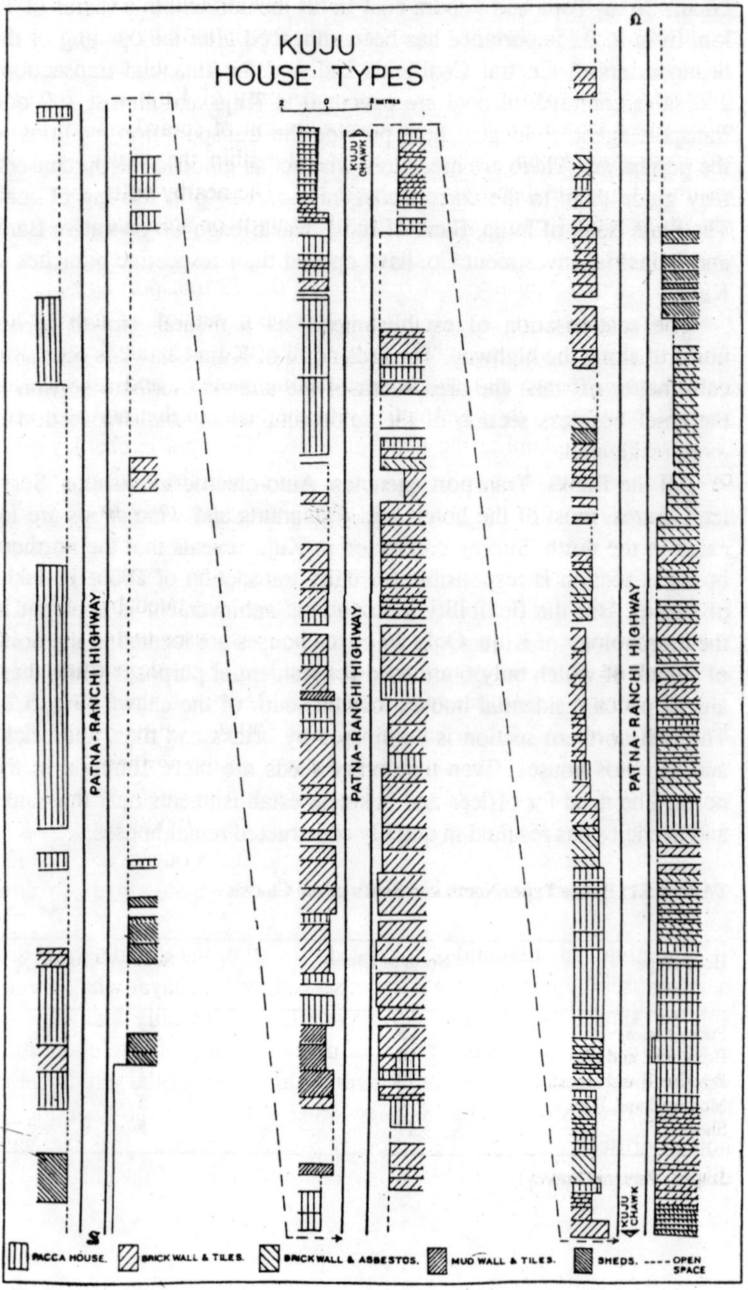
KUJU
HOUSE TYPES
2 0 2 METRES
KUJU CHAWK
PATNA-RANCHI HIGHWAY
PATNA-RANCHI HIGHWAY
PATNA-RANCHI HIGHWAY
KUJU CHAWK
PACCA HOUSE.
BRICK WALL & TILES.
BRICK WALL & ASBESTOS.
MUD WALL & TILES.
SHEDS.
OPEN SPACE

All along the road small houses (without any structural adoption) and agglomeration of units in all sizes and descriptions have been constructed. The leap-frog nature of the growth of built-up area has resulted in destroying the traditional economy of Kuju and is using more space than required. In the outer section of sprawl waste lands are increasing, open spaces between and within the settlements are turning into waste disposal or garbage lots. The nearby cultivable plots are being turned into sewage disposal ground or are used for house construction.

Fig. 5.3 and Appendix I reveal that all the 79 transport agencies of Kuju are located in the north. The northern section is more conspicuous by its specialisation in transport and associated survices. Hotels, motor spare part shops, engineering works , and saloons, all provide services to the chief activity of the area. In this northern section services outnumber the residential use. The area is characterised by over-crowding of services than population along the road.

The southern section is residential and supports only those establishments which serve the local needs.

The survey conducted in Kuju reveals another aspect of urban sprawl. A major portion of its population is constituted by outsiders who came here for business purposes. In most cases their family do not reside at Kuju. They are here to earn, not to reside permanently. The temporary residential requirement has increased the house rent. The house rent varies between Rs. 50 and 500 depending on the size, type of house and its location. Along the road in the northern portion a room of 10′x20′ size costs Rs. 400 per month. The need for space has similarly pushed up the land value which is Rs. 10,000 per 0.1 acre along the road and only Rs. 500 per 0.1 acre at the outskirts. The land value is ten times costly in the north of Kuju chawk as compared to the south.

The civic situation and unregulated growth of the urban sprawl can be visualised by the fact that Kuju is served by Panchayat which is unable to control the migrants and their affairs. The daily incidence of drunken brawls and concentration of unlawful elements are undermining the law and order situation. The drinking water for the settlement is obtained from 30-35 wells. Sewage water collects on the backside of houses or drains into ponds. On every Sunday a doctor visits the state dispensary. The use of electricity is more to the north of the chawk.

FIG. 5.3:

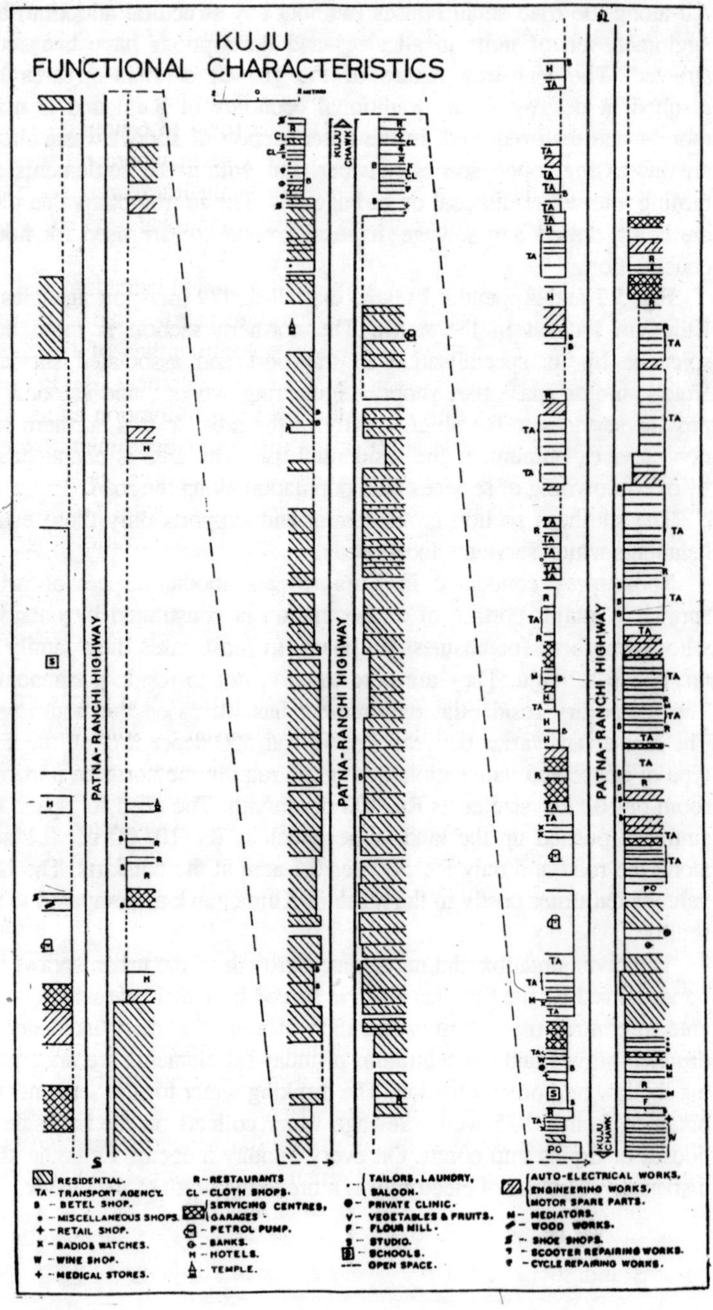
KUJU
FUNCTIONAL CHARACTERISTICS
PATNA-RANCHI HIGHWAY
KUJU CHAWK
RESIDENTIAL.
TA - TRANSPORT AGENCY.
B - BETEL SHOP.
• - MISCELLANEOUS SHOPS.
+ - RETAIL SHOP.
X - RADIO & WATCHES.
W - WINE SHOP.
+ - MEDICAL STORES.
R - RESTAURANTS
CL - CLOTH SHOPS.
SERVICING CENTRES, GARAGES
PETROL PUMP.
G - BANKS.
H - HOTELS.
TEMPLE.
TAILORS, LAUNDRY, SALOON.
PRIVATE CLINIC.
V - VEGETABLES & FRUITS.
F - FLOUR MILL.
S - STUDIO.
SCHOOLS.
OPEN SPACE.
AUTO-ELECTRICAL WORKS, ENGINEERING WORKS, MOTOR SPARE PARTS.
M - MEDIATORS.
WOOD WORKS.
SHOE SHOPS.
SCOOTER REPAIRING WORKS.
CYCLE REPAIRING WORKS.

In absence of local civic authority the entire road side is used as parking space, where 60 to 150 parked trucks greatly hamper road traffic. Sometimes Mandu or Ramgarh police force has to rush here to clear the traffic jams, which sometimes last for 4 to 6 hours. Similar situation can be observed at Demu Tanr, Charhi where traffic gets stalled occasionally by the parked trucks. Along Ramgarh-Gola-Chas road the urban sprawl not only contributes to land-water deterioration but also adds to air pollution.

The general impression of the Kuju urban sprawl is its detached existence in the tribal countryside. It serves the nearby coal fields and distant markets. The rich and resourceful communities of the urban sprawl are not aware of the local needs and development. Entire community shares the responsibility of land-water deterioration and socio-economic disharmony. The indifferent attitude of Government towards a planned development of road-side settlements as service centres in relation to surrounding rural area is behind the growing problems of environmental deterioration, regional disharmony and rural-urban discordance.

Urban Sprawl and Regional Planning : A Need

The problems related to urban sprawls are manifold: land prices are escalating, new lands are continuously being consumed, solid wastes are destroying land-water quality, communal disharmony, cultural conflicts and social disorders are increasing and there is growing indifference to the preservation of cultural as well as physical environment. The growth of urban sprawl in the coal-belts may be precursor to urbanisation, but the utter disregard of socio-economic character of the community and the region has been responsible for generating a variety of problems: problems related to the environment, community and the region.

In the present developmental context one cannot afford to overlook the urban sprawls. But failure of planning is perhaps most obvious at the urban sprawl land as it is neither a town nor a suburb or village. The planning process has failed to recognise the real character of the urban sprawls because they do not provide incentive or leadership to its surrounding rural countryside pertaining to a balanced regional development.

If they are left to themselves people will have to live with the hazards and social ills they engender. Sprawl dwellers will be using more arable lands and forest for development than are needed. The coal belts have plenty of natural land awaiting development, the sprawls pose a danger to them. Also in absence of timely consideration urban sprawls are capable of destroying the possibility for planned construction of an efficient and economic mass transit system.

A systematic trend zoning and regulation is needed for the coal belts. It is not merely a question of restoring or repairing misused environment but of frantic and random growth in the tribal area. If it proceeds unchecked, it might go out of control and pose more serious problems in regional development planning. It is most appropriate to include these urban sprawls into a planning format so that (1) there should be opportunity left for introducing order in the chaos, (ii) a proper land-use, in and around urban sprawl, might be planned to keep the pressure at the lowest, (iii) farming community might be protected from being pushed off from the land, and (iv) assessment of needs related to the growth of artificial landscape might be properly visualised before it is diffused to the level of becoming a problem.

At this stage the problem of regional planning will be less tiring and costly, if urban sprawls are also put under some authorised planning body. It is the imperative need that from the very beginning mining and urban growth should be co-ordinated in the total ecological and regional setting for a balanced regional development.

REFERENCES

1. Whyte, W. H. "Urban Sprawl, Fortune", Vol. 57, 1958, pp. 103-104, 109-194.
2. Coates, D. R. *Environmental Geomorphology and Landscape Conservation*, Vol. II, D. H & Ross Inc., Pennsylvania, 1974, p. 272.
3. Fonseca, R. "The walled city of Delhi", *Ekistics*, Vol. 31, 1971, p. 182.
4. R. D. S. D. V. *An Interim Report for the Western Damodar Valley Region and the Bokaro and Barkakana Sub-Region*, Patna Unit, 1960, p. 144.

APPENDIX I

KUJU Function of Houses

Function of Houses	South of Kuju chawk	North of Kuju chawk
Residential Houses	88	6
Pan Gumtis	10	17
Transport Agencies	x	79
Retail Shops	2	x
Radio & Watches	3	4
Wine Shops	x	2
Auto Electric Works	4	11
Restaurants	10	15
Cloth Shops	3	x
Servicing centres	2	10
Petrol Pumps	1	2
Bank & Investment Co.	2	2
Garrages	1	1
Hotels	3	7
Medical Stores	1	1
Tailors	6	3
Laundries	1	1
Engineering Works	1	5
Private clinics	x	2
Vegetables & Fruits	2	4
Flour mills	x	1
Saloons	x	3
Photo studios	x	1
Motor spare parts	x	3
Wooden Works	2	x
Shoe Shops	2	x
Educational Institutions	1	1
Temples	2	x
Cycle Repairing Shops	2	x
Scooter Repairing Shops	1	x
Miscellaneous Shops	4	6
Iron goods & Hardware	2	x
Tyre Shops	1	x
Mediators	x	1
Police outposts	x	1
Post Offices	x	1
Truck Weighings	x	1

Source: Personal Survey.

SIX

R.N.P. Sharma and **D.P. Singh**

Evolution of Ranchi City

RANCHI is the headquarters of Chotanagpur division and the district headquarters of Ranchi District in the State of Bihar. It is an important commercial as well as industrial centre of the State located in the heart of Chotanagpur plateau. The main object of the present paper is to analyse the physical, economic and cultural factors leading to its rapid growth. An attempt is made here to trace the evolution of the city in the light of morphological and functional structures by bringing into focus the relative importance of different factors in a historical perspective as they have influenced the growth of the city.

Location

Ranchi (23° 23′ N: 85° 23′ E) lies on the north-central part of the Ranchi plateau at an elevation of 649 metres above mean sea level. It is located in the heart of South-East Economic Resource Region of India. The location of the city is at very suitable distances from all the important industrial, commercial and trading centres of the region. Roads radiate from Ranchi in all directions to link it with any other part of the State. Towards north, it is connected efficiently with Patna, the capital of the State, 338 km. away, by a first class metalled road. The southern road is an important highway to Chakradharpur and Chaibasa further leading to the first steel city of Jamshedpur. The efficient connection with the Mica Belt of Koderma, coalfields of Jharia-Dhanbad and the great industrial towns of Sindri, Rourkela and Jamshedpur, all have helped in maintaining the importance of Ranchi. As regards rail communication, it is located advantageously on S. E. Railway.

Site is an important aspect of a town for it "shapes the form and function of the town. Towns exhibit their adjustment to the difficulties as well as to the opportunities presented by their physical setting".[1] Since the foundation of Ranchi about one hundred and fifty years ago, the character of the town and its immediate environs has been altered beyond recognition by the superimposition of the urban profile. So far as the original site is concerned, the problem of defence seems to be of paramount significance. Its actual foundation has been influenced by the safe position amidst the thick cover of forest over the vast plateau country which has a gentle relief. The safety was guaranteed not only by the thick vegetational cover but also by the steep *ghats* on the northern and southern edges of the plateau. Towards the north in the Chutupalu Ghat (32 km. from Ranchi), the edges of the plateau drop to about 213 metres in course of 4.8 km. Similarly in the south, whole Chaibasa road drops steeply down plateau in a stretch of 33.8 km.

Origin

Though it is not easy to trace the cause of origin of the city, it seems, that the political factors have played a greater role than religious ones in its origin and growth. Ranchi does not owe its origin to the Industrial Revolution as many cities of the West and also some cities of India like Kanpur do. The original site of the city was a bi-weekly vegetable market in village Aranchi which gave its name Ranchi. It attracted the trade and performed certain basic functions for the surrounding rural areas, and the plan activities developed there because trade and commerce are active ferments in the origin of a town.

The most important factor responsible for the origin of Ranchi seems to be political one. The region around Ranchi was a seat of political events. The unsettled land was the seat of bandits and outlawed men. So the British Administration realised that the turbulant tract of Chotanagpur was not suitable for administration from distant Sherghati or Chatra. Therefore, in order to rule the country, Captain Wilkinson, the agent of S.W. Frontier's Agency laid the foundation of the town of Ranchi in 1834. He selected the site of Kishunpur, presently the Commissioner's compound, as his headquarters. Later he built a big bungalow in the Chadri village. Lt. Colonel Ousley, the successor of Captain Wilkinson in 1839, extended the compound of the bungalow to include the Ranchi Hill and a Coffee Garden. He excavated the Ranchi Lake. Thus with the permanent establishment of the British, numerous buildings were constructed. And in this way the town of Ranchi got its birth.[2]

Growth

The growth of the city is the result of a change in pattern of economy. Factors that have promoted the growth of Ranchi are of recent origin. It has developed in response to social and economic conditions. The growth of the urban complex of Ranchi can conveniently be classified into following historical phases: (Fig. 6.1)

1. First Phase Before 1891
2. Second Phase 1892 to 1911
3. Third Phase 1912 to 1950
4. Fourth Phase 1951 to 1980
5. Fifth Phase Projection of Urbanisable limit.

These phases indicate the occurrence of significant political events together with the introduction of new economic factors having a marked influence on the growth, forms and functions of Ranchi.

First Phase

The city of Ranchi as it stands today is wholly modern having hardly anything ancient, and dates back to the times of South West Frontier Agency in 1834. The city has grown to its present enormous size during the last one hundred and fifty years. It was originally a village, a biweekly market adjacent to which Kishunpur village developed as administrative centre.

It is rather difficult to give the exact growth contours of the town as it stood in the latter part of the 19th century. Ranchi was a town of moderate stature. It consisted of four nuclei: (i) Purani Ranchi – a trade centre, (ii) Kishunpur – an administrative centre, (iii) Purulia Road side, a Christian Missionaries centre, and (iv) Doranda – a Military Cantonment's Headquarters of Ramgarh Battalion. These were separated from each other by agricultural land. The town showed signs of expansion when in the beginning it was made an important administrative headquarters by the British Administrators. City building during this period was stimulated by the British officers who constructed numerous buildings, established coffee garden, excavated lakes and tanks and encouraged commerce which resulted in a phenomenal growth of the city.

In 1842 the town was raised to be the seat of the district. The Headquarters of the Principal Assistant were transferred from Lohardaga to

Kishunpur. The setting up of the regular court brought other subordinate officers, law agents, mukhtiars and 'Pairvikars' to Ranchi. The district jail was built in 1869 with a capacity to accommodate 200 prisoners. Thus a small hamlet became an important administrative centre.

The advent of Christian Missionaries in this period opened a new epoch in the history of Ranchi. The town expanded from Kishunpur to Purulia Road. Their various cultural institutions like colleges, schools, press etc. and religious institutions helped the expansion of the town. These elements are still active affecting the life and culture of the people. Gradually the land between Kishunpur and Purulia Road on the one hand and between Kishunpur and Chandari on the other were inhabited by people of various walks of life.

In this early period of its growth Military settlement expanded the urban area of Ranchi to Doranda. Gradually the open space between Ranchi and Doranda became dotted with the sporadic growth of residential buildings along the Chaibasa Road. Thus the town grew up from a hamlet in 1834 with a few people to an area of about 6 square kilometres consisting of a total population of about 32 thousand by the end of the 19th century.

2. Second Phase

During the first decade of the present century, Ranchi expanded gradually almost in every direction. The extension was mainly southward due to the following multiplying function in the town. Police College and Police Training School were opened in the year 1905 in Doranda. But later on these were transferred to Hazaribagh and the buildings were utilised for camp Secretariat as Ranchi became the summer capital of Bihar Government. It presented new structures. At present this is the main administrative area of Ranchi. Almost all government buildings are located in this sister town of Ranchi which has a sattelite character. The process of growth was accelerated with the advent of railway in the year 1907. Railway entered the city from the east to its southern margin between Ranchi and Doranda. The Railway station area became another pocket of settlement which was dominated by the railway colonies, commercial godowns, small shops and residences.

The Accountant General office for Bihar and Orissa was opened in 1912 in Ranchi. It extended the town further to Doranda and Hinoo.

During this period it was the most important stimulus which helped the extension of trade and commercial activities in the town. It consequently expanded in all directions. The main road adjacent to Upper Bazar area was lined with single and double storeyed buildings used both as residences and shops. As a result of these developments the area of the town increased to 9.6 square kilometres from Ranchi Lake in the west to Chutia in the east and from Circular road in the north to the bank of Harmu river in the south.

Third Phase

Much of what we observe in the present cultural landscape of the city has been achieved during this period. Major developments took place in the southern part of the city. This part was selected for administrative functions. Similar developments also occurred in Purani Ranchi area. Contiguous to Purani Ranchi, Upper Bazar and Lower Bazar gradually developed as the retail markets along the Ranchi-Chaibasa Road. The marketing area was further extended to the Purulia Road.

On account of its long association with the trade in lac, Ranchi opened two small shellac factories but the enterprise could not be developed largely because of the opening of shellac factories at other places. Except for the establishment of Ranchi Distillery, the period during this phase was quite insignificant in the field of industrial growth. A few engineering and repair shops started functioning. But they could neither impart an industrial character to the city nor could they help its considerable growth.

Several historical factors such as the establishment of a good number of educational and philanthropic institutions by the Missionaries, stationing of a large contingent of troops during and after the First World War etc. boosted up the growth of the city. The establishment of Eastern Command Headquarters during the Second World War which brought about sudden spurt of population helped to a great extent the growth of the city.[3] These factors also provided great fillip to the trading activities of the city and it took the form of an urban central place.

Thus it becomes clear that during this phase Ranchi grew mainly for its political and defence activities together with its religious importance to the Christians. Though cities are regarded as the product of factory system, this principle does not hold good in case of Ranchi.

Fourth Phase

It was only after India achieved Independence that the city advanced to the stage of maturity. It was mainly due to its tremendous potentialities for development as an industrial and commercial centre. Several industries, large and small, were established in and around Ranchi in second and third Five Year Plans. This, by imparting industrial character to the city, has affected its entire fabric. Industrial developments are mainly due to several factors viz; central location of the city in India's richest "coal-steel belt", equitable climate and availability of cheap and ample hard land. This attracted the central government to establish here the Headquarters of National Coal Development Corporation of India and the Hindustan Steel Limited. These establishments developed planned residential colonies for their employees in the form of Gandhi Nagar and Jawahar Nagar on Kanke Road and Shyamli Housing Colony in Hinoo.[4]

Later on the Government set up manufacturing plants and township of the Heavy Engineering Corporation at Hatia on its southern outskirts. Owing to the increased economic pull of Hatia the growth of Ranchi, north of the Railway line, has to a certain extent halted and its axis of growth has turned southward. Besides, the State government has also set up a High Tension Insulator Factory, an Electrical Appliances Factory and an Industrial Estate. These developments increased the population and have affected the growth of the city in many ways. The economy of the area has improved by bringing in sizeable employment.

A very significant development in the evolution of the shape of the town has been the emergence of ribbon settlements along important roads. This necessitated the extension of municipal limits along the road. Thus in 1961 Ranchi covered 26.4 square kilometres of area excluding 14.4 square kilometres of H.E.C. township and 14.4 square kilometres under Military occupation in Greater Ranchi. All these developments, including various educational institutions which sprang up during the period, modified the cultural landscape to a great deal.

Consequent upon the above developments the city naturally experienced a rapid growth of population. The result was congestion in some localities of the city. So the pressing demand for better housing led to the establishment of numerous housing colonies in all directions to accommodate the increased population.[5] Important among them are A.G. Office Colony and H.S.L Colony in Hinoo, Govt. Housing

Colony in Bariatu and in Harmu; Gandhi Nagar and Jawahar Nagar of N.C.D.C on Ratu road and R.M.C.H. Colony in Bariatu. Thus the outer zones of the city were dotted with buildings and the city ushered a rapid lateral growth.[6] The developments of the city started taking a definite form. Semicircular and straggling concentrations appeared. Half a dozen finger like urban projections are also identified along the major roads. Large compact sectors are uncommon. This straggling nature of the urban habitat is to a large extent attributed to the varied nature of the site. The topography helped the growth of settlements but it has dispelled agglomeration and congestion everywhere except in Upper Bazar and Hindpiri.

FIG. 6.1:

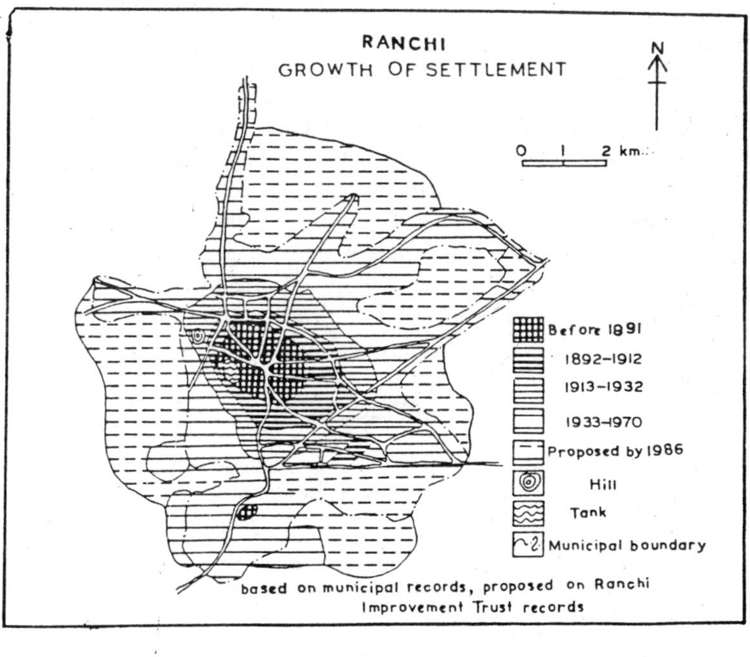

Fifth Phase

Projections of urbanisable limit: The present growth is a mirror image of Ranchi in future. Fig. 6.1 shows the projected urban map by 1986.

The projected areas on every side of the city has been dotted. This Chapter of expansion does not seem to project the urban profile of Ranchi in its proper urban layout.[7] The undulating Ranchi peneplain provides enormous scope for expansion as first class roads radiate from the hub of the present Ranchi city. Industries, as they are growing, ever project multi nuclei for plantscape and townscape.[8] Hatia, Shamlong, Tati-silwai, Hatwar, Ratu, Meshra, Kanke, Getalsud etc. are outstanding interpolations over the plateau face.[9] Do they not indicate a projected urban profile of Ranchi? They do. The city is on its anvil of growth and it is bound to expand as a vast horizontal industrial-cum-urban complex over the Ranchi Plateau.

Conclusion

An analysis of its growth shows that in the beginning it tended to be concentric with the single nucleus of Purani Ranchi. Subsequent development of nuclei like Kishunpur, Doranda, and Purulia Road side enlarged the function of the city. The establishment of Heavy Engineering Corporation at Hatia is a recent hub in its development. It has led to the growth of a separate but significant industrial landscape. Four nuclei of settlements, seem to have existed from its early growth. Each has its defined functions. The present layout and land-use pattern of the city reveal that it is not built around a single centre. Thus Ranchi illustrates the "Multiple Nuclei Theory" of urban growth and development. At the same time, it is also evident from the analysis that in its growth both centripetal and centrifugal forces have acted jointly.

REFERENCES

1. *District Gazetteers of Ranchi District*, Govt. of Bihar, (1970).
2. *Draft Master Plan for Greater Ranchi* - Ranchi Improvement Trust (1964).
3. *District Census Handbooks of Ranchi*, 1891, 1911, 1921, 1931, 1941, 1951, 1961, 1971.
4. *Town Planning in Bihar* - Town Planning Section Government of Bihar.
5. Ahmad, E; Origin and Evolution of Towns of U.P. *Geographical Outlook*, Vol. I, (1956).
6. Burgess, Ernest W. The growth of the city - *The city* - Chicago, (1925).
7. Davis, K. "The origin and growth of urbanisation in the world", *American Journal of Sociology*, Vol. IX, (1955).
8. Dale, Alfred G., What supports a city's Growth, *Texas Business Review 28*, (1954).
9. Manford, L. *City in History* - New York, (1961).
10. Singh, U. Origin and Growth of *Kanpur, N.G.J.I.*, Vol. V (1959).

PART -- III

POPULATION AND SETTLEMENT GEOGRAPHY

SEVEN

Jaymala Diddee and **V.S. Datye**

Process of Population Diffusion in Rural Areas and the Phenomenon of Hamletization
(With Reference to Maharashtra)

Introduction

AN important feature of rural settlements in Maharashtra is the process of population diffusion, resulting from the growth of *Wadis*[1] or hamlets. Like in other parts of the country, even for Maharashtra, the 'gaothan' or 'gaon' is the parent or original settlement, characterised by extreme congestion and smallness of the core area. This was dictated in former times by the need for defence and fortification. In the main village, even today (as a relic of past patterns of settlement) one finds several castes attached to one another by 'Jajmani' or 'Balutedari' rights. This makes for an orderly arrangement of the various castes in the village, in the '*ali*', '*galli*' or '*bol*' pattern. Today, with the withering away of defence needs, the villages in Maharashtra are slowly sprawling into shapelessness, through the erection of structures at will for housing the agriculturists on the lands around the main village, which would eventually develop into what is locally known as 'wadis' or hamlets.

Distinguishing Features of a 'Wadi' or Hamlet

The phenomenon of hamlet development in Maharashtra is of very recent origin, for nowhere does one come across a hamlet which is over 75 years old. Distinction must be made between a 'Wadi' and the 'gaon' or the parent village. A Wadi is a habitation cluster which is usually nearer to the main part of the village. It develops due to convenience of the farming community, to stay as close to their farms as possible. Except for the major cultivating classes, no service or artisan community resides in the hamlets. To distinguish between the hamlet and the parent village, size and nearness to the main village are not always reliable indicators, as many 'Wadis' are often larger than the parent village, and some villages lie closer to one another than to their hamlets. Therefore, size and spatial distance alone cannot serve as the sole criterion to distinguish between a hamlet and a village.

An important distinguishing mark between a hamlet and a village, is the presence of service castes or the 'Balutedars'[2]. So far not many instances of a hamlet possessing an independent set of Balutedars have come to light. On the contrary, it was the authors' personal observation from field visits to several villages that a hamlet depends solely on the main village, of which it forms a part, to provide it with services, while a village, howsoever small, has atleast a few service castes like the 'Mahar' (scheduled caste village servant), and a 'Ramoshi' (the village watchman), as resident Balutedars. Thus, the hamlet looks to the main village for all its socio-economic needs, and religious as well as administrative matters. Hamlets are generally called after the major clan names of the principal landowning families who first settled there. Another important feature of the hamlets is that they are subject to evolution, and in the course of time they achieve independence from their parent village. Instances of hamlets growing into independent villages are numerous in irrigated tracts and industrialised areas. For instance, Mhaswad in Satara tehsil had formerly 12 Wadis in the medieval period. Today, only four Wadis remain, the rest growing into independent villages. Gunwadi is an instance of a hamlet from Baramati tehsil which became a village in its own right, with the introduction of canal irrigation in the area. Similarly, Oglewadi and Kirloskarwadi developed as independent settlements with the location of industry.

Study Area and Data Source

Poona district was used as a representative unit for observing the frequency of hamlet development in the area. In addition, an indepth analysis of the underlying processes of hamlet formation have been made with the help of a case study village (Wagholi), located 15 km to the North-East of Poona on the Ahmednagar highway. The reason for selection, besides proximity and convenience of fieldwork, was that maximum hamlet (12 hamlets) development had taken place at Wagholi. It must be mentioned that any analysis of hamlets, including the present study, must perforce depend solely on data collected from the field; from the hamlets themselves, as no separate published figures for the hamlet as a unit are available either in the census handbooks or even at the village level.

Physical Factors Conducive to Wadi or Hamlet Development

Two sources pertaining to different time periods were used to obtain data for the number of Wadis in each of the thirteen tehsils of Poona District. From the office of the Zilla-Parishad, information for the number of Wadis for 1975 was obtained. The village boundary maps on a scale of 1:100,000, published by the Government of Maharashtra in 1960, were used for an actual count of the number of Wadis for the earlier period.

From Table 7.1, it is observed that the hilly tehsils could be grouped into two categories. The tehsils like Junnar, Ambegaon and Khed, which are only partly hilly, have developed a large number of Wadis (Fig. 7.1). All the Wadis, as evidenced from the map, are invariably situated along the valley sides, where much of the cultivation takes place. In contrast to the above are the tehsils of Velhe, Bhor and Maval which are entirely hilly and devoid of any Wadis. The rest of the tehsils are located mostly in the transitional belt, between the hilly west and the eastern plateau region. Fair amount of Wadi growth is visible in all the tehsils of the plateau, with differential Wadi development taking place either in the irrigated tracts, along the southern boundary of the district, in the command area of the Nira valley, or else in Haveli tehsil (bordering Poona city), where increased demand for perishables has led to intensive truck farming. Haveli tehsil stands out prominently in the region with the highest degree of dispersion, and also with the maximum number of Wadis. Here, inspite of an overall modest agricultural potential, Wadi growth has been rather rapid due to the impetus provided by the forces of urbanisation and industrialisation in the Poona metropolitan region.

Broadly it can be stated that in the hilly villages both, a large number of hamlets, as well as a paucity or total absence of Wadis is found to exist side by side. On the one hand, difficult terrain and poor accessibility may itself be conducive for the inherent settlement pattern in the area to develop in the form of several, dispersed, hamlet-like

FIG. 7.1:

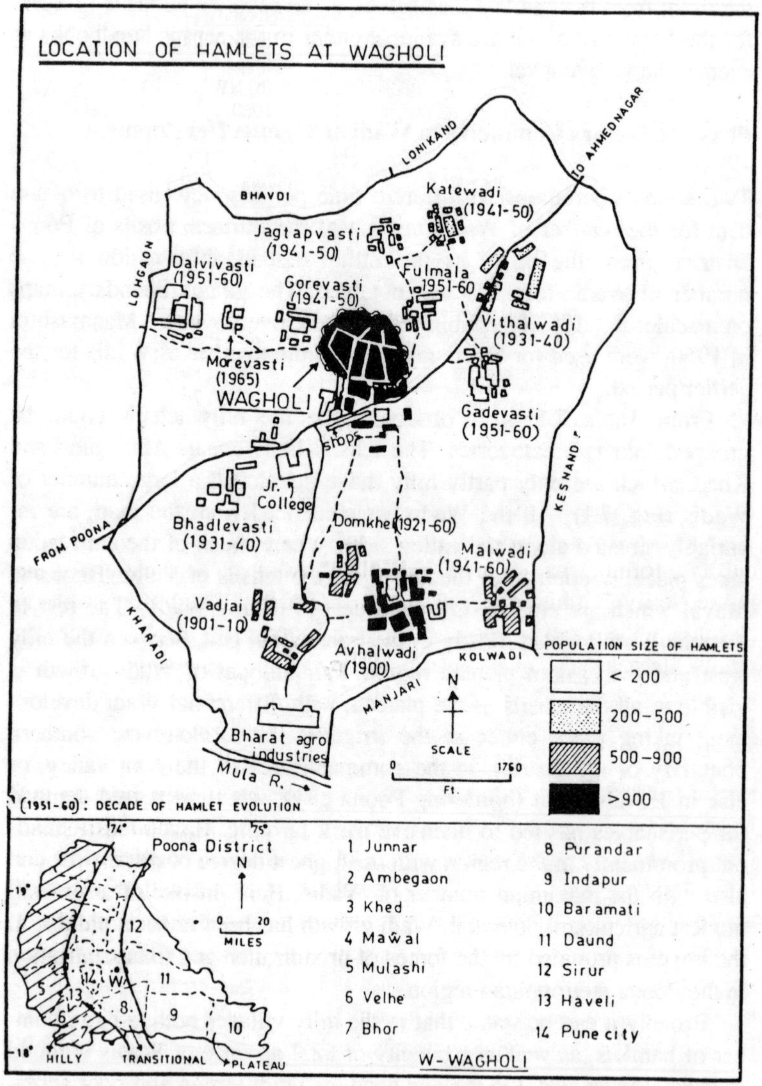
LOCATION OF HAMLETS AT WAGHOLI
BHAVDI
LONIKAND
TO AHMEDNAGAR
LOHGAON
Katewadi (1941-50)
Jagtapvasti (1941-50)
Dalvivasti (1951-60)
Gorevasti (1941-50)
Fulmala (1951-60)
Vithalwadi (1931-40)
Morevasti (1965)
WAGHOLI
Gadevasti (1951-60)
stop
Jr. College
KESNAND
FROM POONA
Bhadlevasti (1931-40)
Domkhe (1921-60)
Malwadi (1941-60)
KHARADI
Vadjai (1901-10)
Avhalwadi (1900)
KOLWADI
MANJARI
N
SCALE
0 1760
Ft.
Bharat agro industries
Mula R.
POPULATION SIZE OF HAMLETS
< 200
200-500
500-900
>900
(1951-60): DECADE OF HAMLET EVOLUTION
74°
75°
19°
18°
Poona District
N
0 20
MILES
HILLY
TRANSITIONAL
PLATEAU
1 Junnar
2 Ambegaon
3 Khed
4 Mawal
5 Mulashi
6 Velhe
7 Bhor
8 Purandar
9 Indapur
10 Baramati
11 Daund
12 Sirur
13 Haveli
14 Pune city
W- WAGHOLI

TABLE 7.1 : Distribution of Wadis and the Degree of Dispersion in each of the 13 tehsils in Poona district[3]

Sr. No. Tehsil	No. of inhabited villages (NV)	No. of Wadis based on data		Degree of
		From Zilla Parishad (a) NW 1975	From Village Maps (b) NW 1960	$\frac{NV+NW(a)}{NV}$
1. Junnar	139	281	100	3.02
2. Ambegaon	100	157	60	2.57
3. Khed	157	100	124	1.63
4. Maval	154	53	47	1.34
5. Haveli	124	227	70	2.83
6. Dhond	64	48	53	1.75
7. Mulshi	133	77	61	1.57
8. Sirur	79	84	84	2.06
9. Velhe	132	0	0	1.00
10. Purandhar	80	89	89	2.10
11. Baramati	62	74	74	1.38
12. Indapur	85	137	81	2.61
13. Bhor	186	0	0	1.00

Source: Alexander Job, A Study of Rural Settlements in the Upper Bhima Basin, Unpublished Ph.D. Thesis (1981).

clusters, forming part of a single village. Also, it is far easier for the farmer to live on his farm, than to cross a stream which may swell up abruptly with a sudden downpour, or to traverse a hill, to reach his minuscule patch of farmland. A very high drainage density, to the extent of there being several streams within the boundaries of the village, has in no small measure encouraged the development of a large number of hamlets, especially along the valleys, as seen in the case of Junnar tehsil. In contrast, the poor development of hamlets in the hilly villages can be attributed to the lack of any scope for diffusion of population, due to the small population size of the villages, coupled with the limited extent of cultivable land. The above, together with the lack of irrigation and subsistence nature of agriculture in these parts, does not provide any further impetus for population to disperse either. Interestingly enough, it is in the hilly villages only that one comes across a total absence of hamlets. This again could be attributed to the constraints imposed by the small size of villages, with even smaller areas available for cultivation (only 10-12 percent of the total area is cultivable). There is no optimum number of hamlets associated with each village as the frequency of villages with varying number of hamlets is highly skewed

(Table 7.2). From the frequency distribution of Wadis in some of the tehsils in Poona district it was seen that the number of villages having more than six hamlets progressively decreases. Tehsils with larger size of villages have greater number of hamlets.

The Impact of Socio-Economic Factors on the Development of Hamlets

Apart from the influence of physical features discussed above, the origin of hamlets is rather intimately linked with the socio-cultural, as well as economic development of the area. As mentioned earlier, the hamlets are a relatively young phenomenon, having made their appearance within the last 50-75 years. A pertinent question at this juncture would be, why there were no hamlets earlier, also, why only some villages develop hamlets and some others do not.

TABLE 7.2: Frequency Distribution of Wadis in Selected Tehsils of Poona District

No. of Wadis in Each Village	Sirur		Junnar		Ambegaon		Mulshi		Dhond	
	A	B	A	B	A	B	A	B	A	B
0	34	-	53	-	20	-	100	-	25	-
1	23	23	33	33	40	40	15	15	33	33
2	11	22	14	28	20	40	2	14	4	8
3	8	24	13	39	9	27	5	15	1	3
4	2	8	6	24	4	16	3	12	1	4
5	1	5	4	20	3	15	1	5	-	-
6	-	-	6	36	1	6	-	-	-	-
7	-	-	4	28	2	14	1	7	-	-
8	-	-	2	16	-	-	-	-	-	-
9	-	-	1	9	1	9	1	9	-	-
10	-	-	-	-	-	-	-	-	-	-
11	-	-	-	-	-	-	-	-	-	-
12	-	-	-	-	-	-	-	-	-	-
13	-	-	-	-	-	-	-	-	-	-
14	-	-	-	-	-	-	-	-	-	-
15	-	-	2	30	-	-	-	-	-	-
16	-	-	-	-	-	-	-	-	-	-
17	-	-	-	-	-	-	-	-	-	-
18	-	-	-	-	-	-	-	-	-	-
19	-	-	-	-	-	-	-	-	-	-
20	-	-	-	-	-	-	-	-	-	-
21	-	-	1	21	-	-	-	-	-	-
Total	79	82	139	284	100	167	133	77	64	48

Source: Same as Table 7.1

A = Village frequency, B = No. of Wadis.

For a reasonable answer to the above queries, a look back into the past conditions of settlements and agriculture becomes necessary. In the light of the earlier social conditions, it seems natural that people should choose to live together in compact settlements, for the prime need of security from invaders, and defence against bandits and marauders, and other dangers to life and property. Added to this was the favourable man-land ratio in the beginning of the 18th century (as land was available for the asking), which did not foster the need for dispersal of population. Poor means of transportation further inhibited mobility, and the various villages in the past must have existed like islands, virtually cut off from one another, and separated by stretches of uncleared forest land. Thus, one finds that the origin of the hamlets can be traced to time after the arrival of the British. The pattern of property rights underwent a significant change during this period, wherein the ownership of land was vested to the cultivator. Also, improved means of communication, together with the establishment of law and order, and greater social security must have comprehensively led to the development of hamlets. More recently, the growth of urbanisation, and the consequent demand for farm produce, provided a further fillip to hamlet development. The farmer today is no longer content with gearing his agricultural production for home consumption along. Instead, the commercial nature of his enterprise vividly reflects that outside forces are responsible for the scale and intensity of agricultural operations which were observed at many of the hamlets visited in course of field-work. Thus, all things being equal, the fertility of the soil, coupled with the availability of water is perhaps of vital significance to the continued diffusion of population in the hamlets today. The increased productivity from land, and gains therefrom, have provided valuable incentives for the rural folks, to forego the 'ambiance' of village life to settle in hamlets. The lucrative nature of commercial agriculture itself acts as the greatest push factor in the flight to the farms; which initially is of a temporary nature, being restricted to periods of hectic agricultural activity. This is slowly extended to larger periods, culminating in the house in the main village lying in disuse for much of the time. The numerous derilict houses and ruins in the parent villages (inspite of a natural increase of population over a period of time), bear testimony to this mass exodus of the cultivator-classes to their fields.

The houses in the fields become permanent fixtures, and it is not long before entire families shift out, giving rise, initially to a 'vasti', named after the major clan who first settled there. With the passage of time, this amalgam of scattered homesteads attracts other migrants, particularly those who work for daily wages and agricultural labourers. Finally, in the course of time, with the increase of population, this habitation cluster gets transformed into a hamlet, or a 'Wadi' of the main village. Instances of a hamlet surpassing the main village, or even growing at the expense of the main village, and assuming the status of an independent village, are not uncommon. This because the location of the hamlets is attuned to the present day economic forces, unlike the main village, whose location was governed by the former needs for defence and safety, and who site today, appears more of an anachronism. More so, when one compares the locational characteristics of the hamlets, which invariably come up on sites with the greatest agricultural potential. Another factor which has inevitably given rise to hamlet formation, is the pressure of population on the existing land resources. This has resulted in the extension of land under cultivation, whereby the marginal lands have also been brought under plough.

Wagholi: A Case Study

Wagholi, lies to the North-East (73° 59′ E and 18°35′ N) of Poona city, on the Poona-Ahmednagar highway, at a distance of 15 km. (Fig. 7.1). With a population of 8,398, according to the 1981 census. It has a total area of 3,367 hectares, out of which only 205 hectares are under irrigation.

Temporal Growth of Hamlets at Wagholi

Wagholi is an old historical village which was given as 'inam' or gift to one of the Maratha generals in Shivaji's times. Before 1891, Wagholi could not boast of a single hamlet, whereas at present, the number of wadis at Wagholi is thirteen.

From Table 7.3, it is seen that within a span of ninety years, thirteen Wadis developed, though the phase of rapid hamlet growth started only after 1930. The maximum number of hamlets were added only during the last thirty years, when ten out of a total of thirteen hamlets came into existence. From the distribution of hamlets, two distinct trends in hamlet development can be discerned. In the first phase, the development of only three hamlets, farthest from Wagholi village took place. Avhalwadi, the oldest hamlet, existed by 1900, followed by

Vadjai, which came up between 1901-1910, and lastly, Domkhel developed during 1920-30. The origin and growth of these hamlets could be attributed mainly to the development of irrigation and introduction of cash crops like onions and vegetables, and later, with the development of life irrigation, sugarcane. All the three hamlets, it is observed, grew at sites which had the greatest potential for agricultural development in the area (over 90 percent of the total irrigated lands are located around these three hamlets).

TABLE 7.3: Temporal Development of Hamlets from 1891 to 1981

	Years										
	1891	1900	1910	1920	1930	1940	1950	1960	1961	1971	1981
No. of hamlets	0	1	2	2	3	5	9	12	13	13	13

During the second phase of hamlet-growth (1930-1961), the remaining ten, or eighty per cent of the total hamlets, were added. From the point of view of the geographical location of these hamlets, it is at once apparent, that unlike the hamlets that developed in the first phase, and which came up on choice agricultural lands, the second generation of Wadis occupy the less productive, second-rate lands. When one delves deeper into the land-use pattern around the later developed hamlets, it becomes clear that on account of the natural increase of population, there was extension of cultivation on more marginal lands,which were formerly given over to either grazing, or were under subsistence grain farming. This was taking place in order to relieve the additional pressure on the existing land resources. Proximity to large urban agglomerations (Poona City), has further encouraged (besides traditional farming) other allied activities like dairying, and to a smaller extent, poultry-keeping, which is gaining in importance at the newly developed hamlets. The pre-eminence of agriculture at these hamlets is missing, unlike their earlier counterparts, where the real *carte de force* was cash-crop farming.

Distribution of Population and Growth Characteristics of Hamlets

Viewing the distribution of population in the different hamlets, it is seen that at the time of the 1981 census, the great bulk (over 77 percent), of the total population of Wagholi was living in its hamlets. In contrast to the above, only 55 per cent of the total population of the village was residing in the hamlets in 1971. The dynamism of the hamlets is clearly reflected in their tremendous potential for growth in relation to the main village, which appears to be losing out heavily to the hamlets. The hamlets in the present context have certainly grown at the expense of the parent village. This could easily be inferred by comparing the share of population of the main village, vis-a-vis its constituent hamlets, for both the decades, 1961-1971 and 1971-1981. With greater diffusion, the centre of gravity of the population is fast tilting in favour of the hamlets (Table 7.4). By the time of the 1981 census, Avhalwadi, the premier Wadi of Wagholi, had surpassed the population of the main village. From a mere figure of 1,700 in 1971, it grew to 2500 by 1981, displaying a growth rate of forty-seven per cent. During the same period, the main Wagholi village declined by an equal amount (47 per cent), from 3,700 persons in 1971 to 1947 persons in 1981.

TABLE 7.4: Population of Wagholi and its Hamlets (Wadis)

Sr. No.	Village/hamlet	Population		% Decadal growth
		1971	1981	
1.	Wagholi village	3700	1947	—47.38
2.	Avhalwadi	1700	2500	47.06
3.	Malwadi	400	750	87.50
4.	Vadjai	350	555	58.57
5.	Kalkewadi	300	450	50.00
6.	Vithalwadi	275	356	29.45
7.	Fulmala	213	290	36.15
8.	Gorevasti	75	165	120.00
9.	Morevasti	75	145	93.33
10.	Dalvivasti	65	130	100.00
11.	Bhadlevasti	200	230	15.00
12.	Gadevasti	120	160	33.33
13.	Jagtapvasti	90	140	55.56
14.	Domkhel	400	580	45.00

The other hamlets displayed varying growth rates, ranging from fifteen per cent for Bhadlevasti to ninety-three per cent for Morevasti. All the hamlets are located within a radius of 1 1/2 miles from the parent village, and except for the three oldest Wadis, namely Avhalwadi, Domkhel and Vadjai, the rest of the hamlets are small in size, with population between 200-400 persons.

Despite the stagnation and decline of the village proper, there is observed an overall growth in the population of the hamlets. This, in the absence of any migration from outside, can only be attributed to the development of the hamlets; which have thus grown largely by the process of diffusion or dispersal of population from the main village, and by natural increase. This is further corroborated with the help of data on place of former residence of hamlet inhabitants. Over ninety per cent of the hamlet dwellers indicated Wagholi village as their home before moving out into the hamlets, whereas, the remaining ten per cent can be accounted for by either, inter-village, or inter-hamlet migration. The general pattern could best be described in the form of a two step migration: initially, from the main settlement to the evolving Wadis; and at a later stage, from the older established Wadis to the newly developed hamlets, or among the Wadis themselves.

Social Morphology of the Hamlets

As seen earlier, three quarter of the total population of Wagholi lives in its hamlets, which are named after the principal landowning families, who first settled there. Also, the hamlets are growing at a much faster rate than the main village. Under the circumstances, it is of vital significance to determine the social structure of these recently evolved dynamic clusters of population.

The main village displays the tightly nucleated, traditional, multi-caste structure, wherein the highest castes occupy the central-most position, followed by other service castes, while the scheduled castes occupy the outer-most fringes. In contrast to the sequential arrangement found in the main village, the hamlets appear like uni-clan, random, population clusters, with no semblance of any order in their spatial arrangement (Fig. 7.2). Viewing the social composition, one finds that in the smallest and most recently evolved hamlets, over 90 per cent of the people are the 'Marathas', the dominant land-owing community, and nearly all of them belong to one agnate clan. In the older established hamlets, though the majority of the population still belongs to the dominant community, different agnates are represented, as also some service castes like the barber, carpenter, blacksmith and water carrier, besides a few scheduled castes. From the sequence of peopling of the hamlets, it can easily be conjectured that the first families to move in are those of the dominant clan with large land holdings. These are followed by the scheduled castes, who are engaged in their time-honoured occupation as agricultural labourers, and lastly, as the hamlet grows in size, some traders and other service castes are eventually attracted. This once again brings to fore the contention that the hamlets grow in response to the need for intensive exploitation of cultivable land, and at the same time to economise on the time and energy spent on commuting daily to and from the house in the village to the farm. And, lately, time has assumed a new significance, with a change from a subsistence to cash economy, as is evinced from the pattern of land utilization near the hamlets.

FIG. 7.2:

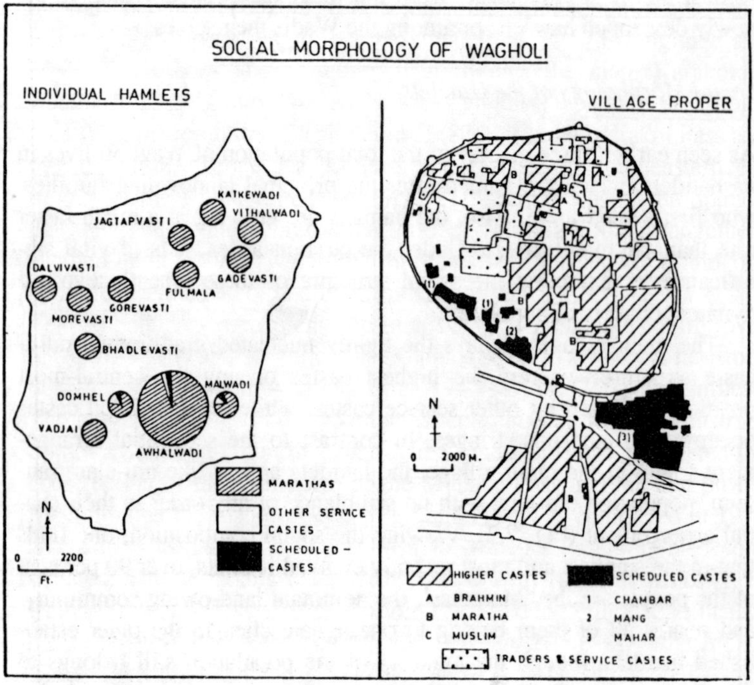

Occupational Structure of the Hamlets

Unlike the main village, where at least twenty to thirty per cent of the people are engaged in services and trade, the hamlets are wholly agricultural, with over ninety per cent of the population, being essentially cultivators (Fig. 7.3). Among the agriculturists, nearly three-

FIG. 7.3:

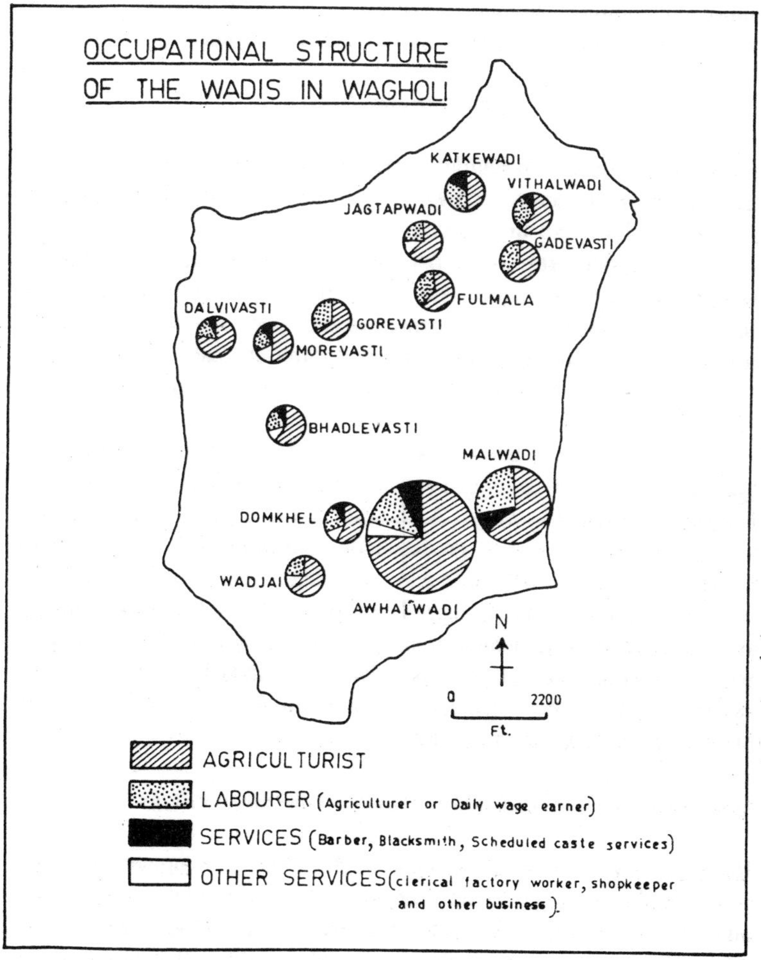

quarters are owner cultivators, while the rest are either daily wage earners or agricultural labourers. Only two hamlets in the area (Katewadi and Vithalwadi), specialize in dairying as the principal activity, with the introduction of a regular bus service, connecting Wagholi to Pune city. Dairying on commercial lines has been developed mainly by farmers with small or medium-size holdings. Worthy of note is its total absence in the irrigated hamlets. Here, the big farmer has his hands already full, coping with the numerous agricultural operations, which leaves him little time to spare for other allied activities.

Trends of Population Diffusion in Hamlets

At Wagholi, maximum hamlet development has taken place. The factors that have favoured such large scale diffusion of population from the main village into the hamlets are the extension of cultivable land, due to increasing pressure of population on the one hand, and the advantages of personal supervision, with the introduction of cash crop economy on the other. Development of transportation, and diversification of allied activities, in response to the increasing demand for perishables from the nearby Poona metropolitan area has further intensified the process.

Avhalwadi, the largest hamlet, having thirty per cent of the total population of Wagholi, is fast showing signs of developing into a full-fledged independent village. Avhalwadi is the only hamlet with services like a primary school, grocery-store and flour mill. It has resident barber, carpenters, blacksmith and the village money-lender, who have migrated from the main village. The rest of the hamlets are essentially small affairs, with populations ranging from as low as 50 to 400 parsons. The small size of their populations inhibits the growth of any functions, as they do not meet the minimum threshold requirement of even the most elementary services.

Some Repercussions of Hamlet Growth on the Main Village

Hamlet growth has in its wake brought about a complete metamorphosis in the socio-economic structure of the main village. It has upset, and virtually stunted, the growth of the parent village, which now shows signs of stagnation and decay. The traditional balance in the socio-economic composition of the village is displaced, as less than five per cent of the farmers now reside in the main village. With the mass exodus, a great contrast between the occupational structure of the main village and its constituent hamlets is seen. The traders, shopkeepers and the scheduled castes who traditionally follow non-agricultural occupations, are left behind to reside in the village proper.

Another consequence, that would have far reaching influence in the future, would be the eroding away of the traditional, tightly knit, cohesive, social structure of the main village. It is already becoming less advantageous (spatially), to reside at the village proper, as there is observed a strong tendency for the new commercial establishments to be located along the main roads and highways, to cater to the increasing clientele from the hamlets. The pace at which the hamlets are growing is likely to tilt the centre of gravity of the population from the village proper towards its peripheries. The process, thus, apart from relieving the pressure of population from the already congested central core, might (with advance of the diffusion process) some day render the main village superfluous. This extreme diffusion from a single compact core might be an adverse element, and pose serious problems for the provision of public utilities and social services, which in the absence of adequate threshold, the government is generally called upon to provide for the rural population.

On the other hand, for the farming community the advantages of living in hamlets are many. Firstly, by living on the premises, the farmer is able to minimise the time lost in daily commuting to the field, and the task of carrying the necessary paraphernalia of agricultural implements, draught animals etc, for farming operations. This leads to increased crop productivity, as seen from the upward trends of several crops. The care and supervision of the fields, which would otherwise be neglected, had they been living far away, also adds up to greater productivity. By living in the hamlets, the farmer also benefits indirectly, in the sense that he escapes from the tradition bound caste ridden social set-up, and in such a situation, there would be greater possibility of attitudinal changes, based on purely economic considerations. This in turn would lead to a more rational outlook on improving one's situation.

Finally, the evolution of hamlets leads to the development of two distinct forms of settlements within the same village, with contrasting features. The earlier traditional pattern, observed in the main village developed within the framework of the need for safety and defence, and on the notion of the religio-ritual model, based entirely on the purity-impurity concept. The hamlets in contrast, owe their origin to economic forces, generating a settlement pattern of greater social homogeneity, rather than spatial propinquity, as is the case with the main village. Since most of the hamlet residents would be landed gentry, differentials in status in the hamlets would be based entirely on economic considerations rather than caste rankings.

Conclusion

With the help of a case study village, the sequence of the process of hamlet development, and its ramifications have been examined at depth. More examples of different kinds of villages, with differential hamlet growth need to be studied, before any definite generalisations can be drawn. Nonetheless, certain recent trends of population diffusion in rural areas, in which the hamlets function as countermagnets to absorb the otherwise increasing population in the central core have emerged.

In Wagholi, inspite of its being a walled village, located on the urban-fringe of Poona city, with a fairly high growth rate of population, the pressure of population is not felt. Within the walls, there is no congestion or even competition for space, as is apparent from the numerous ruins and houses lying in disuse. Almost fifty per cent of all the houses lie abandoned. An interesting feature at Wagholi is that it is the houses of the dominant land-owning community which are lying unoccupied, as they have moved *en masse*, either to the city, or to form the hamlets on their fields, leaving behind a residue of the service castes, agricultural labourers and the traders, who now form the main component of the population of the main village. Curiously, all the scheduled castes are still residing in the village proper. Being virtually landless, they are employed either as unskilled labour in the factories, or as farm labourers in the fields. A clear cut dichotomy exists in the occupational structure of the village and the hamlets, with the village having all the non-agricultural occupations and service castes, while the hamlets having cultivators, specializing in agriculture alone. This heralds the beginning of a new era in which residential as well as occupational segregation, in the context of rural areas, hitherto unknown is taking place. The phenomenon of hamletisation, as observed in the foregoing, led to a complete redistribution of population of the main village. The development, growth and stability of a hamlet, unlike the main village, which today exists more as a vestige of past conditions of settlement, depends on the extent of commercialisation of agriculture.

Acknowledgements

The authors are thankful to Shri D.E. Shinde for assistance in the collection of data and to Mrs. Shrotri for drawing the maps used in the text.

REFERENCES

1. 'Wadi' in Maharashtra denotes an assemblage of houses away from the main village (gaothan), in the fields, but within the revenue area of the village. Gaon, Wadi and Vasti all denote small settlement clusters of varying sizes, from the largest to the smallest.
2. In India, the practice of paying grain at the time of harvest for the services rendered is called the Jajmani system in North India or the Balutedari system in Maharashtra. The service community who receive such payment in kind are called Balutedars. For examples of Balutedari system see, T.N. Atre's Gava Gada (1915) and Dandekar and Jagtap's Maharashtrachi Grameen Rachna (1957).
3. The study excludes Poona City tehsil (14th tehsil), as it is essentially urban.

EIGHT

Arun Kaul

Geographical Factors in the Location and Growth of Settlements in Rajasthan

RAJASTHAN, the land of Rajputs, presents an image very different from the rest of India. The heroism, chivalry and valour of the Rajputs fill many a thrilling pages in our history. The State of Rajasthan (23° 03′ - 30° 12′N and 69° 30′ - 78° 17′E) formed by the Union of the twentytwo princely states and the integration of the former state of Ajmer, covers an area of 341,594 sq. km. Physiographically, Rajasthan exhibits great diversities, ranging from one of the oldest mountains in the world - the Aravallies of today- to the wind-blown sands of the Thar desert interspersed by sand dunes of varying nature. Physiographically the Aravalli range divides Rajasthan into two parts, about three-fifth lies to the north-west and two-fifth to the south-east. As a whole the north-western part is sandy and unproductive, but improves gradually from a mere desert in the far west to comparatively fertile and habitable land towards the north-east. Rajasthan, east and south-east of Aravallis is more diversified in relief, generally consisting of fertile river valleys and dissected plateaux.

In a region of varying physiography, hostile climate and with a history of princely states preserving their glory against the Mughals and Marathas, the factors in the location of settlements are manifold. However under conditions of almost a true desert existing over a major part of Rajasthan, the most effective and dominant factor in the distribution and location of settlements – rural as well as urban – has been availability and adequacy of water supply. Although being a region having mainly an agricultural economy, the distribution of rural settlements is fundamentally related to agriculture: the whole set of conditions affecting the production of crops are a major determining factor in themselves. This is apparent in Ganganagar district where a well-developed canal irrigation has transformed a semi-arid region into the granary of Rajasthan and thereby created the conditions conducive to the concentration of rural settlements.

In a region having an agricultural base, the nature of relief is a domination factor in the location of rural settlements as cultivation is hampered with a negative relief. Thus the Aravalli range with its abrupt rise from the adjoining plains presents an uncompromising condition for the habitat of human beings. However, some concentration of rural settlements in the Aravalli zone is present where gentle relief exists between the Kumbalgarh and Gogunda peaks. The urban settlements in the Aravalli region are likewise located where movement of traffic is easier on account of breaks within the range. It is on account of this that to the north of Beawar, where the range is not continuous, are located several towns of which Ajmer is the most significant. To the west of the Aravallis lies the Thar - the 'Great Desert' of Rajasthan which is however not one single flat waste land. Its surface is diversified by ridges, dunes and hillocks. The sand hills run for long distances varying from 15 to 30 metres in height from the adjoining surface. Besides this, several off-shoots of the Aravalli range appear in Jalor, Jodhpur and Bikaner districts occasionally attaining heights of 600 to 900 metres above sea level. It is all these regions of the Great Desert which apart from the existing arid conditions produce unfavourable sites for human settlements. The region north of the Luni river is to some extent sheltered from drifting sands and so is rather less waste than the 'Great Desert' to the west or the 'Little Desert' to the east. It is here that we find another favourable region for the concentration of rural settlements.

The uplands to the east of Aravallis have a greater concentration of rural as well as urban settlements on account of fertile soils and comparatively higher rainfall. The plains of Jaipur and Tonk are thus studded with rural settlements. However, in the south-east of Rajasthan both the banks of Chambal river have been so much denuded by the gullying action that they could easily be used as a hiding place by the outlaws. Similarly, the Banas banks are not suitable for agricultural practices, due to which only isolated rural settlements have developed along its banks in this zone. The Chappan plains highly dissected by the tribulatries of Mahi has given rise to numerous isolated hillocks where again the rural settlements are dispersed.

In the extreme south-east of Rajasthan is the 'Pathar' or 'Uparmal' (meaning higher plateau). This is the western lobe of the Vindhyan plateau, where on account of comparatively infertile soil and plateau nature of the surface the rural settlements are comparatively dispersed than in the Banas plains to the north. In this region, as the ridges are transversely crossed by the streams flowing eastwards to join Chambal, the settlements are interrupted by the isolated hillocks thus formed.

Contrary to the rural settlements having the tendency of dispersion in areas of rugged relief, the urban settlements in Rajasthan in the Aravalli foothills have been located because of the water carried along their slopes which solves the problem of water, particularly along their western flanks. Several towns in the 'Shekhawati' region have thus grown up along the tributaries of Luni river. In the location of urban settlements to the east of Aravalli range, relief though significant, is not the sole cause. Nearly 40 per cent of the total population of Rajasthan concentrated in the eastern plains, covering only 24 per cent of its area, is of rural nature. The towns located along the eastern flanks of the Aravallis, apart from having a better supply of water, are shielded against the hot and sandy winds of the desert. All such towns were some time or the other capitals of the princely states.

In the distribution and location of human settlements in western Rajasthan the climatic factor is of fundamental importance. The scorching heat with summer temperatures often touching 45°F and an annual rainfall of less than 25cm, sometimes not even falling every year, has turned a greater part of western Rajasthan into one of the least settled parts of India. In this compulsive part of Rajasthan where occasional heavy showers are a miracle for children and existence of old is a struggle against life, the canal water is not only precious than gold but decisive. In the north of this inhospitable part of Rajasthan the water provided by the Bhakra and Gang canals has caused a cluster of rural settlements in Ganganagar district. Here, since the application of canal irrigation, well planned and prosperous villages have come up. If the Bhakra and Gang canals could alone bear an impact on the location of settlements in the arid Ganganagar district then one could well imagine the redistribution of settlements in western Rajasthan after the completion of the Rajasthan canal. In fact the Rajasthan desert which today bears a desolute appearance was once a widely settled area in historic past when the rainfall used to be heavier.

North of Luni and west of Aravalli is a belt of Steppe region, which is comparatively humid and less sandy. The region is generally known as 'Plain of inland drainage' or the Shekhawati tract. It is designated as desert but the ground water conditions and the dense floral growth reveal that the desert is not absolute and bad enough. The fact that a good harvest of Jowar and Bajra can be raised wherever water is available supports this statement. Thus apart from the Ganganagar region in the north, this is the only other part of western Rajasthan where there is greater concentration of rural as well as urban settlements. Similarly in the Luni basin the abundant water supply and fertile soil of the basin has presented favourable sites, for the concentration of rural settlements. However, to the south of the great bend of Luni river, in spite of sufficient rainfall, the settlements are not concentrated to the extent of "the plains of inland drainage' because of the Aravalli off-shoot, which form the highest group of hills in western Rajasthan.

While the urban settlements in eastern Rajasthan are evenly distributed, the towns of western Rajasthan which are in fact bigger villages are very unevenly located over the region. However, in western Rajasthan the number of urban settlements decreases towards the west and north-west where the arid conditions prevail over any other factor in determining their location. The density of rural settlements in western Rajasthan varies greatly as a direct effect of differences in the productivity of the land but this is not ascertained on regional basis. In the location of urban settlements, in western as well as eastern Rajasthan, relief, climate, waterbodies, industrialisation, transport and mining play their part in one or the other regions.

Availability of water is a major factor in determining the site and size of urban as well as rural settlements in Rajasthan. In the desert regions of Jaisalmer, Bikaner and Nagaur even drinking water for human beings is a luxury in summer. Therefore in these arid regions the small rural settlements which are located around a few wells or tanks are abandoned during periods of severe drought. The size of the urban settlements in western as well as eastern Rajasthan depends upon the water supply available during the summer season. The location and development of Ajmer is closely linked with Anasagar, while Jaisamand town situated on the banks of Jaisamand lake exists due to the lake. Similarly, the location and development of Udaipur is mainly due to the group of lakes (Pachola, Fatehsagar and Udaisagar).

Even in the semi-arid zone situated between the Thar desert and the Aravallis, where the drinking water is not a problem during the summer season, the location of bigger villages and towns is related to the availability of water. The towns in the zone are, therefor, located on the Luni or its tributaries. Bali is thus situated on Mitri, Sadri on Sukri,

Pali on the river Bandi and Balotra is located on Luni. The rate of urbanisation has been accelerated in the canal zone of Ganganagar on account of the water available by a network of canals even during the summer season. In Ganganagar district even the dry beds of Ghaggar and Naiwal have determined the location of Suratgarh, Hanumangarh and Gajisinghpur. Apart from these regions, towns in western Rajasthan have been located far apart.

Just as the distribution of rural settlements is influenced by agricultural possibilities, the urban settlements owe their location to the commercial and industrial potentiality of the region. Most of urbanisation in Rajasthan has thus taken place to east of Aravallis on account of the industrial development taking place in this part. Even in the arid district of Bikaner concentration of towns has occurred on account of the development of the cottage and small scale industries. In the arid and semi-arid regions of western Rajasthan, where the opportunities for occupational activities are limited, mineral deposits have been an important factor in the location of towns. The location of Bikaner is determined to a large extent by the deposits of lignite, sandstone and glass. Similarly gypsum has been the most important factor in the location of Lunkaransar and Jaisalmer. Makrana owes its origin and location to the world famous marble deposits.

It is not only a popular belief but also proved on geological grounds that most of Rajasthan west of Aravallis was under the sea during the Jurassic, Cretaceous and Eocene times. The withdrawal of the sea has resulted in the formation of salt lakes called 'Dhands' and Salt pans known as 'Sars'. In western Rajasthan where the salt deposits are of commercial value it has given rise to smaller towns. Most of the smaller towns in the Thar desert not only started their activities as salt centres but also owe their location to the 'Sars'. The names of several of the towns in Thar desert ending with 'Sar' indicate their activity and association with 'Sars'. The names of the towns of Kitasar, Lunkaransar, Dhirdesar, Jaitsar, Sirangsar, and Kansar etc. suggest their association with 'Sars'. Although the names of Sambhar, Didwana and Pachpadra do not end with Sar their existence is to a large extent due to the salt deposits derived from the lakes of their associated names.

The railways although less significant than other geographical factors have given rise to some of the smaller towns particularly in Ganganagar and the arid region of the Thar desert. However, this cannot be taken as a general rule. The location of Jaisalmer in the heart of the desert is not due to the railway line but the railway line has approached the town much after its existence. On the other hand railway line has been a prime factor in the location and development of Barmer, Pokaran and Phalodi. Similarly in the Ganganagar district railway line has been the cause of the location and development of Suratgarh and Hanumangarh. In the eastern Rajasthan, Maoli and Bayana owe their existence to a large extent to the railways. The railways although not the sole cause of the location of Kota, have certainly played a big part in its growth.

The growth of most of the towns in western Rajasthan in their initial stage was retarted due to self-sufficiency and limited occupational activity. It was only when the region was segregated into various princely states that the conditions induced the rise and growth of towns. The most dominant factor in this respect causing the growth and rise of towns was the walled fort (Garh) erected on the top of a ridge rising abruptly from the adjoining ground. This factor has been later on instrumental in the location and growth of several towns in eastern Rajasthan as well. Names of several towns in Rajasthan thus end with Garh indicating their initial association with it, e.g. Chittorgarh, Suratgarh, Kumbhalgarh, Kishangarh, Malgarh, Nawalgarh and Ramgarh.

On the basis of the concentration of rural settlements, Rajasthan can be divided into five zones of comparatively denser concentration:

1. The northern region consisting of the Ganganagar district.
2. The eastern region consisting of Jaipur, Alwar, Bharatpur, Sawai Madhopur and Tonk districts.
3. The south-eastern region consisting of Jhalawar district.
4. The southern region consisting of Banswara, Bhilwara and Chittorgarh districts.
5. The Central region consisting of Ajmer district.

The location of urban settlements in Rajasthan although influenced by the factor of water supply is not affected to the extent of the rural settlements. Thus as compared to the five distinct zones found in the distribution of rural settlement there are only two zones of urban concentration – one to the east of Aravallis and the other to the west of it. Most of the urban centres in the eastern zone have developed due to industrial function while the origin and growth of the towns of the western zone is linked with agricultural activity. Most of the towns in the western region have come up during 1941-51 when the canal irrigation was introduced. With greater emphasis on the development of small scale and cottage industries in the arid and semi-arid zones of Rajasthan, the growth of smaller towns would be accelerated. In the eastern zone Kota has the greatest potentiality to grow, and being on the main railway line would be the second largest city of Rajasthan after Jaipur.

Due to the basic importance of agriculture the pattern of rural settlements in Rajasthan will not be much affected and will not change to a very great extent. However, some remarkable changes shall take place in the districts of Ganganagar and Bikaner which will be benefited by the expansion of canal irrigation. Not only the population will increase in these districts but new villages will develop along the entire length of Rajasthan canal. This development is expected to go a long way in changing the existing distribution of rural settlements in arid and semi-arid regions of Rajasthan.

The search for oil in western Rajasthan is going on and the presence of gas has already been ascertained. The discovery of oil on commercial scale would have far reaching effects on the economy of the region. Not only the smaller towns would have the tendency to grow but new distributing centres would also come up.

NINE

S.B. Sawant and **A.S. Bhole**

Impact of Out-Migration on Population Characteristics of South Konkan

Introduction

Physical conditions of any region including relief, climate, nature of soils etc., influence economic opportunities such as development of agriculture, industrial landscape and transportation network. From the point of view of conducting economic activities, regions with adverse physical setting, which are reflected in not very helpful economic conditions, make the regions unattractive. Such negative regions encourage out-migration. This affects population characteristics such as rate of growth, sex-ratio, literacy etc. To study these relationships, South Konkan has been selected.

The Region

South Konkan is located between lat. 15° 36′ and 18° 50′N and long. 73° 50′ and 74° 36′E. With the total geographical area of 13,040 sq.km., the region is a long narrow strip of land extending in the north-south direction for about 283km. and having an average width of about 55 km. The region is bounded in the west by the Arabian sea, in the east by the Sahyadri escarpment, in the north by the river Savitri and in the south by the union territory of Goa and the Terekhol estuary.

The region is a narrow coastal lowland having numerous low plateaus and hill ranges running in different directions and traversed by innumerable short and swift rivers forming narrow valleys. More than 85% of the land surface is hilly.

South Konkan experiences a maritime climate with high temperatures and high relative humidity (more than 50%) throughout the year. The average annual rainfall for the region is 3,188 mm. bulk of which is received during the four months of S.W. Monsoon season, i.e. from June to September.

Due to excessive leaching, the soils are poor and due to undulating nature of terrain the proportion of land available for cultivation is very low. Area under irrigation is almost negligible, agricultural productivity is low and agriculture is primitive.

The region presently has no railway and the rugged undulating nature of the terrain has hampered the development of an adequate road network. Due to inadequate infrastructural facilities as a result of the difficult terrain, South Konkan has remained industrially backward.

These physical and economic factors have resulted in economic backwardness of the region which in turn has led to sustained and large scale out-migration resulting in peculiar population characteristics. The volume of out-migration has been so large that according to 1921 census more than 3 lakh people born in South Konkan were enumerated in other districts of the state of Bombay particularly the city of Bombay. During the last 50 years the rate has increased rapidly so that the number stood at 6,73,282 in 1971 out of which 5,64,890 were enumerated in Bombay city alone. This flow adversely affected the population characteristics of the region very significantly.

Rate of Growth of Population

Table 9.1 shows that the rate of growth of population in south Konkan has been uniformly lower than the state average throughout these eight decades. With increased volume of out-migration the difference between the two rates has been increasing.

TABLE 9.1: Rate of Population Growth (1901-81)

Decade / Region	1901-11	1911-21	1921-31	1931-41	1941-51	1951-61	1961-71	1971-81
S.Konkan	+2.53	–4.24	+12.68	+6.04	+5.21	+6.73	+8.84	+5.96
Maharashtra	+10.74	–2.91	+14.91	+11.99	+19.27	+23.6	+27.45	+24.36

FIG. 9.1:

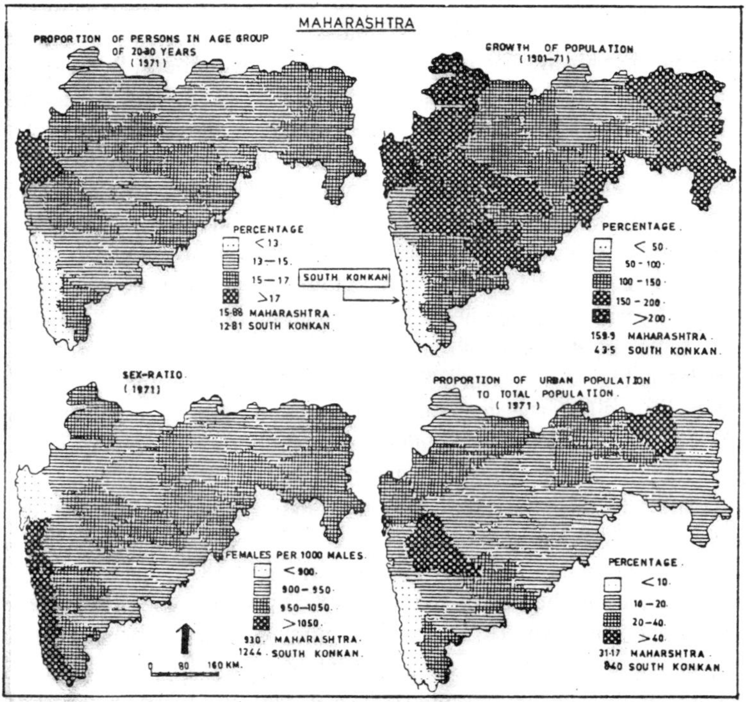

Absence of males in the reproductive age-group due to out-migration on a large scale has affected birth-rate adversely. This is one more reason for lower rate of population increase in the region. In 1975, birth rate per 1,000 person for South Konkan was 18.2 as against 24.9 for the State of Maharashtra. The death rates, however, were almost equal. Hence rate of natural increase of population for the region was significantly lower than that for the State. This low rate of natural increase of population coupled with out-migration on a large scale gave South Konkan the lowest population growth-rate in the State of Maharashtra (Fig. 9.1).

Age-Sex Composition

Migration in South Konkan is primarily due to economic reasons. In such a situation the migration is normally age and sex selective. The impact of age and sex selective migration is clearly seen on the age-sex composition of the region. In 1971, for the State of Maharashtra, the difference between proportions of males and females to their respective totals has always been less than 1% for all age-groups. But proportion of males in South Konkan in the age-group of 0-14 years was higher by about 6% than the State average in the same age-group (Table 9.2). Besides, in South Konkan, proportion of males in this age-group was higher by 9% than that for the females. This is due to poverty which has resulted in neglect of females in this age-group. Although the gap is reduced to less than 1%, the trend continues even in the age-group of 14-19 years. The trend is reversed for the age-group of 20-24 years and continues till the age-group of 40-49 years. Due to large scale out-migration of males in 20-24 age-group the proportion of females is higher by about 2% than that for males in the same age-group. This difference goes on increasing and the peak is reached in 30-39 age-group when for South Konkan, proportion of females in the age-group to total females is higher than that for males by about 4%. Thereafter the difference starts declining and becomes negligible in the age-group beyond 50 years.

This is not a new phenomenon. As early as in 1872, due to age and sex selective out-migration from South Konkan, the age-sex composition was disturbed. In 1872 in the age-group of 0 to 20 years, proportion of males to total males was higher by about 4% than that for females in the same age-group (Table 9.3). This difference increased to about 10% in 1971. This shows that during the last 100 years poverty and consequent neglect of females has increased to an alarming proportion. In 1872, due to age-sex selective out-migration, age-sex composition was disturbed in the age-group of 20-30 years to the extent that proportion of females in the age-group was higher than that for males by about 4%. Age-sex composition remained disturbed till the age-group of 30-40 years, and thereafter there was very little difference, while in 1971 the difference continued till the age-group of 40-50 years. Another change has been that in 1872 the peak was reached in the 20-30 age group while in 1971 the peak was reached in the age-group of 30-40 years.

Proportion of Working Population

Out migration of workers on a large scale for such a long time has resulted in higher proportion of non-workers in South Konkan. While proportion of non-workers in 1971 for the State of Maharashtra was 63.5%, that for South Konkan it was 65%. This has resulted in low per capita income and economic backwardness which has further encouraged out-migration.

TABLE 9.2: Age-Sex Composition (1971)

	South Konkan		Maharashtra	
Age-groups	% males	% females	% males	% females
0-14	46.71	37.15	40.81	41.9
14-19	9.23	8.87	8.94	8.0
20-24	5.4	7.26	8.02	8.27
25-29	5.03	7.47	7.46	8.04
30-39	9.76	13.66	13.03	13.08
40-49	8.96	10.71	9.91	9.06
50-59	7.45	7.33	6.28	5.71
60 and above	7.43	7.54	5.52	5.93

TABLE 9.3: Age-Sex Composition for South Konkan (1872 and 1971)

Age-groups	1872		1971	
	% males	% females	% males	% females
0 to 20	55.85	51.08	55.94	46.02
20 to 30	15.72	19.15	10.43	14.73
30 to 40	11.70	12.2	9.76	13.66
40 to 50	8.59	8.15	8.96	10.71
50 to 60	5.4	5.4	7.45	07.33
More than 60	3.32	3.32	7.43	7.54

South Konkan is a region where proportion of land available for cultivation is very low. Proportion of area under irrigation is negligible. Hence only one crop is possible. Agriculture is primitive and agricultural productivity is very low. In such a region, because of failure of non-agricultural sector to develop, 80% of the workers were engaged in agriculture in 1971. This has further encouraged out-migration from the region.

Literacy

In an economically backward region like South Konkan, job opportunities within the region are very limited. Migration to a region like Bombay city in search of job is the only alternative available. Education makes this task easier. That is the reason why in a backward region like this proportion of literates to total population has almost been equal to the State average throughout the last eight decades (See Table 9.4).

TABLE 9.4: Proportion of literates to total population (1901-1981)

Years	1901	1911	1921	1931	1941	1951	1961	1971	1981
S. Konkan	5.26	4.35	4.64	6.53	14.94	17.7	28.49	37.02	47.63
Maharashtra	4.55	5.0	6.35	7.35	14.35	20.5	29.4	38.74	47.37

Urbanisation

South Konkan is industrially very backward region. Besides, non-agricultural sector has not developed to any significant extent. That is why the region is least urbanised in the State of Maharashtra. Proportion of urban population to total population in 1971 for South Konkan was only 8.4% as against 31.17% for the State of Maharashtra. Not only that, out of fifteen talukas of South Konkan six talukas do not have any urban centre at all.

Sex-ratio

Population character which has been disturbed most due to sex-selective out-migration is sex-ratio. The sex-ratio has been abnormally high for South Konkan than for the State of Maharashtra (see Table 9.5). In 1901 the sex-ratio for the State of Maharashtra was 978 females per 1,000 males. But for South Konkan it was as high as 1119 females per 1,000 males. Due to increase in volume of out-migration this difference has further increased during the last eight decades. In 1981 the sex ratio for South Konkan was 1,242 females per 1,000 males while the same for the State of Maharashtra was only 939. This was highest sex ratio in the entire State of Maharashtra. Hence sex-ratio has been taken as an indicator to represent imbalance created by sex-selective out-migration. Different factors affecting volume of out-migration and consequently sex-ratio were analysed by using taluka-wise data with the help of a correlation matrix. The factors taken into consideration were (i) road density, (2) proportion of literates to total population, (3) proportion of cultivated land to total geographical area, (4) density of population, (5) proportion of non-agricultural workers to total workers, (6) percentage of employment seekers to total population, (7) number of post-offices per 1,000 population, and (8) decadal variation in population. The correlation matrix clearly shows that (see Table 9.6):

(1) Sex-ration is not very significantly affected by road density.
(2) Because of out-migration of literate people, areas where from out-migration has occurred on a large scale show low proportion of literates.
(3) Areas with high sex-ratios as a result of sex-selective out-migration have lower densities, and density of population is directly influenced by road density, literacy and percentage of cultivated land.
(4) Areas where no-agricultural sector has developed have low sex-ratios. Development of non-agricultural sector is directly influenced by road density, literacy, percentage of cultivated land and density of population.
(5) Sex-ratio is not very significantly affected by unemployment. But unemployment is inversely affected by percentage of cultivated land and density of population.
(6) Ease of communication represented by number of post-offices per 1,000 population has positive correlation with sex-ratio. But areas where non-agricultural sector has developed do not have large number of post-offices per 1,000 population.
(7) Decadal variation of population is not very significantly affected by sex-ratio. But decadal variation in population is adversely affected by literacy.

TABLE 9.5: Number of Females per 1000 Males (1901-81)

Years	1901	1911	1921	1931	1941	1951	1961	1971	1981
S. Konkan	1119	1164	1187	1129	1158	1224	1237	1244	1242
Maharashtra	978	966	950	947	949	941	936	930	939

TABLE 9.6: Correlation Matrix

	Sex-ratio	Road density	Literacy	% of cultivated land	Density of population	% of Non-agricultural workers	% of employment seekers to total population	No. of Post-Offices per 1000 pop.	Decade variation in population
	1	2	3	4	5	6	7	8	9
Sex-ratio	1.0000	—0.2492	—0.7846	—0.2718	—0.3431	—0.4754	0.05169	0.5812	—0.1415
2.		1.0000	0.3384	0.5305	0.5898	0.5860	0.0162	—0.4232	—0.2208
3.			1.0000	0.1898	0.5833	0.5892	—0.2646	—0.3803	—0.4858
4.				1.0000	0.8845	0.4974	—0.3500	—0.4881	—0.0780
5.					1.0000	0.7273	—0.5112	—0.4511	—0.2129
6.						1.0000	—0.2813	—0.7628	—0.0129
7.							1.0000	0.3913	0.00045
8.								1.0000	—0.1433
9.									1.0000

Guhagar Taluka : a close up

To study on village level to study the impact of sex-selective out-migration on rural sex-ratio and impact of different factors on volume of out-migration and consequently rural sex-ratio, one taluka Guhagar from South Konkan was selected. This taluka is entirely rural and has the highest sex-ratio. For this purpose, twelve factors were taken and for each factor different categories were fixed. Villages which fell in each such category for all the factors were grouped together. By adding number of males in each such village, total number of males for all the villages falling in one such category was calculated. Similar procedure was adopted to arrive at the total number of females for all the villages falling in the same category. A ratio of these two totals was used to represent sex-ratio of villages coming in that categories of any one factor and for all such factors.

Altitude and Sex-ratio

Villages were grouped according to three altitudinal zones and sex-ratios for villages falling in each zone were calculated (see Table 9.7).

TABLE 9.7: Altitudinal Zones and Sex-ratios (Guhagar Taluka)

Altitudinal zones	No. of villages	Sex-ratio
Less than 100 m	52	1359
100 to 150 m	21	1378
More than 150 m	5	1581

In Guhagar taluka, with increase in altitude, proportion of land available for cultivation decreases. This encouraged out-migration resulting in higher sex-ratios. The sex-ratio was lowest (1359 females per 1,000 males) for villages located in areas with altitude less than 100 metres. Sex-ratio goes on increasing and the highest sex-ratio of 1581 females per 1,000 males was recorded for villages located in areas with altitude more than 150 metres.

Proportion of Land under Cultivation and Sex-ratio

Sex-ratio is inversely affected by proportion of land under cultivation in Guhagar taluka (see Table 9.8).

FIG. 9.2:

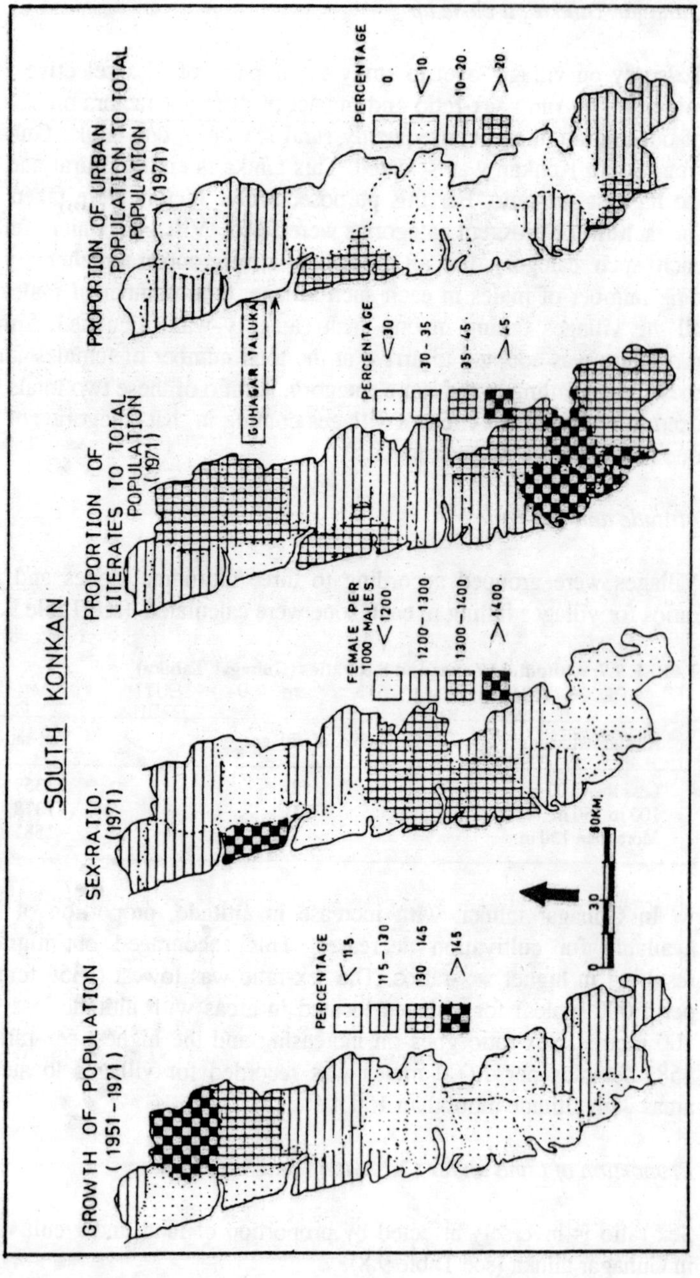
SOUTH KONKAN
GROWTH OF POPULATION (1951-1971)
PERCENTAGE
< 115
115-130
130 145
> 145
SEX-RATIO (1971)
FEMALE PER 1000 MALES
< 1200
1200-1300
1300-1400
> 1400
PROPORTION OF LITERATES TO TOTAL POPULATION (1971)
PERCENTAGE
< 30
30-35
35-45
> 45
PROPORTION OF URBAN POPULATION TO TOTAL POPULATION (1971)
PERCENTAGE
0
< 10
10-20
> 20
GUHAGAR TALUKA
0 30 60KM.

FIG. 9.3:

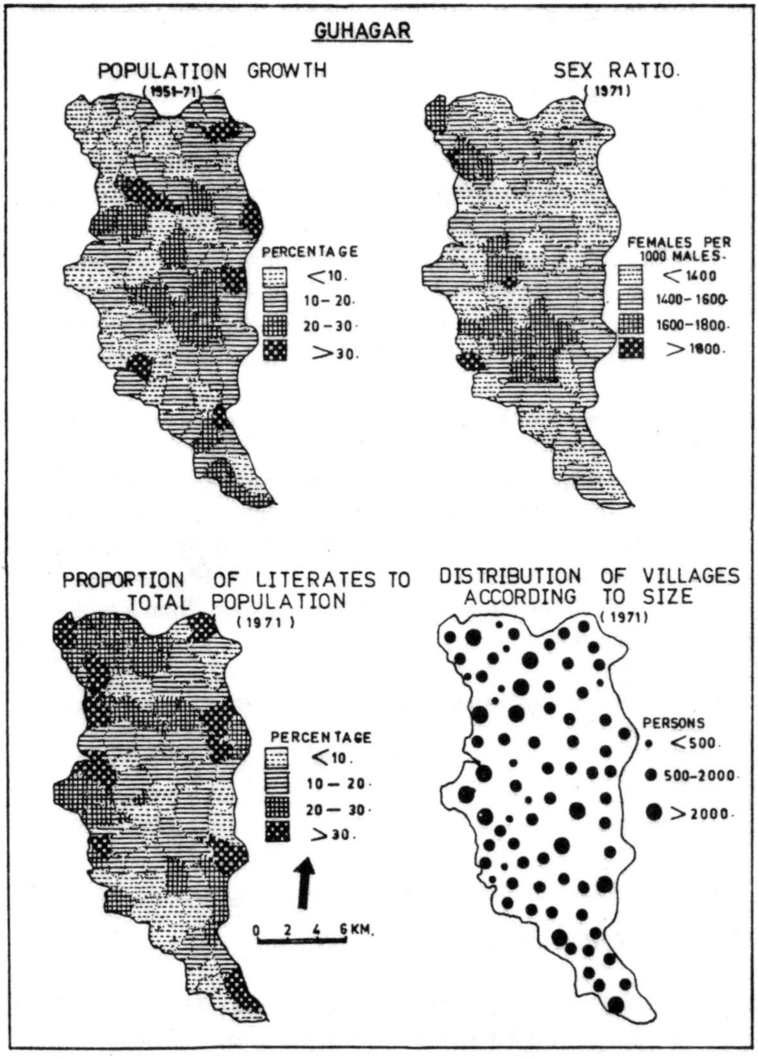
GUHAGAR
POPULATION GROWTH
(1951-71)
PERCENTAGE
<10.
10-20.
20-30.
>30.
SEX RATIO.
(1971)
FEMALES PER 1000 MALES.
<1400
1400-1600
1600-1800.
>1800.
PROPORTION OF LITERATES TO TOTAL POPULATION
(1971)
PERCENTAGE
<10.
10-20.
20-30.
>30.
0 2 4 6 KM.
DISTRIBUTION OF VILLAGES ACCORDING TO SIZE
(1971)
PERSONS
<500.
500-2000.
>2000.

TABLE 9.8: Cultivated Land Sex-ratio (Guhagar Taluka)

Percentage of cultivated land to total geographical area	No. of villages	Sex-ratio,
Less than 30	36	1554
30 to 45	28	1441
More than 45	14	1326

Low proportion of land under cultivation encourages out-migration resulting in adverse sex-ratio. In Guhagar taluka, for villages where proportion of land under cultivation is less than 30%, there are 1554 females per 1,000 males. As proportion of land under cultivation increases, sex-ratio decreases. Lowest sex-ratio of 1326 is recorded for villages where proportion of land under cultivation is more than 45%.

istance from Road and Sex-ratio

Better accessibility has encouraged out-migration in Guhagar taluka. Villages located within 2 km. from a motorable road have high sex-ratio of 1654 females per 1,000 males. As accessibility decreases, sex-ratio also decreases. Relatively low sex-ratio of 1321 females per 1,000 males is recorded for villages located beyond 4 km. from a motorable road (see Table 9.9).

TABLE 9.9: Distance from a Motorable Road and Sex-ratio. (Guhagar Taluka)

Distance from a motorable road	No. of villages	Sex Ratio
Less than 2 km.	41	1654
2 to 4 km.	26	1427
More than 4 km.	11	1321

Distance from Port and Sex-ratio

In the absence of railway, another mode of transportation available in South Konkan is steamer service connecting small and medium ports on the Konkan coast with the port of Bombay. Hence distance from port also influences volume of out-migration significantly. In Guhagar taluka, villages located within 5 km. from a port have high sex-ratio of

1572 as a result of out-migration on a large scale. As distance from a port increases, sex-ratio also decreases. Relatively low sex-ratio of 1372 females per 1,000 males is recorded for villages located beyond 10 km. from a port (see Table 9.10).

TABLE 9.10: Distance from a Port and Sex-ratio: (Guhagar Taluka)

Distance from a port	No. of villages	Sex Ratio
Less than 5 km.	24	1572
5 to 10 km.	44	1377
More than 10 km.	10	1372

Decadal Population Variation during 1951-71 and Sex-ratio

Volume of out-migration influences decadal population variation and sex-ratio. Villages from where there has been out-migration on a large scale show low decadal variation in population and high sex ratio (see Table 9.11).

TABLE 9.11: Decadal Variation in Population and Sex-ratio (1951-71) (Guhagar Taluka)

% Population Variation 1951-71	No. of villages	Sex Ratio
Less than 0	7	1855
0 to 10	22	1443
10 to 20	30	1339
More than 20	20	1205

In Guhagar taluka, villages which have shown negative decadal variation in population during 1951-71 due to large scale out-migration, have high sex-ratio of 1855 females per 1,000 males. With increase in decadal variation of population sex-ratio declines. Relatively lower sex-ratio of 1205 females per 1,000 males is recorded by villages which have shown decadal increase in population of more than 20% during 1951-71 due to relatively less out-migration.

Settlements by Population Size and Sex-ratio

In South Konkan there has been large scale out-migration from smaller villages than from larger villages. In Guhagar taluka, small villages each with population less than 250 have an abnormally high sex-ratio of 2116 females per 1,000 males. As population size of settlements increases, sex-ratio declines. Large size villages, each with population of more than 2,000 have relatively low sex-ratio of 1324 females per 1,000 males (see Table 9.12).

TABLE 9.12: Settlements by Population Size and Sex-ratio (Guhagar Taluka)

Settlements by population size	No. of villages	Sex-ratio
0 to 250	2	2116
251 to 500	9	1587
501 to 1000	22	1513
1001 to 2000	30	1418
More than 2,000	14	1324

Average Family Size and Sex-ratio

Villages from where there has been out-migration on a large scale have smaller average family size and higher sex-ratio (see Table 9.13).

TABLE 9.13: Average Family Size and Sex-ratio (Guhagar Taluka)

Average family size	No. of Villages	Sex Ratio
Less than 4	7	1533
4 to 5	59	1525
More than 5	12	1297

In Guhagar taluka villages with average family size of 4 have high sex-ratio of 1533 females per 1,000 males. With increase in average family size, sex-ratio decreases, so that villages with average family size of more than five have relatively low sex-ratio of 1297 females per 1,000 males.

Density of Population and Sex-ratio

High density of population has encouraged out-migration on a large scale which has resulted in high sex-ratio (see Table 9.14).

TABLE 9.14: Density of Population and Sex-ratio (Guhagar Taluka)

Density of population per acre	No. of Villages	Sex Ratio
Less than 1	12	1203
1 to 2	34	1438
2 to 3	26	1519
More than 3	6	1577

Villages in Guhagar taluka with relatively high density of population of 3 persons per acre, due to out-migration on a large scale, have abnormally high sex-ratio of 1577 females per 1,000 males. Sex ratio decreases with decrease in density of population. Thus villages with low population density of less than 1 person per acre have relatively low sex-ratio of 1203 females per 1,000 males.

Proportion of Non-workers to Total Population and Sex-ratio

Migration due to economic reasons is normally age and sex selective. Areas from where there has been out-migration on a large scale have high proportion of non-workers and high sex-ratio.

In Guhagar taluka, villages with high proportion of non-workers of more than 80% have abnormally high sex-ratio of 1591 females per 1,000 males. Sex-ratio decreases with proportion of non-workers so that in villages where proportion of non-workers is relatively low (less than 60%), sex-ratio also is relatively low (1422 females per 1,000 males) (see Table 9.15).

TABLE 9.15: Proportion of Non-workers to Total Population and Sex-ratio (Guhagar Taluka)

% of non-workers to total population	No. of Villages	Sex Ratio
Less than 60	24	1422
60 to 80	46	1451
More than 80	9	1591

Proportion of Workers Engaged in Non-agricultural Occupations to Total Workers and Sex Ratio

There has been relatively less out-migration from areas where non-agricultural sector has developed to some extent. In such areas, sex-ratio is relatively less disturbed. But from areas where non-agricultural sector has not developed adequately, there has been sustained and large scale out-migration resulting in abnormally high sex-ratio (see Table 9.16).

TABLE 9.16: Proportion of Workers Engaged in Non-agricultural Occupations to Total Workers and Sex-ratio (Guhagar Taluka)

% of workers engaged in non-agricultural occupations to total workers	No. of Villages	Sex Ratio
Less than 10	38	1540
10 to 20	18	1398
More than 20	22	1342

In Guhagar taluka, villages where non-agricultural employment is more than 20%, sex-ratio is relatively low (1352 females per 1,000 males). Due to out-migration, sex-ratio increases with decrease in proportion of non-agricultural employment so that villages where proportion of non-agricultural employment is low i.e. less than 10%, sex-ratio is abnormally high (1540 females per 1,000 males).

Proportion of Literates to Total Population and Sex-ratio

Literate people are normally more mobile than illiterate people. Hence in areas where proportion of literates is high due to sex-selective out-migration, sex-ratio is normally high (see Table 9.17).

TABLE 9.17: Proportion of Literates to Total Population and Sex-ratio (Guhagar Taluka)

% literates to total population	No. of Villages	Sex Ratio
Less than 20	19	1373
20 to 40	48	1387
More than 40	12	1557

As expected, in Guhagar taluka, villages where proportion of literates is high i.e. more than 40%, sex-ratio also is high (1557 females per 1,000 males). Sex-ratio decreases with proportion of literates so that villages where proportion of literates is less than 20%, sex-ratio is relatively low (1373 females per 1,000 males).

Existence of a Post-office and Sex-ratio

Existence of a post-office results in a better communication with outside world which encourages out-migration and consequently disturbs sex-ratio (see Table 9.18).

TABLE 9.18: Existence of a Post-office and Sex-ratio (Guhagar Taluka)

Villages	No. of villages	Sex-ratio
With post-office	31	1534
Without post-office	47	1345

In Guhagar taluka, villages with post-office have an abnormally high sex-ratio of 1534 females per 1,000 males, while villages without a post-office have a relatively low sex-ratio of 1345 females per 1,000 males.

Conclusions

Preceding discussions clearly show that in South Konkan sustained and large scale out-migration has adversely affected population characteristics such as rate of growth of population, birth-rate, proportion of workers and sex-ratio. Village-level analysis showed that volume of out-migration and resultant sex-ratio are influenced by factors such as proportion of area under cultivation, accessibility, settlement-size, density of population, literacy and communication in the region.

PART – IV

MARKETING GEOGRAPHY

TEN

Howard F. Hirt

Planning and Retailing in South Delhi: A Personal Appraisal

the householders in the planned residential colonies of South shopping for daily needs often presents problems. Planned shopping centres, although present in many cases, do not provide a solution. They are often inconveniently located, and they often do not provide adequate numbers of shops or selection of family necessities. In Greater Kailash, for example, the M-Block market has mostly luxury goods, such as television, appliances, saries, and fancy restaurants. The problem of planned shopping centres is particularly difficult in the case of perishables, such as fruits, vegetables, meat, fish, and similar goods.

In response to this situation, the "informal" or "unorganized" sector has proliferated. Vendors of perishable and non-perishable foods, and of a variety of non-food items, have moved in and settled illegally on the roads and footpaths. Some of them have erected stalls of canvas, wood, or brick, and some display their merchandise in baskets or on burlap sacking on the ground. Itinerant peddlers have claimed their place in the retail scheme, moving daily on the roads and lanes of residential areas with their bicycles, carts, and headloads, and their distinctive calls.

Some planned shopping centres do provide adequate facilities for daily needs. The I.N.A. market and the Sarojini Nagar Market have a multiplicity of shops selling vegetables, fruits, meat, fish, and other necessities in great variety and of high quality. Shoppers from distant residential areas, including the diplomatic enclave, come by car and scooter rickshaw, or send their servants to these markets.

From the householder's standpoint the optimal situation would be to have a selection of shops selling perishable foods within about five minutes walk for daily shopping, and a larger, more diversified market within roughly fifteen minutes walk for periodic or weekly shopping. But at present, for the average householder lacking a car or a servant, shopping for daily needs often means dealing with small vendors in a contaminated environment, characterized by garbage, smells, excrement, animals, birds, insects, and dust.

This essay is a brief personal appraisal of some of the factors that may underlie the situation described above, based on four months of observation in 1981. The factors may be classified as economic, administrative, conceptual, and cultural, but there is overlap between the groups.

Economic Factors

The most important factors are the economic. Sellers of perishable foods in India are characterized by: (a) small scale of operations; (b) intense competition; and (c) lack of capital investment. The scale of operations ranges from the part-time vendor with a few tired-looking vegetables set out on the footpath, up to the merchant with carefully arranged pyramids of fruit on a concrete plinth protected by an asbestos-cement roof. But in no case is there any substantial investment in inventory, store fixtures, rent, or sales force. Under such conditions entry into the business is easy at the lower end of the scale. All that is needed is the wholesale price of one day's merchandise.

Retail prices of perishable foods are established by vigorous competition between merchants and hard bargaining by the customers. Prices vary from season to season, from day to day, and from morning to evening, depending on the quality, quantity, and freshness of the fruits and vegetables. Under these conditions, the business tends not to be highly profitable. The smaller, more marginal merchants move in and out of the business, depending on conditions.

Administrative Factors

By administrative factors are meant the methods by which the retail spaces in planned shopping areas are allotted, and by which municipal, sanitary and land use rules are enforced.

The Delhi Development Authority is the agency responsible for planning shopping centres and allocating retail space to merchants. The method of allocation is the auction. The highest bidder gets the space. The highest bidder most often is the merchant with the highest potential profitability--in other words, the seller of luxury or high cost goods. The seller of perishables, whose profit margins are relatively low, cannot afford to pay for the high cost space in planned shopping centres.

Occasionally, as in Greater Kailash, M-Block and Defence Colony markets, a seller of fruits or vegetables does manage to find a place. This merchant then has a "monopoly" position, and can and must charge higher prices.

Another administrative factor is the lack of enforcement of rules concerning land use, sanitation, and encroachment. There are no markets in South Delhi where the footpaths and roads are free of encroachment by shopkeepers and small vendors. Instead of consistent rigorous enforcement of the rules, there are occasional police raids that have no long-term effect.

Conceptual Factors

Under the heading of conceptual factors are included some of the planning ideas embodied in the Master Plan for Delhi, 1961-1981.[1] The Plan was prepared with the assistance of a team of American consultants provided by the Ford Foundation. The Plan adopted Zoning and Subdivision Regulations of the type that are almost universally used the United States. These regulations are an example of the uncriti adoption of a western practice without adequate consideration of t Indian context.

Zoning is a technique used to prevent the "harmful" invasion c residential areas by commercial and industrial land uses. The Plan established twenty-four "Use Zones," of which nine were residential zones of various population densities, and the rest were non-residential.[2] Within each zone there were certain permitted land uses. There were provisions for dealing with non-conforming uses in each zone, so that they could be phased out within a specified number of years. Under certain circumstances non-conforming uses were permitted if allowed by competent authority after special appeal. There were also prohibited uses. The end result of the enforcement of the zoning regulations would be zones whose land uses would be relatively uniform within the zone. This is the objective for American cities where zoning regulations are in effect.

Zoning regulations are a necessary limitation of the landowner's right to do what he wishes with his land. Their justification is the promotion of public health, safety, and welfare. To be effective, there must be: (a) the informed agreement of the majority of the population; and (b) an enforcement procedure that is certain, just, and uniformly applied to all property.

The planners publicised the Draft Plan and dealt with objections, but the persistence of non-conforming and impermissible uses in the use zones is clear evidence that the general public knows little and cares less about the zoning regulations. The householders of South Delhi do not seem to object to the presence near their homes of the various shopkeepers, vendors, and service providers that they need. They don't generally object to the nuisances caused by the conversion of residences into professional or business offices or commercial establishments. Even if an activity emits noxious smoke, fumes, noise, or effluents, there seems to be relatively little objection in lower income group areas. The enforcement of the zoning regulations seems to be haphazard, uncertain, and subject to irregularities.

Another error in the Master Plan was in the numbers of retail shops that were allocated to the various levels of shopping centres in the planned development areas. The smallest centre, the "Convenience Shopping Centre," catering for 3,500 to 5,000 population, would have 4 to 6 shops, or one shop for about 850 persons. The next larger centre, the "Residential Planning Area Centre," now called the Local shopping Centre, would have 15 to 20 shops to cater for 12,000 to 15,000 population, or one shop for about 800 persons. The "Community Centre," serving 40,000 to 50,000 population, would have 80 to 100 shops, or one shop for 500 persons.[3]

It is obvious to those with knowledge of Indian cities that these numbers are too small. They do not take account of the shoppers, desire to compare prices and quality. They tend to give the merchants a near monopoly position in their location. With the passage of time the planners have revised their norms upward. A recent study showed that in the combined formal and informal sectors there was one shop for 30 persons.[4]

Cultural Factors

In addition to the economic, administrative, and conceptual factors, there are cultural influences that appear distinctive to the Delhi Metropolitan Area and perhaps also to Indian cities in general.

Possibly the most important of these factors is the continued rapid growth of Delhi by in-migration and natural increase. It is the fastest growing metropolis in India. The present population of about 62 lakhs is expected to reach 128 lakhs by the year 2001 A.D.

The rapid growth of Delhi has been accompanied by an increase in the share of the informal sector in the total working force from 58% in 1961 to about 63% in 1980.[5]

The demand for housing, employment, shopping facilities, education, health services, transportation, water, electricity, and sanitation by this rapidly growing population would soon outstrip the abilities of even the most powerful and wealthy municipal administration. It is small wonder then, that the in-migrating unemployed workers and petty traders have continued to build *"jhuggie-jhonprie"* shack communities and to establish informal small-scale industries and retail shops.

The second cultural factor seems to be a certain ambivalence regarding the roles of planning, maintenance, and the enforcement of municipal regulations. The Delhi Development Authority has completed many housing and commercial projects. They have contributed much to ameliorating Delhi's housing and economic problems. But, after the projects are completed, the quality of maintenance is very low, and the enforcement of municipal regulations regarding sanitation, encroachment, bill-sticking, etc., is very poor. There seems to be a lack of commitment on the part of the authorities to carrying a project through to its planned objectives. Perhaps it is recognized that illegal constructions and unauthorized shops serve a genuine need, and that it would be cruel to displace them.

Finally, there is the nature of Indian society, which has been described[6] as a "free-for-all" society. The term is useful in characterising the public behaviour of Indian businessmen. They are independent, aggressively competitive, and eager to succeed. They do not allow the rules and regulations – which they have not had a hand in framing – to stand in their way.

Conclusion

Does this situation require some form of corrective action? What form should it take? What should be its objectives?

With the cooperation of the Delhi Development Authority the writer is seeking to develop a technique for optimizing the numbers, types, and locations of shops in the two lowest levels of the retail hierarchy. The technique will use the results of a survey of consumer and merchant behaviour and preferences. If the technique is successful, the householders in new residential areas will have a selection of competing shops selling necessities within a maximum of five minutes walk for daily purchases and fifteen minutes walk for less frequent purchases.

In addition, the writer will recommend that the Delhi Development Authority construct these shops and lease them to the merchants at nominal rent.[7] The Delhi Development Authority must ensure that they are kept clean and orderly, and are not diverted to some other type of use.

Will measures such as these discourage the proliferation of the informal sector? Probably not. But if they are carried out with consistency and thoroughness, they might give the shopper a better chance to purchase necessities conveniently, at competitive prices, and under sanitary conditions.

REFERENCES

1. Delhi Development Authority, *Master Plan for Delhi*. New, Delhi : Delhi Development Authority, (1962), 108 pp.
2. *Master Plan*, pp. 44-45.
3. *Master Plan*, pp. 66-67.
4. Delhi Development Authority, Perspective Planning Wing, "Background paper - 2,"Seminar on employment, Delhi 1981-2001, (October 24, 1981) p. 23.
5. Atreyi Majumdar, "In-migration and Informal Sector: A Case study of Urban Delhi,"(1980) quoted by Sayed S. Shafi and S.S Dutta, "Some Conceptual Issues in the Study of Delhi's Economic Base," Seminar on Employment, Delhi 1981-2001, (October 24, 1981)
6. By Prof. R. Ramachandran, Geography Department, University of Delhi
7. Suggested by M.N. Buch, Director, Nat. Inst. Urban Affairs, New Delhi.

ELEVEN

R.C. Srivastava

Periodic Markets and Intra-Urban Mobility: A Case Study of Kanpur Metropolis

Introduction

IN urban societies which are spatially confined, only localized interaction and shorter movements take place. But the million cities on account of complicated nature of intra-urban movements are facing different types of traffic problems. Intra-urban moves are short and the unit of travel is customarily the trip i.e. a one way journey that proceeds from an origin to a destination by a single type of vehicular transportation. Yeats & Garner[1] have concluded from their regional transport study of Toronto that personal trips undertaken for variety of purposes, involve multitude of origins and destinations and can be grouped into four main categories: (i) trip to and from home, (ii) trip to and from work, (iii) social and recreational trips and (iv) trips for shopping, school and personal business. Shopping trips are different in many ways since they account for only a small part of total pattern of urban movement; much shorter in terms of time and distance; much regular in time; spatially dispersed; and direction varies depending upon the specific demands.[2] The movement of population for shopping in cities most vitally concerns the nature of consumer's demand, differences in societal habits, nature of organizational methods of the retail supply and locational structure of shopping centres. There is a close relationship between the level of development and spatial shopping behaviour and patterns.[3]

The area of consumer behaviour, particularly the travel patterns for shopping, is becoming the most important frontier in geographical research into service activities.[4] Much attention has already been focussed on the attitude and perception of consumers to different shopping opportunities, patterns of movement behaviour in reference to permanent retail markets and CBD area business activities of a city but studies have been hardly done in reference to periodic markets of a city on the these lines. Although Wheeler[5] and Scott[6] studied the spatial behaviour of the traders of London city but no work has been done so far about the travel patterns of traders and consumers of periodic markets of an Indian city. For the first time attempts were made by Srivastava & Gupta[7, 8] to analyse the typical visit patterns of traders and consumers in reference to periodic markets of Kanpur metropolis. The author has already tried to review the studies done on the travel patterns of traders and consumers in relation to markets in his previous research papers.

The objectives of the present paper are (i) to analyse the role of travel patterns (spatial and temporal) of the consumers and traders which are largely responsible for the survival of several periodic markets in this important metropolis of northern India, (ii) to identify the factors that affect the consumers and traders travel decisions, (iii) to examine the relative degree of interdependence and need of such traditional markets in the existing business structure of the city and (iv) to advocate the case of their patronisation and improvements by the civic authorities. The ultimate aim of the present study is to recognise the importance of periodic market trader and consumer movements as a part of intra-urban mobility, though quite small in length but highly significant to a particular group of population.

Methodology

One of the unique characteristics of the business structure of Kanpur metropolis is the existence of nine small and large periodic markets (Fig. 11.1) which are nursed mostly by the consumers of low income class. Out of 9 markets only 6 markets viz; Parade, Bakerganj, Beconganj, Sisamau, Jajmau and Dwarkapuri have been selected on the basis of their location, hierarchy, periodicity, range of goods and the characteristics of their market influence area.

The data for the markets under study were collected under extensive field surveys exclusively for identifying trader and consumer travel behaviour and patterns. The main tool of the data was questionnaire prepared both for consumer and trader separately. 5 to 10 per cent of consumers on the basis of the size of the market were covered by applying random sample technique. Only city area consumers representing different occupation groups as well as mainly purchasers of low order convenience goods such as vegetables (47.7%), grains (28.6%) and kirana (16.0%), high order shopping goods particularly cloth and apparel and *kabār** have been included in the present study as they all represent more than 90% of the total consumers interviewed. On the other hand 10% of the shopkeepers representing only cloth (67%), garment-cum-hosiery (58%), vegetables (53%), grains (34%), kirana (13%) and *kabār* (11%) were covered on the basis of spatial stratified random sample technique. Only these 6 categories of traders which represent more than 75% of the total traders, have been taken into consideration.

Fig. 11.1:

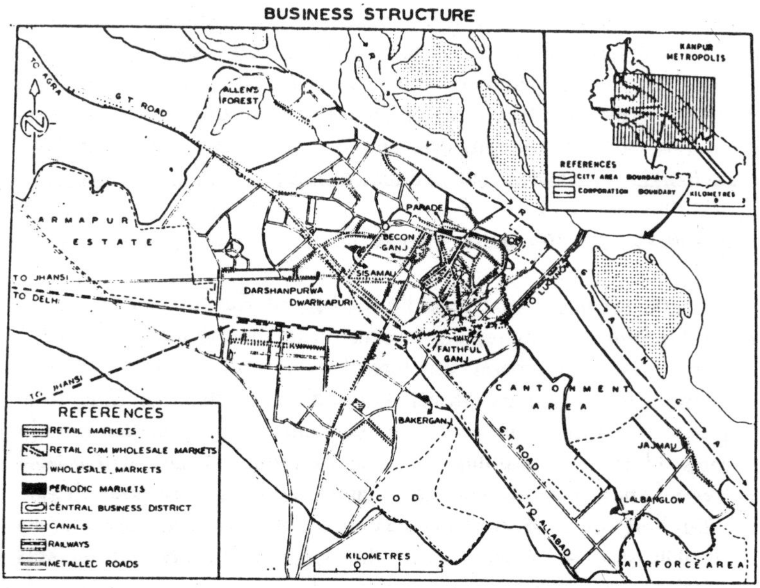

* Old, broken and used articles.

The trader's and consumer's questionnaires contained a detailed inquiry on their spatial travel patterns viz., respondants, place of origin, mode of conveyance and walking distance from residence to market place and markets from where traders purchase their consignments. Under the temporal travel pattern only two variables i.e. frequency of visit and inter-market visit have been included. Besides these, questions were also asked about caste, religion, occupation and income of both the consumer and trader. In the case of consumer particularly, the purpose of market visit other than purchasing was given due importance.

In the tabulation of data those questionnaires were excluded which were either incomplete or provided incorrect information. Moreover, the consumers and traders residing out of the city have not been included in the study. The data were tabulated, analysed and cartographically depicted. Spatial travel patterns of traders and consumers have been shown in Figs. 11.2 and 11.3. In order to draw visit lines from the respondent's place of origin, the centre of the mohalla* has been taken into consideration to join them with the market place in question. Number of consumers/traders coming from a place within the city was noted along the visit line to reveal the intensity of travel from different directions. Analysis of temporal and spatial travel patterns has been done market-wise as well as commodity-wise.

Characteristics of Periodic Market

The characteristics of the periodic markets of Kanpur metropolis are quite different from its regular markets in relation to their site, shape, size, range of goods, spatial structure of shops, traders' socio-economic structure and consumers' travel and shopping behaviour. The rural migrants and labours, who reside in the slums, labour colonies and old villages of the city continue to nurse their old culture, need typical markets.[9] These markets have still maintained their indigenous character. The periodic markets of this city, in the real sense, are the markets of low income group population who depend upon periodic markets not only for daily consumable goods but also for some high order shopping goods. Shopping behaviour of the consumers of these markets is more or less similar to rural area consumers.

* Residential locality of a particular name.

FIG. 11.2:

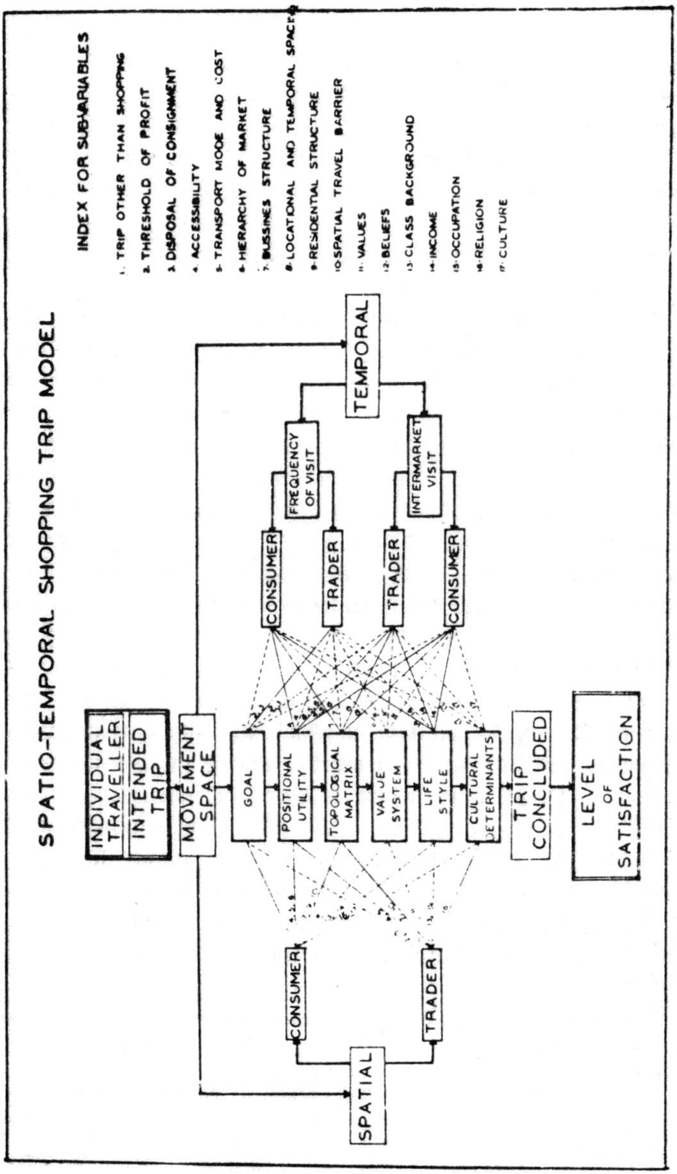
SPATIO-TEMPORAL SHOPPING TRIP MODEL
INDIVIDUAL TRAVELLER
INTENDED TRIP
MOVEMENT SPACE
GOAL
POSITIONAL UTILITY
TOPOLOGICAL MATRIX
VALUE SYSTEM
LIFE STYLE
CULTURAL DETERMINANTS
TRIP CONCLUDED
LEVEL OF SATISFACTION
TEMPORAL
FREQUENCY OF VISIT
INTERMARKET VISIT
CONSUMER
TRADER
TRADER
CONSUMER
SPATIAL
CONSUMER
TRADER
INDEX FOR SUBVARIABLES
1. TRIP OTHER THAN SHOPPING
2. THRESHOLD OF PROFIT
3. DISPOSAL OF CONSIGNMENT
4. ACCESSIBILITY
5. TRANSPORT MODE AND COST
6. HIERARCHY OF MARKET
7. BUSSINES STRUCTURE
8. LOCATIONAL AND TEMPORAL SPACE
9. RESIDENTIAL STRUCTURE
10. SPATIAL TRAVEL BARRIER
11. VALUES
12. BELIEFS
13. CLASS BACKGROUND
14. INCOME
15. OCCUPATION
16. RELIGION
17. CULTURE

Periodic markets which are located in different parts of the city have typical sites, viz; Parade on the edge of CBD, Beconganj and Sisamau in the central densely populated area, Jajmau and Bakerganj in the outer zone while Dwarikapuri in a 'āhatā*' near factory area. The intermarket distances are small, the average comes to 5.5 km., while the minimum value comes to 1 km.[10] (Fig. 11.1). Markets are managed by urban landlords who collect the rent from the shopkeepers on each market day. Schedules** of periodic markets are in such a way that traders can easily dispose of their consignments during the week period. There is also a good spatio-temporal synchronization among the markets. Except Jajmau which is a bi-weekly market, all the selected markets are tri-weekly.

The shape, size and spatial structure of shops of the selected markets vary from each other. Parade, the largest market with 1300 shops, is rectangular in shape while Bakerganj, the next largest market with 1200 shops, is extended in a pentagonal shape and also presents a ribbon pattern. Beconganj (800 shops) and Sisamau (764 shops) sprawl along the residential and commercial streets besides their original rectangular shape. Almost all shopkeepers arrange their shops on the space allotted to them. Though all the markets deal in vegetables, grains, kirana, cloth, hosiery-cum-ready-made garments, footwear, cosmetics, utensils and commodities of domestic use, yet each of the markets have some specialities regarding the variety of goods. Parade, Beconganj and Sisamau are primarily cloth and apparel markets where 59, 42, and 43 per cent of the shops respectively come under this category. Bakerganj and Jajmau which specially deal in grains and vegetables, fulfil the needs of nearby villages and low-income group population. Dwarikapuri, which is losing its importance as periodic market due to nearby regular markets (Fig. 11.1), is now reduced to a vegetable (54% of the total shops) market. Moreover, Bakerganj and Parade are the only two markets which specialise in *kabār* for which consumers come from distant localities and even out of the city. The spatial structure and morphology of some of the shops are gradually

* Big enclosures cosisting of a group of tenants, with one or two rooms intended for human residence.

** Periodicity of the markets: Sisamau (Sunday, Wednesday, Fri.) Parade (Tuesday, Thursday, Saturday), Bakerganj (Sunday, Wed., Friday), Beconganj (Monday, Wednesday, Friday), Jajmau (Sunday, Tuesday), Dwarikapuri (Tuesday, Thursday, Saturday).

changing and some portions are taking the shape of daily retail market.

Consumers' purchasing behaviour in these markets definitely varies from daily retail markets. Majority of consumers stress upon the price of the goods rather than their quality. In a recent survey of the consumer's shopping behaviour in these markets conducted by the author, 78% of the consumers were found indulged in bargaining.[11] Consumers prefer bargaining whether it is profitable or not. Due to low quality of goods the question of band preference does not arise among the consumers. Traders also prefer bargaining as it becomes profitable for them in every case. Some of the cloth and apparel shopkeepers employ brokers to attract the customers but there is absence of advertisement.

Travel Patterns

Analysis of consumer travel behaviour has preceded under the rubric of 'the range of a good' within the framework of central place theory. According to Christaller[12] four main groups of factors influence the consumer's travel decisions: (i) the size and the importance of central place, (ii) the 'price willingness' of a purchaser, (iii) subjective economic distance and (iv) the type, quantity and price of a good. Later on Baker, Marble, Mayfield, Woroby and Berry have indicated in their studies that the forces influencing consumer travel behaviour would also include (i) socio-economic status and (ii) time effort. Peter Scott[13] presented a highly generalized analysis of consumer travel behaviour which is based on (i) establishment by type of trade and (ii) population distribution. Murdie[14] has included (i) the nature of local transport technology, (ii) consumer need, and (iii) the geographic and cultural environment as the controlling factors for consumer travel preferences. Hurst[15] suggested a conceptual framework for movement space based on earlier works on consumer travel patterns, space preferences and movement decisions in geography and other social sciences. He stressed on six factors which are significant to micromovements especially in intra-urban mobility. These are (i) goals, (ii) positional utilities, (iii) topological matrix, (iv) value system, (v) style of life, and (vi) cultural or socio-economic determinants.

Consumer motivation and purchase pattern have been explained through different models and theories, such as; (i) Land-use model, (ii) Trip purpose model, (iii) Regression model, and (iv) Horton's[16] analogy expression approach model. Some of the models emphasise on the social milieu and state of individuals, while others stress on the economic constraints and psychological components. Shopping trips which are the result of consumer decision process, are generally influenced by distance and travel cost. The socio-psychological factors also affect the spatial travel behaviour to a great extent because each consumer keeps his own highly personalised behaviour space. Consumer space perception has a dominant role on shoping pattern. Huff[17] formulated a 'sui-genesis model' of consumer space preference and has tried to emphasize certain psychological concepts. His topological model attempts to structure the interplay of factors affecting consumer behaviour in urban areas. By connectivity analysis of graph representing all possible linkages between these factors, he suggests that age is the single most important influence followed by personality, sex, education, mental synthesising abilities, occupation and income.

Rustan[18] used scaling technique to analyse the consumer space preference. Gravity models which have been used to predict and delimit the market area regions and even for metropolitan area, are being used for intra-urban purposes. Bucklin[19] evaluated some facets of 'simple gravity model' for consumers in reference to intra-urban movements. Huff later on developed a behavioural model from the view point of the consumer to find out the total utility of all shopping centres. Lakshmanan & Hansen[20] developed another model* with the probability that a consumer residing in zone 'i' patronize a centre 'j'. His model differs from Huff's equation only in terms of their use of a distance friction factor. Recently Cadwallader[21] in his model** of consumer spatial behaviour suggested the interplay between 'attractiveness', 'distance' and 'information' in the context of patronisation of a particular store.

---

* A Retail Market Potential Model:

$$Pij = \frac{Aij^a / dij^b}{J^n - iA\, j^a / dij^b}$$

Where Aij = the attractiveness of shopping centres located in zone j
dij = the distance between residential zone i and centre j
a & b = empirically derived exponents.

** Cadwallader model can be expressed as: Pi = f(Ai, Di, Ii)
where Pi is the proportion of consumers patronising store i
Ai is some measure of attractiveness of store i
Di is some measure of the distance to store i from the consumer's home
Ii is some measure of the amount of information generated by store i

The study of traders space preferences, travel decisions and patterns have been covered by anthropologists, sociologists and a few geographers but suitable model could hardly be developed like consumer shopping behaviour models. The positional utility of the market place i.e. size, hierarchic level, subjective economic distance, location, periodicity, range of good (the type, quality and price), mode of transport and spatial travel barriers are some of the significant factors which affect the space preference and travel patterns of trader. Personality, style of life and sometimes the cultural determinants also influence the trader's mobility to some extent. In fact the factors which decide the travel patterns of consumers of daily markets vary from those of periodic markets. Usually the traders do not play significant role in the intra-urban mobility but Kanpur metropolis is an exception where about 5500 local traders of periodic markets visit a market (periodic) place twice or thrice and 2 to 4 different periodic markets in a week. Their spatial and temporal movements differ from travelling traders because of the small intermarket distance. Hence in the present study the author has developed a spatio-temporal travel purpose model which clearly shows the relationship between the affecting factors and the different types of movement both of consumers and traders (Fig. 11.2)

(A) **Spatial**

The model used in the present study suggests that the trip, whether it is for work or shop, must have a purpose, objective or goal. In case of shopping trips the *goals* are usually confined to individual trip maker but sometimes may be set by the joint participation of household. The goal is an intended action that is expected to be fulfilled at a particular point in space and time.[22] Goal is a more prominent factor in case of consumer than a trader because the traders of the markets under study remain almost bound to sell their goods daily in some of the markets to achieve the threshold of profit. A shopping trip may be simple i.e. an interrupted journey from origin to destination, and multiple (a one way trip). In the present case only 7.6% of the consumers have been found in practice of multiple trips which include the journey to work, to meet relatives and other type of social visits. Traders hardly show the tendency of multiple trips.

The concept of utility represents the stage of travel motivation and differs from 'goals'. The travel decision in a spatial context can be termed as '*positional utilities*' which indicates the net utilities derived from the trip maker's integration at some point in space. The planning of a trip from an origin to a destination is the result of a decision making process which recognises differences in utility associated with different places.[23] Whether the positional utility is negative or positive, it is indicated by trip maker's satisfaction or dissatisfaction. The movement space includes the range of choices of trip maker who attaches a utility to his present position and assigns relatively higher or lower utilities to the alternative destinations, but in the present context a few variables were found relevant to positional utilities. Accessibility or proximity of periodic markets from the consumer's and trader's place of origin is the most forceful factor and relevant too as it influences their travel patterns to a great extent. The hypothesis 'consumer visits the nearest place at which a good is offered' has been strongly supported by Christaller's work. He is of the opinion that if the consumers are rational being who want to consume as much as they can for their money, they will visit the closest store to save transport cost.[24] Barnum's[25] studies reveal that in German case 96% of the population sampled outside the major centre Heilbronn, generally purchased food in their centres of residence. Clark[26] tested this 'nearest centre hypothesis' for each of the levels of business centre for each of the three goods i.e. grocery, vegetable and meat, and found that as few as 46% of the consumers in the sample study used the nearest offering of good (meat) and as many as 62% in the other case i.e. vegetables.

In the present study for each of the five goods i.e. vegetables, grains, kirana, cloth-cum-apparel and *kabar*, the nearest centre hypothesis has been tested. From the analysis of consumer travel distances it is clear that for vegetables, kirana and grains, 76, 75 and 73.5 per cent of the total consumers of respective items covered a distance less than 2 km. while in the case of cloth-cum-apparel and *kabār* this distance is covered by 62 and 25 per cent consumers respectively. A study of the consumer's behaviour in Iowa (Colledge and Rustan)[27] reveals that this relationship holds good to a greater extent for low order convenience goods than for high order shopping goods. As the selected markets primarily deal in vegetables, kirana, grains and cheap quality of high order shopping goods, major percentage of consumers want to minimize their travel cost by weighing the nearest market visit cost. Marketwise data and Fig. 11.3 also support this hypothesis as majority of consumers visit these markets from nearby residential areas. Correlation and the significance of the correlation coefficient of each market and consumer travel distance are given in Appendix 1A.

The results show that there exists a high correlation as the computed values are greater than even the 10% of level of significance in case of all markets.

FIG. 11.3:

CONSUMER TRAVEL PATTERNS

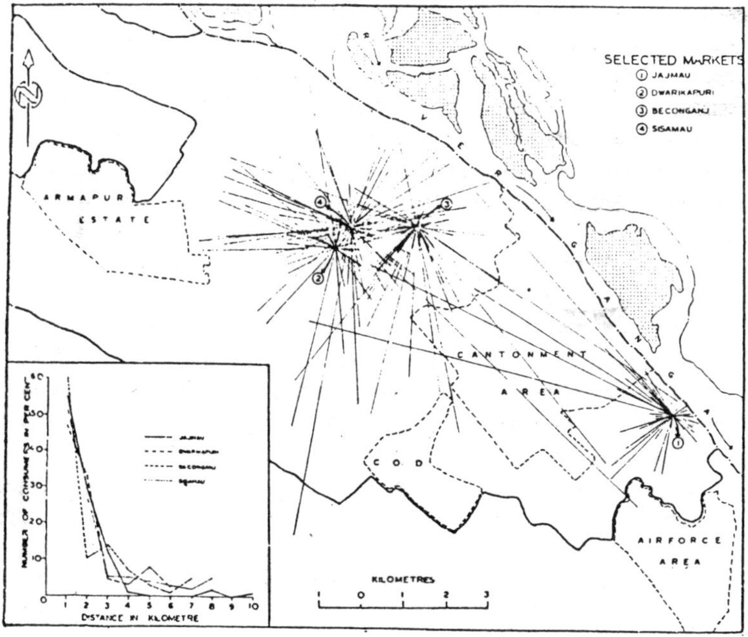

The hypothesis 'a trader will prefer that market where he gets maximum net profit inspite of long travel distance' does not seem correct in case of the traders under study as 82, 75, 75 and 71 per cent of the traders of Parade, Bakerganj Jajmau and Dwarikapuri respectively cover a distance less than 2 km. (Fig. 11.4). Smith's[28] analysis of the traders travel distances and market preference in the countries of West Africa concludes that traders actually visit that market which is closest to them on a given day. This statement is correct in the present case as there is a high correlation between the number of traders and their travel distances. The correlation coefficient is quite significant as it is clear from Appendix 1B.

The mean walking distance in case of both the consumers and traders of all markets under study which comes below 2 km., also supports the hypothesis of preferences for nearest centre. Moreover, the mean walking distances of different categories of consumers (on the basis of the range of good) do not exceed 1.8 km. except in case of the *kabār* purchasers who show a mean distance of 3 km. because *kabar* is not an item to be sold in retail shops. Except the grain trader, 60% of the traders of all selected categories visit different periodic markets from a distance less than 2 km. On the whole the length of shopping trip is directly related to the order of good or service and it does seem to a certain extent consumers attempt to minimise their travel cost by visiting nearby urban centres (Lloyed & Dicken).[29] The analysis of consumer and trader travel distances support that both patronise the nearest periodic market. Mean walking distance of traders and consumers in relation to markets and commodities is clear from the Table 11.1.

Mode of transport and travel cost have been found relevant to positional utility. The markets under study, except Jajmau, are well connected by metalled roads and streets with different residential areas of the city (Fig. 11.1). Mode of conveyance, other than cycle and scooter, are rickshaw, *kharkhara** tempo** and city bus which are readily available on reasonable fare. Inspite of the thick road net and cheap transport cost, the percentage of consumers covering long distance (above 4 km.) is low in the case of selected markets i.e. Sisamau (9.7%), Beconganj (7.3%), Jajmau (7%) and Dwarikapuri (3%). In his study Murdie[30] evaluated the differences in the means and cost of transportation as an important factor affecting the consumer travel. The analysis of data reveals that only 6, 2, and 6 per cent of the consumers visit different markets by rickshaw, city bus and scooter respectively because the travel cost by these modes is difinitely higher than cycle and *kharkhara*. The local traders of these markets bear a nominal travel cost on account of the small inter-market distances and the mode of conveyance preferred by them. The analysis makes it clear that only 15, 8, and 2 per cent of the traders bring their consignments in the market by rickshaw, *kharkhara*, and city bus respectively.

---

* A rectangular shape wooden cart driven by a horse.

** A three wheeler autovehicle.

FIG. 11.4:

TRADER TRAVEL PATTERNS

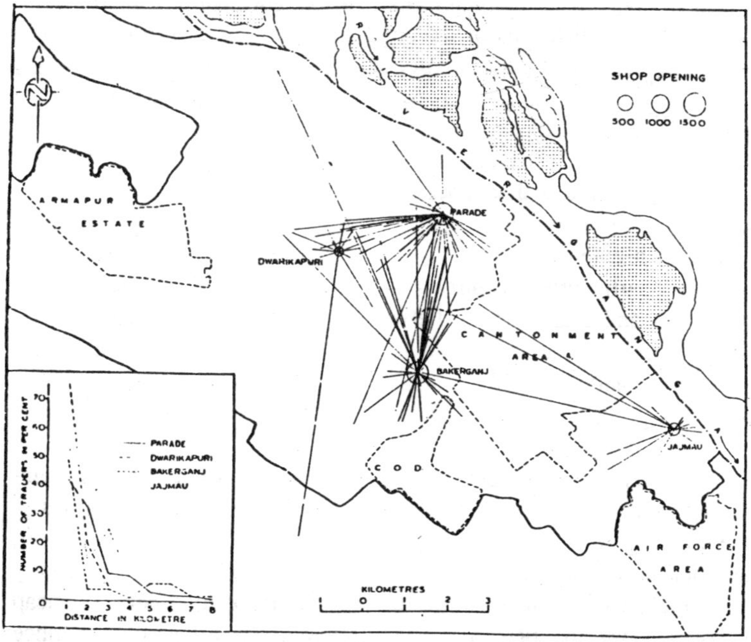

The hierarchy of markets is not only relevant but also an important variable of positional utility. Consumer travel pattern is also influenced by the level of the markets hierarchy.* The hypothesis that 'the distance travelled increases as the hierarchy of the business centre increases' has already been tested by researchers working on consumer behaviour. Clark examined this hypothesis in his study of the market of Christchurch metropolis and came to the conclusion that there was no significant difference in the distances travelled for the same good from different level of hierarchy of business centre.[31] The present data reveal

* Four hierarchic orders of the periodic markets of this metropolis have been identified on the basis of their establishment size, number of shop opening, range of good, intensity and frequency of trader's and consumer's visit. *I Order*. Parade & Bakerganj, *II Order*. Sisamau & Beconganj, *III Order*. Jajmau & Faithfulganj, *IV Order*. Darshanpurwa, Dwarikapuri & Lal Bungalow.

that the length of shopping trip (more than 4 km.) has increased as the hierarchy of the market has also increased. In Sisamau and Beconganj which belong to II order hierarchy, only 7 and 7.3% of the consumers respectively cover a distance above 4 km. whereas in Dwarikapuri the percentage of this long distance decreases as it comes under the IV order hierarchy. In case of traders this factor does not play a significant role because the traders sell their consignments on each day whether the market is of highest or lowest order.

TABLE 11.1: Mean Walking Distance (in km.)

(A) Marketwise

	Parade	Baker-ganj	Sisamau	Becon-ganj	Jajmau	Dwarika-puri
Consumer	—	—	1.58	1.42	1.65	1.42
Trader	2.40	1.60	—	—	2.10	1.80

(B) Communitywise

	Cloth & apparel	Vegetables	Kirana	Grains	Kabar
Consumer	1.27	1.45	1.67	1.71	3.00
Trader	2.60	2.30	3.40	7.00	0.66

Location in respect to the total urban structure, literally a '*topological matrix*'; has been stressed in all earlier studies of micromovement. The existing spatial distribution of markets, residences and travel barriers are the three important variables of topological matrix which affect the shopping trips and movements of consumer and trader of the periodic markets of this metropolis. Kanpur metropolis has large specialised wholesale markets in CBD area along with important retail markets. About 75% of the commercial establishments of the city lies in CBD attracting large number of buyers and sellers which swell to several lakhs at times.[32] The intensity of business actively declines towards the edge of the CBD where some of the large periodic markets are not only situated but also surviving. Besides CBD markets, several planned and unplanned commercial ribbons also do a good deal of business (Fig. 11.1). Small regional shopping centres and isolated store clusturs which deal in almost all essential commodities, are scattered throughout the city for catering to the needs of sorrounding residential areas. Consumers of Sisamau and Beconganj market areas are partly diverted to the nearby commercial ribbons and main business thoroughfare markets i.e. P. Road, Mestan Road, Parade and Chamanganj, because they have greater gravitational force than periodic market on account of their establishment size, quantity and quality of commodities and shop opening days. On the other hand, in Jajmau and Dwarikapuri where more than 90% of the consumers belong to low income group, they show a low frequency for daily markets. Location of wholesale and retail-cum-wholesale markets influence the mobility of traders, as 85% of cloth, 71.4% of apparel, 77% of kirana and 64.2% of vegetable traders do their regular purchasing from the wholesale markets.

The spatial distribution of residential areas in this metropolis is quite uneven due to its typical land-use. Railway yards in the central part, defence areas in eastern and western sectors, and haphazard concentration of industrial establishments have made the residential localities segmented. Old slums and *ahātās* are concentrated in the core area, around CBD, in concentric form, and in the industrial areas. The slum dwellers are mostly factory workers and manual labours who can satisfy themselves on the low quality of consumer goods generally available in periodic markets. About 60% of the residences in the old unplanned areas are occupied by low income population. Besides slums, there are still 30 old villages within the city area where rural immigrants and labour class population reside and they are still nursing the rural culture. Shopping trips to the periodic markets by the consumers of these residential areas are higher than the high class residential areas which are in the river front section, defence area and in a few planned residential localities. The consumers of posh and planned residential areas which are in the outer zone of the city, are hardly concerned with these traditional markets as they have their own local shopping centres. The uneven distribution of population is also responsible for the variations in the intensity of consumers mobility in reference to periodic markets. Mobility of traders and consumers decreases from middle sector where the density of population is 67975/km.^{2} (Singh)[33] towards rivers front and southern sectors where the density of population is much lower than the former.

The cultural barriers of the city obstruct the mobility of the traders of the periodic markets in particular and the consumers of different categories in general. As the traders under study move along with their consignments, they face difficulties to cross some of the barriers and are compelled to follow much longer and circuitous routes to reach their destinations. Among cultural barriers defence areas, large industrial establishments, railway yards, parks and gardens and, to some extent, the administrative blocks are significant. For example: Jajmau market area is surrounded by river Ganga in the north and defence areas in the west and south-east (Fig. 11.5). Due to these barriers 54% of the consumers and 55% of the traders of this market come from a radius of 1 km. only. Similar is the case of Bakerganj where the traders residing to the north of G.T. Road and eastern parts hardly visit because of C.O.D, a defence area in the east and railwayyards in the north. Most of the consumers of Beconganj, Sisamau and Dwarikapuri come from nearby localities on account of presence of cultural barriers in their southern and western parts.

The judgement between various positional utilities involves the *value system* of a trip maker. The related concepts, of individual value system are the 'beliefs' and 'impulses'. Impulses influence action space with regard to value systems or beliefs.[34] In the travel patterns of the traders and consumers the value system is insignificant and their relationship cannot be shown empirically. But 'life style', which is an important source of stability in the flux of urban stratification, affect the movement space of an individual. Boscoff[35] in his sociological study of urban region has identified seven life styles.* Besides life styles, the *'Socio-economic or cultural determinants'* influence space perception of an individual which ultimately affect the movement behaviour. Webber[36] is of the opinion that culture plays a major role in establishing the propensity to interact as distance varies.

As manufacturing, services and trade and commerce predominate in the occupational structure of the city, Kanpur may be included in the category of M.S.T.** In 1971 the city had 71.4% of non-productive population[37] comprising a large number of dependents. According to Majumdar's sample survey, manual labours represented 85.02% of the total workers.[38] The highest percentage of workers i.e. 86.2% is engaged in industry while it is 31% in other services, 21% in trade and commerce and 3.9% in agriculture and other primary activities.[39] A majority of the population of the city lives below the poverty line on account of its occupational structure. The percentage of slum dwellers is more than 25 of the total population and their standard of living is

* The styles of life are: the social elite, nouveaux, riches, exurban, middle class, social or aspiring lower group and marginal life style.

** M.S.T. stands for Manufacturing, Service and Trade & commerce.

FIG. 11.5:

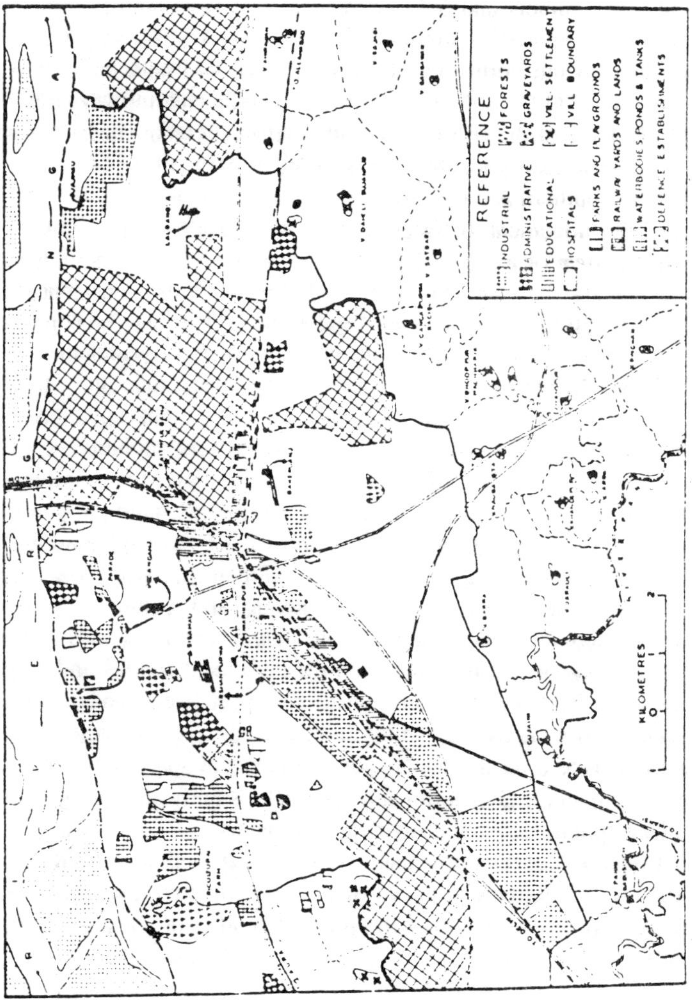

TRAVEL BARRIERS

very low. Majority of slum dwellers are rural immigrants who have still maintained their culture and contacts with rural areas. The low income group population mostly depends on the periodic markets not only for daily consumable low order convenience goods but also for high order shopping goods. Religion and caste structure in the city is spatially integrated. In certain localities caste segregation in the form of social prestige worked so effectively that certain *chaks** have become the concentration of castes and religions. Hindus constitute about 88% of the population while Muslims represent only 10.7%.[40] Muslim population is concentrated in the central western part of the city. Their life style and culture entirely differ from the Hindus. Moreover, like social movements their shopping trips are largely decided by their life style and culture.

Hurst has emphasised the role of three variables of life style i.e. class background, income and occupation, which have their influence on micro movement in urban areas. He is of the opinion that 'social elite' have a more extensive movement space than the 'exurban' style.[41] Numerous studies have demonstrated that socio-economic status and life styles affect traders' and consumers' mobility, especially the shopping trips. In U.S.A, Britain and Denmark, for example, consumers with higher social status living in the metropolitan fringe patronize the city centres more and show more favourable attitudes to it than do those with lower social status (Jonassen,[42] Pahl[43] and Hess[44]). Consumers of different social, economic and cultural background select different levels of hierarchy to obtain required goods and services. Low income consumers shop in small local centres and only occasionally visit higher order centres for specialised goods (Murdie)[45] because different groups exhibit diverse needs of interaction with other groups and as a result, display varying levels of space preference. Life styles and cultural determinants are less significant in the case of traders' spatial movements than the consumers'.

Under the assumption that mobility is related to income and increase with hierarchic level of origin and destination it seems correct in the context of consumers of the periodic market of Kanpur metropolis that low-income consumer shops in the local centres. 66% of the total consumers in question, who belong to low income group, are mostly factory workers, manual labours and low paid government servants,

* Chak stands for those city administrative areas which are managed by municipal corporation.

while consumers of high income group represent only 3.5% of the sampled respondents. Dwarikapuri market which is situated in a *ahātā*, is patronised by manual labours and factory workers who represent 70.8% of the total sampled consumers. Similarly Jajmau is another market where 85% of the consumers belong to low-income group population. Generally the consumers of low income group in this city who have their associations and attachment with rural culture, satisfy themselves on cheap goods of poor quality and give preference to these traditional markets. They seldom visit higher order business centres for more specialised goods. On the other hand, the picture of high income group consumers is different. They visit such markets for low order convenience goods such as vegetables, grains, meat and fish. Both in U.S.A. and Britain the spatial distribution of income has been found to be a significant factor influencing the structure of shopping centres and retail markets. Yuill[46] and Davies[47] have supported this fact in their studies.

Traders sometimes patronise those markets where they get some cultural affinity and homogeneity. In this metropolis at least two markets i.e. Beconganj and Sisamau which are situated 2.5 km. apart, are patronised by Muslim traders (72.5%) and Hindu traders (86.5%) respectively because the former is located in Muslim dominated area and the later in Hindu dominated locality. Muslim traders of these markets generally show smaller travel distances than Hindus because the former give much weightage to their culture in transactions. Moreover, the Muslim traders of Parade and Beconganj markets usually deal in those cloth which are preferred by their community and thus their spatial mobility is of shorter distance. Hindu traders are not rigid in their religion and visit all periodic markets whether it is patronised by Hindus or Muslims and deal in each and every type of commodity.

(B) **Temporal**

The spatial system of market integration usually includes some forms of temporal synchronization (Bromely).[48]One of the important aspects of the periodic markets is their relative position in time and space. It is useful to examine the relationship between temporal and locational spacing. On account of small intermarket distances (average 2.5 km.), the hinterlands of these markets overlap, though their meeting days do not coincide. Spacing values differ from trader's and consumer's point of view. As a trader has to dispose of his consignments, he is bound to visit other markets while in case of a consumer it is not essential that he will visit another market which is situated at a longer distance. Temporal travel patterns of the traders and consumers have been studied from the point of view of their frequency of visits and inter-market visits during the period of a week. In case of traders both types of distances i.e. mobility (i) for buying goods from the wholesale and retail markets and (ii) for reselling them in periodic markets, have been included in the present study. The spatio-temporal travel purpose model explains that the temporal travel patterns are affected by goals, positional utilities, typological matrix, life style and cultural determinants. Moreover, economic factors play a more dominant role in temporal mobility than the personal and psychological factors.

(I) Frequency of Visit

Consumers' frequency of visit is largely affected by positional utility and locational factors. Consumer actually visits that market twice or thrice in a week which is closest to him on a given day or will weigh the advantages of waiting until a later date when a market nearer to him will be meeting (Ukwa).[49] As proximity in space implies separation in time, an indirect relation exists between temporal and locational spacing of periodic markets (in case of consumer). Among the variables of positional utility, proximity or accessibility is the most influential factor. The hypothesis that 'there is a decrease in the number of shopping trips as the distance to a centre increases' (Murdie)[50] has been found correct even in the case of consumers' travel distances and the frequency of their visit to a market. There is a high correlation between the travel distances and frequency of visits in case of all selected markets as it is clear from Appendix 2. Again this high correlation can be marked in the case of Sisamau market where out of 299 consumers 95 visited this market on all the market days and individually covered a distance less than 1 km. On the other hand, when the distance has increased (above 4 km.) it was found that only 2 consumers visited a market thrice.

The markets under study are purely local markets of low order convenience goods hence the purchasers of these goods show a high frequency (all market days) of visits. Maximum frequency of visits to a market is marked in case of vegetables, meat and fish, kirana and grain purchasers. It is the commodity which largely decides the number of shopping trip to a particular market. Hierarchy of the market is an insignificant variable as consumer only weighs the waiting and travel cost. Location and network of periodic market in the spatial structure of an area is of much significance because the consumer will prefer the nearest market for two or three trips in a week. The relation between the spatial distribution of the periodic markets and the distribution of population indicates the degrees to which people have access to marketing facilities. In the area under study three selected markets are situated in the central zone while Jajmau is situated in that zone which is rather detached from the main city. Consumers of eastern zone show a high frequency of visit to this market as they have no other alternative except to choose Lal Bangalow periodic market (3 km. away). Consumers of the central zone also show a high frequency. Income is the main variable relevant to life style which decides the consumer's mobility in time. In this city the low income consumer shows a higher frequency of visit to a periodic market in comparison to high income consumer as the former minimises his travel cost by visiting nearby markets.

Traders' frequency of visit to a periodic market, whether in rural or urban environment, is decided by positional utility and locational factors of the market in question. The proximity or accessibility do influence the traders' frequency of visits but are overshadowed by the two important factors i.e. threshold of profit and disposal of consignments. The markets situated at a comparatively long distance to the traders residence are hardly visited twice or thrice a week by him as he weighs the waiting cost against travel cost. In all the selected markets traders' frequency of visit is very high as more than 90% of the traders (Parade – 94%, Bakerganj – 89.70%, Jajmau – 90% and Dwarikapuri – 93.8%) visit a particular market on all market days because they want and try to dispose of their consignments and achieve threshold of profit. Traders dealing in cloth and apparel show the highest frequency of visit as their percentage comes to 91 and 88 respectively. Life style of the traders, especially their income, is significant to their frequency of visit. While studying the travel patterns of traders of Northern Nigeria, P. Scott concludes that 'high income farmers are assumed to be economically more rational, visiting few markets often, and low-income farmers are assumed to be less rational visiting more markets often'.[51] In the present study it does not seem correct because a trader, whether he belongs to a high income group or low income group, will visit thrice his nearest market rather than the markets located at a longer distance.

(II) **Intermarket Visit**

Consumers market travel patterns reveal a low range of spatial interaction, usually a distance of 5 km. The selected markets, except Jajmau, are located in the central zone within a radius of 3 km. (Fig. 11.1). There is a substantial number of consumers who visit regularly more than one periodic market whether it is large in establishment and range of good or of lower hierarchy. Intermarket visit of a consumer is decided by small intermarket distances, spatio-temporal synchronization, range of goods, hierarchy of market, mode of conveyance and his life style. The analysis of the questionnaire data reveals that more than 50% of the consumers of all categories (vegetables – 52.7%, cloth & apparel – 59.5%, kirana – 56%, grain – 60% and *kabār* – 50%) were found indulging in intermarket visits only due to small intermarket distances. Majority of the consumers of all selected markets, except Sisamau, showed a high percentage for intermarket visits viz; Dwarikapuri – 84.3%, Beconganj – 73.6%, Jajmau – 62.8% and Sisamau – 38% .

Smith has investigated the synchronization of market schedules using data from several areas in West Africa to ascertain whether the minimisation of consumer travel or trader travel distance is most important consideration in the establishment of market schedules. The results of Smith's analysis were inconclusive. Support for the consumer hypothesis is much stronger than for the trader hypothesis although there is much unexplained variation.[52] As the periodic markets of this metropolis have narrow average locational spacing, the consumers attempt to cover more markets on different days of the week. These markets have a good spatio-temporal synchronisation such as in Sisamau (Sunday, Wed., Fri.) situated at a distance less than 1 km. from Dwarikapuri (Tues. Thurs. Sat.). Consumers residing in the market area of these two markets usually do intermarket visit as all the days of the week are occupied except Monday which remains occupied by Darshanpurwa market quite near to them. If a consumer, infact, weighs waiting cost against the travel cost (as Ukwa suggests), then he would presumably consider the distance from the nearby market X being held today, which he might attend on the nearest adjacent-day, adjacent-day plus one and so in the markets held both before as well as after the market in question (Fagerlund & Smith[53] and Smith[54]). Most of the consumers follow this pattern as the present study indicates. The hierarchy of the markets and the types of transactions which one wishes to conduct, are important in the intermarket visit activity (Mc Kim).[55] When a consumer's desire is normally not satisfied in the nearest (in time and space) market, he chooses the next market and does not weigh the waiting cost. Consumers do intermarket visit not on account of the hierarchy and range of goods of the markets but simply on the ground of their temporal spacing. Income does play a significant role in intermarket trips but mostly in rural areas where the spatial distances involve travel cost. In the present case this factor is not significant.

Horizontal exchange synonymous to interregional trade is performed by the periodic markets of this metropolis. Traders move along with finished goods and locally grown foodstuffs from one market to another market within the same region. The question of itinerant traders who move around a net of periodic markets throughout the week and return home after the disposal of bulk consignment, does not arise in the present case. The traders in question are local traders who visit two or three markets and sometimes more in a week but return home each night. The average percentage of the traders involved in intermarket visits is 63.5 with maximum of 100% in Dwarikapuri and minimum of 28% in Bakerganj. Stine[56] has given explanation as to why traders must sell in more than one market. This explanation is based on the fact that in an area the maximum range of a good around one market may be smaller than the minimum range required in order to make the trader viable. The factors which compell the traders of these periodic markets to indulge in intermarket visits are proximity or accessibility, range of good, hierarchy and spatio-temporal synchronisation of the markets, and life style (particularly income). But, ultimately, the main purpose behind this movement is to achieve profit threshold.

For the trader who returns homebase each night, the precise sequence in which markets occur in a network is immaterial, his total movement cost will be the same regardless of the order in which markets are visited but for the 'travelling trader' the movement costs vary with the spatio-temporal sequence of markets (Hill & Smith).[57] The ideal spatio-temporal sequence from the trader's point of view is one in which periodic markets are adjacent in space and time. The traders travelling hypothesis suggests a direct relationship between locational and temporal spacing. As the periodic markets in question also present a good spatio-temporal sequence, the majority of the traders practise intermarket visit. A trader of the central zone bears the minimum travel cost because the temporal and spatial spacing is low. The hierarchy of the markets and the type of the transactions are important in the intermarket visits of traders. A trader selects the next market only on that ground when he becomes sure the commodity which he deals in, will be partly disposed of. It depends upon the range of goods and the hierarchy of the markets in question. Selected markets deal in almost the same commodity but the number of their dealers vary. Beconganj and Parade are the two markets where *kabăr* is sold and the intermarket visit of *kabăr* traders is low in comparison to other traders. The cloth and apparel traders usually move in two or three markets and sometimes more than three.

Peter Scott is of the opinion that low income traders visit more markets than high income traders. High income group traders select a small number of markets to visit, thereby minimising the distance while lower income traders choose to interact in different markets and dispose of their consignments. Vegetables, kirana and *kabăr* traders generally belong to low income group and they have been found visiting different markets. Moreover, the 100% traders of Dwarikapuri who generally belong to low income group, were found practising intermarket trips.

The temporal movements are more often the result of social needs of the sellers than a desire for profit (Hodder).[58] This may be true in the context of rural markets but in the case of traders in question it is quite different. The main objective of the trader's visit is to achieve the threshold of profit. The study done by Underwood[59] also reveals that traders might visit several markets per week in order to increase their margin of profit and presumably their cash income. Scott in his study of Northern Nigeria concludes that an increase in the number of market visits results in increased cash income of profit. Traders of these markets move in different markets in a week till the major portion of their consignment is disposed of.

Besides intermarket and frequency of visit, the travel distance covered by a trader during a week has also been calculated with the help of questionnaires. A trader's temporal travel distance includes his movement from residence to large retail or wholesale market centres (to purchase the goods in bulk quantity) and back, and his frequency of a market and intermarket visits. Weekend movement analysis reveals that kirana, apparel, vegetables and cloth traders cover a mean distance of 45.9, 43.9, 43.3 and 42.1 km. respectively. 50 to 80 km. distance in the week end is covered by 41% appareal dealing traders and 29% by the cloth and kirana dealing traders. Thus the temporal travel distance of a trader becomes greater than a consumer.

REFERENCES

1. Yeats, M. & Garner, B., *The Northern American City.* 2nd. edition, Harper & Raw. Newyork. (1976), pp. 347-76.
2. Pachauri, M.K., Intra-urban Interaction Pattern: An analytical Review: *Indian Geographic Review.* Vol. 3 & 4 (1979), p. 43
3. Lantnek, B, Lieber, S.R. & Sheskin, Ira. Consumer travel behaviour in different areas, *Annals of the Association of American Geographers.* 65. No. 4 December (1975), p. 538.
4. Thompson, D.L., Future directions in retail area research. *Economic Geography.* 42, (1966), pp. 1-19.
5. Wheeler, P.T, 'Travelling Vans and Mobile Shops in 'Southerland'. *Scottish Geographical Magazine.* 76. (1960), pp. 147-55.
6. Scott, P., *Geography and Retailing.* Hutchinson & Co. (1970), London.
7. Srivastava, R.C. and Gupta, J.P. Consumer Travel Patterns in the Periodic Markets of Kanpur Metropolis, *National Geographer,* Vol. XIV, No. 2 (1979), pp. 147-58
8. Srivastava, R.C., and Gupta, J.P., Visitation Patterns of the Traders of Periodic Markets of Kanpur Metropolis. *Geographical Viewpoint,* Vol X. (1979) No. 1-2.
9. Singh, H., *Kanpur: A Study in Urban Geography.* Varanasi (1972), p. 65.
10. Srivastava, R.C. & Gupta, J.P. 'Consumer Travel Patterns in the Periodic Markets of Kanpur Metropolis. *op. cit.* p. 150.
11. Srivastava, R.C., 'Consumer Buying Behaviour in the Periodic Markets of Kanpur Metropolis', *Abstracts of the National Seminar & Symposium Papers,* V Indian Social Science Congress. Udaipur. (1980), pp. 7-8.
12. Christaller, W. *Die Zentralen Orte in Siiddentschland* (Jena 1933); Carlisle, W. Baskin (Trans): *A Critique and Translation of W. Christaller's Die Zentralen Ortein Sddentschland* (unpublished Ph.D. Dissertation, University of Virginia, (1957), pp. 58-108.
13. Scott. P., Geography & Retailing. *op. cit.* (1970) p. 60.
14. Murdie, R.A., Cultural Differences in Consumer Travel. *Economic Geography.* 41. (1965) pp. 211-33.
15. Hurst, M.E. Eliot, Micromovement and urban dweller. in *Transportation Geography: Comments & Readings* (Ed.), Hurst, M.E.E. Mc. Graw-Hill Book Co. (1974) p. 495.
16. Horton, F.E. Location Factors as Determinant of Consumer Attraction to Retail Firms. *Annals of the Assoc. of American Geographers.* Vol. 59. (1968) pp. 391-401.
17. Huff, D.L., A Geographical Model of Consumer Space Preferences. *Papers of the Regional Science Association.* Vol. 6. (1960), pp. 159-74.
18. Rushton, G., Analysis of the Spatial Behaviour by Revealed Space Preference, *Annals of the Association of American Geographers.* Vol. 59. (1969) pp. 391-401.

19. Bucklin, L.P., Retail Gravity Model & Consumer Choice: A Theoretical & Empirical Critique. *Economic Geog*. Vol. 47. (1971), No. 4.
20. Lakshmanan, T.R. & Hansen, W.C., A Retail Market Potential Model. *Journal of the American Institute of Planners* 31. (1965), pp. 134-43.
21. Cadwailader, M, A Behavioural Model of Consumer Spatial Decision Making. *Economic Geog*. Vol. 51. (1975), No. 4
22. Hurst M.E.E., Micromovement & Urban Dweller: *op. cit*. (1974), p. 496
23. *Ibid*. p. 498
24. Berry, B.J.L., *Geography of Market Centres & Retail Distribution*. Prentice Hall. INC. Englewood. Cliffs. (1967), p. 62.
25. Barnum, H.G., *Market Centres and Hinterlands in Baden Wrttenberg*. University of Chicago, Department of Geography Research Paper. (1966) p. 103.
26. Clark, W.A.V., Consumer Travel Patterns & Concept of Range. *Annals of the Association of American Geographers*. Vol. 58. No. 2 (1968), p. 386.
27. Colledge, R.G., Rustan, G & Clark, W.A.V., Some Spatial Characteristics of Iwo's Dispersed Farm Population and their Implications for the Grouping of Central Place Functions. *Economic Geog*. 42. (1966), pp. 261-72.
28. Smith, R.H.T., The Theory of Periodic Market: Consumer & Trader Behaviour. *Preconference Publication of Papers Canadian Association of Geographers*, Waterloo. (1971), p.336.
29. Lloyd, E.F. & Dicken, P. : *Location in Space: A Theoretical Approach to Economic Geography*, Harper & Row, INC New York (1972) p. 30.
30. Murdie, R.A. *op. cit*. pp. 24-33
31. Clark, W.A.V., *op. cit*. p. 396.
32. Singh, H., *op. cit*. p. 5.
33. *Ibid*., p. 38.
34. Hurst. M.E.E., *op. cit*. p. 499
35. Boscoff, A., *The Sociology of Urban Regions*, New York, Appleton Century Crafts. (1962).
36. Webber, M.M., Culture Territoriality and the Elastic Mile. *Papers & Proceedings, Regional Science Assoication*. Vol. 13. (1964), pp. 54-69.
37. District Census Handbook, Kanpur. Part 10. B. (1971). p.5
38. Majumdar, D.N. (1962). Social Contours of an Industrial City. Asia Publishing House. Bombay. (1962), p. 111.
39. District Census Handbook, Kanpur. *op. cit*. pp. 4-5.
40. Singh, H., *op. cit*.
41. Hurst, M.E.E., *op. cit*., p. 500
42. Jonassen, C.T. *The Shopping Centres Versus Downtown: A Motivation Research on Shopping Habits in three Cities*. Columbus. Ohio. (1955).
43. Pahl, R.E., Urbs in Rure: The Metropolitan Fringe in Hertfordshire, London School of Economics & Political Science, *Geographical Papers* No. 2. (1965).
44. Hess, C.F. Geographical Aspects of Consumer Behaviour in Retail Service Area of Greater Alberg; *Geograpiska Tiddsstrift*, 65. (1965), p. 128.
45. Murdie, R.A., *op. cit*. pp. 212-13.
46. Yuill, R.S., Spatial Behaviour of Retail Customer: Some Empirical Measurements. *Geografiska Annaler*, 49. B. 1967 pp- 105-15.
47. Davies. R.L., Effects of consumers Income Differences and the Business Provision of Small Shopping Centres. *Urban Studies* 5. (1967), pp. 144-64.
48. Bromley, R.J., Markets in Developing Countries: A Review, *Geography*. 56. (1971), p. 128.
49. Ukwa, U.I. & Hodder, B.W.: *Markets in West Africa*. University of Ibadan Press. (1969)
50. Murdie, R.A. *op. cit*. 212-13.

51. Scott, E.P., The Spatial Structure of Rural Northern Nigeria: Farmers, Periodic Markets & Villages'. *Economic Geography*. Vol. 48 No. 3. (1972), p. 229.
52. Smith, R.H.T., *op. cit.* p. 186.
53. Fagerlund, B.G. & Smith, R.H.T., A Preliminary Map of Market Periodicity in Ghana. *Journal of Developing Areas*. 4. (1970), p. 333-38.
54. Smith , R.H.T., West African Market Places, Temporal Periodicity and Locational Spacing. *Development of Indigenous Trade & Markets in West Africa* (Ed.). C. Meillasseux, (1971). London.
55. Mc. Kim, W., The Periodic Market System in Northeastern Ghana. *Economic Geography*. Vol. 48. No. 3. (1972), p. 336.
56. Stine, J.H., Temporal Aspect of Tertiary Production Elements in Korea, in *Urban System & Economic Development* (Ed.). F.R. Pitts. Eugene University of Orogon. School of Business Administration. (1962)
57. Hill, P. & Smith, R.H.T., The Spatial and Temporal Synchronization: Evidence from Four Emirates in Northern Nigeria, *Economic Geography*. Vol. 48. No. 3. (1972), p. 351.
58. Hodder, B.W., Distribution of Markets in Yorubaland. *Scottish Geographical Magazine* (1965), pp. 48-58.
59. Underwood, F.W., *The Marketing System in Peasant Haiti*. Yale University Publication in Anthropology. No. 60. (1960), pp. 3-33.

APPENDIX 1

	Market	r value	t value	Levels of significance		
(A) *Correlation between consumer number and travel distance*						
				0.10	0.05	0.01
1.	Beconganj	–.67	2.02	2.13	2.78	4.40
2.	Sisamau	–.92	4.75	2.35	3.18	5.34
3.	Jajmau	–.74	2.21	2.35	3.18	5.34
4.	Dwarikapuri	–.71	2.01	2.35	3.18	5.34
(B) *Correlation between trader number and travel distance*						
1.	Bakerganj	–.62	2.28	1.94	2.45	3.71
2.	Parade	–.87	4.76	1.94	2.45	3.71
3.	Jajmau	–.81	2.41	2.92	4.30	9.92
4.	Dwarikapuri	–.71	2.01	2.35	3.18	5.34

APPENDIX 2

Correlation between consumer frequency of visit and travel distance.

	Market	r value	t value	Levels of significance		
(A) Once a week						
				0.10	0.05	0.01
1.	Sisamau	–.91	4.41	2.35	3.18	5.34
2.	Jajmau	–.78	2.56	2.35	3.18	5.34
3.	Beconganj	–.73	2.38	2.13	2.78	4.60
4.	Dwarikapuri	–.85	3.21	2.35	3.18	5.34
(B) Twice a week						
1.	Sisamau	–.84	3.12	2.35	3.18	5.34
2.	Jajmau	–.89	3.85	2.35	3.18	5.34
3.	Beconganj	–.76	2.45	2.13	2.78	4.60
4.	Dwarikapuri	–.76	2.35	2.35	3.18	5.34
(C) Thrice a week						
1.	Sisamau	–.81	2.78	2.35	3.18	5.34
2.	Jajmau	—	—	—	—	—
3.	Beconganj	–.73	2.38	2.13	2.78	4.60
4.	Dwarikapuri	–.77	2.01	2.35	3.18	5.34

PART – V

ECONOMIC GEOGRAPHY

TWELVE

N.G. Jain

Road Pattern in Akola District (Maharashtra)

Introduction

CHARACTERISTICS of roads radiating from a central place towards the surrounding regions are the indicators of level of economic progress of a region. Central place and its umland are inter-dependent and their interaction is through the media of transport lines. This leads to the growth of network of roads around a central place.

The network so developed does not attain the same level on all sides of the central place as number of factors – both physical and cultural – modify its development. Roads are classified as national highways, State highways, district roads and local roads. This classification seems to be arbitrary. Instead, the road pattern can be considered on the lines of streams. Small streams make a bigger stream and further combination of them make a river. The analysis of road network on this line can prove to be useful for understanding economic status of the region.

Given a map of a complete stream channel network, the individual lengths of channel or channel segments are arranged according to a heirarchy of orders of magnitude, assigning a sequence of numbers to the orders. Each finger-tip channel is designated as segment of the first order. At the junction of any two first order segments, a channel of the second order is produced and so forth. By this linear analysis, it is possible to make some generalisation about the form and dimensions of the network characteristics of a particular region.

In the present paper an attempt is made to analyse, using the Strahler's method of stream order, the road pattern in Akola district, as a planning unit, with Akola as the central place.

Methodology

General

The method used in this paper is the Strahler's 'Stream Order method'.[1] The road network is usually in the form of circuits. Haggett[2] has suggested a five-stage algorithm for the breaking down of circuit type networks into trees. The algorithm is based on the concept of accessibility and shortest distance paths. These five stages are: (i) 'Pole' identification, (ii) Polar network isolation, (iii) Determination of network hierarchies, (iv) Circuit decomposition, and (v) Path ordering. This method is used in determining the path orders in this paper.

Path Orders

Akola city is identified as Growth Pole in Purna Basin. The roads leading to Tahsil places (Secondary Growth Poles) are presumed to be important ones. For each of these important roads path orders are determined by breaking the circuit road by the principal of equidistance from the Growth Pole. Breaking of the circuit network also determines distinct road systems in the region.

Quantitative analysis of stream geometry has been introduced by Horton. He recognised stream orders. His method was further modified to a simpler comminatorial system by Strahler. The success of the Horton-Strahler approach in the recognition of fundamental regularities in drainage systems suggests that the search for comparable ordering systems for more complex networks – notable transport circuits – would be worth pursuing.

Village roads are taken as the segment of first order roads. The convergence of two first order roads produces the second order road and the junction of two second order roads makes the third order road and so on. Following this method path orders are decided for the region (Figs. 12.1 and 12.2.)

Average Order Index

The magnitude of roads can be observed and established in relation to Average Order Index which can be obtained by formula:

$$\text{Average order Index } (O) = \frac{\sum (iu)}{\sum i}$$

where u = length of path order

i = number of orders.

Σ = total length of path of all orders.

FIG. 12.1:

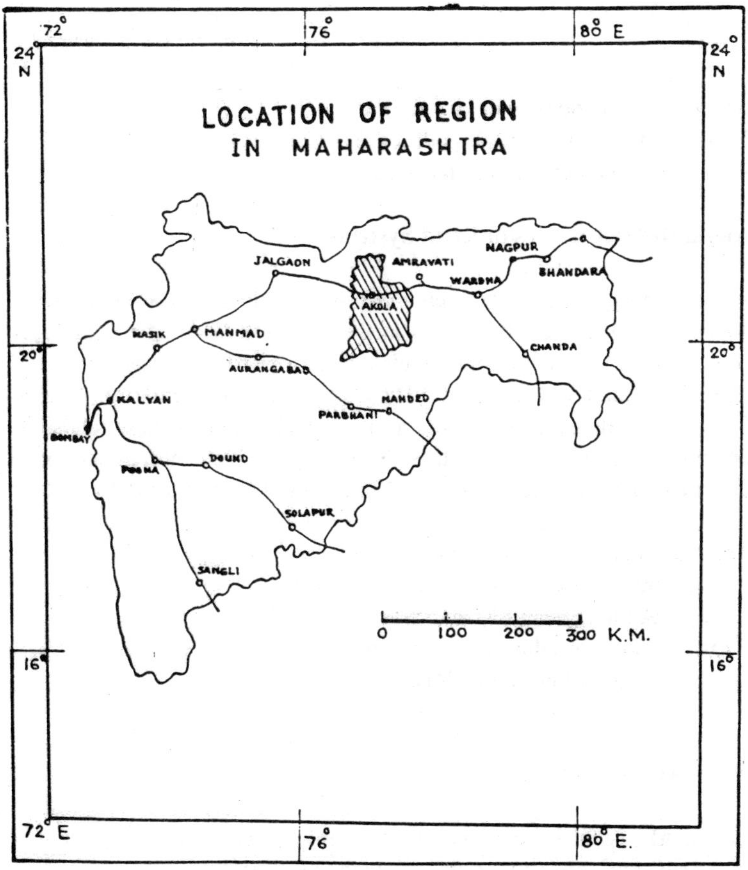

Density

If, for the road network map, we measure the total length (in kilometres) of all the paths, and divide this figure by the total area in km^2 of the catchment area, the road density can be found. Thus:

$$D = \frac{\Sigma Lk}{Ak}$$

where D = road density in km. per km^2.
ΣLk= the total length of all paths of all orders,
Ak= total catchment area of the road.

Akola District: Zones of Road Systems

At the central place of the area under study is located Akola city (Fig. 12.1). The road network pattern in the region is oriented towards this 'Pole'. From this centre main roads radiate towards Secondary Poles of tahsil headquarters (Fig. 12.2). These roads joining Primary Pole with Secondary Pole have been taken as main roads. Each of these roads has developed its own road system. Boundary of each system has been demarcated by joining points equidistant from the primary Pole.

The region has following road-systems:

(i) Akola-Akot Road System.
(ii) Akola-Balapur Road System.
(iii) Akola-Washim Road System.
(iv) Akola-Mangrulpir Road System.
(v) Akola-Murtizapur Road System.

Akola-Akot Road System

This road system is developed to the north of Akola, covering an area of 220.40 km^2. and comprising 93 paths of all orders with total length of 365.7 km. (Table 12.1). Orderwise distribution of number of paths is 1 path with 26.8 km. of length in fourth order; 6 paths with 54.4 km. of length in third order; 17 paths with 102 km. of length in second order and 69 paths with 182.5 km. of length in first order.

FIG. 12.2:

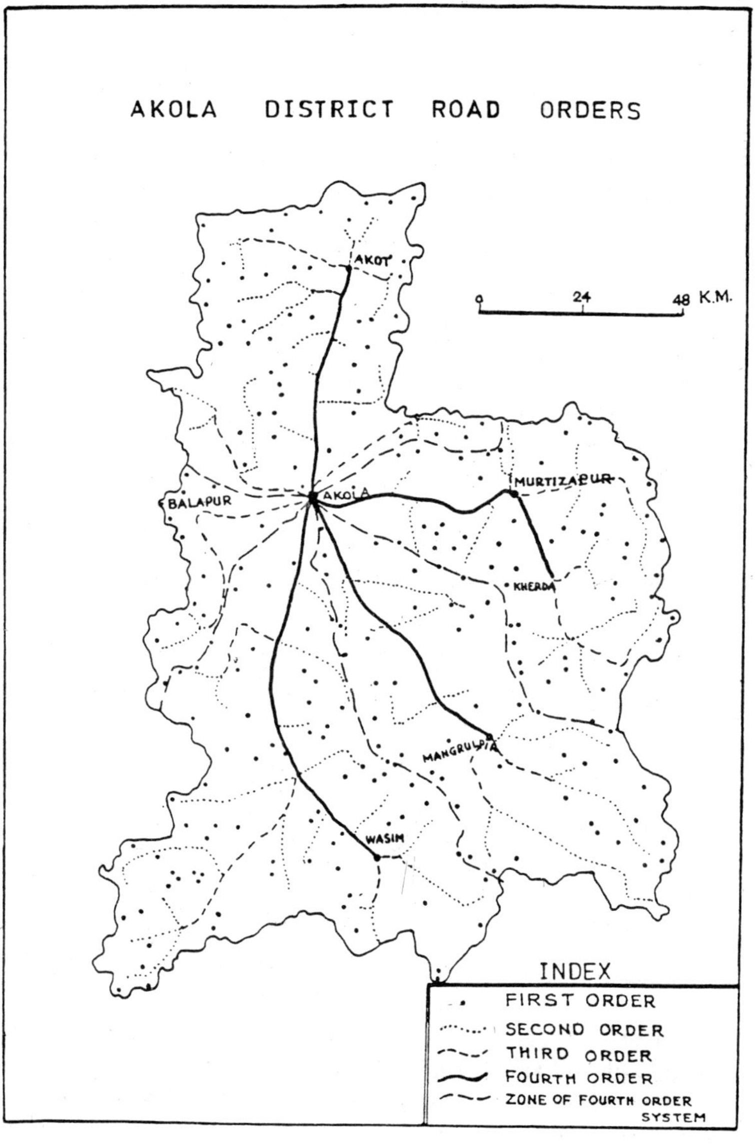
AKOLA DISTRICT ROAD ORDERS
AKOT
0 24 48 K.M.
MURTIZAPUR
BALAPUR
AKOLA
KHERDA
MANGRULPIR
WASIM
INDEX
FIRST ORDER
SECOND ORDER
THIRD ORDER
FOURTH ORDER
ZONE OF FOURTH ORDER SYSTEM

The length of the Fourth Order path is less as compared to other Road System Zones. The third order paths have comparatively more length. The average length of paths in this order comes to 9,06 km. per sq. km. The average length of paths for the next two orders is 2.6 and 2.64.

The distribution of number of roads and their length in each order indicates that there is still scope for development of first order roads.

TABLE 12.1: Number and Length of Roads Radiating from Akola and Area of Road Systems

Sr. No.	Road System	Path Order	Number	Length	Average Length km.	Area of Road System km.^{2}
1.	Akola-Akot	I	69	182.5	2.64	
		II	17	102.0	6.00	
		III	6	54.4	9.06	220.40
		IV	1	26.8	26.40	
2.	Akola-Balapur	I	15	44.8	2.98	
		II	3	9.2	3.06	50.0
		III	1	29.2	29.20	
3.	Akola-Washim	I	96	304.5	3.18	
		II	19	136.0	7.22	324.0
		III	4	40.8	10.20	
		IV	1	46.0	46.0	
4.	Akola-Murtizapur	I	74	191.8	2.59	
		II	18	91.6	5.08	200.4
		III	4	39.4	9.85	
		IV	1	36.0	36.00	
5.	Akola-Mangrulpir	I	57	185.2	3.24	
		II	12	112.8	9.40	218.0
		III	2	17.6	8.80	
		IV	1	35.6	35.60	

Akola-Balapur Road System

To the west of Akola city this system covers an area of 50 km.^{2}, with 19 roads with 832 km. of length. The region is rugged and unproductive. In this system only three order paths are developed. Akola-Balapur is the third order path with only 29.2 km. of length. Second order paths are 3 with 9.2 km. of length. Paths of the first order are 15 with 44.8 km. of length.

Road network is less developed in this zone.

Akola-Washim Road System

This road system is developed to the south-west of Akola, covering an area of 324.0 km². – highest in the region. There are 120 roads with 527.3 km. of length. The zone is having one road in fourth order with 46.00 km. of length. Medasi and Kalegaon are the two important villages on this road. Third Order roads are 4 with 40.8 km. of length; the second order roads are 19 with 136 km. of length and first order roads are 96 with 302.5 km. of length.

This zone shows highly developed system of first order as the region is economically progressive with agriculture at the base.

Akola-Mangrulpir Road System

To the south-east of Akola this system covers with 72 roads an area of 218 km². Here again we find only one road of fourth order (Akola-Mangrulpir) on which Kapasi, Baran, Mahan and Shelu are the important villages. It has a length of 35.6 km. There are 12 (112.8 km.) of second order and 57 (185.2 km.) of first order roads.

The development of first and second order roads seems to be conspicuous in this zone.

Akola-Murtizapur Road System

To the east of Akola this road system is developed with Murtizapur as the important node. The system covers an area of 200.4 km².

There is one road of fourth Order with 56 km. of length joining Murtizapur with Akola. This is the second important road in the region. The number of roads of other orders is 4 (39.4 km.) in third order; 18 (91.6 km.) in second order and 74 (151.8 km.) in first order. The average length of all these paths is only 2.51 km. the lowest for the region as a whole.

Comparative Analysis

The comparative analysis of all road systems in the region reveals uneven distribution. In some systems though the number of paths is more, their total length is less and average length is more.

Amongst fourth order roads Akola-Washim road (46.0 km) ranks first followed by Akola-Murtizapur (36 km.), Akola-Mangrulpir (35 km.) and Akola-Akot (26.5 km.).

Amongst third order roads Akola-Balapur road is important as it has the highest average length of 29.20 km. for the order. Next in importance are Akola-Washim, Akola-Murtizapur, Akola-Akot and Akola-Mangrulpir.

Amongst second orders roads, Akola-Washim system is important. This system has the highest number of roads and lengths of this order as compared to other systems. However, an average length of roads (9.40 km.) in this order is found in Akola-Mangrulpir system.

First order of roads are developed most in Akola-Washim road system. There are 96 roads. Next orders are Akola-Murtizapur, Akola-Akot, Akola-Mangrulpir, and Akola-Balapur. First order roads are most significant as they cover mostly rural areas.

Relative Importance of Road Systems

The degree of development of roads radiating from the central place can be measured by correlation of coefficient of path orders and length of that path order. However, each road system has varied path orders which makes it difficult to establish their relative importance. There is no direct method for such measurement. Gauri Dutta[3] devised a formula to calculate Average Order Index and by establishing relationship between Average Order Index and length of path, relative importance of road systems can be established.

By using this formula Table 12.2 and Fig. 12.3 are drawn.

From the figures it is obvious that in no road system of the region total length of road and average order index is high. Co-efficient of average order index and length is 119.1 in Akola-Washim Road system which is the highest for the region as a whole. Next to it is 119.0 in Akola-Murtizapur Road system; 118.33 in Akola-Akot road system; 90.99 in Akola-Mangrulpir Road system; and 24.01 in Akola-Balapur Road system. This shows that it is the southern part of Purna Basin which is most important.

FIG. 12.3:

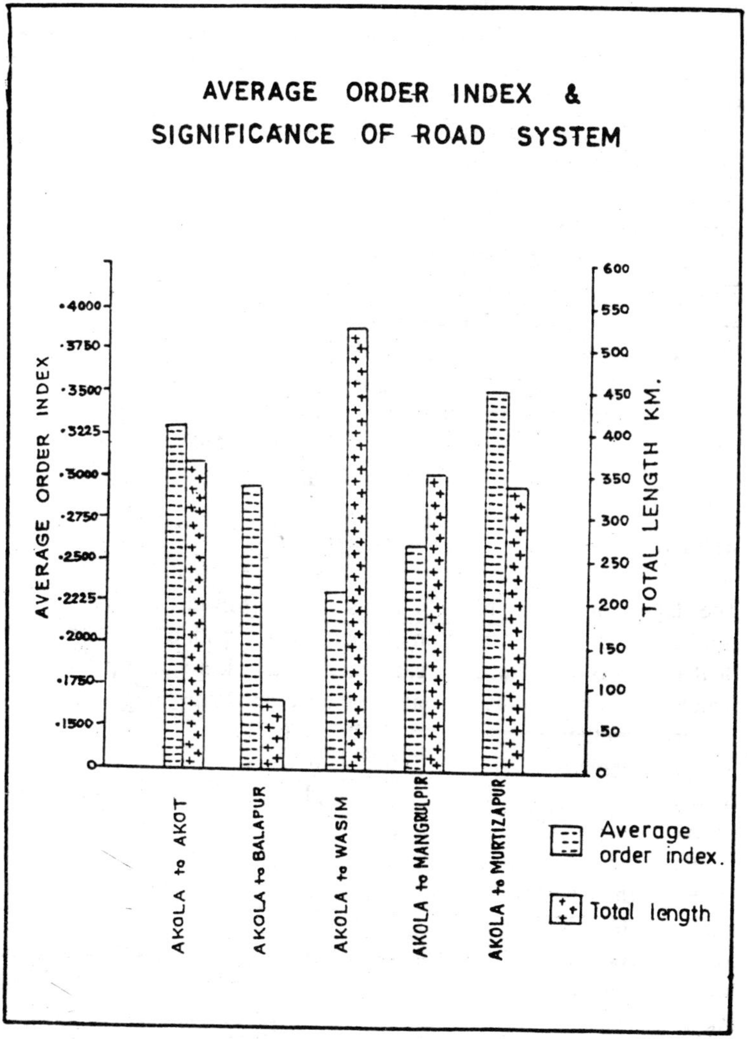

Road Density

Road density is calculated with the help of Strahler's formula and is tabulated in Table 12.3 and represented in Fig. 12.4. The density for

FIG. 12.4:

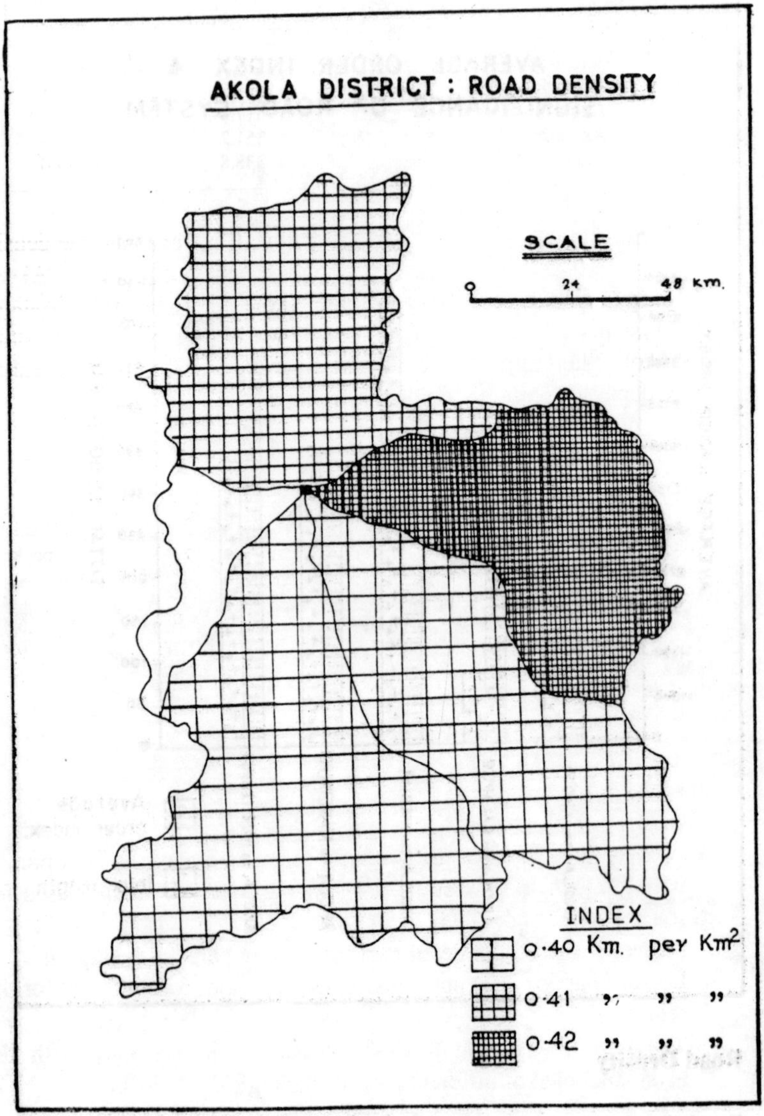
AKOLA DISTRICT : ROAD DENSITY
SCALE
0
24
48 Km.
INDEX
0·40 Km. per Km²
0·41 ” ” ”
0·42 ” ” ”

TABLE 12.2: Average Order Index and Significance of Road System

S.No.	Road System	A.O.I (km.)	Total Length (km.)	Significance Index
1.	Akola-Akot	0.3241	365.7	118.33
2.	Akola-Balapur	0.2885	83.2	24.01
3.	Akola-Washim	0.2260	517.3	119.10
4.	Akola-Mangrul	0.2591	351.2	90.99
5.	Akola-Murtizapur	0.3512	338.8	119.0

the whole region comes to 0.41 km. per km^2. If we consider the density for each road system it is found that highest density (0.42) is in Akola-Murtizapur road system. Next to it are Akola-Akot and Akola-Balapur road systems indicating 0.41 km. each, while that of Akola-Washim and Akola-Mangrulpir it is 0.40. The figures of road density reveal no major departure from normal in different parts of the region.

TABLE 12.3: Road Density

Road System	Area	Total length (km.)	Density per km.^{2}
Akola-Akot	881.60	365.7	0.41
Akola-Balapur	200.00	83.2	0.41
Akola-Washim	1296.00	527.3	0.40
Akola-Mangrulpir	827.00	351.2	0.40
Akola-Murtizapur	801.60	338.8	0.42
Region	4051.20	1686.2	0.41

Conclusion

1. The analysis of network in Akola district with Akola as a pole is done by path order method. This method can be suitably used for road network of complex nature.
2. Network patterns are developed in different parts of the region.
3. Density pattern does not show major departure from normal for the region.
4. The regional pattern of road network is in harmony with the economic level of different parts of the region.

REFERENCES

1. Strahler, N.: *Physical Geography,* (1965) Wiley International Edition, pp. 481-492.
2. Chorley and Haggett: *Integrated Models in Geography,* (1969) Methaen Co. Ltd. London, pp. 659-663.
3. Gauri Dutta : The Network Pattern of Indian National Highways from Major Urban Centres to the National Capital. *Geographical Review of India.* Vol.38, No.2, (1975) pp. 121-131.

THIRTEEN

Suman Kumar

Industry and Segregation: A Case Study of Gaya (Bihar)

INSPITE of the intrinsic stagnation of its economic system, the industrial economy of Gaya city is commanding considerable attention both in policy decisions and in geographical deliberations. Its industrial economy is characterised by some peculiar symptoms, one of which is segregation in industrial pursuits. Single castes and communities monopolise many of the industries and affect to a considerable extent the optimum industrial growth and welfare of its industrial society. The present paper attempts to measure the segregation in industries and analyse its impact on profitability and industrial welfare in the study area.

The Study Area

Gaya is not the archetypal manufacturing industrial city with industrial establishments along the urban fringe. Industry is jumbled here with housing and tertiary activity centres[1]. Hence, the limit of the study area is chosen to be the municipal boundary of the city. For the purpose of the present study, it is defined as the cluster of 1-km grid squares that corresponds to the municipal limits. This produces an irregularly shaped area covering 49 square km. Each of these grid squares are further subdivided into four smaller squares of 1/2-square km. each and all the spatial computations and analysis have been made with reference to them.

Data and Methodology

One serious limitation of many spatial industrial studies is that most data are tied to administrative units and only reveal a picture describable in terms of net aggregate analysis[2]. The data used here, however, are both spatially independent of administrative units and are based on individual industrial establishments. However, for reason of confidentiality, details are aggregated after the event to the level of 1/2-square km. grid squares and this is, therefore, the lowest level of spatial desegregation permitted in subsequent discussion.

The coefficients of segregation are calculated on the basis of two variables, plant ownership and input, according to the following formula:

$$\frac{2A}{B} \times \frac{C}{D}$$

where A= No. of plant owners of the caste* that owns maximum No. of plants.

B= Total No. of plant owners.

C= No. of input suppliers of the caste that qualifies for A.

D= Total No. of input suppliers.

Plant ownership is given double the weight that of input because it has more direct bearing upon character of industrialization.

Measurements of Segregation

Industrial composition of Gaya can be classified under two major heads - traditional industries and modern industries. Segregation coefficients derived both for each grid square and for each major industrial order indicate that the traditional industries are characterised by high segregation, and the modern industries are almost free from segregation.

Spatial measurements of segregation

Spatial values of segregation coefficient in the study area vary from 0.01 to 0.62. Classified into four categories – low (0.00 to 0.20), medium (0.21 to 0.40), high (0.41 to 0.60) and very high (0.61 and

* Religion in case of Muslims and Sikhs as caste subdivisions among them are insignificant from the stand point of segregation.

above), they reveal greater segregation in west, north-west and south (see Fig. 13.1). The areas of high segregation are dominated by incense stick making, brick making and stone carving industries respectively. The incense stick making is almost exclusively monopolised by the Muslim both in plant ownership and input. In many cases the input suppliers also take back the bulk of the products. The stone carving industry is monopolised by Gaud Brahmins as a hereditary occupation. Bespoke garments, textiles and fibres and metal engineering industries are responsible for medium segregation in the west and east. The three western grid squares of medium segregation west of Phalgu river represent bespoke garments industry monopolised to a high degree in plant ownership and labour force by Muslims (Fig. 13.1). Similarly, the three north-eastern grid squares of medium segregation are highly monopolised in plant ownership and labour by Patwa, Tatwa and Bhumihars in cotton weaving, rope making and metal engineering industries. However, monopoly in labour force is less marked in metal engineering.

In the inner city, spatial location of different industries is highly jumbled up and there is hardly any specific zone for any industry except automobile engineering along the Phalgu riverside. Consequently, segregation is less marked here (Fig. 13.1). Areas of low segregation east of Phalgu river represent cotton weaving, calendaring, processing and sizing which are again monopolised in plant ownership, and to a certain extent in labour force, but not in materials and output. The southern ribbon of low segregation running parallel to the river (Fig. 13.1) consists of brick making, lime kilns and various other industries which, though each segregated to a certain extent, offset each other's segregation in spatial analysis.

Industrywise Measurements of Segregation

For the purpose of the present study, industries in the area are classified into fifteen major industrial orders based on the classification by the Department of Industries, Government of Bihar[3]. Certain modifications are made to suit the present purpose. Measurements of segregation according to the method indicated above

$$\frac{2A}{B} \times \frac{C}{D}$$

reveal two orders highly segregated, two having medium segregation and the remaining eleven having low segregation. The two highly segregated orders are tobacco wrapping and plastic and chemicals. The former is highly monopolised by the Muslims in plant ownership and input. The latter is a group of industries, but is largely constituted by the incense stick making which has similar characteristics as tobacco wrapping and thus the order is highly segregated. The two orders with medium segregation, namely, garments and tailoring and leather products, are again monopolised by Muslims but only in plant ownership and labour force. As for the remaining eleven orders, their small bits are distributed among different castes and communities and are not significant from the standpoint of segregation.

FIG. 13.1

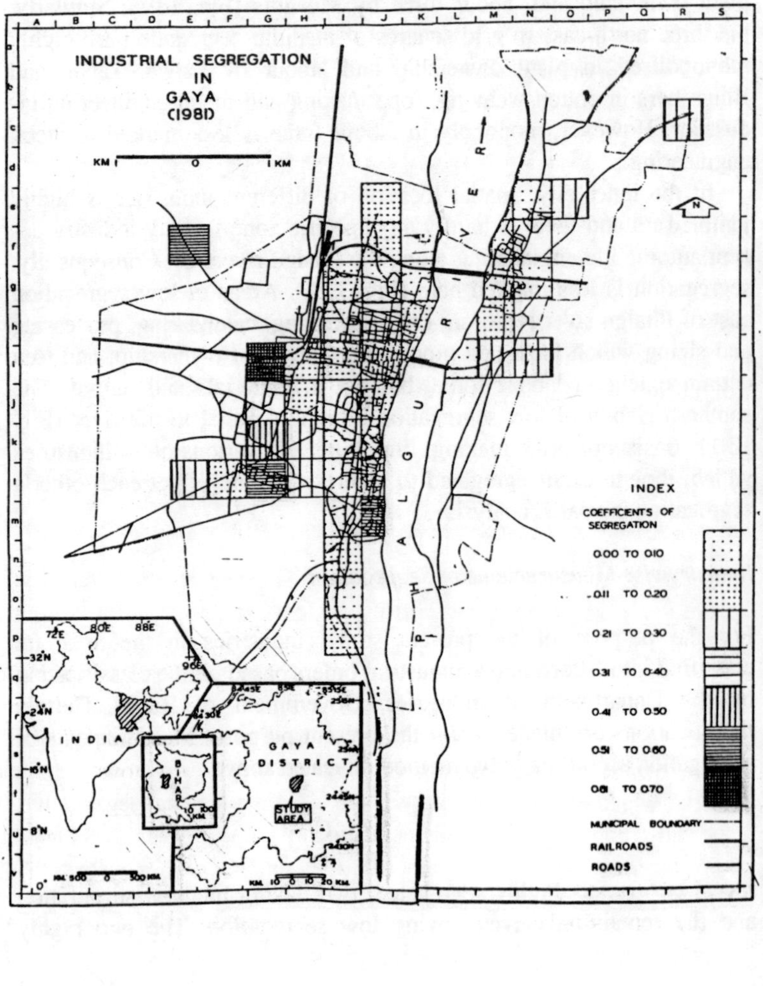

Effects

Industrial segregation in the study area has a marked relevance in the study of prosperity of its industrial society and in micro level industrial planning. In the present study, the coefficients of segregation are correlated with the profitability (as a percentage of input) to analyse their relationship. The method used is the Pearson's Product Moment Correlation Coefficient (4.5) which follows:

$$r = \frac{n \sum xy - (\sum x)(\sum y)}{\sqrt{\{n \sum x^2 - (\sum x)^2\} \{n \sum y^2 - (\sum y)^2\}}}$$

where r = Pearsonian correlation coefficient.

$\sum x$ = Sum of all x values.

$\sum x^2$ = Sum of squares of all x values.

$\sum y$ = Sum of all y values.

$\sum y^2$ = Sum of squares of all y values.

$\sum xy$ = Sum of products of all x and y values.

n = Total number of observations.

The result thus obtained is r–0.670 which indicates that there is a negative relationship between segregation and profitability in the study area. The value 0.670 suggests a strong correlation. The significance of the correlation is tested according to the formula

$$t = \frac{\sqrt{n-2}.r}{\sqrt{1-r^2}}$$

where this student's test of significance is made at 5% level. The t value is 3.254 with 13 degrees of freedom. The correlation is highly significant.

Thus, from the above analysis it is inferred that there is a close relationship between segregation and profitability in Gaya. There are other factors like old operational techniques and machinery, small scale operation, and "fossilised" attitude of workers towards their work[6], which affect profitability in the same manner, but segregation is the most dominant single element hindering the welfare of industrial society. Plant owners get materials from suppliers of their own caste, employ labour of their own caste and sometimes sell output to the same material suppliers. The situation persists even when there are more advantageous alternatives. Thus, they deprive themselves of competitive market for minimum input cost and maximum profits.

Conclusion

The industrial economy of the study area is plagued by the segregation which has led it to industrial stagnation. Its industrial society is denied its due reward and this situation eventually hinders the balanced economic growth of this area.

In order to achieve the goal of micro level regional development, following measures are suggested for the study area and other areas suffering from similar industrial agony:

1. Introduction of simple, modern techniques and supply of necessary equipments by the government at low cost on credit.
2. Establishment of public sector material supply system for industries in which it is difficult to break monopoly in plant ownership and labour force.
3. Promotion of modern resource based (leather garments, bonemeal) and demand based (drawing boards and T-squares, annodised aluminium and brushware products, and plaster of paris replicas and statues) industries[7] in areas dominated by highly segregated traditional industries.

REFERENCES

1. Roy Chaudhury, P.C. Bihar District Gazetteers, Gaya, pp. 90-93, 134, (1957) Patna.
2. Lloyd, P.E. and Mason, C.M. Manufacturing Industry in the Inner City: A Case Study of Greater Manchester, *Transactions New Series, Institute of British Geographers,* Vol. 3., pp. 72-73 (1978) London.
3. Directorate of Public Relations, *Industrial Directory of Bihar,* (1969) pp.17, 74-81 Bihar, Patna.
4. Gregory, S. *Statistical Methods and the Geographer,* pp. 181-186, Longman, (1978) London.
5. Ram, L.N. Correlation Analysis of Regional Parameters in Geography, *Indian Geographical Studies, Research Bulletin No:3,* (1974) pp. 34, Geographical Research Centre, Patna.
6. Jarret, H.R. A Geography of Manufacturing, (1977) pp. 84, 85, Macdonald and Evans Ltd., Estover, Plymouth.
7. Sinha, Chakradhar. "Industrial Landscape of Gaya District", *Souvenir, 55th Annual Conference, Indian Economic Association,* pp. 44, 45, Magadh University, Bodh Gaya (1972).

PART – VI

CULTURAL GEOGRAPHY

FOURTEEN

Ashok K. Dutt and **Allen G. Noble**

Religious Diversity Patterns: Rajasthan and India

RELIGION has formed a topic of research for several geographers, although only one has attempted a world overview (Sopher).[1] On a more restricted areal scale, Zelinsky,[2] Pillsbury[3] and Shortridge[4] all have analyzed religious patterns in the United States and several geographers have produced studies of religious phenomena in other countries. Nonetheless, religion has made far-reaching imprints on the peoples and landscapes of the world. Those imprints vary from the establishment of *pinjrapoles* and *jivat khans* in Gujarat, as part of the Jain manifestation of *Ahimsa* (Lordrick)[5] to the widespread destruction of magnificent abbeys and monasteries in England as a result of Henry VIII's war against Catholicism, the remnants of which can still be seen as ruins. Similarly, attitudes of peoples have been moulded largely by religious beliefs; the Hindu reliance on fate in contrast to Sikh adherence to pragmatism in just one example.

Introduction

Several studies have been made of religious patterns in India. A common theme in each has been the identification of greatest religious diversity at the periphery of the country. Join Brush[6] was the first social scientist to provide a comprehensive spatial analysis of religious communities in India. Among his observations was that after Partition, the northwestern provinces of India (i.e., Punjab and Kashmir) had the greatest concentration of minority religions (Sikhism and Islam). Portions of the northern border of Rajasthan confront Sikh-dominated Punjab.

Kingsley Davis[7], a demographer, using the data base of the 1931 Census of India, noted that the peripheral areas throughout South Asia contained the principal concentration of non-Hindu groups. In part, the present study will examine the effect of Rajasthan's location on its religious pattern to determine if Davis' and Brush's observations hold true on a less than sub-continental scale.

Gosal and Mukerji[8] confirmed, with 1961 census data, that two minority communities (Sikhs and Christians) continue to be concentrated along the periphery of the country. Recently, Dutt, Chatterjee and Geib[9] have reiterated that Jains, a distinctive religious group believing in strict non-violence to animate life, are concentrated in Rajasthan and adjacent Gujarat. The 1971 Census of India provided confirmation of religious diversity in Rajasthan, although at the same time indicating less diversification than in all India (Table 14.1). Finally, Davgun[10] applying factor analysis techniques, noted that only one factor, which included negative concentrations of Hindus and Jains and positive concentrations of Christians and other religions was statistically significant in India. All other religious groups stood in independent relationship to each other.

Dutt and Davgun[11] identified the reasons for the confinement of Sikhism in the Punjab area: (1) Nanak and other Sikh gurus operated from headquarters in Punjab, (2) most gurus were selected on family lines which necessarily limited dispersion, (3) *Gurumukhi*, the script of the Punjabi language, was chosen for Sikh religious use, and (4) the Sikhs retained a preoccupation for combating Mughal persecution. In another study, Dutt and Davgun[12] delineated India's religious regions, dividing the country into five major sub-regions : Hindu, Buddhist, Muslim, Sikh and Mixed. They used 1971 census data and applied factor analysis technique.

The present study will analyze the existing geographical pattern of religions in Rajasthan, and offer measures of the diversity of those patterns (Fig. 14.1 and Fig. 14.2) in comparison to the country as a whole. The State is unique as a meeting ground for major religions. Madhya Pradesh, to the southeast, has long been known as a centre for tribal groups and as a centre for Christian missionary activity. Muslims predominate in Pakistan to the West, Sikhs to the northwest in Punjab, and Hindus on all other sides, with an important concentration of Jains to the south in Gujarat. Each of these neighbouring groups potentially affects the religious pattern of Rajasthan itself.

FIG. 14.1:

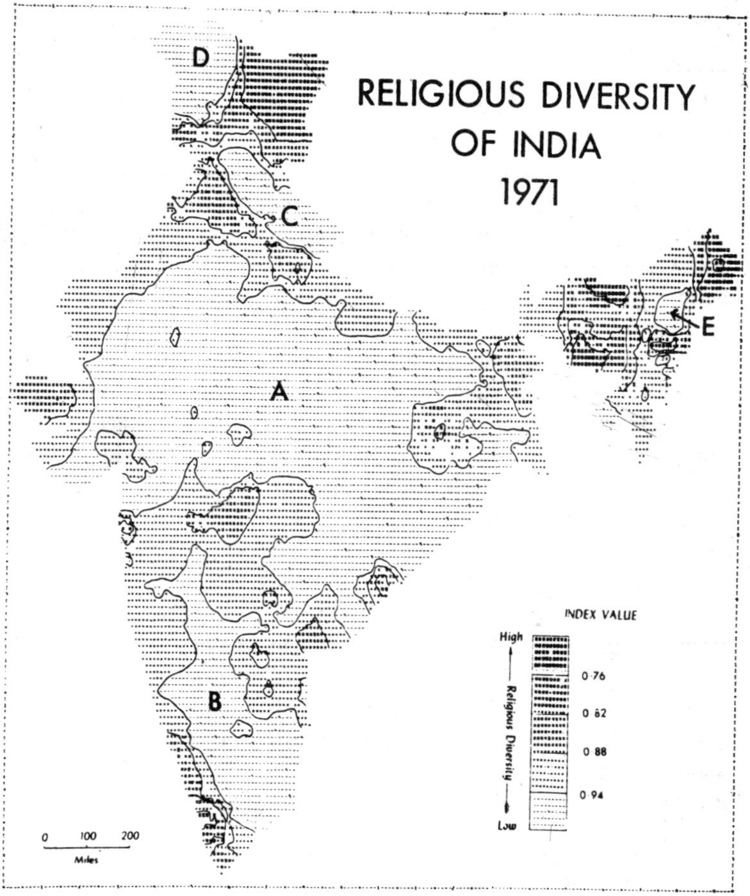

FIG. 14.1: Religious Diversity Index of India by district based on Lorenz Curve and as applied by Shortridge. Lower Index value indicates higher religious diversity, while the higher value indicates lower religious diversity. Map drawn on a computer based SYMAP. Data Base: 1971 Census of India.

Research Design

The 1971 Census of India provided, for the first time in forty years, official information on the district composition of religions in India and its States. Useful as such data are, a more detailed, and thus meaningful, analysis is possible by assembling and analyzing data for smaller units than districts. Therefore, unpublished, but officially collected, religious data (i.e., number of adherents to each region) was obtained from the Rajasthan State Census Office for each minor civil division (*tahsil*), of which there were 196 in 1971.

FIG. 14.2:

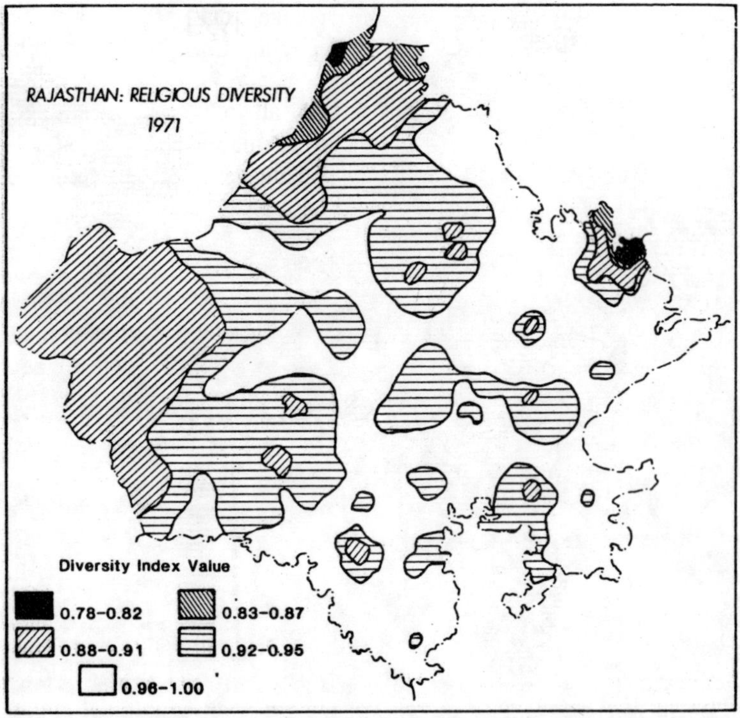

FIG. 14.2: Religious Diversity Index of Rajasthan State by *Tahsil* based on Lorenz Curve and as applied by Shortridge. Lower index value indicates higher religious diversity, while the higher value indicates lower religious diversity. Map drawn on a computer based SYAMP. Data Base : 1971 Census of Rajasthan.

Within each tahsil, the percentage of each religion's adherents to total tahsil population was calculated and SYMAPS of these were prepared (Figures 14.3, 14.4, 14.5, 14.6 and 14.7). Furthermore, a diversity index at the tahsil level also was calculated, following the method proposed by Shortridge. The index is a refinement of the "Lorenz Curve", which is generally used to describe industrial diversification. The "Index of Diversity" may be determined by the following general formula:

$$D = \frac{T-1}{M-1}$$

where D = Index of Diversity (or Concentration),

T = Tahsil cumulative percentage total of six religions (Hindu, Muslim, Sikh, Jain, Christian, and other religions)

I = Cumulative percentage of all religions, assuming a hypothetical, or ideal even distribution and

M = Maximum cumulative percentage total assuming 100 percent of frequencies in rank 1.

An index value of 1.00 represents an absolute concentration of one religion; similarly a zero value of the index indicates an even distribution signifying complete diversity (Fig. 14.1). The same technique was applied to measure the diversity index for India by districts, where T represented district cumulative percentage and R the national cumulative percent.

Analysis of the Results

India

The map of religious diversity for India was based on 356 districts and reveals several spatial characteristics. First, five areas (A, B, C, D, E) have very low religious diversity. The central area (A), which extends into the Indo-Gangetic plain, is largely a Hindu dominated country where 80 percent and more of the people are Hindus. This area is the home of tribal populations, some of whom are animists, but recorded in the census as Hindus. This also includes the northern and central parts of the Deccan Plateau which were relatively unattractive to the Muslim rulers of Delhi-Agra core areas because of rugged topography, thick forest cover, and infertile soils. The southern region (B) is the heartland of the southern Hindu kingdoms of Tamilnadu. This area, being far away from the Delhi-Agra Muslim core, was relatively little influenced by Islam. Moreover, being on the eastern side of the Western Ghats barrier, this region was away from the main Christian and Islamic trade-cum-seaborne influence routes, giving greater opportunities to the Hindus to evolve themselves unobstructed. Such unobstructed evolution can further be observed in a detailed stage by stage development of Hindu temple form during the past two thousand years, in Tamilnadu.

Area C lies in the Himalayas, i.e., Siwalik Hills, Middle Himalayas, and Great Himalayas. Being mountainous country, the Muslims treated this locale as unattractive because of its inaccessibility and agricultural infertility. Thus, in spite of its nearness to the Delhi-Agra core and regular Muslim route ways, the Himalayas remained over 90 percent Hindu.

The fourth area (D) is Muslim dominated Western Kashmir, with the Srinagar Valley as its core. Here Muslim conversion began in the thirteenth-fourteenth centuries. The Muslim rulers were attracted by the agricultural fertility and Himalayan beauty of the Srinagar Valley; small wonder that the Mughals laid out the beautiful Shalimar gardens here.

The fifth area (E), almost at the eastern end of the Brahmaputra Valley, had been under Hindu kingdoms of Assam for several centuries and was not attractive to Bengal Muslims because of distance, nor to Tibetan Buddhists living in high altitudes because of lowland, unhealthful, hot and humid climates. The northern (Kashmir-Punjab), northeastern (Assam and adjoining Hilly States and Union territories) and the extreme southwestern (Kerala) fringes possess greater religious diversity than the rest of India. Eastern Kashmir is mainly Buddhist, but with a strong mixture of Islam. Buddhist influence in the Ladakh part of Kashmir is an extension of Tibetan Buddhism. Punjab is strongly Sikh with some Hindus. In the northeastern part of India, Christianity, Animism, Buddhism, Islam and Hinduism are intermixed with each other. Here the spread of Christianity is the result of western missionary activities and conversion of local tribal people. Muslims in this area represent migratory extensions from nearby Bengal. Buddhism in Arunachal Pradesh, adjacent to Tibet, is the result of direct contacts with Tibetan Buddhists. The Burman Buddhists are responsible for the spread of Buddhism in the border territory of Mizoram. In the southwestern coasts, sea-borne contacts from the Middle East and Europe have produced sizeable Muslim and Christian populations respectively (Dutt and Davgun).[13]

Several areas of intermediate level diversity exist. In the middle and Upper Gangetic plain, the existence of central and regional Muslim kings diluted the Hindu populations. Lower down the Gangetic plain, adjacent to Bangladesh, Muslim influence is evident. In the Chotanagpur plateau of south Bihar, diversity results from Christian conversion of the native tribes. In the Deccan peninsula around Aurangabad, the influence of regional Muslim kingdoms can be seen, along with that of recent conversion of Hindu Scheduled Castes to Buddhism through Ambedkar's Neo-Buddhist effort. Along the Andhra coast, Christian missionary activities have reduced the Hindu base. Kutch in Gujarat demonstrates the earlier extension of Islam from Sind, where Islam established its first base in South Asia (Dutt and Davgun).

FIG. 14.3:

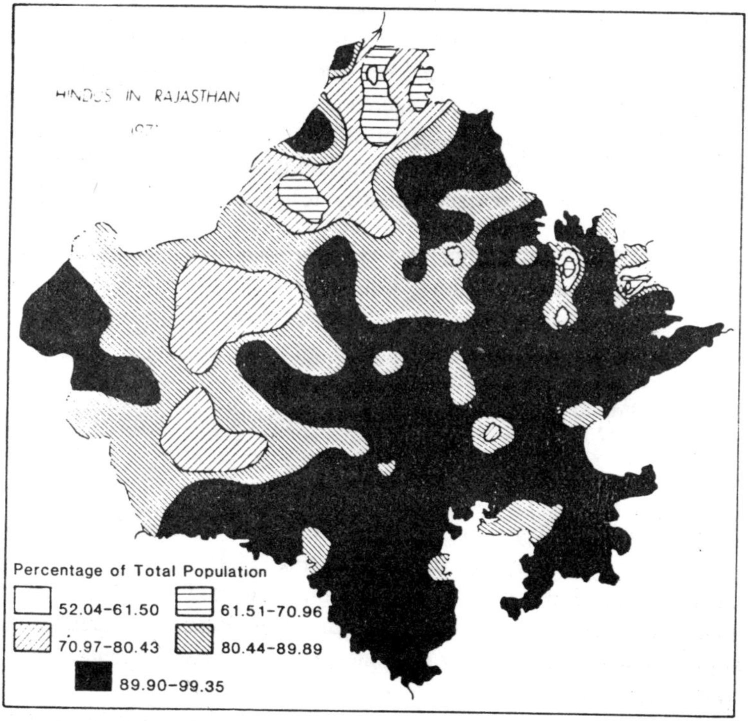

FIG. 14.3: Percentage of Hindus to total population by *Tahsil* of Rajasthan State based on computer produced SYMAP. Data Base: 1971 Census of Rajasthan

Rajasthan

Hindus form almost 90% of Rajasthan's population (Fig. 14.3), a proportion significantly higher than that of the balance of the country. Noteworthy in this regard, is that the other peripheral States of India, such as Punjab, Kashmir, Arunachal Pradesh, Nagaland, Mizoram and Meghalaya, all have more sizeable minority religious communities, when measured in proportional terms. In Rajasthan, significant areas of religious diversity occur only in the extreme north, extreme northeast and to a lesser degree in the west (Fig. 14.1). Thus, Rajasthan represents something of a special case in analyzing religious diversity along India's fringe zones.

Several factors, some geographical and some environmental, help to explain these phenomena. First, the victorious Muslim invaders during their rule in western India avoided the arid, desolate lands of Rajasthan in preference to the better watered sections of Gujarat, the Indus Plain and Punjab. Furthermore, the already well-ensconced Rajput kingdoms, such as that of Maharana Pratap Singh in the 16th century, successfully created strong anti-Muslim buffers in the region sufficient to discourage conversion from Hinduism to Islam. Still, Muslims are the only important minority religious group in Rajasthan (Table 14.1).

TABLE 14.1: Percent of Population by Religion (1971)

	Hindu	Muslim	Christian	Sikh	Buddhist	Jain	Others
Rajasthan	89.63	6.90	0.12	1.32	0.01	1.99	0.03
India	82.72	11.21	2.60	1.89	0.70	0.47	0.41

Source : 1971 Census of India.

The present-day distribution of Muslims in Rajasthan occurs primarily in two widely separated areas (Fig. 14.4). Along the western border of the State, adjacent to Muslim-dominated Pakistan, is one zone, more or less a spill-over from the Indus Plain, with settlement largely based upon herding settlements tied to small scattered localized oases. Total population is low, however.

Perhaps, because of the sparse, population, the poor quality of the land, and the backward nature of the region's economy, Muslims from this area were not forced out to Pakistan during the communal frenzy

FIG. 14.4:

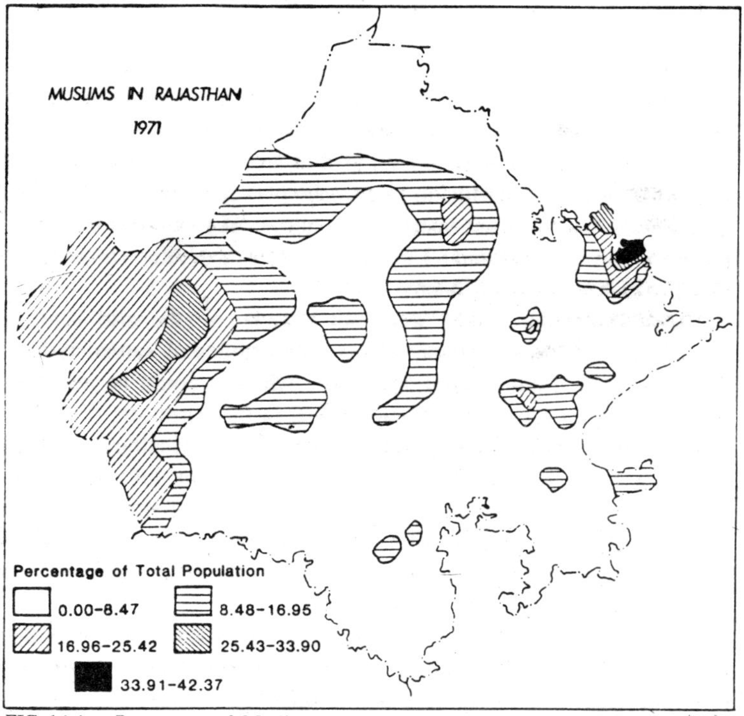

FIG. 14.4: Percentage of Muslim's to total population by *Tahsil* of Rajasthan State based on computer produced SYMAP. Data Base: 1971 Census of Rajasthan.

associated with Partition in 1947. The successful survival of a small, minority community of Muslims in the dry plains of western Rajasthan may also be related to Islamic religious and social customs. A religion which originated in the desert and which flourished initially in semi-desert and desert environments, required lesser water than Hinduism in various ceremonies and social situations. Perhaps these circumstances permitted a better adjustment of Muslims than Hindus to the dry conditions of western Rajasthan.

The other, more discontinuous, zone of Muslim settlement follows the "historic transport corridor" which once linked the Delhi-Agra Muslim core area, an outlying portion of which occurs in northwestern Rajasthan, with strategically positioned seaport centres, such as, Surat, at the mouth of the Tapti River and Bharuch at the mouth of the Narmada. Traders, partly Muslim, moving back and forth along this routeway established a number of important trading and administrative centres (Spate).[14]

Udaipur, Jaipur, and Ajmer developed as the principal focal points along this corridor, located in response to a line of springs outcropping along the eastern flanks of the Aravalli Ranges. Ajmer, situated in the heart of this corridor, while not an area of large Muslim concentration, is an especially sacred Muslim pilgrimage place containing the tomb of a venerated Muslim saint visited by hundreds of thousands of Muslim pilgrims during the annual Urs festival. Muslims refer reverently to this city as Ajmershariеf (Sacred Ajmer).

As with Hindus, Sikhs were not attracted to the arid lands. A people derived by conversion within communities of settled farmers, the Sikhs sought arable land, especially where it could be improved. Today, the Sikh religious community lies in the northwest (Fig. 14.5) where former desert lands have been opened for agricultural colonisation as a result of Sikh refugees, farmers from the Pakistan Punjab plains, who migrated to this area with the opening of new agricultural opportunities in the 1950s. Sikh concentrations are remarkably absent in the balance of the State, probably due to the recent nature of the migration and its agricultural orientations.

Jains are a slightly larger group than Sikhs in Rajasthan, with their proportion (1.99 percent) being considerably higher than in all India (0.47) (Table 14.1). In point of fact, Rajasthan contains the largest concentration of Jains in the world. Originating in Bihar in the 6th Century B.C., the Jain community found security in the semi-arid zone of Gujarat and southern Rajasthan where several important Jain kingdoms gave cohesiveness to this community. Jains are now widely dispersed across the State (Fig. 14.6). A northerly zone, particularly in Bikaner, is an outlier of a much larger and more concentrated settlements toward the southern border near Gujarat, the centre of which is Mount Abu, the highest point of the Aravalli Mountains, a peak sacred to Jains, and studded with profusely carved temples of delicate white marble and alabaster.

No other religion is important numerically in Rajasthan (Table 14.1). Tiny pockets of tribals and Buddhists are widely scattered, mostly as isolated families in larger cities or in the remote vastness of the mountain ranges.

FIG. 14.5

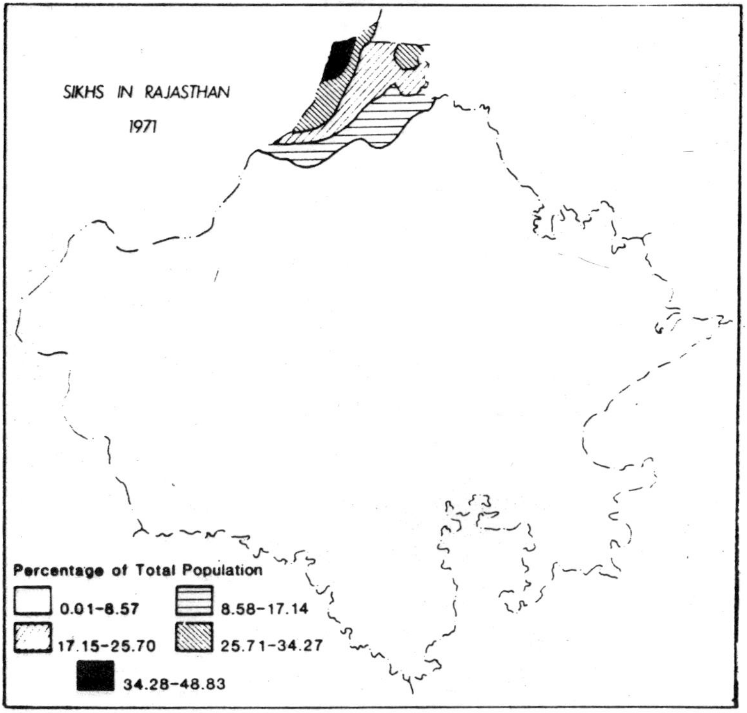

FIG. 14.5: Percentage of Sikhs to total population by *Tahsil* of Rajasthan State based on computer produced SYMAP. Data Base: 1971 Census of Rajasthan.

The pattern of distribution of Christians has certain similarities to those of tribals and Buddhists. In the south and east of Rajasthan are small, widely scattered clusters among the jungly sections where tribal groups are found. Especially noteworthy is the concentration in Banswara district, a remote, hilly area through which no major road or rail link passes. Missionaries, arriving late on the scene in India, were generally most successful in securing converts among those groups who had not fared well with the established religions (the Scheduled Tribes and Untouchables, were one such group). Given the official British policy of restricted approval of missionary activity, especially in more remote areas, Christian conversion was never a smashing success.

One community, however, was established within Christianity, the Anglo-Indians, many of whom gravitated to engineering, transportation, and minor administrative careers. The effects of these

FIG. 14.6:

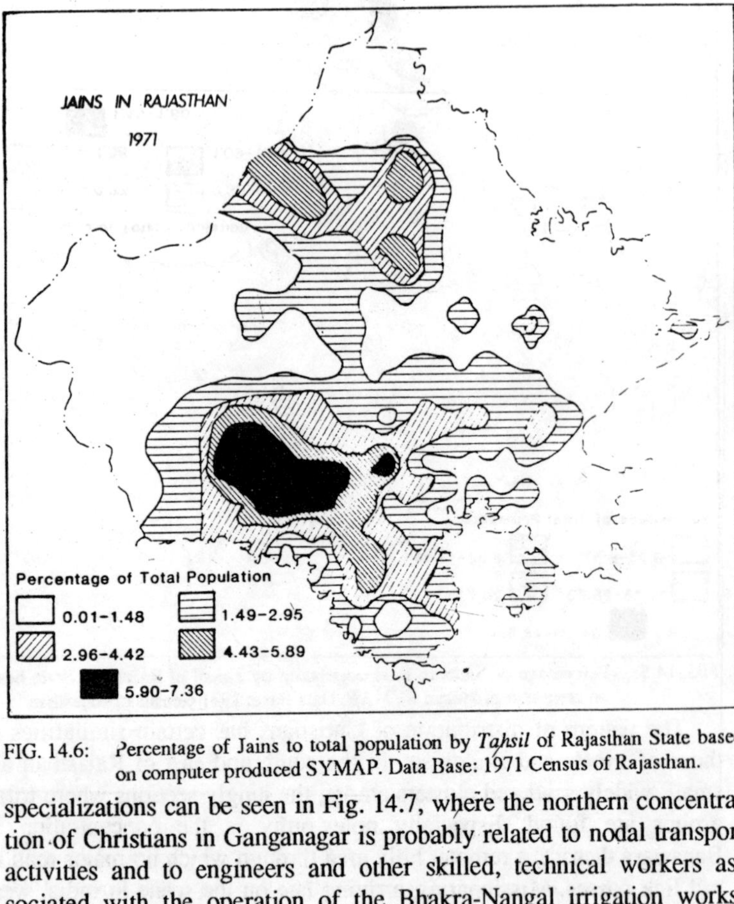

FIG. 14.6: Percentage of Jains to total population by *Tahsil* of Rajasthan State based on computer produced SYMAP. Data Base: 1971 Census of Rajasthan.

specializations can be seen in Fig. 14.7, where the northern concentration of Christians in Ganganagar is probably related to nodal transport activities and to engineers and other skilled, technical workers associated with the operation of the Bhakra-Nangal irrigation works. That around Ajmer is probably related to the presence of early British administrative functions and to the important railway facilities.

Conclusion

The measure of diversity employed by Shortridge when applied to marginally-located Rajasthan, confirms the observations of Brush and Davis that peripheral areas demonstrate greater diversity, whereas, centralized locations illustrate greatest unity or homogeneity. In

FIG. 14.7:

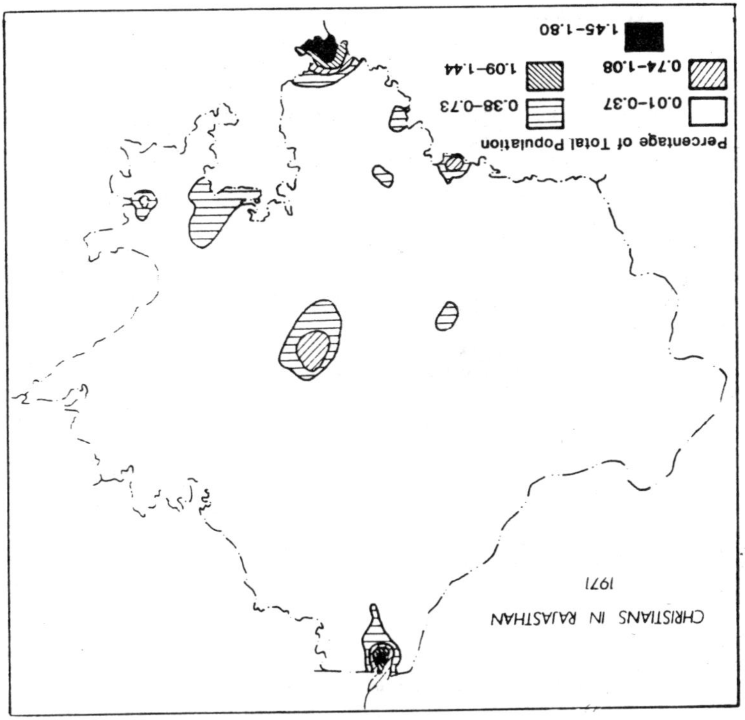

FIG. 14.7: Percentage of Christians to total population by *Tahsil* of Rajasthan State based on computer produced SYMAP. Data Base: 1971 Census of Rajasthan.

Rajasthan, such diversity is mainly caused by the relatively larger concentration of Muslims and Sikhs, whereas, for India its peripheral diversity reflects not only Muslim and Sikh concentrations, but both Tibeto-Burman Buddhists and Christians who have also diluted religious composition in those areas. Lower diversity areas in Rajasthan, like India, are associated with Hindu predominance. Therefore, the more the non-Hindu population, the greater the diversity.

REFERENCES

1. Sopher, David E., *Geography of Religions*, Prentice-Hall, Inc., Englewood Cliffs, New Jersey. (1967).
2. Zelinsky, Wilbur, "An Approach to the Religious Geography of the United States", *Annals of the Association of American Geographers*, Vol. LI, pp. 139-193 (1961).
3. Pillsbury, Richard, "The Religious Geography of Pennsylvania: A Factor Analytic Approach," *Proceedings of the Association of American Geographers*, Vol. 3, (1971) pp. 130-134.
4. Shortridge, James R., "Patterns of Religion in the United States", *Geographical Review*, Vol. 66, No. 4, (1976), pp. 420-434.
5. Lodricks, Deryek O., "Cultural Landscapes in Western India," eds. Allen G. Noble and Ashok K. Dutt, *India : Cultural Patterns and Processes, Ibid.* (1982)
6. Brush, John E., "The Distribution of Religious Communities in India," *Annals of the Association of American Geographers*, Vol. 39, No. 2, (1949) pp. 81-98.
7. Davis, Kingsley, *The Population of India and Pakistan*, Princeton University Press, Princeton, New Jersey (1951).
8. Gosal, Gurdev S. and A. B. Mukerji, "The Religious Composition of Indian Population - A Spatial Analysis," *Tydschrift voor Economische en Sociale Geogrfie*, Vol. 61, (1970), pp. 91-100.
9. Dutt, Ashok K., S. P. Chatterjee and M. Margaret Geib, *India in Maps*, Kendall-Hunt Publishing Company, Dubuque, Iowa (1976).
10. Davgun, Satish, *The Religious Structure of the Indian Population, 1971 : A Spatial Perspective*, unpublished Masters' thesis, Department of Geography, University of Akron, (1977), pp. 89.
11. Dutt, Ashok K. and Satish Davgun, "Diffusion of Sikhism and Migration Patterns of Sikhs in India," *Geojournal*, Vol. 1, No. 5, (1977), pp. 81-89
12. Dutt, Ashok K. and Satish Davgun, "Religious Patterns of India with a Factoral Regionalization," *Geojournal*, Vol. 3, No. 2, (1979), pp. 201-214.
13. Dutt, Ashok K. and Satish Davgun, "Patterns of Religious Diversity," in eds. Allen G. Noble and Ashok K. Dutt, *India : Cultural Patterns and Processes* (Boulder, Colorado : Westview Press), (1982), pp. 221-246.
14. Spate, O.H.K. and A.T.A. Learmonth, *India and Pakistan*, Methuen and Company, Ltd., London (1967).

FIFTEEN

K.M. Kulkarni

Geography of Crimes: A Study of Ahmedabad City

Introduction

THE statistics on crime all over the world confirms the urban bias though it does not recognise geographical boundaries. The time and space are two important dimensions of crime investigation. The crime can take place at any time of the day and at any place on the globe. It does not respect class and caste structure of the society. On the contrary its methods keep pace with the developing scientific and technological knowhow. It ranges from a local petty theft to a skyjacking of passenger airliner on an international level depending on the scale of operation. In more crowded cities it has a greater ability to increase fear and tension among the residents. The greater occurrence of crimes in urban areas is perhaps due to its heterogeneous social conditions and diversified economic activities and class structure which can be traced in language, religion, caste and culture. However, it is interesting to study in depth the socio-economic conditions prevailing in the neighbourhood of the criminal's residence as well as the dominant areas of crimes. The crimes recorded in different parts of the crowded cities can be identified into three major areas of occurrence. Firstly, the crimes occur in the same socio-economic neighbourhood where the criminal resides. Secondly, the crimes occur in the area where high socio-economic conditions exist. The criminal considers such areas as favourable fields for his purposes. Lastly, the crimes occur over an interacting space where the criminal and the possible victim come in contact.

In the present study, the limitation of data on crimes inhibits the analysis of the locality of criminals. However, an attempt is made to relate the reported crimes of all types to the social environment, such as density of population (external living environment), internal living density (number of persons per room), non-residential land-use (interacting space), literacy condition (including the female literacy), major non-agricultural activity (manufacturing, trade and services), distribution of textile mills and areawise distribution of car owners.

The social reasons, especially the strained social relations, due to economic gains (property or huge assets), and social injustice invariably end in severe crimes. The psychological reasons like the pent up frustration, disgust, disappointment, disregard, deep fear and tension lead to the destruction of property and human-lives. In case of economic reasons the sole purpose is to gain wealth and material and the victim could be any one who possesses wealth. With the economic purpose the crime rarely ends in murdering the victim. The social, psychological and economic aspects mentioned above have geographical bearing especially in relation to the core periphery aspects, distance decay concept and urban land-use and functional aspects. The present study aims at understanding the patterns of crimes in the background of socio-economic environment.

Data Base and Methodology

The data related to crimes were collected from the Divisional Commissioner's Office, Ahmedabad. There are different types of crimes. These can be grouped broadly into two major categories. The major crimes include different categories such as murder, dacoity, robbery, house breaking (during night hours), house breaking (during day hours), and motor cycle robbery. The minor crimes include gambling (roadside), gambling (at house), gambling (Satta) and blackmarketing of cinema tickets. The data were collected under the above mentioned headings for the year 1979. The crimes of different types which were reported at different police stations (sixteen in number) of the City were grouped according to major areas, namely, walled city, Eastern outer area (excluding the walled City) and Western outer area. All the three spatial units display distinct patterns of density of population, functional land-use, interaction and socio-economic level including literacy, language, religion, economic condition and social backwardness.

The study takes into account the variety of socio-economic factors of micro urban area for the analysis of crime phenomenon. The cartographic presentation of the data on crimes helps us in comprehending the spatial patterns and processes.

Conceptual Framework

In the field of Social Geography the issues such as social well-being, social justice, social equalities and orders are discussed in detail. Crime is an important and severe social deviance which erupts to the surface as a result of underlying social disharmony. The reasons for crime could be social, psychological, economic or a combination of all. Hence, it is necessary to relate the crime statistics of different areas to their social, psychological and economic conditions respectively. The crimes ranging from black marketing of cinema tickets to murder show certain associations with socio-psychological and economic factors. The following possible associations can be evaluated by analysing the data.

1. The higher the density of population, the higher will be incidence of crime.
2. The higher the proportion of illiterate people, the higher will be the rate of crime.
3. The higher the proportion of people belonging to the backward communities, the higher will be incidence of crime.
4. The higher the proportion of persons per room, the higher will be the rate of crime.
5. The higher incidence of crime is associated with the higher proportion of labourers engaged in industrial activity.
6. The less severe crimes (house breaking, robbery, and gambling) occur in the more prospective areas (upper class residential areas.).
7. The black marketing of cinema tickets is higher in older cinema houses (of old areas) than in the newer ones (of newer areas).
8. The areas of constant and intense interaction (frictional areas) are prone to conflict and crimes.

Social Attributes of Areas

The patterns of density of population, internal living density, literacy, religion, caste, and communities have evolved over a period of time depending upon the functional emphasis. In case of Ahmedabad City the areas of pre-industrial, industrial and the post-industrial nature can be identified distinctly as walled city, outer areas to the east of Sabarmati river and outer areas to the west of Sabarmati river. The walled city is characterised by high density of population, moderate density of persons per room, higher literacy, high proportions of houses under non-residential land-use, high concentration of homogeneous population (Muslims, Jains, Hindus) and low caste Hindus at the outskirts of the walled city (Table 15.1). The outer area in the east is characterised by moderate density of population, high internal living density (with labourers' chawls), low level of literacy, high concentration of low caste Hindus (in Asarwa and Saraspur areas), cosmopolitan nature of societies (reflected in South Indian Housing Societies and the large number of Primary Schools having different languages as medium of instruction) and the newer industrial pockets. The area lying on the western side of the Sabarmati river is quite different from the areas mentioned earlier. This area is characterised by low density of population, low internal living density, moderate to high literacy, moderate female literacy and large number of educational and cultural institutions. The types of buildings and residential structures, shopping arcades, the number of cars and the English medium schools indicate the high socio-economic status of residents and their style of living. These social areas can be synthesised for the better understanding of incidence of crime, if the functional or economic aspects are introduced.

Functional Areas

By and large, the urban workers in Indian cities are compelled (by economic forces) to choose residential locations closer to their place of work because of their economic conditions. This fact is more true in case of working class engaged in manufacturing and construction activities. Persons engaged in trading activity prefer to stay in the same building for the convenience and security. The patterns of functional land-use (manufacturing and trading) and the distribution of workers engaged in such activities are related (Table 15.2). The census data reveal the predominance of workers engaged in manufacturing activity on the eastern outer area. Similarly the urban land-use data and maps reveal the intensive industrial activity (especially the textile, chemical and engineering) on the eastern outer area. The predominance of workers engaged in trade and commerce is observed in the walled city where the retail and wholesale marketing is a dominant feature. The workers and the agencies engaged in transportation and storage of industrial and commercial goods are conveniently located midway between industrial and commercial core areas. Table 15.2 also reveals the distribution of car owners having a bias to the outer areas. Nearly 72 per cent of the total car owners reside in outer areas with a slightly higher proportion in the eastern outer area. This is probably due to the large number of companies owning cars. The three areas discussed above (walled city, eastern outer area and western outer area) have the predominance of commercial activity, industrial activity and the educational, cultural and administrative activity respectively. It will be interesting to know the incidence of various types of crimes with a background of social and economic attributes of these areas.

TABLE 15.1: Some Selected Social Indicators (Areawise)

Localities	Density of population per hectare	Number of persons per room	Sex Ratio	Percentage Literacy	Percentage Female Literacy	Percentage of S.C. Population	Percentage of Residential Houses
Walled City	875	2.92	894	67.96	60.71	4.03	21.15
Outer Area (East)	178	3.43	793	51.80	40.00	17.32	15.25
Outer Area (West)	66	2.66	852	65.49	58.61	8.59	11.94
Ahmedabad City	171	3.21	833	59.02	50.06	11.77	16.21

Source: Census of India Gujarat, 1971.

Patterns of Incidence of Crimes

The data on crimes has been collected in major and minor categories from all police stations of the city. Table 15.3 and Table 15.4 show certain interesting spatial associations. The total number of major and minor crimes is high in the eastern outer area compared to the other two areas. The major crimes are relatively low in number in the walled city compared to the two outer areas. This phenomenon is partially due to homogeneous and heterogeneous nature of the areas. Gambling, especially roadside gambling and satta, is a common feature of the industrial areas. Similarly black marketing of cinema tickets is associated with the crowded environment of the walled city. The dense locality, small lanes and by-lanes are favourable for such activities. Among the major crimes murder is by far the extreme one. Nearly 50 per cent of the total murders recorded in the city during 1979 have taken place in the eastern outer area (industrial environment). The intensity of robbery and house breaking during night time is also quite high in the same area. The major crimes of the western outer area are mainly house breaking (during day and night times) and motor cycle robbery (Fig. 15.1). The area is inhabited by fairly well-to-do families. Out of the total number of minor crimes committed in the city about 40 per cent occur each in the walled city and the eastern outer area. The gambling, especially the roadside gambling and satta, accounts for more than 60 percent of the total number of minor crimes within the mentioned areas, as well as in the whole city. The gambling at house is not significant in any area but relatively it shows a bias to the walled city. Even within the crowded area such activities can thrive without making it public (Fig. 15.2). In brief, it can be stated that the total number of crimes show high incidence in the eastern outer area.

TABLE 15.2: Some Selected Economic Indicators (Areawise)

Localities	Percentage of Workers in				Female Participation in work	Dependency Ratio	Percentage of car owners
	Manufacturing H.H & Construction	Trade & Commerce	Total Storage & Commerce	Other Services			
Walled City	24.22	41.61	23.12	27.59	6.59	2.79	27.5
Outer Area (East)	66.12	39.29	57.03	46.11	7.48	2.35	37.0
Outer Area (West)	9.43	19.09	19.85	26.29	9.56	2.66	35.6
Ahmedabad City	50.84	19.91	7.39	21.85	7.57	2.62	–

The walled city ranks a close second in the total number of crimes committed. The western outer area, though has a high number of major crimes recorded next to eastern outer area, the overall intensity of crimes is only to the extent of 13 per cent of the total crimes recorded in the city during 1979. The emerging pattern of crimes shows a fairly reasonable association with the social and economic aspects of the areas.

TABLE 15.3: Major Crimes in Ahmedabad City during 1979

Localities	Murder	Dacoity	Robbery	Sub Total	Day	House Breaking		Sub Total	Total
						Night	Motor Cycle Robbery		
Walled City	19(59.4) (29.2)	7(21.8) (87.5)	6(18.8) (23.0)	32 (32.3)	22(17.5) (22)	42(33.3) (18.1)	62(49.2) (38.5)	126 (25.5)	158 (26.7)
Outer Area (East)	32(65.3) (49.2)	1(2.0) (12.5)	16(32.7) (61.5)	49 (49.4)	33(17.0) (33)	21(62.4) (52.1)	40(20.6) (24.8)	194 (39.3)	243 (41.0)
Outer Area (West)	14(77.8) (21.6)	—	4(22.2) (15.5)	18 (18.3)	45(15.0) (45)	69(39.9) (29.8)	59(34.1) (36.7)	173 (35.2)	191 (32.3)
Ahmedabad City	65(65.6)	8(8.2)	26(26.2)	99	100(20.3)	232(47.1)	161(32.6)	493	592

Source: Police Commissioner's Office, Ahmedabad.

Note: Figures in parentheses indicate percentages.

TABLE 15.4: Minor Crimes in Ahmedabad City during 1979

Localities	Gambling			Sub Total	Black marketing (Cinema Tickets)	Total
	Road side	At house	Satta			
Walled City	1309(53.6) (41.6)	27(1.1) (61.3)	1106(45.3) (41.3)	2442 (41.6)	1253(33.9) (49.1)	3695 (43.9)
Outer Area (East)	1545(54.2) (49.1)	13(0.4) (29.5)	1295(45.4) (48.4)	2853 (48.6)	874(23.5) (34.2)	3727 (44.3)
Outer Area (West)	291(51.1) (9.3)	4(0.7) (9.2)	274(48.2) (10.3)	569 (9.8)	422(42.6) (16.7)	991 (11.8)
Ahmedabad City	3145(53.6)	44(0.8)	2675(45.6)	5864	2549(30.3)	8413

Source: Police Commissioner's Office, Ahmedabad.
Note: Figures in parentheses indicate percentages.

Table 15.5 shows the incidence of crimes in relation to the unit of population. The proportion of crimes per ten thousand population (projected) show correspondence with the density of population and concentration of heterogeneous population belonging to different linguistic States and religions of India. The incidence of major and minor crimes is quite conspicuous in the walled city. In the walled city gambling and black marketing activities per ten thousand population is more than twice than that of the eastern outer areas as the crowded lanes and by-lanes provide ample opportunities to maintain privacy in the mixed land-use of the walled city. Nearly 21 per cent of the houses are used for non-residential purposes such as commercial, trading, household industries and miscellaneous. The gambling and black marketing activities thrive in the old residential areas perhaps in the name of commercial or trading activity.

The proportion of non-Gujarati medium primary schools indicates the underlying cosmopolitan nature of the society. The walled city has large number of Urdu medium primary schools (46 in number) reflecting the large proportion of Muslim population, especially in the areas of Kalupur, Dariapur and Jamalpur. The eastern outer area has 38 schools having Urdu as medium, 45 schools with Hindi medium and 8 schools have different South Indian languages as medium of instruction. A high incidence of crimes in the walled city and Eastern outer area is mainly correlated with the concentration of heterogeneous population.

FIG. 15.1:

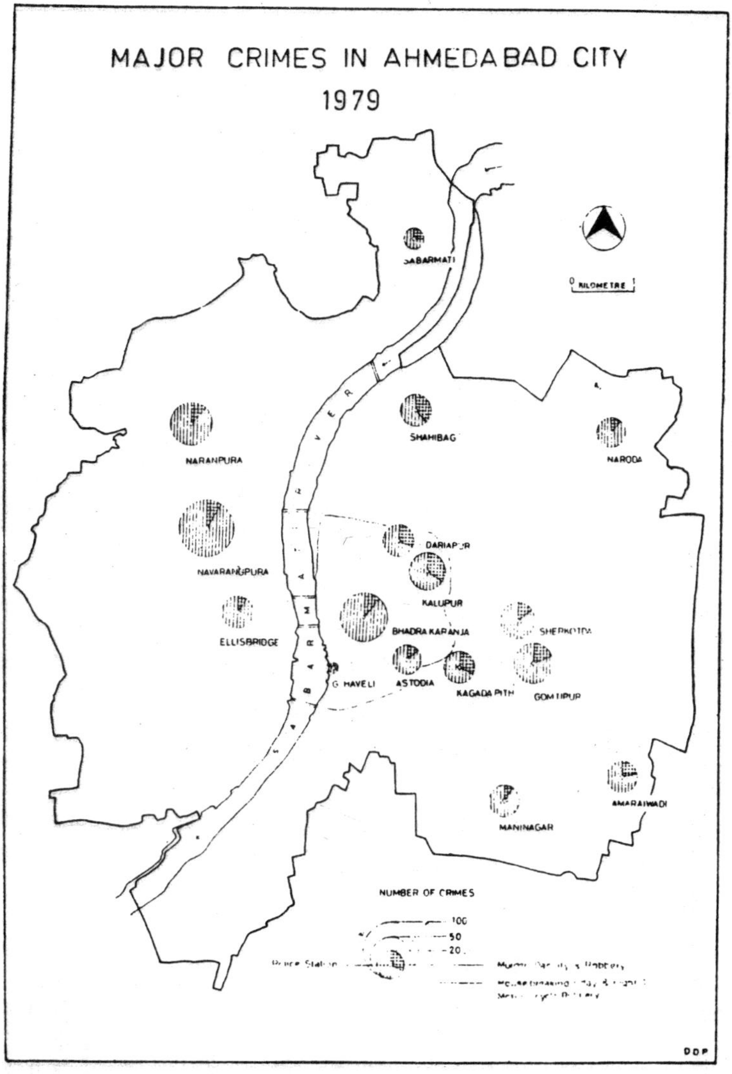

Thus the incidence of crime is most often an urban phenomena which is characterised by: regional and religious diversities, mixed land use, high density of population, substandard housing, high dependency ratio and high proportion of females.[1]

TABLE 15.5: Crimes and Some Indicators

Locality	Projected Population for 1979	Density per Hectare	Number of Crimes Per 10,000 Population: Major Crimes: Murder, Dacoity and Robbery	Major Crimes: House Breaking (Day and Night) Motor Cycle Robbery	Minor Crimes: Gambling, (Roadside, at house) Satta	Minor Crimes: Black Mktg. Cinema Tickets	Number of non-Gujarati* Primary Schools	Percent of non-residential houses	Number of Police Stations
1. Walled City	4,98,718	908.03	0.6	2.5	48.9	25.1	71	21.15	5
2. Outer Area (East)	12,47,840	265.4	0.4	1.6	22.9	7.0	124	15.25	6
3. **Outer Area** (West)	5,54,168	136.9	0.3	3.1	10.3	7.6	20	11.94	4
Ahmedabad City	23,00,726	247.4	0.4	2.1	25.5	11.1	215	16.21	15

Note: *Where medium of instruction is other than regional language.
Walled City has Primary Schools having other mediums: Urdu-46, Sindhi-5, Hindi-5, Marathi-4 and English-11.
Outer Area (East): Urdu-38, Sindhi-6, Hindi-45, Marathi-13, English-14 and South Indian Languages-8.
Outer Area (West): Sindhi-3, English-16 and South Indian Languages-1.

FIG. 15.2

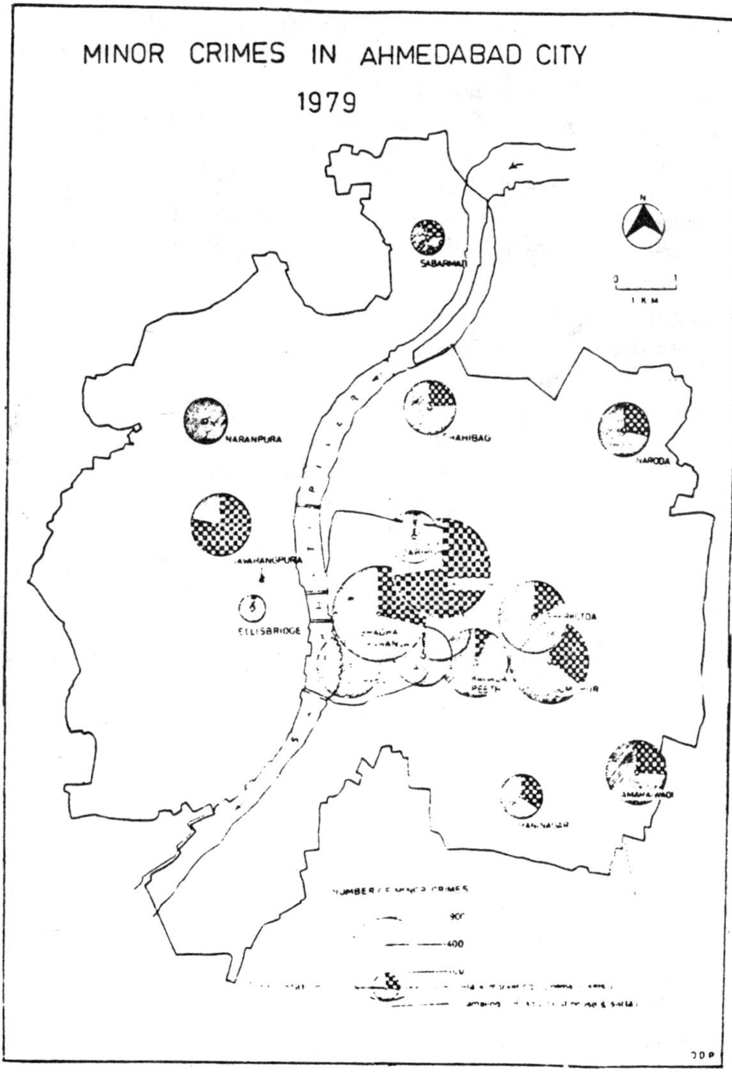

Conclusion

The foregoing analysis brings out certain interesting results which can be further tested under similar situations elsewhere in India and abroad.

1. The eastern outer area, where high incidence of crime is recorded is characterised by high internal living density (more number of persons per room), high proportion of illiterate population, high concentration of socially backward communities and high proportion of workers engaged in industrial activity.
2. The densely populated walled city also experiences high rate of crimes but of less severe nature. The blackmarketing of cinema tickets and gambling (roadside and satta) are the important crimes of the area.
3. The walled city being the core of the city for commercial, administrative, religious and cultural purposes has an intensive interaction resulting into social conflicts and tensions.
4. The western outer area which is inhabited predominantly by the residents of middle and upper economic class shows insignificant proportion of crimes. However, the housebreaking and motor cycle robbery are relatively important in the area.

REFERENCE

1. Murray R. and F.W. Boal: The Social Ecology of Urban Violence in D.T. Herbert & R.J. Johnston (Eds) *Social Areas in Cities*, John Wiley & Sons Ltd. (1979).

PART – VII

HISTORICAL GEOGRAPHY

SIXTEEN

Paul B. Wilson and Darshan S. Kang

The Sources of Jadeite in Middle American Cultural Artifacts: A Geographical Approach

Introduction

THE stone called Jade[1] has been found in connection with many of the prehistoric civilisations of the world. Numerous primitive people singled out this stone apparently for its toughness and durability in making knife blades, axe heads, and other implements needing that quality. More advanced societies have used jade for the material used in figurines, jewellery, and similar art forms. Some incorporated jade into their religion and mythology to the extent that it came to be considered sacred and symbolised purity, power, and authority. Beginning with the Shang Dynasty in China (1200-1400 B.C.), Jade has played an extremely important role in Chinese Civilisation. Attributed to it were extraordinary healing powers and its value was set higher than gold. Similarly, the jade of early Meso America was apparently held in high esteem, and only those of high rank and authority possessed it. At the time of the Spanish Conquest of Mexico, Cortes was surprised to find that jade was the most valued of any of the objects in Montezuma's treasury.[2]

As a gem stone jade has a number of unusual properties that are of interest to its context with early civilisation. Jade is a hard stone, varying from about 6.5 (Nephrite) to 7 (Jadeite) on the Moh scale of hardness. This may be compared with a hardness of 2.5 for amber, 5 for diopside, 6 for turquoise, 7 for quartz, 8 for spinel or topaz, 9 for corundum, and 10 for diamond.[3] While jade does not rank at the top of the hardness scale, still it is one of the world's toughest stones and fractures only with extreme difficulty. The internal structure of jade is fibrous and it largely lacks zones of weakness along cleavage planes. Because of this, jade is a very poor stone for chipping. If it is made to fracture, it splinters into a myriad of irregular shapes. On the other hand, jade is one of the finest stones for grinding since its toughness allows harsh treatment in handling without breaking. Fine grinding and cutting on jade may give the impression that it is carved or sculptured; and, consequently, it is a favoured stone for producing intricate art works. It is these characteristics, along with the natural beauty of the stone, that most likely made it so valuable to the people of early civilisations. Once the early jade worker had managed to shape the stone, it had the durability of iron and was vastly favoured over other stone items. In addition, jade easily takes and retains a high polish from either wood or leather. Many jade artifacts that have been buried thousands of years still retain their polish.

Jade was a ubiquitous material among the pre-conquest civilisations of Meso America. As an artifact, it has been found in most of the major excavations dating from the early Olmec civilisations in Tabasco or Veracruze and before. It apparently circulated widely in trade, and as tribute throughout the area to the extent that numerous varieties and qualities of jade have been thoroughly intermixed. Even so, individual excavations have yielded distinct jades that may be recognised on the basis of their shading, mottling, colour, and mineralogical composition. Many of the jade specimens from Kaminaljuy, the Peten, Copan, and British Honduras, for example, are a clouded green and white colour with flakes of brilliant green sprinkled throughout. Many of the Olmec jades, on the other hand, are a fine blue-green colour; while the jade from Teotihuacan is almost entirely of a dull grey colour.[4]

The different Meso American Jades would tend to suggest that they came from a number of distinct sources. While the colour and composition of jade may vary strikingly within the same lens or vein and even within the same stone or boulder, it is hardly likely that such gross differences on the scale of the findings in Meso America could be explained in that manner. This problem is over-shadowed, however, by the fact that to date there has been no confirmed discovery of a natural occurrence of jade any where within Meso America. So, it becomes not simply a question of where the different grades of Meso American jade came from, but where any of it came from. While mention was made by the Spanish of a "piedra verde" or green stone called "chalchihuitl" by the Aztecs, the question of the source of jade did not seriously come to the attention of anthropologists until the beginning of the present century.[5] After the important discoveries of the Leyden Plate and the Tuxtla Statuette, however, the question of the source of Meso American jade became very important . A communication to W.H. Homes in June 1892 concerning the discovery of the Tuxtla Statuette reveals some of the consternation created by the matter:

Dear Sir:

I send you herewith two photographs of a jade idol which was dug up by the plow in the district of San Andre's Tuxtla on the Gulf of Mexico, about 100 miles southeast of Veracruz. I have had it photographed on account of its material and of the hieroglyphics in the hope that both may be of some archaeological value. I believe that jade is not found in this country, so that the material and the design and possibly the hieroglyphics would seem to be points in the favor of the theory of an Oriental origin for some of the inhabitants of ancient Mexico.

Yours very truly,
Alfred Bishop Mason[6]

Most archaeologists and anthropologists currently working with the problem no longer adhere to the theory that Meso American jade came from the Orient. This conclusion has been drawn partly on the fact that so much jade has been found in Meso America, and so much more is likely to be found; that a source somewhere in Asia would not only have involved trans-Pacific contacts, but a mature shipping industry of some consequence as well. Still, this paper will not rule out the possibility. Current thought has it, rather, that Meso American jade had an indigenous source and that at some time in the future, this source will be discovered.[7]

Jade, like most things in nature, does not occur without design unless disturbed and scattered by man. Accordingly, there must be parts of the earth more likely to have jade than others; depending upon the factors of its genesis and the type of minerals, geologic structure, and landscape with which it may be associated. The purpose of this paper is to explore the possible sources of jade in Meso America. If existing world source areas of jade can be inventoried and other possible source areas suggested, a major step will have been made toward the ultimate solution of the problem. Orderly field investigation, of course, will be necessary to eventually find the actual source of Meso American jades; and the object here is to only narrow that search by indicating likely places to look. The method employed is to start with a world-wide jade universe and eliminate all but the possible source areas, after which these areas are roughly ranked according to the authors' view to the likelihood of their being the source of Meso American jade.

What is Jade?

Before any inventory of actual and possible source areas of jade can be made, it is first necessary to establish the characteristics and varieties of the material along with the nature of its origin and associated mineral and rock complexes, and geologic structure. The term jade is actually a general term loosely applied to several distinct minerals and mineral complexes which are similar in appearance. The two major jade minerals are Nephrite and Jadeite, each belonging to separate mineral groups.[8]

Nephrite belongs to the amphibole group of minerals and is actually a compact, fibrous variety of the actinolite-tremolite series. Tremolite is a calcium-magnesium silicate [$Ca_2Mg_5\ Si_8O_{22}(OH)_2$], usually white or grey in colour. Actinolite is essentially the same mineral except that part of the magnesium is replaced by ferrous iron. The ferrous iron may replace any proportion of the magnesium, and it is responsible for the green colour of the complex. In one form the actinolite-tremolite series is a type of asbestos well known for both its heat and acid resistant properties. Nephrite is chemically the same mineral, but is extremely hard (6–6.5) and amounts to one of the most difficult to break of all of the minerals. Its durability is explained by the fiberous and interwoven complex of crystals that appear almost like felt beneath the microscope.[9] Nephrite is the more common of the jade minerals, and occurs in a number of places about the world (Fig. 16.1). Among the more notable locations are New Zealand, Tibet, Wyoming and Alaska.[10]

Jadeite is a member of the pyroxene group of minerals and chemically is a sodium aluminum silicate ($NaAISi_2O_6$). Jadeite is commonly associated with the related pyroxenes of diopside ($CaMgSi_2O_6$) and acmite ($NaFeSi_2O_6$), which blend with the mineral in varying amounts to give it its colour and variable translusence. Varieties of jadeite have been assigned the names diopside-jade or tuxtlite when mixed with diopside, or chlormelanite or mayatite when mixed with acmite; but

FIG. 16.1:

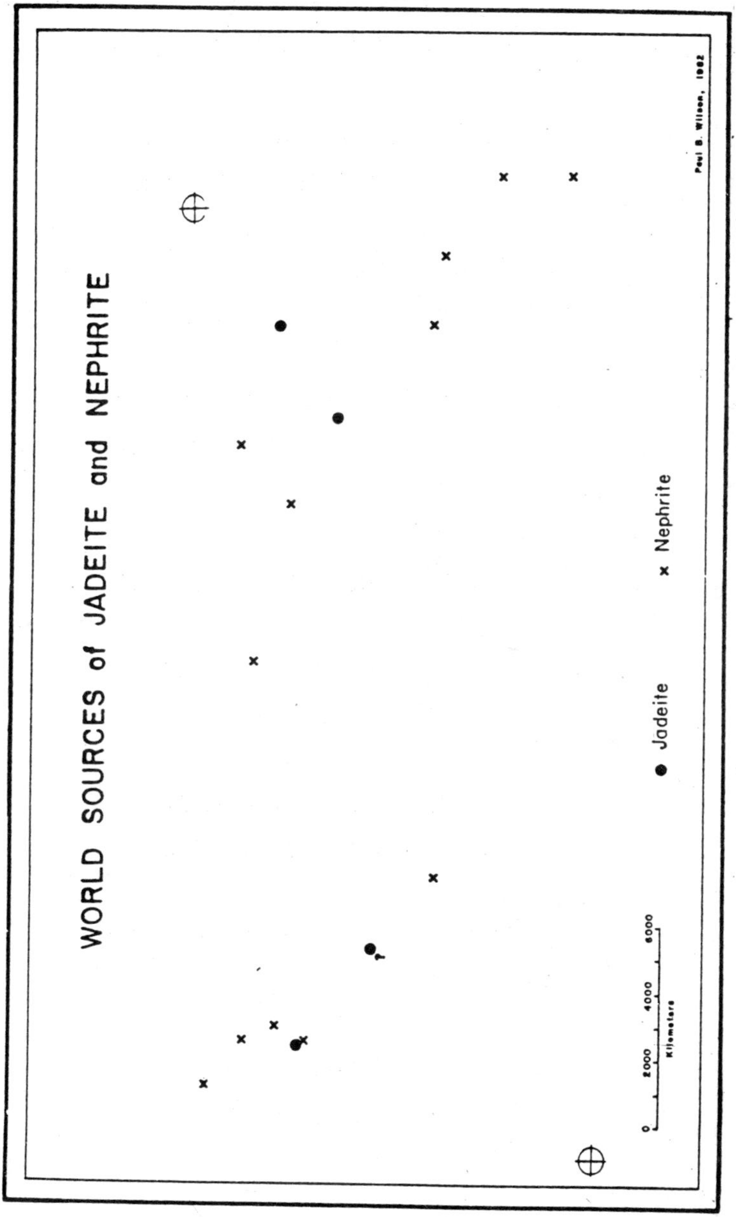
WORLD SOURCES of JADEITE and NEPHRITE
Jadeite
Nephrite
0
2000
4000
6000
Kilometers
Paul B. Wilson, 1982

FIG. 16.2:

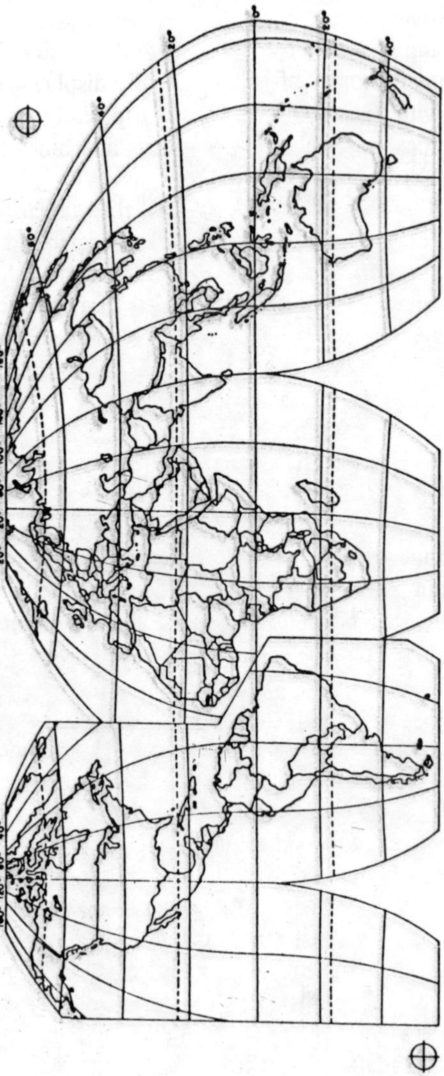

many mineralogists feel this is an unfortunate duplication of terminology.[11] Although jadeite is harder than nephrite, it lacks the same toughness and is inclined to break with a sharp blow somewhat more easily. This is mainly due to the crystalline composition. Instead of the interwoven, fibrous arrangement of crystals, as in nephrite, jadeite is composed entirely of anhedral or subhedral grains of pyroxene. Many examples of jadeite actually display crystal grains that may be seen with the naked eye. This is especially true of the lighter-coloured varieties, while the darker greens and blues tend to be finer grained.[12]

Jadeite is a much more scarce mineral than nephrite, and there are only few sites in the world that provide appreciable amounts suitable for commercial production (Fig 16.1). The most notable of these is the deposit at Tawmaw, Burma, which consists of a vein or dike of almost pure jadeite measuring roughly 182 mt wide and 1315 mt long at the surface.[13] Today, the Burma jadeite makes up the bulk of jade used by China, but before 1784 when it was introduced into the market, virtually all of the Chinese jade consisted of nephrite from Tibet.[14] A second locality is found in Japan near the village of Kotaki. This deposit was first discovered in 1938 along the bed of the Kotaki River and there was no evidence of it having been previously worked.[15] A third notable finding of jadeite was made during the summer of 1950 in San Benito County, California by H.S.Yoder.[16]

Only jadeite has been found among the jade artifacts of ancient Meso America. Nephrite, apparently, was unknown to these early people even though it has since been found at several sites in the Americas. A number of early anthropological sources actually refer to Meso American nephrites, but more careful work since has revealed that this must have been a misuse of terminology. A confirmed deposit of jadeite still remains to be found anywhere within Meso America. While no deposits have been found, however, it is interesting to note that a number of apparently natural nodules of jadeite have been reported found in river beds in the Mexican states of Morelos, Buerrero, Oaxaca, and Chiapas; not to mention adjacent Guatemala. Still, these finds are scanty and mainly unconfirmed, and can hardly explain the abundance of jade artifacts in Meso America.[17]

The Genesis of Jadeite

Where the deposits of any mineral are not actually found, the point of its origin still remains in doubt even though the mineral appears widespread in fragmentary form. Purple quartzite, apparently from the Laurentian Shield in Canada, is spread over thousands of square km. in the northern United States, for example; yet, the only way one may actually be certain of its point of origin would be to find the deposits in Canada. The same is true of the jadeite in Meso America. Until the actual deposits are found, their point of origin is in doubt even though they may appear abundantly as artifacts, and on rare occasion as natural pebbles. If jadeite actually was deposited in Meso America, clues to its point of origin surely must be found in the nature of its genesis. If one understands how a mineral is formed, he must surely better understand where it was formed; or, at least in what type of situation it was formed.

Unfortunately, mineralogists are not altogether certain how jadeite came to be. As of yet no one has been able to produce a synthetic jadeite; where the synthetic saphire, emerald, ruby and diamond have been mastered long ago. It was originally thought that jadeite was formed as a result of great pressure and heat. A relatively recent study by Hatten S.Yoder, however, has established that jadeite is unstable at greater than 800°C. at virtually any pressure, and crystallises into nepheline and albite. Yoder concluded that jadeite must form at temperatures below 800°C. in the presence of volatiles. The composition of the volatiles is apparently the unknown in the formula, for Yoder was unable to pin it down. He did make a number of interesting associations between the occurrence of jadeite and related minerals and geologic structure, however. Even if these do not provide the key for the origin of jade, at least they indicate the type of situation in which it may be expected to occur.[18]

The most adequately studied jadeite deposit is the one located in Burma. This deposit is intimately associated with the minerals serpentine, amphibolite, and albite; which in turn form part of a metamorphic matrix. The jadeite deposit was found in the form of a vein either intruded into or compressed between a surrounding mass of serpentine. The following figure taken from Yoder shows a cross-section of the Burma deposit (Fig. 16.2).[19]

The metamorphic environment of the formation of jadeite at this location is further accentuated by the fact that serpentine is, itself, a metamorphosed version of olivine, which in turn is a plutonic rock.[20]

The jadeite deposit in Japan is located in a strikingly similar situation to the Burma deposit. Again, the jadeite was found in serpentine and was partly mixed with albite. In this instance, however, the relationship to surrounding metamorphics was less clear, since the serpentine was bordered on at least one side by limestone. It is felt, however, that the serpentine and the jadeite both were a product of contact metamorphism of the faulted limestone.[21]

The recent discovery of jadeite in California did little to alter the concept of the jadeite environment outlined above. At this site the jadeite was found in numerous small lenses varying from several cm to several mt in diameter. In each instance the jadeite was found within a serpentine mass, which in turn was surrounded by schist.[22] Thus, the correlation of jadeite with serpentine and a general environment of metamorphic rock would appear to be consistent. This relationship is fundamental to the thesis developed in this paper, since it is used to establish the pattern of possible sources of jadeite.

The Possible Source of Jadeite: The Orient

The point was made early in this paper that one of the arguments against the hypothesis that Meso American jadeite originated in the Orient was the very quantity of jade artifacts found. It has been suggested that this would represent more than casual contact between Meso America and the Orient, which is not supported by laboratory evidence. It should be pointed out, however, that this alone is not satisfactory evidence for the rejection of the Orient jadeite hypothesis. Instead, there are a number of more serious obstacles making it unlikely that the Orient was the source of the Meso American jadeite. One of these has to do with the mineralogical composition of the jadeite itself. Most of the Meso American jadeites are distinctive in that they contain a higher percentage of the mineral diopside ($CaMgSi_2O_6$) than do other representative jadeites about the world. This is shown by Table 16.1 of jadeite analyses taken from Japan, Burma, and Meso America.[23]

Table 16.1 gives a kind of fingerprint test that would not tend to support the theory that the Meso American jades were Oriental in origin; or, if they were they must have come form sites other than the present ones.

Another problem with the Oriental jadeite source hypothesis is simply historical. If Meso America received its jadeite from the Orient, it must be assumed that the Orient in effect shared the jade that it was using at that time. The difficulty here is that jadeite, itself, is a relatively new item in the Orient. It may be recalled that virtually all of the

FIG. 16.2:

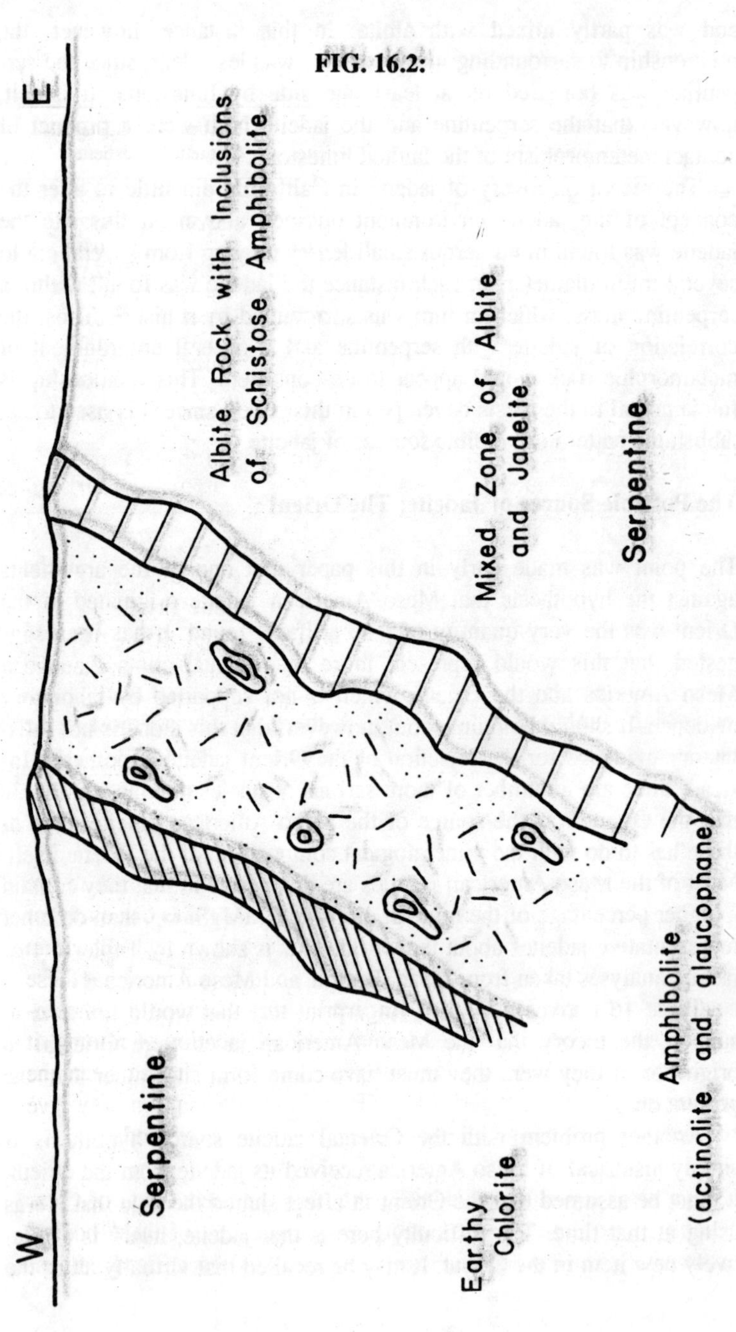
W
E
Serpentine
Earthy Chlorite
Amphibolite (actinolite and glaucophane)
Albite Rock with Inclusions of Schistose Amphibolite
Mixed Zone of Albite and Jadeite
Serpentine

TABLE 16.1: Table of Jadeite Analyses

	Theoretical Composition	Burma Jadeite	Japan Jadeite	Tuxtla Statuette	Guatemala Jadeite
SiO_2	59.4	59.51	58.02	55.50	56.28
TiO_2	----	0.01	0.04	----	0.03
Al_2O_3	25.2	24.31	22.96	12.33	12.18
Cr_2O_3	----	0.01	----	----	----
Fe_2O_3	----	0.35	0.77	1.41	0.85
FeO	----	0.03	0.18	1.33	1.28
MnO	----	0.01	0.01	0.05	0.13
MgO	----	0.58	1.70	8.72	9.02
CaO	----	0.77	1.58	12.76	12.60
Na_2O	15.4	14.37	12.38	6.94	6.32
K_2O	----	0.02	0.16	0.25	0.11
H_2O	----	0.06	0.87	0.30	1.00

jade worked in China prior to 1784 was nephrite.[24] It was not until the discovery of Burmese jadeite that it appeared there in great quantities. The discovery in Japan was even later. It has only been since 1938 that this area has added any jadeite to the world market. Unless Meso America received its Oriental jade form a separate source than China, it seems highly unlikely that it came from there. Otherwise, most of the Meso American artifacts would necessarily be nephrite.

The Possible Source of Jadeite: California

Outside the Orient the only other place that deposits of jadeite are known to exist is in San Benito County, California. The discovery of jadeite in California is remarkable in that it places jadeite well within access of ancient Meso America. What is more remarkable is that these deposits do not appear to have been mined. While the reports concerning this area by Yoder and Chesterman make no mention of mining, it may safely be assumed they would have done so if it had been the source of the Meso American jadeite. Rather, the description they give of the site would lead one to believe it had never been touched:

> Eight large exposures of jadeite were found in the canyon of Clear Creek ... and there are, no doubt, many more. Six of these bodies, completely surrounded by highly sheared and brecciated serpen-

> tine, are lens shaped and do not exceed 50 by 200 feet in outcrop. The seventh, a veinlike body, was found at the contact of the serpentine with an enclosed mass of schist ....Detailed collections of specimens were made across the jadeite bodies where possible. Although an effort was made to secure representative samples, some outcrops did not yield samples, even to heavy sledging.[25]

This passage does not sound like one describing the scene of several millennia of jadeite mining by ancient Meso Americans. Still, a careful field examination should be conducted in this area and other potential sites before California is rejected as the possible source of Meso American jadeite.

The Possible Source of Jadeite: Meso America

Although confirmed deposits of jadeite have not been found in Meso America, this does not rule out the possibility that the source was from there all along. The idea that jade came from Meso America itself is appealing in that this overcomes the problems of trade, transport and foreign connections. Until the actual site of the deposit is found, however, the issue can never be settled one way or the other.

There are a number of localities throughout Meso America and adjacent to it that very possible could have provided jadeite. It will be recalled that in every other instance that jadeite is found intimately associated with serpentine and metamorphic rock. Indeed, it is generally held that jadeite is the product of some phase of metamorphism, as is serpentine. The appearance of the combination of serpentine and metamorphic rock is not uncommon in Meso America, and simply because jadeite has not been discovered in association with them does not rule out the possibility that at some point in the future it may. So far as is ascertainable, in fact, it would not appear that a systematic search has been conducted in these areas to locate either the jadeite or evidence of its extraction. It is the opinion of the authors that such a search would likely establish one or more local sources for Meso American jadeite.

The following map (Fig. 16.3) is taken from a multiplicity of sources which when put together, hopefully shows with some accuracy the known areas in Meso America where metamorphic rock and serpentine coincide.[26] The most notable of these areas of coincidence is in Guatemala north of Guatemala City in the vicinity of the Sierra de las

Minas adjacent to the Motagua river. Extensive deposits of serpentine have long been known to exist as part of the metamorphic complex of these mountains. The great quantity of serpentine located here alone would indicate that this may be a desirable place to begin the search for Meso American jadeite.

Other areas in Meso America which contain associated deposits of serpentine and metamorphic rock include parts of the Mexican states of Chiapas and Puebla. These may also be possible source areas. Another area far to the southeast in Nicaragua also has associated serpentine and metamorphic rock, as does a prominency on the Guajira Peninsula of Columbia. Each of these areas should be examined as well.

The geology of Meso America and surrounding areas is at best not exactly known. Although the areas in which serpentine and metamorphic rocks are known to coincide are probably the best place to begin to search for the source of Meso American jadeite, these are likely not the only places where jadeite may exist. More is known about the distribution of metamorphic rock than about the distribution of serpentine. Consequently, it may be necessary to more exactly establish the total distribution of serpentine in Meso America before the source of jadeite is found.

In the course of this investigation, the authors were led repeatedly to the likelihood that Guatemala is the source of Meso American jadeite. While to date no confirmed deposit of jadeite has been established, a footnote appearing in an article by the late William F. Foshag is of interest. This footnote reads as follows:

> Since this has been written, fine jadeite of a lichen-green colour has been found *in situ* near Manzanal, Guatemala, By Robert Leslie, Guatemala City.[27]

If this report can be confirmed, the subject matter of this paper becomes purely academic.

Conclusion

Existing data on the jadeite of pre-Columbian Meso America would suggest that there are three possible general sources of that mineral--the Orient, California, and Meso America. In the opinion of the authors, the most likely source for the jadeite is Meso America, itself, followed by California and the Orient in that order.

FIG. 16.3 a:

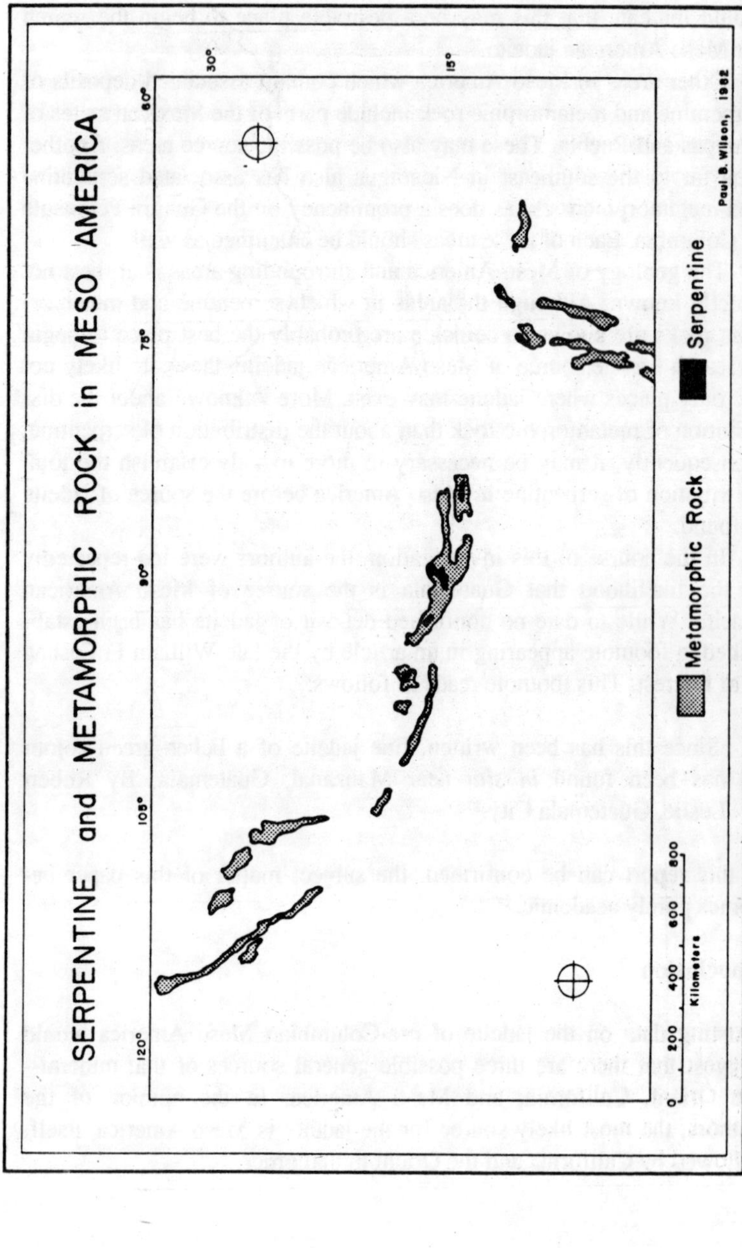
SERPENTINE and METAMORPHIC ROCK in MESO AMERICA
120°
105°
90°
75°
60°
30°
15°
0 200 400 600 800
Kilometers
Metamorphic Rock
Serpentine
Paul B. Wilson, 1982

FIG. 16.3 b:

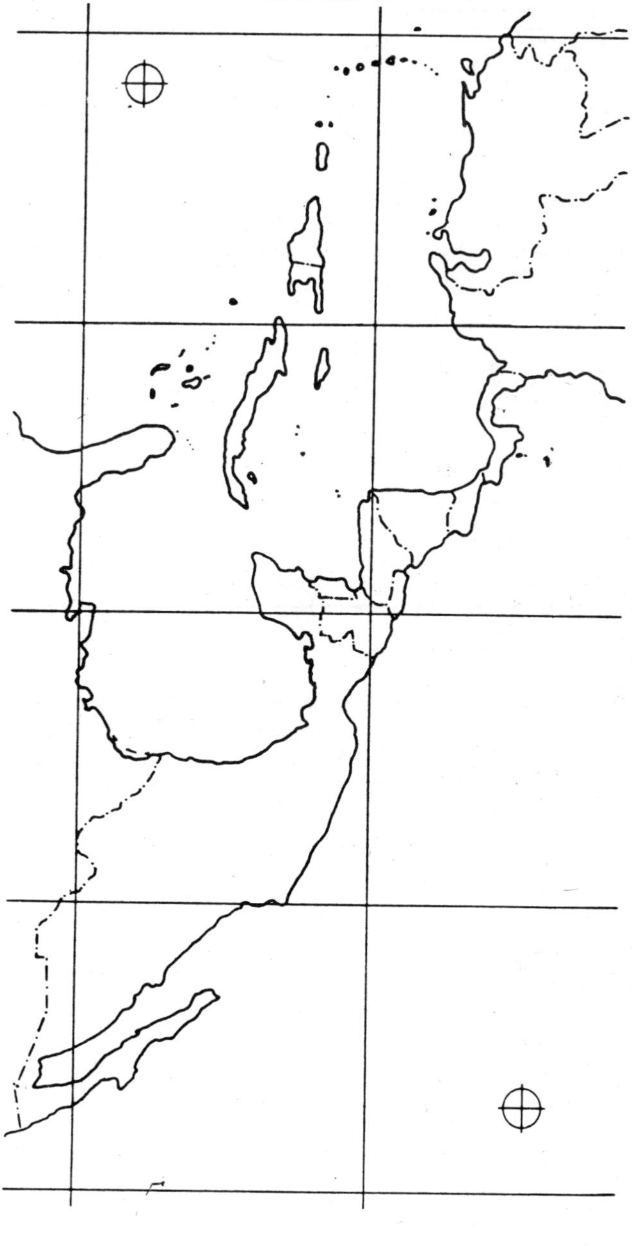

REFERENCES

1. The root of the name jade lies in the end word of PIEDRA DE HIJADA, the Spanish name for jade. See Webster, Robert, *Gems - Their Sources, Description and Identification,* Hamden, Connecticut: Archon Book, (1975), pp.233-234.
2. Gump, Richard, *Jade: Stone of Heaven,* New York: Doubleday and Co., Inc., (1962), pp. 14-19.
3. Anderson,B.W., *Gem Testing* New York:Emerson Books Inc, (1948), pp.234-239.
4. Kidder, Alfred V., Jennings, Jesse D., and Shook, Edwin M., *Excavations at Kaminaljua, Guatemala,* Washington: Carnegie Institution of Washington, Publication 561, (1946), pp. 104-105.
5. Foshag, William F., "Mineralogical Studies on Guatemalan Jade,"*Smithsonian Miscellaneous Collections,* Vol. 135, No. 5 (December, 1957), pp. 7-11.
6. Holmes,W.H.,"On a Nephrite Statuette from San Andres Tuxtla, Vera Cruz, Mexico,"*American Anthropologist,* Vol. 9 (1907), p. 691.
7. Foshag, *op. cit.,* pp. 11-12.
8. In this paper the term "Jade" has been used to refer to two mineral species, - nephrite and jadeite. For details of differences in their chemical and physical properties see Webster, *op. cit.,* pp. 223-234; and Lapedes, Daniel N., *McGraw-Hill Encyclopedia of the Geological Science,* New York: McGraw Hill, (1978), pp. 394-395.
9. Crippen, Richard A., Jr., "*Nephrite Jade and Associated Rocks of the Cape San Martin Region, Monterey County California,*" State of California, Department of Natural Resources, Division of Mines, Special Report 10-A (May, 1951), p. 4.
10. Gump, *op.cit.,* pp. 39-44.
11. Foshag, *op. cit.,* pp. 14-17.
12. Washington, Henry S., "The Jades of Middle America, "*Proceedings of the National Academy of Sciences,* Vol. 8 (1922), pp. 319-321.
13. Yoder, Hatten S., Jr., "The Jadeite Problem,"*American Journal of Science,* Vol. 248 (1950), pp. 237-240.
14. Gump, *op.cit.,* pp.181-184.
15. Yoder, *op cit.,* pp. 240-242.
16. Yoder, H.S. and Chesterman, C.W., "*Jadeite of San Benito County, California,* "State of California, Department of Natural Resources, Division of Mines, Special Report 1--C(September, 1951), pp.3-8.
17. Kidder, *op. cit.* p. 105.
18. Yoder, *op, cit.,* p. 318-323.
19. *Ibid.,* p. 238.
20. Hurlbut, Cornelius S., *Dana's Manual of Mineralogy,* New York: John Wiley and Sons, Inc., (1959), pp. 516-519.
21. Yoder, *op. cit.,* pp. 240-242.
22. Yoder and Chesterman, *op. cit.,* pp. 3-8.
23. Foshag, *op. cit.,* p. 16 and Yoder, *op. cit.,* p.241.
24. Webster, *op. cit.* p. 223.
25. Yoder and Chesterman, *op. cit.,* p.3.
26. Schuchert, Charles, *Historical Geology of the Antilleon-Caribbean Region,* New York: John Wiley and Sons, Inc. (1935), pp. 31, 367-368, 323, 338.
    Garfias, Valentin R. and Chapin, Theodre C., Geologia de Mexico Mexico: Editorial Jus, (1949), pp. 109-115.
    Ministero de Minasy Petroleos, Servicio Geologico Nacional, Mapa Geologico de Columbia, Bogota, D.E. (1962).
    Cserna, Zoltan de, *Tectonic Map of Mexico,* The Geological Society of America (1961).
27. Foshag, *op. cit.,* p.11.

SEVENTEEN

O.P. Singh

Origin and Evolution of Urban Central Places in Uttar Pradesh

UTTAR PRADESH (U.P.), a major part of the ancient 'Madhya Desa' or the middle land, is one of the oldest settled parts of India, which has a long continuous history and civilisation.[1] Even in the palaeolithic period (the old stone age), human beings are supposed to have been inhabiting the Ganga valley, leading a nomadic life. Evolutional developments continued through the neolithic period until the Aryan civilisation was fully established with its fortified and well-defended capital towns, most of which were developed at pre-historic ancient sites but whose reasonable account is lacking. A majority of ancient centres of Uttar Pradesh originated or evolved as administrative strongholds, religious places, clan centres or political capitals. Locations of these centres were also governed, in most cases, by the physical bonds of site and situation.

The account of origin and evolution of the urban central places in U.P. can be divided into three major and nine smaller periods based on the prominent breaks in historical chronology of the State such as:

A. Ancient Period	M. Medieval Period	Z. Modern Period
A_1 Pre-historic	M_1 Early Medieval	Z_1 Pre-British Transition
A_2 Hindu	M_2 Mughal	Z_2 Early British
A_3 Pre-Muslim Transition		Z_3 Post-Revolution Z_4 The Present Century

Further the centres of each period have been divided according to their nature, with four or five groups as under:

1. **Centres found as existing in a period for the first time**

A. As a place (a place, rather than a settlement, with one or two central activities, with or without a small settlement)
B. As a village settlement or a small central place.
C. As a town in the antiquitarian sense or a flourishing large central place.

2. **Centres that originated or established anew in a period**

A. As a settlement (mostly rural in nature and smaller in size, originated in a natural process or by arbitrary human agencies).
B. Built (or rebuilt) as a town or as an important central place.
C. Founded anew as a town ('town' in the old sense)

3. **Centres that developed and grew**

A. Developed or grew into a town (by natural or human forces).
B. Grew and expanded naturally (radially, vertically and qualitatively).
C. Developed or extended by human hands (by introduction of new patches or sectors or by additions of new parts or contiguous areas).

4. **Centres that flourished and prospered**

A. As an important centre or town.
B. As an administrative centre or as political headquarters.
C. As a regional capital or full-fledged central place.

5. **Centres stagnant or decadent**

A. Centres stagnating (or maintained).
B. Centres declining (or decayed).

Thus the distinguishing symbols A_1 to Z_3 indicate the periodicity of the central places, while 1A to 5B indicate their nature of growth. The Appendix gives a consolidated picture of the evolution and growth of the central places in the State indicated by the symbols. Let us review them in their historical perspective.

A_1: The Pre-historic Period

We have little or no authentic historical information of those centres existing before the Buddha period (i.e. before sixth or seventh century B. C.). We have, therefore, grouped them as pre-historic centres. Centres which were existing then as places or small settlements (1A) are Ramnagar, Chitrakut Dham, Sitapur, Vrindavan, Kosi Kalan, Soron, Deoband and Rishikesh. Centres which are supposed to be existing before the Buddha period as small central places (1B) are Sultanpur, Mahoba, Banda, Lucknow, Mainpuri, Hardwar, Meerut, Mawana and Amroha. Meerut, a place of Mahabharat age (named so perhaps after 'Maye', an architect in the days of king Yudhisthir), got a fort in 11th century A.D. and continued to develop upto the Mughal period and again with the establishment of cantonments in 1806, the town grew very fast.

Centres which were existing as large flourishing centres or as 'cities' in the old sense (1C) are: Ayodhya (or Ajodhya, now a part of Faizabad), Prayag (a part of Allahabad), Kashi (Varanasi), Mathura (or Muttra, as called in early days), Kannauj and Sambhal, the first four being also the most important and great places of pilgrimage. Sambhal rose to be an important political seat in Delhi Sultanate and also remained as the capital of Sultan Sikandar Lodi for many years. Kannauj also named as 'Kanyakubja' (in Sanskrit) meaning 'The City of humpbacked maidens; is mentioned by the two Chinese travellers Fa Hian and Hiuen Tsang. The latter visited the town in the 7th century A.D. when it was flourishing most as the capital of Northern India under Harshavardhana. It continued to enjoy an important political and strategic status till the foundation of Farrukhabad in early 18th century, when it was deprived of its former grandeur and magnificence.

The name of Kashi, popularly known even now as 'Banaras' was officially changed to 'Varanasi' on 24.5.1956: It has been, from time immemorial, a great religious and cultural centre of the Hindus. It is a sacred place also for the Jains and the Buddhists. It had remained for centuries the capital of the ancient Kashi kingdom.

Prayag has been more a sacred place of religious worship than a city, till the rise of Allahabad in medieval period. Ayodhya, (meaning 'invincible') which is identical with 'Saket' of the Buddhists and is said to be the chief of the seven cities ('Saptapuri'), is very intimately related with the story of God Rama and the 'Suryavanshi' (solar) race. It was the capital of the Muslim rulers of Avadh till the foundation of Faizabad in about the middle of 18th century. Mathura also is a great religious and old city associated closely with the story of Lord Krishna.

A_2: **Hindu Period** (6th century BC-1018 A.D.)

The real authentic history of the State (as well as of the country) may safely be said to begin with the establishment of the Kingdom of Magadha and several other small republics and kingdoms in about 7th century B. C. and with the commencement of the Buddha period in about 6th century B.C. This period was marked with the rise of Buddhism and Jainism, development of monasteries and growth of several capital centres mentioned also in ancient texts. Old capital cities like Sravasti and Kausambi, which in these early days were among the largest world cities, are non-existent today. The political stability, the interest of kings in urban growth and the good administration of the Mauryan dynasty induced much the rise and growth of towns. Many roads were constructed by Ashoka, including the highway now known as the Grand Trunk Road (running from Peshawar to Calcutta). Many roadside centres, fortified and planned towns and monastic centres came into existence.

The Chinese pilgrim Fa Hian visited the country between 400 and 413 A.D. and he has referred to the greatness of the mighty Gupta kingdom as well as the favourable conditions and growth of various townships. The grandeur of Harshavardhana's (600-647) reign and other conditions have been described by the Chinese traveller Hiuen Tsang who visited the country between 629 and 645 A. D.

Before and after these two periods mentioned above, the entire country was characterised by unstable conditions created by the multiplicity of small chiefs. After Harsha, many clans (including the unaforeseen Rajputs of the west) and aborigines were locally ruling the country also establishing several towns as their strongholds. We have little or obscure historical account of the period between the death of Harshavardhana and the invasion of Mahmud of Ghazni in 1018 A.D.

This whole period is, therefore, sometimes known as 'the dark period'. 'Bhars' who were ruling around Oudh are said to have developed many important towns (viz. Bahraich, Bhadohi, Bara Banki, Rae Bareli). Chandels of Bundelkhand (with capital at Kalinjar) and the Rajputs of the west also developed many centres as strategic points.[2]

Most of the centres or towns of the Hindu period (Fig. 17.1) were founded or developed as administrative capitals or as political strongholds. Again a majority of these centres belong to the dark period (647-1018 A. D.) where again the Rajputs developed perhaps the largest number of centres. Kannauj (4BC), being the capital city, was at the zenith of its prosperity and the most important city in Northern India.[3]

A_3: Pre-Muslims Transitional Period (1018-1206)

This whole period was characterised by political instability and destructive raids and wars, and, therefore, very few towns could be developed in this period. Instead, the towns subjected to battle (viz. Kannauj, Mathura) suffered very much. Certain small towns were, however, developed by the dispersed Rajputs of this period. Ganj Dundwara (1B) was existing as a small settlements. Hamirpur (2A), and Hardoi, Debai, Amroha and Badaun (2B) all these towns were built in this period. Aligarh or 'Koil' (3A) and Meerut (3C) experienced growth before they were captured by the Muslims (Fig. 17.1).

M_1: Early Medieval Period of Delhi Sultanate (1206-1526)

In their attempt to rule and hold the area, the Muslim Sultans built forts and developed certain towns as strategic points (viz. Sambhal) and as administrative centres. Badaun and Ayodhya enjoyed the status of a provincial capital. On the other side, the local and dispersed Rajput clans including the Rajputs of Katehar (or Rohilkhand), in their attempts to strengthen themselves, built and extended several strongholds (viz. Etah, Jalesar, Chhibramau, Biswan, Utraula, Aonla etc.).

Very few towns appear to have been developed under the Khilji dynasty of rulers (1290-1321 A.D.). Ala-ud-din (1295-1316), however, is reported to have taken some interest in the improvement of towns. The succeeding Tughlak sultans (1321-1388 A. D.), established and built a number of centres in their regime [e.g. Khurja, Laharpur,

Saharanpur (founded by Shah Haran Chishti), Fatehpur (Barabanki), Bisauli (Badaun) etc.]

FIG. 17.1:

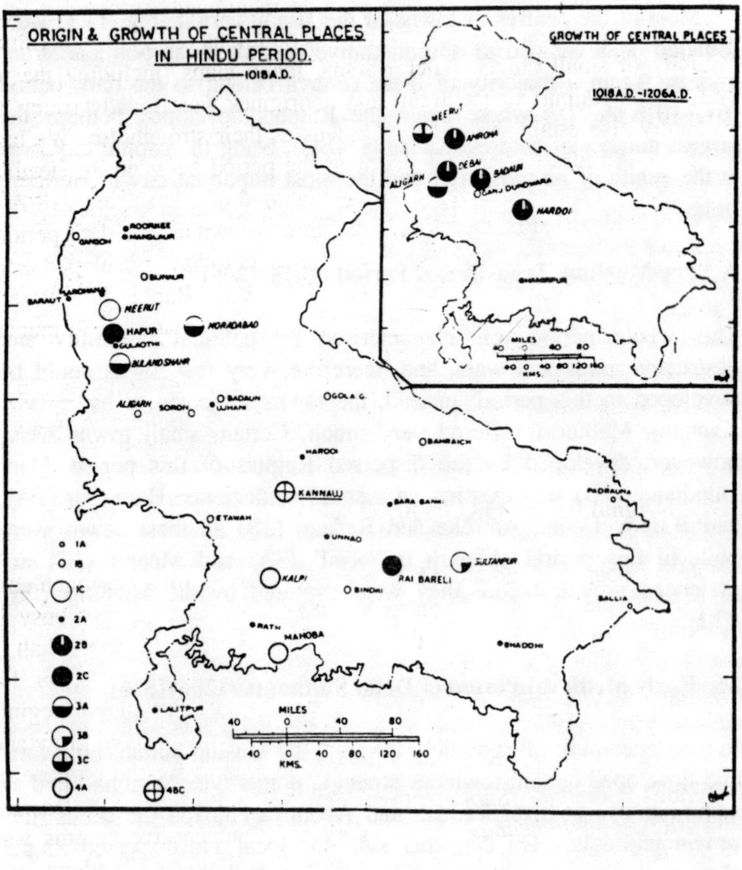

Firoz Shah Tughlak (1351-1388) built the famous city of Jaunpur which later on became the capital of the Sharki (i.e. eastern) kings. The city was built between 1359 and 1364[4] and he named it after 'Juna', the proper name of Mohammad-bin-Tughlak, the preceding emperor.

The Sharki kings later built in the capital city numerous unique and glorious mosques and buildings after demolishing the Hindu temples and palaces. Jaunpur in these days was perhaps the most flourishing city in the country and, therefore, known as the 'Shiraz of India'.[5] The famous fort built by the emperor Firoz Shah was further decorated and developed by these kings. The royal bridge ('Shahi pul') over Gomati wtry between 629 and 645 A. D.

Before and after these two periods mentioned above, the entire country was characterised by unstable conditions created by the multiplicity of small chiefs. After Harsha, many clans (including the unaforeseen Rajputs of the west) and aborigines were locally ruling the country also establishing several towns as their strongholds. We have little or obscure historical account of the period between the death of Harshavardhana and the invasion of Mahmud of Ghazni in 1018 A.D. This whole period is, therefore, sometimes known as 'the dark period'. 'Bhars' who were ruling around Oudh are said to have developed many important towns (viz. Bahraich, Bhadohi, Bara Banki, Rae Bareli). Chandels of Bundelkhand (with capital at Kalinjar) and the Rajputs of the west also developed many centres as strategic points.[2]

Most of the centres or towns of the Hind viz. Sikandra Rao, Sikandrabad, Shikarpur, Kiratpur, Sikandarpur (Ballia) etc. A majority of the centres were developed by Sikandar Lodi (Fig. 17.2).

M_2 : Mughal Period (1526-1707)

Before Akbar, we find a confused picture of the regime not much conducive to the growth of centres, as the rulers were always busy in political turmoils except in the good administration of Sher Shah, a great reformer, who provided an impetus for towns to grow; but his regime was very brief. It is in Akbar's good, stable and tolerant regime (1556-1605) that we find the maximum number of towns to grow and develop (Fig. 17.3). He divided the whole empire for the purpose of administration, into *Subas* (provinces), *Sarkars* (divisions), *Dasturs* (districts) and *Parganas*. A hierarchy of administrative centres was thus established. Old religious centres like Banaras, Mathura and Ayodhya were revived. Akbar built the fort of Agra and made Agra his capital, which, therefore, began to flourish perhaps as the most important city in India.[6] Agra continued to remain as the capital of the succeeding Mughal emperor Jahangir and also of Shahjahan, for a considerable part of his reign. Since the latter part of Shahjahan's reign, Delhi had been enjoying the status of the Mughal capital. In about 1572, Akbar built a fort and a city at the confluence of the Ganga and the Yamuna and the city was named by him as Allahabad or Ilahabad, which became the capital of a province (Suba). Lucknow was made the capital of a 'Sarkar' and was developed much under him.

FIG. 17.2:

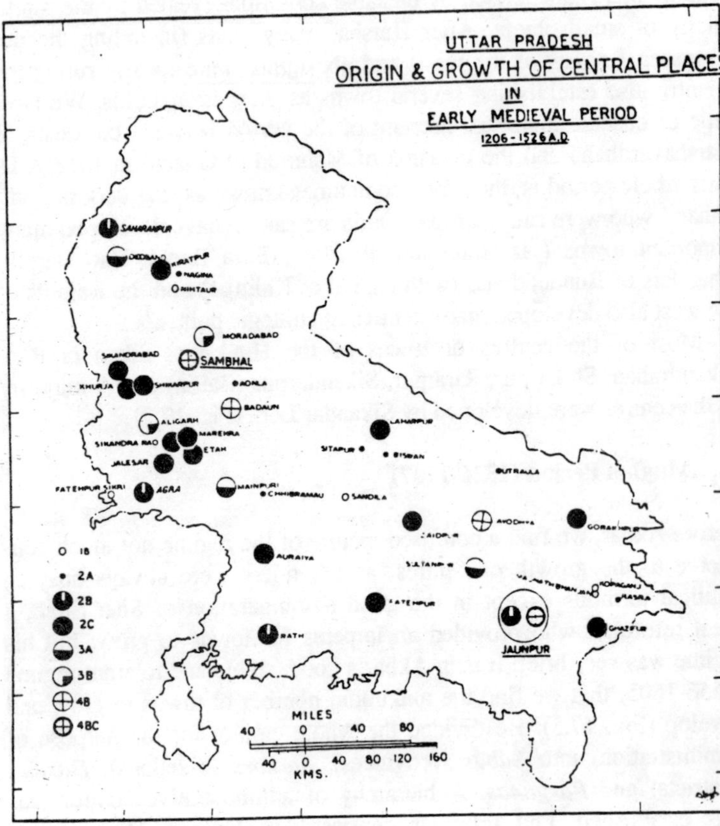

Other important centres (Fig. 17.3) which are ascribed to his reign are Fatehpur Sikri, Firozabad, Itmadpur, Jalalabad (Meerut and Shahjahanpur), Tilhar, Akbarpur and Jalalpur (Faizabad). Mughal Sarai came into existence as a sarai post on the Mughal road, which ran from Delhi to Bengal via Agra and Etawah. Rivers were still serving as important means of communication, though certain roads and roadside inns were also developed.

FIG. 17.3:

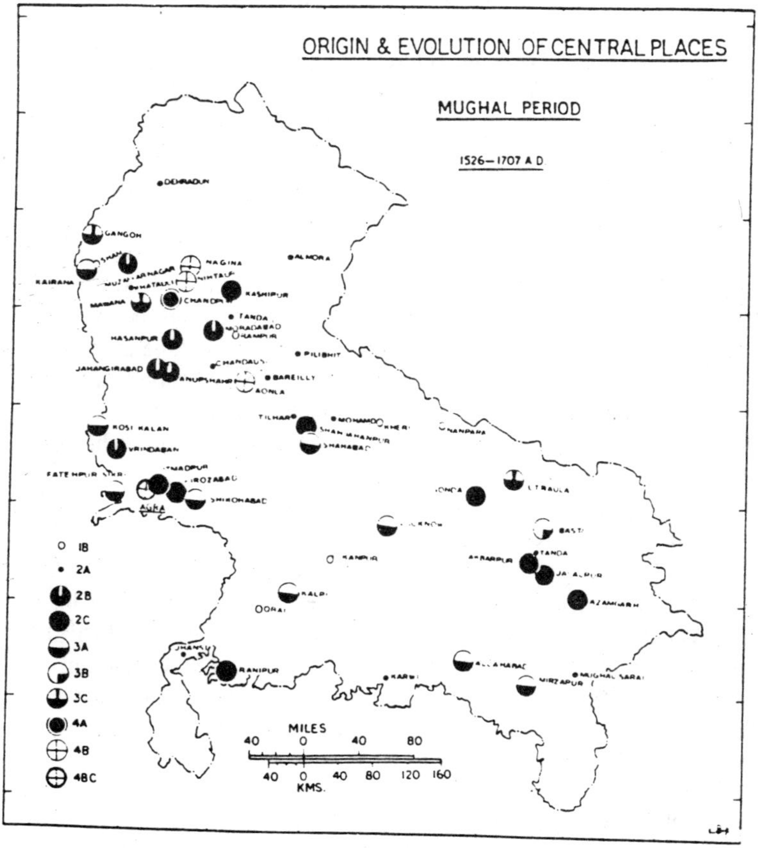

The comparative politico-economic stability of the regime established by the great monarch continued during the reign of his son Jahangir (1605-1627), and also during the time of his grandson Shahjahan (1627-1658). Anupshahar, Jahangirabad, Gonda (founded by a Rajput) and certain other small centres were developed in Jahangir's regime. Much more centres were evolved under Shahjahan, viz. Shahjahanpur (named after the emperor), Muzaffarnagar, Bareilly, Kairana,

Khatauli, Sadabad (Mathura), Shahabad and Moradabad (named so after the emperor's son Murad Bakhsh).

With the development of Bareilly and with its selection as the capital of Katehar (Rohilkhand) in 1657 by Makrand Rai, the then governor, the significance of Sambhal decreased very much. With the decay of the Mughal power in the 18th century, the Rohillas were consolidated under Ali Muhammad who made Aonla his capital, and Bareilly, therefore, was neglected, until Hafiz Rahmat Khan succeeded Ali Muhammad in the Rohilkhand, when Bareilly again rose to prominence as he was living alternately, at Pilibhit and Bareilly which, after its cession to the British in 1801, was made the headquarters of a district and of a provincial court.

During the reign of the succeeding Mughal emperor Aurangzeb (1658-1707), only a few towns could be established and developed, and some of the existing centres suffered seriously, as he was intolerant in his policies and he devoted about half of his time in the task of campaigning in Deccan. Azamgarh is the most important town founded in his regime by Azam Khan (named also after him) about 1665 A.D. Mohamdi (Kheri) and Aurangabad (Bulandshahr) are among other centres developed during his rule.

Z_1: Pre-British Transitional Period (1707-1801)

Owing to highly disturbed conditions and the existence of various local regional authorities, most of the towns founded or developed in this period owe to the rulers and Nawabs of the individual States and only a few to the Mughal rulers. Ghaziabad was founded in 1740 by Wazir Ghazi-ud-din and was formerly known after him as 'Ghazi-ud-dinnagar'. Tanda (Faizabad) was much more developed. Thakurdwara in Moradabad was also developed under the Mughals.

The origin of Faizabad as a settlement was due to Sadaat Khan, the first Nawab Wazir (1732-1739) of Oudh, who built here a *bangla* (shooting box) and initiated the construction of Dil Kusha palace, which could not be completed till his death in 1739. Abul Mansur Khan or Safdar Jang (1739-1754) the next successor, founded the city of Faizabad and made it his military headquarters and residence. His son Shuja-ud-daula (1754-1775) shifted his capital from Ayodhya or Avadh to the new city of Faizabad, which flourished under him as a city of 'unparalleled prosperity and rivalled Delhi in magnificence'. The now dismantled fort was built by him. The glory of Faizabad began to decay with accession of his son Asaf-ud-daula in 1775, as he at once shifted the capital of his province to Lucknow, which under him then entered into a new era and began to enjoy the status of a city. "During his reign, very great extensions were made: all the central parts of the city were built and 52 villages are said to have been taken up"[7]. The famous Imambara is his creation. He also constructed a bridge over the Gomati to connect the capital with Faizabad and Sitapur. Other rulers did comparatively much less for Lucknow. Some of the important places founded by the Oudh rulers are Nawabganj (Bara Banki), Shahganj (Jaunpur), Kakrala and Bilsi in Badaun and Nawabganj in Gonda (Fig. 17.4).

Bangash Nawabs (1713-1801) of the central Doab (extending from Aligarh to Fatehpur) developed certain very important towns. The most important of these centres is Farrukhabad, which was founded in 1714 by Nawab Muhammad Khan, the founder of the territory of the Bangash rulers. He made it the capital of his territory. Other important towns which they founded are Kaimganj, Kamalganj (Farrukhabad), Kasganj, Dundwaraganj and Aliganj (Etah).

The important centres which were developed by the Rohillas (1720-1774) are Pilibhit, Chandausi, Najibabad and Afzalgarh (Bijnor). The Bundels (1680-1791) built certain forts in their times, but no large centre was, however, founded by them. The Marathas could also hardly found any important town. Jhansi rose to be a large town under them. The walled town of Jhansi is said to have its origin in about 1553 A.D., when on the Bangra hill some huts were built by two 'Ahirs', Birsa and Asole, to watch their herds. A fort was built on this hill by Bir Singh Deo of Orchha in 1613 A. D., and gradually it began to grow. Its importance suddenly increased, when the Marathas appeared here (about 1742), and it grew as one of the most important towns of Bundelkhand under them.

Kanpur, the largest city of the State, had its origin in this very period. It was existing as an unimportant village without any antiquity upto the time of the first British annexation in U. P., when this village named 'Kanhpur' or 'Kanhaiyapur' was selected as the site of a trading factory by the East India Company. Mainly for the protection of European traders and trading houses, the place was selected in 1778 as military cantonment for Oudh local forces, which were previously stationed near Bilgram in Hardoi. Since then, the place began to experience a continuous rapid growth. Its size, including the cantonment, in 1847 is estimated to be 1,08,796.

FIG. 17.4:

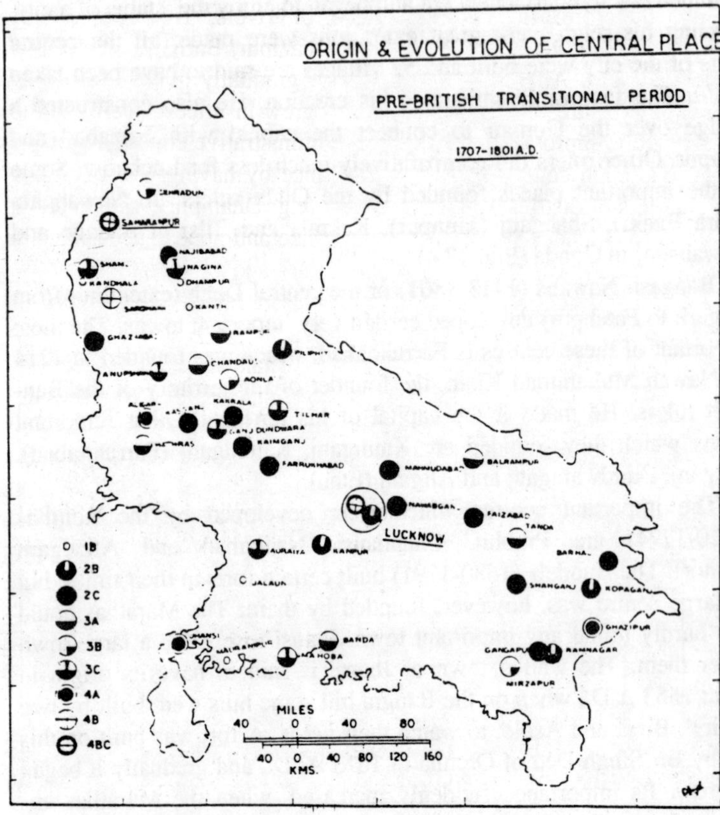

Z_2: Early British Period (1801-1858)

By this time also, there were no metalled roads except in the city areas, and most of the few roads that existed were not suitable and secure for communication and trade. There were only two bridges on a large river in the State and both of them lay on the Gomati (in Jaunpur and Lucknow). Rivers, therefore, continued to be the main expeditious arteries of trade. The first regular settlement was started after 1833 in the

State, except in Oudh, where it was done between 1860 and 1878 (as it was annexed late, and this is one of the reasons why the Oudh districts have fewer number of centres, mostly small and less developed). Owing, therefore, to the importance of rivers, riverside centres flourished much, viz. Mirzapur, Kalpi, Ghazipur, Barhaj, Farrukhabad etc. (Fig. 17.5). Allahabad began to rise gradually as a flourishing commercial centre. Certain other centres grew in importance owing to the relatively improved economic and administrative conditions of the country. Certain centres rose to significance by having administrative headquarters of district, tahsil or pargana (e.g. Dhampur); while certain others were extended much in their total size and appearance owing to establishment of cantonments (e.g. Meerut) and other administrative departments. Extension of roads also caused rapid development of many centres and revival of certain others.

Mirzapur, which is referred by Tieffen Thaler to be a mart on the Ganga between 1760 and 1770 and which contained an important custom house in 1788, increased rapidly to be the most important trading centre in Upper India in the first half of the 19th century[8] owing principally to its position at the highest point of navigation by large steamers on the Ganga. But its decline began with the opening of the East Indian Railway in 1864 as far as the Yamuna in Allahabad. The importance of the great river route of trade offered by the Ganga declined. Because the trade activities were now controlled more economically and swiftly by the railway, the significance of Mirzapur as a great emporium of trade for cotton, grains and other goods serving Upper India, the Deccan and the east, declined fast.

Ghazipur on the Ganga and Barhaj on the Ghaghara (near the confluence of Rapti with it) were also important commercial centres for their respective regions. Varanasi, however, suffered from heavier import duty and the merchants were, therefore, much more attracted by Mirzapur. Kalpi, along the Yamuna in Jalaun district, flourished as one of the largest commercial marts in Northern India. Konch was also an important trade emporium of Bundelkhand, as it is said to be having 52 banking houses.

The most remarkable developments which took place during the early British period, were those belonging to the northern mountainous region. Immediately after its annexation to the British regime in 1814-16, the British people entered the Himalayan region with a hope to get certain suitable sites to be developed as resort centres, and they got many. Before these events took place, Almora was the only real 'town' in the whole of the Himalayan region, and a huge village was existing at the site of the present Dehra Dun city. Most of the present significant centres of this region came into existence as a result of the British efforts.

FIG. 17.5:

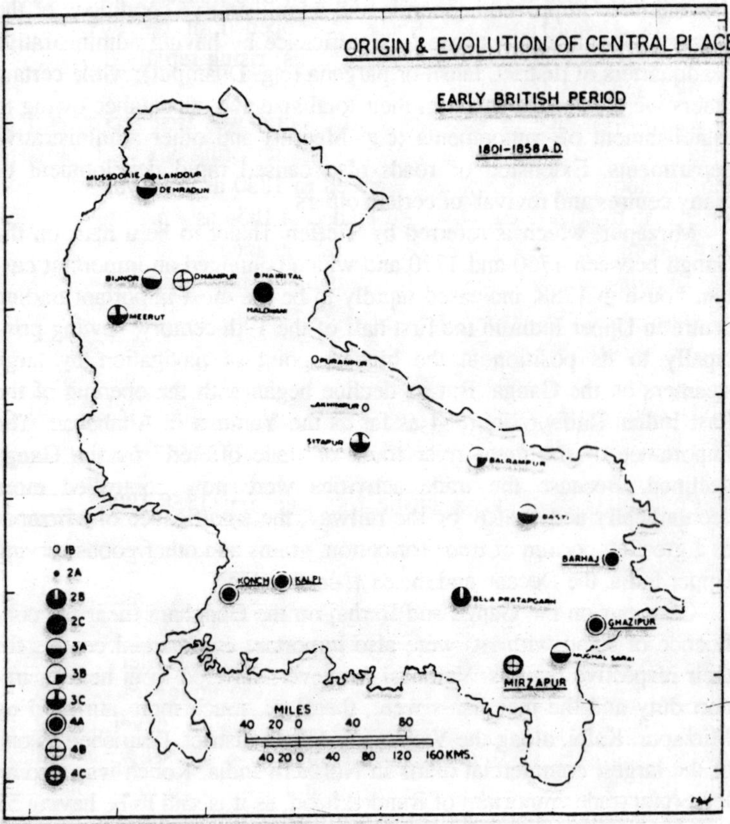

Dehra Dun the largest centre of the Himalayan region, dates from 1699, when Ram Rai, a dissentient Sikh, after his failure to succeed as *Guru*, made this place his residence and attracted many dissenters as his devotees, and soon the place grew in the form of an important town called Gurudwara or 'Dehra'. But the place relapsed into insignificance following frequent incursions by the Sikhs and Gujars. In 1808, when Captain Raper visited the place, he described it as an 'extensive village'. With its formal annexation to Saharanpur district in 1815, certain administrative sections (viz. the revenue and police) were opened here, but its real development began in February 1823, when it was made a district centre and it was developed as a resort town. In 1827, it possessed 2,126 persons living in 518 houses, and by 1900, when the Dehra-Hardwar railway was opened, it contained about 28,000 persons (30,995 in the 1901 census) rising rapidly to 1,56,341 by 1961 and 2,03,464 by 1971.

The importance of the site of Mussoorie was first recognised in 1823, when the first house in the form of a shooting box was stationed here. Landour (or Landhaur) originated in 1830 as a convalescent site for British troops. Haldwani was founded in 1834 as a mart to serve the surrounding local population of the sub-montane region. Naini Tal lake was first discovered in 1841, and realising the importance of the site in the surroundings of the lake, a resort town was installed.

The great revolution of 1857-58 against the British regime caused serious setbacks to the existing centres, particularly those which were directly involved as battle places, as some of the places which might have functioned as strongholds for the rebels were destroyed.

Z_3: Post-Revolution Period of the 19th Century (1858-1901)

The second half of the preceding century has contributed certainly much more towards the development and extension of centres than any other single century. (1) The fast construction of many metalled and unmetalled roads in and out of the towns immediately after the revolution, (2) establishment of civil lines and other administrative, educational and other types of institutions for healthy development of towns–mostly by 1870, and (3) development of the railways – these three factors are peculiar to this period and have acted in a composite way to increase rapidly the sizes of a majority of towns. On the contrary, only a few towns have seen stagnant or decaying owing principally to their functional momentum being lost. Riverside trade centres, for example, were adversely affected by the advent of the railways (Fig. 17.6).

FIG. 17.6:

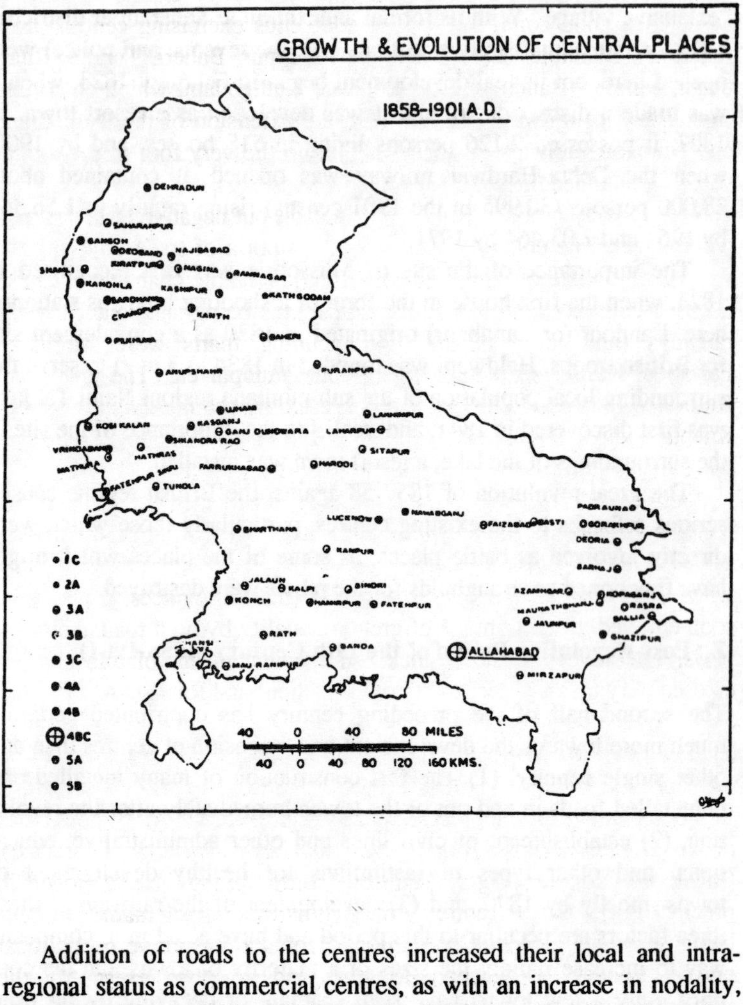

Addition of roads to the centres increased their local and intra-regional status as commercial centres, as with an increase in nodality, the relative accessibility of the centres for the surrounding dependent population also increased; while the introduction of the railways, in addition to strengthening and enhancing the town-country relations, also brought in the extension of far influencing inter-regional relations of trade and transport. Centres which also began to act as railway stations or important railway junctions, experienced remarkable growth.

It was owing to the effect of the railways that some of the rural settlements and railway stations grew rapidly into towns and some of them attracted a good commercial population thus exercising central place functions. Examples include Deoria, Puranpur, Baheri, Tundla, Bharthana, Naraini (Banda), (Fig. 17.6), and Kathgodam, which came into existence as a railway terminus with the extension of the Rohilkhand and Kumaon Railway (now N. E. R.) upto the very foot of the mountains. It contained, in 1901, only 375 persons.

The railway produced another important but negative effect on certain centres. The erstwhile flourishing emporia of trade enjoying the special advantage of being located along navigable channels began to decay owing to significance of river routes being supplanted by the railways (and the roads). Such declining marts were Mirzapur, Faizabad, Kalpi, Farrukhabad, Ghazipur, Jaunpur etc. The growth of Kalpi and Farrukhabad was further arrested by the rapid emergence of Kanpur, whose size increased from 1,13,601 in 1865 to 2,02,797 in 1901.

The growth of Allahabad is remarkably interesting. Its size increased very fast from 72,093 in 1853 to 1,05,926 in 1865 and to 1,72,032 in 1901. Its significance began to increase just after 1858, when it was made capital of the North Western Provinces. It also very soon enjoyed the advantage of greater nodality by both roads and railways. The advent of these quick and efficient means of transport increased very much the centrality of Gorakhpur and Rasra (4A) also.

Z_4: The Present Century (1901-)

In the beginning of the present century, there were in the State 7 cities above 1,00,000 population, viz. Lucknow, Benares (Varanasi), Cawnpore (Kanpur), Agra, Allahabad, Bareilly and Meerut (given in order of rank). Larger centres grew by this time owing mainly to their being seats of religious activities and of administrative or political power. Varanasi, Allahabad, Mathura and Ayodhya exemplify the former, while Agra, Lucknow, Faizabad and Jaunpur were developed under patronage of the great rulers. Very few centres, however, seem to have thriven purely on account of their trade activities. Certain towns like Kanpur, Agra, Hathras and Mirzapur flourished also owing to their industrial bases.

Factors of the politico-administrative impetus, the nodality of transport routes and the functional bases continued to control the growth and development of central places in the present century also. All those centres, where the old industries declined, or where small scale cottage industries could not cope with the modern factory industries introduced in some of the centres in the present century, and where no other important function was added to the morphological landscape of the centre, began to decay. Centres formerly established as religious places but which caught no new economic base of industry or commerce or the administrative bias, could not maintain their growth. On the other hand, all those where their former bases of origin or evolution were not lost and those which got industrial bases owing to private or public enterprises, continued to rise. Riverside markets, where rail facilities could not be extended, lost their former status and stagnated.

The additions of numerous government institutions and services in most of the towns particularly after the Independence provided new forces for their growth. The beginning of the Five Year Plans and the establishment of improvement trusts in certain cities also enhanced directly or indirectly the growth of centres. Earlier part of this period (1901-1921) was, however, a period of decline or stagnation for a majority of centres, and this was affected by the general decrease in the total population of the State and also by a decrease and stagnation in the total urban population of the State. This may be owing to constant succession of epidemics, effects of World War I, the conditions of famines owing to the worsened economic conditions and the bad harvests caused by the irregularities in the advent, distribution and return of the monsoon.

Taking the percentage of the population growth from 1901 to 1961 as the base (Population of 1901=100), the sizable central places[9] of the State were divided into 7 categories as shown in Table 17.1.

The total population growth of the State between 1901 and 1961 is 150%, while the urban percentage is 176. All the centres, therefore, lying below 150% were not considered as grown. The mean percentage of central places came to be 219.

Ghazipur (94) is the only centre which has been called a decaying centre. Some of the important stagnating centres are Jalesar (105), Zaidpur (107), Sandila (109), and Vrindaban (111). Those which are extremely overgrown are Deoria (1321), Ghaziabad (625), Firozabad (585), Kathgodam (507) and Dehra Dun (504). Deoria is a unique example which grew from a village into an important town and central place owing to the extension of transport lines, particularly the railways, administrative functions and also owing to absence of any sizeable centre in the region. The growth of Ghaziabad may be attributed to the factors of transport (specially the railways) and industrial development. The industrial base worked as the impetus to the growth of Firozabad. Kathgodam and Dehra Dun grew as regional capitals in the mountainous region, where there was also a natural necessity of such centres to develop. Other important centres which experienced a very high development are Muzaffarnagar (372), Shamli (353), Orai 350 and Ganj Dundwara (350). Kanpur (479) also is a separate example of growth. The main factor of its growth is the industrial base supported by the trade activities, which naturally followed, and also subsequently by its transport nodality and the administrative functions.

TABLE 17.1: Growth of Sizeable Central Places (1901-61) in % (1901=100)

Order of Growth	Name of the Category	% Range assigned	Number of Centres
1.	Decadent Centres	Below 100	1
2.	Stagnant Centres	100-125	10
3.	Maintained Centres	125-150	21
4.	Grown Centres	150-200	41
5.	Much grown Centres	200-300	34
6.	Highly developed Centres	300-500	10
7.	Extremely overgrown Centres	500 and above	5

Growth of Centres in the Post-Independence Period (1947-)

Growth of centres in the post-Independence period can be very well analysed with the help of the census data (1951-71). The mean percentage growth of population of sizeable towns (20,000 and above) during the period from 1951 to 1971 came to be 60.9 while the median value was 59.3. Modinagar (with 43,470 persons in 1971), an industrial town located on the Delhi-Meerut rail route in Meerut district, has grown by 253%, the highest record of the period (and by 79% in 1961-71 decade). Ghaziabad, a bi-functional town of the new Ghaziabad district (specialising in manufacturing and transport), has grown by 192% in the same period, and is now the fastest growing ever-flourishing city of Uttar Pradesh (81% in 1961-71 decade), its present growth rate being exceeded by none of the remaining 21 cities with or above 100,000 persons in 1971. Fatehpur (125% in 1951-71) has also grown extremely, particularly during 1961-71 decade, when its growth percentage was 93. Other highly growing centres are : Haldwani-Kathgodam (108%), Pilkhuwa (108%), Firozabad, Shamli, Gola Gokarannath (each 105), Kashipur (102) and Orai (100). Other significant centres worth mentioning are: Baheri (94), Naini Tal (92), Mainpuri, Auraiya (both 91), Roorkee, Deoria (both 89), Sultanpur, Baraut, Mughal Sarai, Bela Pratapgarh (each 85), Maunath Bhanjan, Etah (both 84), Kanpur (81), Muzaffarnagar (79), Varanasi[10] Aligarh (both 78), Sardhana (76), and Lakhimpur (75). Rudrapur, located in Naini Tal district, became a town for the first time in 1961 with 9662 persons; and it grew in size so rapidly by 1971 (161%) that it has surpassed the growth percentage of all towns of the State.

The slow growing centres of the last decade (61-71) include Balrampur (14%), Mathura (12%) and Chandausi (10%). Three towns have been found to be growing very slowly all the time since the very beginning of the present century – Kannauj, Tilhar and Mirzapur. Mirzapur, a separate and unique growth example, has grown in the pre-Independence period by 51%, in the post-Independence period by 22%, and in the latest decade merely by 6% (when the mean growth percentage or all sizeable towns was 29.8).

A model has been prepared to show the influence of prominent factors upon origin and evolution of towns in various historic periods (Fig. 17.7). A time-scale has also been inserted in the model. It is very clear from the model that starting from pre-historic sites and settlements, towns have grown first as administrative strongholds and religious-cultural centres in the ancient period; administrative origins and growths have dominated the medieval scene; while transport specially the railways, manufacturing and planned development efforts have shaped the destiny of towns in modern times.

FIG. 17.7:

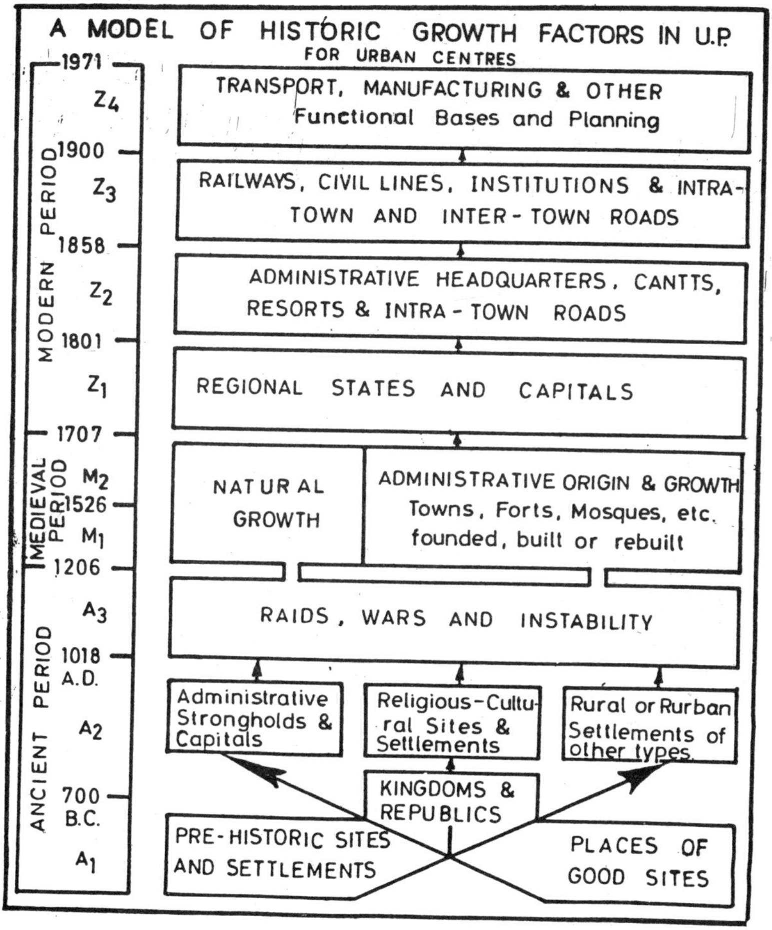

REFERENCES

1. Smith, V. A., The Oxford History of India, 1919, p. 43.
2. Ahmad, Enayat, *Origin and Evolution of the Towns of Uttar Pradesh*, Geographical Outlook, Vol. 1, No. 1, 1956, pp. 38-58.
3. District Gazetteer, Farrukhabad, (1911), p. 120

4. District Gazetteer, Jaunpur, 1908, p. 152
5. *Ibid.*, p. 238
6. District Gazetteer, Agra, 1905, p. 191.
7. District Gazetteer, Lucknow, 1904, p. 148.
8. Singh, O.P., *Growth of Population in Sizable Towns of Uttar Pradesh*, Geographical Outlook, Vol. XI, 1975-76, pp. 111-126.
9 130 sizable centres have been selected here for specific study, all of them being towns with and over 10,000 persons in 1961. Owing to non-availability of data, 8 centres could not be classified.
10 The population of Varanasi (1971) includes here that of Maruadih and Ramnagar too.

APPENDIX

List of Central Places with their symbols indicating origin and nature of growth

1. Faizabad $Z_1$2C & 4B, $Z_3$5B
Ayodhya A_1 1C, M_1 4B.
Tanda M_2 2A, Z_1 3A
Jalalpur M_2 2C.
Akbarpur M_2 2C.

2. Sultanpur A_1 1B, A_2 3B, M_1 3A.

3. Bela Pratapgarh Z_2 2B.

4. Allahabad M_2 2B & 3AC, Z_3 4BC.
Prayag A_1 1C.

5. Azamgarh M_2 2C, Z_3 3B.
Maunath Bhanjan M_1 1B, Z_3 3B.
Kopaganj M_1 1B, Z_1 2B & 3A, Z_3 5A.

6. Jaunpur A_2 1B, M_1 2B & 4BC, Z_3 5A.
Shahganj Z_1 2C.

7. Ghazipur M_1 2C, Z_1 4A, Z_2 4A, Z_3 5A, Z_4 5A.

8. Ballia A_2 1A, Z_3 3AB.
Rasra M_1 2A, Z_3 4A.

9. Varanasi (Kashi) A_1 1C.
Mughal Sarai M_2 2A, Z_2 3AB.
Bhadohi A_2 2A.
Gangapur Z_1 2C & 4B.
Ramnagar A_1 1A, Z_1 2B & 4B.

10. Mirzapur M_2 1B & 3A, Z_1 3B, Z_2 4C, Z_3 5B.

11. Deoria Z_3 3A & 4A.
Gaura Barhaj Z_1 2C, Z_2 4A, Z_3 3AB & 4C.
Padrauna A_2 1A, Z_3 1C.

12. Gorakhpur M_1 2C & 3A, Z_3 4A.

13. Basti M_2 1B & 3B, Z_2 3A, Z_3 3B.

14. Gonda M_2 2C.
Balrampur Z_1 3AB, Z_2 3B.
Utraula M_1 2A, M_2 2B & 3C.

15. Jalaun Z_1 1B, Z_3 5B.
Orai M_2 1B.
Konch Z_2 4A, Z_3, 5A.
Kalpi A_2 4A, M_2 3A & 4A, Z_2 4A, Z_3 5B.

16. Hamirpur A_3 2A.
Mahoba A_1 1B, A_2 4A, Z_1 3C.
Rath A_2 2A, M_1 2B, Z_3 5B.

17. Banda A_1 1B, Z_1 3AB, Z_3 5B.
Chitrakut Dham A_1 1A.
Karwi M_2 2A.

18. Jhansi M_2 2A & 3AC, Z_1 4AB, Z_3 3B.
Lalitpur A_2 2A.
Mau Ranipur Z_1 1B, Z_3 5B.
Ranipur M_2 2C.

19. Lucknow A_1 1B, M_2 3AC & 4B, Z_1 2B & 4BC, Z_3 5A.

20. Rai Bareli A_2 2C.

21. Unnao A_2 2A.

22. Bara Banki A_2 2A.
Nawabganj Z_1 2C, Z_3 4B & 3A.
Zaidpur M_1 2C.

23. Kanpur M_2 1B, Z_1 2B & 3AC, Z_3 3B & 4ABC.

24. Fatehpur M_1 2C, Z_3 5A.
Bindki A_2 1B, Z_3 3B.

25. Pilibhit M_2 2A, Z_1 2B & 3A.
Puranpur Z_2 1B, Z_3 3A.

26. Shahjahanpur M_2 2C.
Tilhar M_2 2A, Z_1 3C.

27. Lakhimpur Z_2 1B, Z_3 3ABC.
Kheri M_2 1B.
Gola Gorannath A_2 1B.
Mohamdi M_2 2A.

28. Hardoi A_2 2A, A_3 2B, Z_3 3AC.
Sandila M_1 1B.
Shahabad M_2 3A.

29. Sitapur A_1 1A, M_1 2A, Z_2 3C, Z_3 3B.
Laharpur M_1 2C, Z_3 5A.
Biswan M_1 2A & 4B.
Mahmudabad Z_1 2C.

30. Bahraich A_2 1B.
Nanpara M_2 1B & 3C.

31. Aligarh (or 'Koil') A_2 1B, A_3 3A, M_1 3B, Z_1 3C & 4A.
Hathras Z_1 3A, Z_3 3B.
Sikandra Rao M_1 2C, Z_3 5A.

32. Agra M_1 2B, M_2 4BC.
Firozabad M_2 2C.
Tundla Z_3 3A.
Fatehpur Sikri M_1 1B, M_2 3A, Z_3 5B.
Itmadpur M_2 2C.

33. Mathura A_1 1C, Z_3 5A.
Vrindaban A_1 1A, M_2 2B & 3A, Z_3 5A.
Kosi Kalan A_1 1A, M_2 3A, Z_3 5B.

34. Etah M_1 2C & 4B.
Kasganj Z_1 2C & 3A, Z_3 3B.
Soron A_1 1A, A_2 1B.
Jalesar M_1 2C & 4B.
Ganj Dundwara A_3 1B, Z_1 3C, Z_3 5B.
Marehra M_1 2C.

35. Mainpuri A_1 1B, M_1 3A.
Shikohabad M_2 3A.

36. Farrukhabad Z_1 2C & 4AB, Z_3 5B.
Kannauj A_1 1C, A_2 4BC.
Kaimganj Z_1 2C.
Chhibramau M_1 2A & 4B.

37. Etawah A_2 1B.
Auraiya M_1 2C, Z_1 3C.
Bharthana Z_3 3AB.

38. Saharanpur M_1 2B & 4A, Z_1 4BC, Z_3 3B.
Hardwar A_1 1B.
Roorkee A_2 2A.
Deoband A_1 1A, M_1 3A, Z_3 5A.
Gangoh A_2 1B, M_2 3C, Z_3 5A.
Manglaur A_2 2A.

39. Muzaffarnagar M_2 2B & 3A.
Kairana M_2 3A.
Shamli M_2 1B, Z_1 3C, Z_2 5B.
Khatauli M_2 2A.
Kandhla Z_1 1B, Z_3 5A.

40. Meerut A_1 1B, A_2 1C, A_3 3C, Z_2 3BC.
Ghaziabad Z_1 2C.
Hapur A_2 2C.
Baraut A_2 2A.
Mawana A_1 1B, M_2 3C.
Sardhana A_2 2A, Z_1 3B & 4B, Z_3 5A.
Pilkhuwa Z_3 1C.

41. Bulandshahr (or 'Baran') A_2 1B, 3A & 4B.
Khurja M_1 2C.
Sikandrabad M_1 2C.
Debai A_3 2B.
Sikarpur M_1 2C.
Jahangirabad M_1 2B.
Gulaothi A_2 2A.
Anupshahr M_2 2B, Z_1 3C, Z_3 5B.

42. Bijnor A_2 1B, Z_2 3ABC.
Najibabad Z_1 2C, Z_3 5A.
Nagina M_1 2A, M_2 4B, Z_1 4A & 3C, Z_3 5A.
Chandpur M_1 1B & 4A, Z_3 5A.
Kiratpur M_1 2C, Z_3 3B.

Dhampur Z_1 1B, Z_2 3B & 4B.
Nihtaur M_1 1B, M_2 4B.

43. Moradabad (or 'Chaupal') A_2 3A & 4B, M_1 3BC, M_2 2B.
Amroha A_1 1B, A_3 2B.
Sambhal A_1 1C, M_1 4BC.
Chandausi M_2 2A, Z_1 3A & 4A.
Hasanpur M_2 2B.
Kanth Z_1 1B

44. Rampur M_2 1B, Z_1 3A.
Tanda M_2 2A.

45. Bareilly M_2 2A & 4AB.
Baheri Z_3 3AB.
Aonla M_1 2A & 4B, M_2 4B, Z_1 3B & 4AB.

46. Badaun A_2 1B, A_3 2B, M_1 4B,
Ujhani A_2 2A.
Kakrala Z_1 2C.

47. Almora M_2 2A.

48. Nainital Z_2 2A.
Haldwani Z_2 2C.
Kathgodam Z_3 2A, Z_4 3A.
Kashipur M_2 2C, Z_3 5A.
Ramnagar Z_3 1C.

49. Dehra Dun $M_2$2A, Z_1 3B, Z_2 3AC & 4A, Z_3 3C.
Rishikesh A_1 1A.
Mussoorie Z_2 2A.
Landaur Z_2 2A.

EIGHTEEN

B.G. Tamaskar

Ports and Harbours of Shivaji's Kingdom

Introduction

THOUGH there is an ever-growing volume of literature on the history of Shivaji, the geography of his times still remains a neglected aspect of study. A systematic study of harbours and ports of the territory controlled by him has been attempted as a part of the spatial organisation and phenomena of his times.

The initial problem posed by the proposed study concerns itself with the precise definition of areal extent of Shivaji's kingdom. The territorial limits may be fixed on the basis of document No. 78, the *Maratha Itihasachi Sadhane*, Vol. 8 (*Rajwade*), and the *Swarjya Jabta of 1718 A.D.* (*Mawjee, 1903*). The north-south extent of his kingdom ranged between the Tapti River on the north and Bednur on the south, on the west coast with the exception of Bombay, Janjira and the Portuguese possessions. On the East coast, his sway sprawled over the territory in the vicinity of Parto Novo, Nagapatam, Pondicherry and Tanjore.[1] All harbours and ports falling within the above-mentioned territorial extents have been taken into account.

Secondly, the identity of all harbours and ports, directly alluded to in the contemporary Marathi, English, Portuguese, Dutch and French historical documents has been established for plotting their spatial locations on a map (Fig. 18.1). The unidentified ones have been listed in Appendix-I. The depiction of spatial locations of 77 ports, including 16 ports in the Bombay-Port Complex, on the est coast and 5 ports in the Pondicherry region on the East coast has enabled the author to make a systematic and close analysis.

In the present paper an attempt has been made to study the relative significance of maritime activities of Shivaji's time, his maritime policy, locational and regional classification of the ports and harbours, their functional variables, their hierarchical class system and locational spacing.

FIG. 18.1:

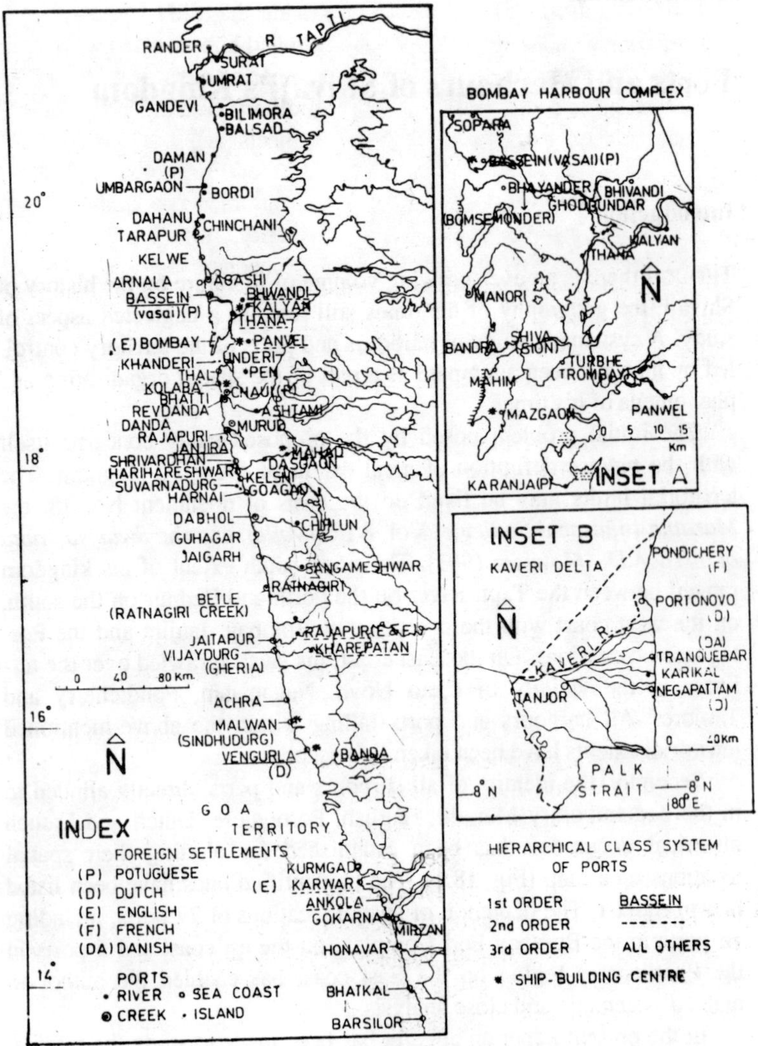

The Relative Significance of Maritime Activities

The Nizamshahi premier, Malik Ambar (1600-1626 A.D.), as a predecessor of Shivaji, had the cognitive preception of the necessity of naval activities. He had made humble beginnings on the West coast and entered into naval rivalry with the contemporary Portuguese, English and Dutch intruders. It is not surprising that Shivaji, as a far-sighted statesman and administrator, had followed him to enlarge naval activities on the West coast. He set up a number of naval bases, (Fig. 18.1). The navy, as a part and parcel of his military system, and a merchant fleet, served to protect his ports, subjects and traders of his kingdom from the high handedness of the European settlers, entrenched on the West coast. They also promoted his kingdom's economic development, growth and prosperity, which ultimately resulted in augmenting revenue of his state exchequer. The port establishments on the sea board, creeks and river-banks comprised new cultural features on the landscape. Shivaji acquired the power "to impose his right of sovereignty over territorial sea and thus claim the wrecks of all ships in his ports".[2]

We may take a note of the significance of a few outstanding ports as follows:

1. *Achara:* was an important coconut trading centre.
2. *Ankola:* (Anchla, Hanabla, Unclelah) was considered to be a place of strength.
3. *Banda* (Bande) on the R. Terekhol, about 9 km south of Vadi (Sawantvadi), was a place of considerable importance in the 16th and early 17th Century. It was the old capital of Sawantvadi State, 32 km upstream the sea.[3]
4. *Bhatkal:* Famous for cheap rice.
5. *Bassein:* Under the Portuguese control was a ship-building port.
6. *Bhivandi* (Islamabad): was a textile manufacturing centre[4] specialising in bleached cottons, *sele* and turbans. It was a supply centre for wood needed for the construction of navigational vessels. It had a route linkage with Aurangabad.
7. *Chaul* (Murtzabad): "This city, or citadel rather, is built circular, the whole being encompassed with 9 bastions, some after the old manner of 1/2 moons but angular,... and are said to be very good... it hath been furnished with buildings but now 2/3 parts thereof are ruinous and the rest hardly two families in a street ....

it is not less suited for commerce, as it is watered by two rivers which – facilitate trafficking in merchandise. The merchants of this place are very rich and live in opulence there were ..... many weavers with the most curious merchandise".[5] Chaul was extremely prosperous and famous for its imports, horse traffic, silk weaving, wood carving and lacquer work.[6]

8. *Dabhol* : situated on the river Vasishti was a seat for trade in salt.
9. *Guhagar* : was supplier of coconuts.[7]
10. *Kolaba* : had Shivaji's shipbuilding and repairing yards.
11. *Janjira* : is an island fortess, which was the stronghold of the Nizamshahi naval armada during Malik Ambar's regime. As the bay of Rajpuri is nearly 23 km in length with sufficient width, it had become a safe refuge for the naval armada of the Siddis of Janjira. The immediate proximity of the island is hilly, forest-clad and swampy, to render the movements of men and animals by no means easy.[8] The impregnable stronghold held out its own during the life-long struggle of Shivaji. The port dealt in wood, salt and several sorts of cloth.
12. *Kalyan* : not unlike Bhivandi, close by it, was an industrial centre concentrating on the manufacture of textile. It had a profuse supply of timber for the construction of navigational vessels and was one of Shivaji's centres for ship-building. It was the home of great merchants.[9]
13. *Karwar* : yielded the biggest and weightiest pepper. The proximity of the port had coconut plantations.
14. *Kharepatan* : was reckoned to be the best port of the Bijapur Kingdom.[10]
15. *Kelshi* : was considered to be of exceeding and indispensable necessity for the trade of Bombay.
16. *Mahad* : was made as an emporium of the vicinal coast and a naval base for ship-building industry.[11] Within an easy distance from Mahad, Raigarh could obtain supplies of war-materials, as the former had been linked with sea ports.[12]
17. *Malwan* : with its shipbuilding and repairing yards,[13] was the principal port of Shivaji.[14]
18. *Nagothana* : had a supply of wood, corn and other commodities.[15]
19. *Panvel* : was a mart for salt,[16] as well as was equipped with ship-building and repairing yards.[17]
20. *Pen* : on the Bhogavati creek, about 16 km from its mouth has a strategic location[18] and had been a notable mart for salt.[19]

21. *Rajapur* : was a livestock market for the sale of buffaloes and cows. Lead, copper and cloth were also available to consumers. It was a wealthy emporium with merchandise of Arabia, Persia, Egypt, Africa, China and Europe, etc.
22. *Shrivardhan* : seems to be an occasional shelter for Shivaji's navy, with a strong castle, defending a deep bay.[20]
23. *Thana* : "was the chiefest, nearest and the best pass", near the island and port of Bombay. The Portuguese collected excessive duties on goods through Thana to Bombay, which were an eyesore and hindrance to all trade, indeed, wholly destructive to Bombay . . ."[21].
24. *Vengurla* : traded in cinnamon and cotton yarns,[22] and had been one of Shivaji's centres for ship-building and repairs.[23]

A close scrutiny of the map brings out that the string of ports ranged on the sea board paralleled the inner ports on the stream-banks.

The Bombay-Port Complex is of equally absorbing interests to both geographers and historians. It appears to bear the imprint of spatial interactions of maritime activities from times immemorial. Viewed in this perspective, one can easily recall to one's mind the ancient and celebrated port of Sopataka (Sopara) on the northern part of the Port Complex.

The seven Deccan lava islets, which are now united to form Bombay Island, were held by the Portuguese, who made little use of them, though the local officials had been quite aware of their value and put every obstacle in the way of their cession as a part of Catharine of Braganza's dowry in 1661.[24]

Though the deep waters off the coasts of the Bombay islets with a promise of outstripping the premier port of India at Surat on the Tapti River, rapidly silted up, it had to encounter the bitter rivalries of the Portuguese, the Dutch and the Siddis of Janjira; insecurity caused by raids of Malabar and other pirates; and not the least, the enlarging sphere of Shivaji's conquests in the Konkan littoral. "... neither the Portuguese nor the Siddy's Fleet, nor Savages, nor any other whatsoever do offer any the least violence from Hunry Cunry (Underi-Khanderi rocky islands off the coast to the S.E.) and Chaul inwards. For otherwise you will utterly discourage all merchants from trading unto or entering into the Porte."[25] The English factors in Bombay adhered to a well-calculated and wise policy of religious tolerance to attract traders and colonisers, particularly, those fleeing from the religious persecution and tyranny of the Portuguese. The Portuguese had correctly forecasted : "India will be lost the same day on which the English nation is settled in Bombay."[26] The port of Bombay by slow degrees stole a march over not only the vicinal Portuguese ports of Bassein, Salsette, Chaul, and Daman but also over the Moghul port at Surat. The shipbuilding activity of Bombay was dependent upon the supply of wood from Kalyan and Bhivandi held under the sway of Shivaji with their linkage through the Portuguese settlement at Thana. Mocha, Persia, Arabia, etc. constituted the forelands of the port. It had been decided consistent with the interests of the English factors to settle their chief Government on their own Island of Bombay.[27] It was deemed to be prudent to build a granary for provisions, and laying in a constant store for times of danger, without which it were impossible for the fort and island ever to be safe.[28] The granary was in a position to supply foodstuffs to Rajapur, Goa and other places.[29]

Shivaji's Policy

Navy had been recognised by Shivaji as an independent organ of the State,[30] The *Agnapatra*, relating to the State Policies, had laid down a few advisory measures regarding the assignments of lands to the European traders as follows:

> "Their individual principals are in the main rulers. How can it be expected that rulers have no ambition about land? However, hatwearers (i.e., the Europeans) have displayed ambitious prestige for entering into this land (country), extending their sway on the ground (under their occupation). Accordingly, *they have succeeded in their activities at several places.* Once some ground has been acquired they will not allow it to slip out from their hands till their last breath. Their public movements should be confined only to their coming and going. They should not be given land every time. They should not be allowed to approach close to Janjira (islands?). If land is allotted for erecting factories, it should not be at mouth of a bay on sea-coast. If they procure land at such a place, so long as they remain within their limits, it is well or else, at their opportune time, they can wield power with the aid of their navy and artillery to erect new fort at that port, procure the resultant cessation of that ground from the State. Hence, the land should be allotted to them at a distance from the bay. In principle, one or two villages such as

> assigned to the French at Rajapur, or in two or more big towns, grounds may be set apart to them. Moreover, it should be on the periphery of the town in a lowland site. They should be immune from troubles of the town at the site of the factory. They should not be permitted to construct substantial/massive houses. So long as they behave in this manner, it is well and good or the action, otherwise, cannot be wise. Their entry and exit may not be interrupted; they should not come our way and this is all."[31]

While evaluating the statement of policy of Shivaji towards the control over harbours and ports, it has been already admitted explicitly that the Europeans could not be fully restrained from their irredentist activities. The empirical evidence reveals that the sites at Bassein, Majgaon, Thana, Vengurla and others had passed into their possessions. It must be fully appreciated that Shivaji had been able to maintain friendly relations with the European powers for the defence of his navy and merchant-shipping, for the protection of his coast, for encouraging trade, and for obtaining war-materials.[32] The English settlement at Bombay, being in its infancy, could not successfully resist Shivaji's onslaughts on it, but he had realised the importance of every European nation which was carrying on commerce with India. He occasionally threatened the English, but actually did not harass them, though they had been offering refuge to Siddis' fleet. Only at the end of 1679 he occupied Khanderi, and successfully kept it in possession against the combined fleets of the English and the Siddi.[33]

In other words, the focus on the orientation and extension of political and economic activities towards littoral regions found expression with the advent of the European traders on the Indian sea-coasts. It markedly invited the attention of some Indian rulers, particularly of Shivaji, to the gains and advantages of marine resources and resultant economic activities and prosperity. There had been a powerful realisation of the fact that the mastery of the sea could be in the hands of any political power which possessed the strongest navy[34], and its humble beginning had been already anticipated and made by Malik Ambar in the preceding Nizamshahi Kingdom (1600-1626 A.D.). The remarkable upshot of the institution of navy was equal and successful competition of the Maratha rulers in naval and maritime activities in the Arabian Sea against their determined and avowed European rivals, particularly, the Portuguese strongly entrenched on the western coast of India, claiming to issue to navigation permits, known as *cartaz* to all

Indian navigators. "Right from the beginning of their coming to India the Portuguese regarded themselves lords of the seas".[35] The mastery of the seas was challenged by the Maratha rulers with the result that the concept of pushing coastal boundary seawards into territorial waters could be sensed and began to crystallise into existing pattern, unconsciously and consciously to lay claim on all wrecks in their ports. The increased shipbuilding and commercial activities, fishing, salt-making, and collection of custom duties improved the State finance to a considerable degree on this account.

Locational and Regional Classification

According to spatial locations, the harbours and ports of Shivaji's Kingdom reveal the following typology :

(1) River, (2) Creek, (3) Island, (4) Sea Board and (5) Delta ports. The numbers and names of ports under these categories have been incorporated in Appendix-II.

The Regional Classification of ports may be as follows :

Ports				
(I)	(II)	(III)	(IV)	(V)
North of Bombay.	The Bombay Port Complex.	South of Bombay.	From Goa to Karwar.	South of Karwar.

The above table needs no elaborate comments, as the regional characteristics of harbours, on which port locations are sited have been already alluded to including the Bombay-Port Complex. The Bombay-Port Complex had been and it still outstandingly significant landscape feature, falling in a category of its own, with not a single port but a group of ports on the combined 'islands' and adjacent main land. The islands of Underi-Khanderi and the Janjira in the proximity of Bombay constituted cockpit among Shivaji and his rival powers.

Functional Variables of Ports

A delineation of functional variables of ports is an essential approach to their study. A rigid classification is impossible to attain for a few ports performed only one function. Their multi-functional character is the normal feature and multiplication of functions usually increases as the activity of the port increases. A study of port functions of Shivaji's regime gives an insight into what ports did. The unifunctional ports, restricted to commerce only, numbered 36, giving a percentage of nearly 44 to the total. The functional attributes of ports covered industry, administration, naval base, foreign settlement, and fortification.

Apart from the functional variables listed above the Bombay harbour played the significant role of a temporary refuge port for the Siddi's fleet, wintering in the rainy season to the annoyance of Shivaji and chagrin of the English.

As coast-wise shipping had been of significance, most of the ports fall into what may be designated as coastwise and short sea-voyage ports, except Bombay, Revandanda, Chaul, Janjira and the ports with foreign settlements. A certain number of harbours had outports with their related interior river ports as noted under.

Sr. No.	Outports	Interior River Ports
1.	Bassein	Kalyan and Bhivandi
2.	Revadanda	Chaul
3.	Harihareshwar	Mahad and Dasgaon
4.	Dabhol	Chiplun
5.	Jaigarh	Sangmeshwar
6.	Jaitapur	Rajapur
7.	Vijaydurg	Kharepatan.

It may be noted that fishing did not figure as a significant functional variable during those times, though it was not entirely absent.

The hierarchy of ports has been based on and derived from their functional characteristics. For determining the relative hierarchy, the function/functions performed have been tabulated in Appendix-II and the scores have been totalled in the last column. The following hierarchical order has been recognised and plotted on the Fig. 18.1.

Sr. No.	Order	Range of Score
1.	1st Order	Above 4.
2.	2nd Order	3 - 4
3.	3rd Order	1 - 2.

7 per cent of the ports and harbours belong to the 1st Order, 18.3 per cent to the 2nd Order and 74.7 per cent to the 3rd Order.

Locational Spacing of Ports

The locational spacing of the ports, plotted on the Fig. 18.1, denotes that the coastal ports appear like a string of beads, unevenly spaced. The ports on the West coast, together with those sited on river banks, have been computed to be spaced at an average distance of 46.6 km with the maximum and minimum spacings of 114 and 12 km Table 18.1 shows average spacings of ports in different parts of Shivaji's Kingdom.

TABLE 18.1: Spacing of Ports in Shivaji's Kingdom

Sr. No.	Region	Spacing in km
1.	The West Coast (excluding river ports)	27.1
2.	The Bombay Port Complex	22.4
3.	The East Coast (Kavery Delta)	96.

Table 18.1 clearly shows the closest spacing of ports in the Bombay-Port Complex, followed by that on the West coast. The East coast (Kaveri Delta) ports are much farther apart. This is due to physical differentiations on the two coasts and incentives for increased maritime activities in the Konkan region.

Impediments to Ports

The frequent wars among the political powers and onslaughts on the Moghuls in the Deccan had been responsible for political instability and interruption the growth and development of ports which, even resulted into their marked decline, beyond recovery. The maritime activities were not immune from dangers, risks and losses, as the adjacent seas were infested with pirates.[36]

Conclusion

The ports of the Konkan ranked among contemporary towns with their locations on the coast or on rivers or at or near the heads of navigation.

Most of them, as enumerated above, were centres of trade. The gradual accumulation of silt rendered most of the harbours, on which the ports are located, shallow and unfit for the anchoring of ships. The development of steamship rendered these shallow ports useless. Quick road transport has been an active factor responsible for the ports declining in importance. With the firm hold of the English on the Bombay island, commercial activities tended to concentrate into the port of Bombay. (*Sita*, 1972).

REFERENCES

1. Balkrishna :*Shivaji the Great*. Arya Book Depot, Laxmipuri, Kolhapur. (1939). Avalaskar, S.V., 1944: *Shiva-Charitra-Sahitya*, Vol. 9, Bharat Itihas Samshodhak Mandal, Pune.
2. *Ibid.* 1953: *Shiva-Charitra-Sahitya*, Vol. 10. (Sources of the History of Konkan) Bharat Itihas Samshodhak Mandal, Pune.
3. Balkrishna, 1932: *Shivaji the Great*. D.B. Taraporevala Sons & Co., Kitab Mahal, Hornby Road, Bombay.
   Sen, S.N., *Foreign Biographies of Shivaji*.London, Kegan Paul, French, Trubner & Co. Ltd. (1927).
4. Tamaskar, B.G.: *The Life and Work of Malik Ambar*. M/S. Idrah-i-adabiyat-i, Delhi, 2009 Qasimjan Street, Delhi (1978).
5. Sen, S.N. *op.cit.*
6. Kalle Dinkar Vinayak: *Forts of Maratheshahi* (in Marathi Shivaji Souvenir, Edited by G.S. Serdesai, (Keshav Bhikaji Dhawale, Girgaum, Bombay.
7. Joshi, S.N. (Ed.) : *Siva-Kalin-Patra-Sar-Sangrah.* Part III Bharat Itihas Samshodhak Mandal, Pune. (1937).
8. Kelkar N.C. and Apte D.V. (Ed.) : *Siva-Kalin-Patra-Sar-Sangarah.* Part-I & II, Shiva-Charitra Karyalaya, Pune (1930).
9. Mawjee, P.V., 1903 : *Shivaji's Sivarajya.* Caxton Printing Works, Bombay.
10. Kelkar, N.C. and Apte D.V.: *op.cit*. cited from Tavernier's account of Shivaji.
11. Balkrishna : *Shivaji the Great* B.D. Taraporewala Sons and Co., Kitab Mahal, Bombay. (1932).
12. Balkrishna : *Ibid.*
13. *Ibid.*
14. *Ibid.* Sen : *Administrative System of the Marathas*. Bagchi & Co., Calcutta (1970).
15. Balkrishna, *op. cit.* (1939).
16. Joshi, S.N., *op. cit.*
17. Balkrishna, *op. cit.* (1939).
18. Balkrishna, *op. cit.* (1932).
19. Joshi, S.N., *op. cit.*
20. Balkrishna, *op. cit.* (1939).
21. *Ibid.* (1932).
22. *Dagh Register*, p. 455, 20th July, 1663, cited by Balkrishna, *Ibid.*
23. Balkrishna. *op. cit.* (1940).
24. Spate, O.H.K. : *India and Pakistan*. Methuen & Co. Ltd., London. (1964).
25. *Original Correspondence* Vol. 36, No. 4115, (28th Sept. 1675).

26. E.F. India, 1661-64, p. 339, The Viceroy of Goa to the Kind of Portugal, (26th Dec., 1664).
27. *Original Correspondence* : Vol. 32, No. 3624, (3rd Feb. 1671/2).
28. *Ibid*, Vol. 37, No. 4258, 22 Jan. 1676/7.
29. *Ibid*, 24 Jan.
30. Subnis Keshao Govind : *Pant Amatya Bawda Dafter*. Vol. I. (1937).
31. *Ibid.*
32. Balkrishna, *op. cit.* (1940).
33. *Ibid.*
34. *Ibid.*
35. Shastry, B.S. : The System of Cartaz. *Journal of Indian History, Vol. LI, Part-II*, Sr. No. 152 (1973).
36. *Original Correspondences, op. cit.*

APPENDIX I

Unidentified Ports and Harbours

Sl. No.	Name	Reference(s)	Remarks, if any
1.	Mochimbo (Monchumbo, Monchimbo.)	Balkrishna: Shivaji the Great, I-427 & II-324-25., F.R.Bombay, Vol. 8, p. 26, dated 20 July,1678.	Sion and Mochimbo occur jointly.
2.	Bomesemoender	Balkrishna: Shivaji the Great, I-533-34.	
3.	Morttuges (Martherges.)	F.R. Surat, Vol. 88, Fol. 122, dated 30 April, 1674.	
4.	Betle	Sen, S.N. : Foreign Biographies of Shivaji, p. 163.	
5.	Kurmagad	Kale, D.V. *Maratha-shahitil Kille*.(in Serdesai,G.S.: Shivaji Souvenir.)	2 Miles north of Karwar. Partially costructed fort, named Siddhagad by Shivaji.

N.B. : It is not ascertained whether Jiwal, Pabal and other ports in the vicinity of Surat were under Shivaji's unbroken control, after their capture in 1665 (Bal-Krishna : *Shivaji the Great*, I-236 and also included in the *Jabita Swarajya* of the 9th Sept., 1718 A.D.)

APPENDIX II

Spatial Locations

Group of Ports	River Ports	Creek Ports	Island Ports	Sea Board Ports	Delta	Total
1	2	3	4	5	6	7
(A) West Coast.	(1)Randher 2. Gandevi 3. Bilimoria	1.Agashi Bassein Thana	Bhati Chenia *alias* Vijaydurg. Goagad.	The Rest. (29)		61
	4. Balsad	Chaul	Kase *alias* Padamdurg.			
	5. Bhivandi 6. Kalyan	Revadanda Murud	Kurnagad. Suvarnadurg. --------- (6)			
	7. Panvel 8. Pen	Dabhol (6) Ratnagiri --------- (8)				
	9. Ashtami. (8) 10. Dasgaon 11. Mahad 12. Chiplun. 13. Sangmeswar. 14. Satvali 15. Rajapur 16. Kharepatan. 17. Banda. 18. Nagokhan. ----- (18)					
(B) Bombay-Port Complex.		The rest (13)	1.Karanja 2.Khanderi 3.Underi.	—		16
(C) Pondicherry Region 'Karikal'		—	—	—	(The rest (4)	5
Total	19	21	9	29	4	82

APPENDIX III

Functional Variables of Ports

Name of the Port	Comm-erce	Indu-stry	Admini-stration	Naval-base	Fore-ign settl-ement	Forti-ficat-ion	Total
1	2	3	4	5	6	7	8
1. Achara	1	-	-	-	-	-	1
2. Agashi	1	-	-	-	-	-	1
3. Ankola	1	-	1+1	-	-	-	3
4. Arnala	1	-	-	-	-	1	2
5. Ashtami.	1	-	1	-	-	-	2
6. Banda	1	-	1	-	-	1	3
7. Bhati.	1	-	-	-	-	-	1
8. Bhatkal	1	-	-	-	-	-	1
9. Barsilor.	1	-	-	-	-	-	1
10. Balsad	1	-	-	-	-	-	1
11. Bassein	1	-	1	1	1	-	4
12. Bhivandi	1	1	1	1	-	-	4
13. Bilimoria	1	-	-	-	-	-	1
14. Bordi	1	-	-	-	-	-	1
15. Chaul	1	1	1		1	1	5
16. Chinchini	1	-	-	-	-	-	1
17. Chiplun	1	-	1	-	-	-	2
18. Dahanu	1	-	-	-	-	-	1
19. Daman	1	-	-	-	-	.	1
20. Dabhol	1	-	1	-	-	-	2
21. Dasgaon	1	-	-	-	-	-	1
22. Gandevi	1	-	-	-	-	-	1
23. Cheria (Vijaydurg)	1	-	-	-	1	-	2
24. Goagad	1	-	-	-	1	-	2
25. Gokarna	1	-	-	-	-	-	1
26. Guhagar	1	-	-	-	-	-	1
27. Kolaba	1	1	-	-	1	-	3
28. Harihare-shwar.	1	-	-	-	-	-	1
29. Harne	1	-	-	-	-	-	1
30. Honavar	1	-	-	-	-	-	1
31. Janjira	1	-	1	1	1	1	5
32. Kalyan	1	1	2	1	-	-	5
33. Karwar (Kadwad)	1	-	1	-	1	-	3
34. Kase (Padamdurg)	1	-	-	-	-	1	2
35. Jaitapur	1	-	-	-	-	-	1

(Contd.)

1	2	3	4	5	6	7	8
36. Kelshi	1	-	-	-	-	-	1
37. Khare Patan	1	1	1	-	-	1	4
38. Kurmagad	1	-	-	-	-	1	2
39. Mahad	1	1	1	1	-	-	4
40. Mahim Kelwe	1	-	-	-	-	1	2
41. Malwan	1	-	-	-	-	-	1
42. Mirzan	1	-	-	-	-	-	1
43. Murud	1	-	1	-	-	-	2
44. Nagothana	1	-	1	-	-	-	2
45. Panvel	1	1	-	1	-	-	3
46. Pardi	1	-	-	-	-	-	1
47. Pen	1	-	1	-	-	-	2
48. Randher	1	-	-	-	-	-	1
49. Rajapur	1	-	2	-	1	-	4
50. Ratnagiri	1	-	-	-	-	1	2
51. Revadanua	1	-	-	-	-	1	2
52. Satvali	1	-	-	-	-	-	1
53. Sindhudurg	i	-	-	-	1	-	2
54. Sangmeshwar	1	-	-	-	-	-	1
55. Shrivardhan	1	-	1	-	1	-	3
56. Suvrandurg	1	-	-	-	1	-	2
57. Tarapur	1	-	-	-	1	-	2
58. Thana	1	-	-	1	1	1	4
59. Umbargaon	1	-	-	-	1	-	2
60. Umrat	1	-	-	-	-	-	1
61. Vijaydurg	1	-	-	-	-	1	2
62. Vengurla	1	1	1	-	1	1	5
63. Mahim	1	-	-	-	1	1	3
64. Godbundar	1	-	-	-	-	-	1
65. Karanja	1	-	-	-	1	-	2
66. Shiva (Sion)	1	-	1	-	-	1	3
67. Sopara	1	-	-	-	-	-	1
68. Turbhe (Trombay)	1	-	-	-	-	-	1
69. Bandra	1	-	-	-	1	-	2
70. Bhayander	1	-	-	-	-	-	1
71. Khanderi	1	-	-	-	-	1	2
72. Underi (Jayagad)	1	-	-	-	-	1	2
73. Sashti	1	-	-	-	-	1	2
74. Thel	1	-	-	-	-	-	1
75. Manori	1	-	-	-	-	-	1
76. Majgaon	1	-	1	1	1	1	5
77. Karanja	1	-	-	-	1	1	3
78. Pondicherry	1	-	-	-	1	1	3
79. Karikal	1	-	-	-	-	-	1
80. Tranquebar	1	-	-	-	-	-	1
81. Negapattam	1	-	-	-	-	1	2
82. Porto Novo	1	-	1	-	1	-	3

Bharatajanapada. The Panchavinsa Brahmana refers to the journey of Visvamitra to the *janapada* of the Bharatas.[4] According to Rigveda, the Bharatas crossed the rivers Vipasa and Sutudri and got settled in the region which was called Kurujanapada (region from Kurukhsetra to Hastinapur, 22 miles north-east of Merath on the bank of Ganga).

Besides Bharatvarsha, another name of our country is Hindustan which has been given by the Iranians. The antiquity of this name may be traced atleast to *C.* 5th century B.C. when emperor Darayavausha I was ruling over Iran. The Nakh-i-Rustam and Persepolis inscriptions,, written at least 1200 years before the birth of Islam, refer it as Hindu. This term has been derived from the Vedic word *sindhu.* In old Iranian language *Sa* of Vedic language changes into *ha*, thus the word Sindhu which was used for the people of India by the Iranians came to be called as Hindu. This tradition continued in Persia, China, Turkistan and Afghanistan atleast upto the *C.* 10th century of Vikram era. The Paikuli inscriptions of the Sassanian kings invariably use the word Hindu for our country. Further, the Jain work *Nishitha churm* written in 733 Vikrama era, refers to the journey of Jain muni Kalkacharya who visited Parasadesa and invited the ruler of Parsia to visit Hundugada एहि हिन्दुगदेशे वच्चावो . The Chinese continued the Vedic term Sindhu only. They used the word *Sin-tu.*

After this discussion the data about the boundary[5] of Bharatvarsha may be taken. In Bhishmaparva, Sanjaya, while describing Bharatvarsha, gives the following colophon:

अत्रते कीर्तयिष्यामि वर्षं भारत भारतं ।
प्रियमिन्द्रस्य देवस्य मनोर्वैविस्तवस्यच ॥

Bhishmapurva, 9,5. Gorakhpur

At first he describes the mountains, rivers and the janapadas of Bharata. This data gives an idea of the geographical boundary of Bharata. He describes the *Kulaparvatas* and *Varshaparvata.*[6] His Kulaparvatas are Malaya, Sahya, Suktiman, Rikshavan, Vindhya and Pariyatra. After this he describes many unimportant mountains. Then he takes up the names of rivers and the tribes (jana) drinking their water. In this long list there are one hundred-sixty names of the rivers, many of them have not yet been identified. The janapadas enumerated by him are also numerous and produce a vivid account of all the regions of India from north to south and east to west. The Mahabharata refers that Bharatvarsha had mixed population consisting of Aryans, Mlechchhas and the Varnasankaras.

The geographical boundary of India at the time of the completion of the Mahabharata geography may be ascertained on the basis of the rivers and the janapadas described within the limits of Bharata. Taking for example the north-western boundary of Bharata, we find that the geographer has included the rivers which flow out of the limits of undivided India: These rivers are Suvastu, Gawri and Gomal. The river Suvastu has been identified with the river Swat which emerges from the Hindukush mountain and joins the river Kabul. The Suvastu river used to irrigate the janapada of Odra which has been located in Swat or ancient Uddiyana.[7] Mention has been made of Odra in the Bengali version of Valmiki Ramayana, River Gawri has been identified with Panjkora, one of the tributary of Kubha (Kabul) river. The river Kubha (Kabul), mentioned in the Rigveda(5, 53, 9), emerges from Koh-i-baba and passing through Kabul joins the river Indus to the north of Attock. The river Gomati has been identified with Gomal which has been mentioned in the Rigveda also. The river Krumu has been identified with Kurram, one of the tributaries of Indus. All these rivers emerge from Hindukush mountain. The river Panchami which has been identified with the river Panjshir, emerges from the Khawak spurs of Hindukush and joins the river Kubha (Kabul) at Charikar. All these rivers used to flow on the north-western boundary of India.

Besides this, Sanjaya describes those janapadas of North-western region which were included in India. These Janapadas were of the Hunas, Tukharas, Kankas, Sakas, Khashikas, Gandharas and the Kambojas. Taking the Hunas into consideration, it is to be noted that these Hunas were different from those who invaded India during the Gupta period. Dr. Motichandra has identified these Hunas with Hiung-nu who were settled in Mongolia and were responsible for driving the Ta-yiie-chis from their country on the northern foot of Nan-shan Mountain.[8] Next in this series are the Tukharas. In the Sabhaparva, they are mentioned with the Sakas and the Kankas. Sylvain Levi remarks that Indian writers have identified them with the Tocharians.[9] Ptolemy locates Tochari at several places where the Yiie-chi are known to have been on their journey. They may be located here in Sogdiana (Samarkand).[10] The Kankas have been identified with Ka'ng-Kiu - the inhabitants of Sogdiana placed in the company of Sakas and Tukharas. Chang-kien remarks that the Ka'ng-Kiu were under the political influence of the Yue-chi,[11] on the the south and under the Hung-nu on the east. The Sakas have been mentioned in the Mahabharata Sabhaparva in the order as China, Huna, Saka and Odra, the inhabitants of mountanous country (*parvatantara vasinah*). At another place, they are placed with the Tukharas and Kanikas. Herodotus points out that their earlier home was to the east of Caspian and north of Jaxartes, in the Pamirs to the north of Hindukush. During the 3rd and 2nd century B.C. they were settled in Seistan and have been mentioned as Sai in the Chinese annals. According to Chinese sources they had several states, one of their group settled with the Tukharas and has been identified, as Sai-wang. Next the Khashikas have been located near Kashgar in Central Asia. Thus from the above discussion it may be concluded that valleys of the rivers Swat, Kurram, Kabul, Lora, Arghanbad, Kunar, Kokacha and Surkhan etc. were in India. This included a considerable portion of Afghanistan and Chinese Turkistan, The north-eastern boundary of India has not been changed as yet. The Mahabharata describes that the river Lohitya and Kartoya which flow in the north-east[12] formed the north-eastern boundary.

The Adiparva and Sabhaparva mention that the rulers of Simhaladwipa paid tributes to Yudhisthira at the time of the coronation ceremony, but in Bhishmaparva Simhala has not been included in the geographical limits of India. The southern boundary of Bharata was Kanyakumari, the place where goddess Parvati performs her *tapsya* to marry Siva, the lord, residing at mount Kailasa. In Indian tradition Siva performing his *tapsya* on mount Kailasa and Parvati at Kanyakumari have been considered as the symbol of fundamental unity of India.

The northern limit was Meru mountain. The location of Meru is a matter of controversy. Prof. S.M. Ali has identified it with Pamir but on the basis of the data of the Mahabharata it is difficult to agree with him. Meru has to be identified with the mountain from which river Ganga emerges.

Puranas

The Puranas have tried to explain the tradition of the Mahabharata. The Matsyapurana and Markandeyapurana record that Lampaka (modern Laghman), Chulika (Kashgar) and Jaguda were important centres of north-western region. The river Vankshu which flow to the north of Afghanistan formed the political boundary of India since the region of Chandragupta Maurya. There was a regular route which used to pass through the janapadas of Kamboja, Kapisa (Kafiristan), Bamiyan, Balkh and connected China and Europe. The shape of Bharata in the

Puranas has been described as *tiryogyama*. By the time of the compilation of the Puranas China janapada was not included in the geographical boundary of Bharata. The Markandeya and Matsyapuranas have described it as *bahyatodara*, i.e. of the boundary of India. The importance of the Pauranic geography in ascertaining the political limits of India may be recognised from the following sloka:

उत्तरं यत्समुदुस्य दिमोदेशचैव दक्षिणम् ।
वर्ष तद्‌भारतं नाम भारती यत्र सन्तति ॥

Vishnupurana, II, 3, 1.

i.e., "the land north of the ocean and south of the Himalaya is Bharat and its offsprings are Bharati".

Another most important contribution of the Puranas is the conception of Greater India which is purely cultural. Here they have included all the islands of South East-Asia including Malaya, Java, Sumatra, Bali, Andaman and Nicobar islands.[13]

The Puranas commissioned the sentiments of Indians to regard it as their motherland where even the gods crave to take their birth in order to acquire final salvation from the cycle of birth and death.

गायन्ति देवा किलगीतिकानि
धन्यास्तु ते भारतभूमि भागे
स्वर्गापवर्गास्पद् मार्गभूते
भवन्ति भूयः पुरूषाः सुरत्वाद्

Vishnupurana, 2, 3, 24.

Ancient thinkers of India established several *tirthas* in India particularly on the borders, in order to safeguard the boundaries of India. This tradition of the Puranas found vent even in the literature. Kalidasa in Kumarsambhava eulogised the high Himalayas and the seas of India and regarded them equal to gods:

अस्यउत्तरस्यां दिशि देवतात्मा
हिमालयो नाम नागाधिराजः
पूर्वापरो तोयनिधि वगाह्य
स्थिति पृथिव्याम् इव मानदण्डः

Kumarsambhava[14]I, I.

Thus the tradition of ancient Indian geography which was conceived by Sauti, the editor of the third recension of the Mahabharata, continued in India for more than two thousand years. The regions of Afghanistan and Chinese Turkistan and lately Pakistan and Bangla Desh slowly got sliced out due to the rise of Islam, leaving the tradition of the existence of Indian culture in the Persian and Arabic works.*

REFERENCES

1. Important centres of the *rishis* were as follows: In the eastern region of India the *rishis* who got settled were, Kausika, Yavakriti, Gargya, Galava and Kanva. In the South were Svasyatreya, Namuchi, Agastya, Atri, Sumukha and Vimukhi. In Western India there were Naishangu, Kavasha, Dhaumya and Kausheya. In northern India were Vasishtha, Kasyapa, Visvamitra, Gautama, Jamadagni and Bharadvaja. *The Ramayana of Valmiki, Uttarakhanda* 1, 2-5.
2. Earliest name of the science of geography in ancient Indian literature is *bhuvanakosha*, its modern name *bhugol* is still later. The word 'bhugol' for geography has been used in Suryasiddhanta of Varahamihira in *C.* 5th or 6th century A.D.
   मध्येस्वमन्तादण्डस्य भूगोलो व्यम्नि तिष्ठति ।
   विभ्राणः परमाशक्तिं ब्रह्मणोधारणात्मिकाम ॥
   The commentator of Suryasiddhanta identifies both the terms
   भुवनकोष भूवनस्यकोष इव भूगोल ।
   cf. Vachaspatyam, Vol. VI, p. 4679; *Sabdakalpadrum*. Vol. VI, p. 522.
3. भरताद् भारती कीर्तियभेदं भारतं कुलम् ।
   अपरे ये च पूर्वे वै भारती इति विश्रुताः ॥
   Mahabharata, Adiparva, 74, 131, Gorakhpur; 69, 49 B.O.R.I. Poona
4. The *Panchavinsa Brahmana*, 14, 3, 13.
5. The concept of the boundary of the country developed in India many centuries before the Christian era, In Rock Edict No. II Emperor Ashok gives a clear picture of the boundary of his empire as under:
   सर्वत विनितम्हि देवान प्रियसि पियदसिनो राजो एवमपि प्रंचतेसुयथा ।
   चोड़ा पाड़ा सतियुतो कतलयुतो श्रा तनपंजी प्रतियको
   यातराजा धे वापि श्रतियकडस मामयि राजानो
   He calls it as *pratyanta* (Prakrit *prachanta*). In Raghuvamsa Kalidasa has used the word *pratyanta* for the purpose.
6. His Varshaparvatas are Nishadh (Hindukush), Meru (Himalaya), Chaitra and Sringavan. The Varshaparvatas separate two countries.
7. Stein Archaeological tour in Upper Swat and Adjacent hills, pp. 34-35 *Memoirs of the Arch. Survey of India*, No. 42 cf. *Journal Asiatic*, 1915, Jan - Feb. pp. 105-110.
8. Motichandra, *Geographical And Economic Studies in the Mahabharata: Upayanaparva*, Lucknow, (1945), p. 61.
9. Sylvain Levi, *Journal Asiatic*, (1897), I, p.10
10. Motichandra, *op. cit.*, p. 23

---

* After Prof. Suryavanshi submitted this paper he left his mortal coil on Nov. 12, 1989. Our heartfull condolences

11. Hirth, *Journal of the China Branch of the Royal Asiatic Society*, (1886), p.96.
12. लोहित्यां करतायां च वृषसध्वियाम
Bhishmaparva, 9, 35; Gorakhpur;
10, 33, B.O.R.I. Poona.
13. भारतस्यास्य वर्षस्य नव भेदान्निवोधत ।
समुद्रान्तरिता ज्ञेयास्ते त्वगभ्याः परस्परम् ।
दन्द्रद्वीपः कसेरूश्च ताम्रपार्णि गमस्तिमान्
माम द्वीपस्तथा सौम्यो गन्धर्वस्तथ वारूणाः
प्रयन्तु नवमस्तेषां द्वीपः सागर संवृता
Matsyapurana, 114, 7-9; *Vayupurana*, 1, 45, 78-80;
Markandeyapurana 57, 6-7; *Garudapurana* 27, 3-4.
14. The *aparajitaprichchha* has explained the traditions of the Puranas further

त्रिकूट हिमदन्तर्वर्षो भारतः उच्यते
Aparajitaprichchha, 37, 7.

This means that from the Trikuta parvat of Simhaladvipa to Himalaya is Bharatvarsha. To its north is Himalaya and in the south are both the seas. (Bay of Bengal and Arabian sea).

अत्रकूटं हिमायन्तं योनिनैः शत पंचभिः ।
पूर्वापरो तोयनिधि हिमदण्डस्पश्च भारते
-*Aparajitaprichchha*, 38, 19.

PART – VIII

POLITICAL GEOGRAPHY

PART – VIII

POLITICAL GEOGRAPHY

TWENTY

Sudeepta Adhikari

Mountain Boundaries: A Case Study of China-Pakistan Boundary

Introduction

THE term 'boundary' refers to certain well-established limits (the bounds) of a given political unit, and all that which is within the boundary is bound together, that is, it is fastened by an internal bond.[1] They are points of contact of territorial power structures. Boundaries are, therefore, lines of equilibrium owing to their position at any time to the pressures exerted from either side, reflecting the spatial relationship of neighbouring states. The boundaries bind together an area and a people which live under one sovereign government and law and are integrated economically and administratively by means of a state-idea justifying the *raison d' etre* of the state unit. An attempt is made here to analyse the spatial characteristics of mountain boundaries with special reference to the China-Pakistan boundary alignment across "Occupied" Kashmir. Mountain boundaries belong to the morphological group of boundaries or for that matter, they are the significant constituents of "natural boundaries" for they correspond to distinct, as well as conspicuous physical features of the surface of the earth.

The doctrine of natural boundaries seems to be an outcome of the Age of Reason and of Nationalism chafing at old restraints, though natural marks were used for boundaries for millennia before there rose a doctrine about them. When the revolution of 1789 swept away the remnants of French feudalism, the concept of natural boundaries took predominance over historical claims.[2] In ancient period, too, the physical features, particularly, the mountain ranges of conspicuous height including the accessible passes, did perform significant functions of separation as well as contact. In the *Arthasastra*, Kautilya (321-300 B.C.) seemed to have advocated strongly in favour of natural boundaries for strategic purposes.[3] Natural boundaries are seldom straight, they in most cases zigzag continuously. This is specially seen in the older parts of the political world that boundaries follow the natural features.

Methodology

There is no distinct methodology to interpret the spatial characteristics of mountain boundaries but when we analyse the evolution of a particular boundary alignment between two distinct spatial territorial structures, we follow a definite analytical frame. The most pertinent method to study the evolutionary characteristics of new pattern of spatial interactions is that which embraces an approach to cognitive behaviourism. This concerns with the pattern of individual behaviour of the plenipotentiaries who initiate negotiation and finally agree to a settlement.[4] There are two distinct aspects of boundary studies: the position and the character of the boundary which influences the character of of the landscape of which it is a part; and the development of policies of the separated states. The behavioural analysis of the boundary study requires a systematic approach to the problem.[5] It is proposed to make an analysis of the evolution of the China-Pakistan boundary across 'Occupied' Kashmir within the framework of the behavioural approach. The author tries to avoid controversial issues such as those related to the territorial rights, the question of exclusive jurisdiction, and the competency of the contracting parties to arrive at a boundary settlement regarding the alignment. Another significant aspect of the study will be to assess the geographical implications of the collective political decision that have brought about the settlement.

Spatial Characteristics of Mountain Boundaries

Boundaries based upon mountains, are able to perform their separating function more effectively than those marked by other physical features. Mountains usually exert strong barrier effects. It is the scarcity of the people in the mountainous regions rather than the physiographic feature that encourages people to use them as base for their boundary lines.[6] Mountains, specially in the most rugged regions, usually separate cultural groups by virtue of the relative difficulty in crossing them. For centuries they have been thought of as good strategic or military boundaries.[7]

There are four distinct spatial criteria or the possibilities for the definition of mountain boundaries:

- that it runs along the crest of the main range, it may include passes or parts of passes subject to bilateral negotiation and settlement;
- that, it may be along the hydrographic divide;
- that it may be drawn near the foot of the slope;
- that it may be drawn on the basis of the ethnographic structure, and distribution of the sparse population.

Sometimes nations extend their territory beyond their mountain boundaries in an attempt to obtain double protection, a type of territorial extension known as a "glacis". The Russians have a glacis south of the Carpathian Mountains that extends to the Danube plain. The former Austro-Hungarian Empire once had a glacis in Galicia against the Russians.[8]

The boundary that runs along a hydrographic divide is usually preferred. A definite line of watershed carried by a conspicuous mountain ridge, or range, is undoubtedly the most lasting, the most unmistakable and the most efficient as a barrier.[9] A water-divide on the map is usually marked upon without much problem. The geographical coordinates which are of special significance in the process of boundary-making are easily identified on the maps. Where a sharp crest exists and where it coincides with the parting of waters, such a boundary line is of the most stable and satisfactory type.[10]

It is a rare coincidence that the high crest should conform to the hydrographic divide, thus making it difficult for a proper delimitation of the boundary line. There is no conspicuous crest line in the Andes; and the hydrographic divide does not conform with the higher ranges. Glaciation has left a drainage pattern often unrelated to the crests and there are many instances of bifurcation. This peculiar geomorphological condition had created tension between Argentina and Chile, on the precision of a political boundary along the Andes.

However, the final award, approved in 1902 was commemorated by the Christ of the Andes, a huge statue erected where the boundary crosses the summit of the Uspallata.[11] This is the longest mountain based boundary in the world.

Another example of one of the longest mountain based boundaries is that of the Tibeto-Indian boundary which runs along the main crest-cum-watershed alignment. In fact, the whole Sino-Indian boundary is based on the difficult terrain of the Himalayas and the Karakoram ranges, and the lack of coincidence between the crest and the watershed at various places has been one of the reasons for the boundary dispute between the two countries.

It is now a well established and recognised principle of customary international law that when a mountain range separates two countries and there is absence of any boundary treaty or a specific agreement, the boundary then tends to take shape along the crest that divides the major volume of the water flowing into the two countries. Sometimes, it so happens that the mountain crest and the watershed differ in position by tens of miles, particularly when the process of demarcation begins, the difference on the ground finally leads to contradictory definitions and bitter controversies between the states. The hydrographic divide which corresponds with the permanent snowfields, shows minor to wide fluctuation in its areal disposition. The spatial nature of the fluctuation of the snowfields usually occurs when the glaciers either retreat or advance which may also lead to the truncation of the spur causing bifurcation. Glacial retreats, particularly in the tropical regions, usually result in the sporadic spatial growth of the grazing grounds which normally attract the mobile frontier people. The boundary line which runs along such hydrographic divide requires to be adjusted in the background of such natural changes. Such phenomena usually occur in the Karakoram region.

Frequently mountain valleys and high pastures have been slowly included in the economic system of adjacent areas and actual boundary line developed gradually. Such boundary lines do not usually coincide with the crest line. It may be practical to reach high pastures by means of a mountain-crossing pass: or people living on one side may have used, or be entitled to, areas on both sides of the crest; or a common economic way of life may bring together a population living on both sides of the crest line. In mountain ranges which lack sharp, continuous crests, it can be shown that the boundary line is usually a late development, developing from an original frontier zone. The mountain may not even be the primary frontier zone, which may have dense forests.[12]

In some of the cases, boundary lines run along the foothills of the mountains. Before World War I the boundary line between Austria and Italy extended along the northern rim of the eastern plains of northern Italy. It was on the lower slope of the Alps, that the line left the bulk of the range in Austria. This gave Austria a strategic superiority over Italy during the First World War. The boundary line between India and Bhutan run along the low angle slopes of the Siwaliks. Where boundaries are set up in mountain country strategic factors are also important. If such a line is imposed by a more powerful state on another, the former will seek to obtain a location which will secure military advantage irrespective of traditional rights and distribution of peoples. The foothill boundaries seldom act as cultural barriers and they often provide examples of adjustment and reconciliation.

Commenting on the spatial characteristics of the mountain boundaries Spykman[13] argued: "mountains provide a barrier zone in which it is comparatively easy to draw as the boundary the line of the peaks or that of the watershed. These two lines will not necessarily coincide but that divergence will create problem of only minor adjustment. "Such a boundary has an economic as well as strategic justification", for there is always an unmistakable orientation of a population towards a valley which they can see from the mountain crest". But another important fact should not be overlooked, that most of the formidable mountain ranges constitute minute cultural regions rather than cultural divides. A political alignment across the mountain ranges causes disintegration of human societies, thereby creating tension along the political boundary between the states.

China-Pakistan Boundary: A Case Study

Many boundaries are drawn with a view to eliminate a potentially dangerous situation and to secure peace between the flanking states.[14] The China-Pakistan boundary has been drawn in order to maintain the balance of power in South Asia, particularly in the Kashmir region which has immense geostrategic significance because of its "crossroad geographical position" on the threshold of the maritime and the continental spatial political patterns. Lamb[15], and Janaki[16], studied the historical spatial characteristics of the China-Pakistan boundary alignment across occupied Kashmir in the background of the territorial claims of the flanking states. It is essential, and equally necessary, to understand the circumstances leading to the boundary agreement between China and Pakistan particularly when the Kashmir problem had yet to be solved.

The ceasefire of 1949 across Jammu and Kashmir between India and Pakistan left Pakistan with an area of 78215 sq. km. (30200 sq.

miles) under its control. The same year China came under communist rule which by 1951 led to communist domination over Tibet and Sinkiang and flight of Dalai Lama to India. The process of territorial accretion, thus, brought, both China and Pakistan close to each other across Kashmir. The ceasefire line of 1949 seemed to be an implicit recognition for the division of Jammu and Kashmir which Pakistan thought of immediately after the alignment of the truce line. The ceasefire line gradually became a *de facto* superimposed boundary because it resulted from confrontation and is without any confirmity to the cultural landscape. The alignment of the cease fire line of 1949 has greatly affected, rather controlled, the pattern of settlement and also the land-use pattern particularly after the alignment was achieved. The alignment of the ceasefire line, undoubtedly gave Pakistan a control over some 'strategic areas' of Kashmir. Confronted with China along its 'newly aligned boundary' in Kashmir, Pakistan got suspicious about the Chinese intention. Yet in 1959, when the shooting incident at Longju revealed the dangers to India of a Chinese invasion, President Ayub Khan of Pakistan made a bid for joint defence of the Indian subcontinent, but the proposal found no admiration and recognition in India.[17] China, a victim of an "expanding British frontier pilosophy" in the early part of twentieth century, wanted to settle down the vaguely defined Sinkiang-Kashmir boundary". India's rejection of Pakistan s joint defence proposal, followed by Chinese willingness to resettle "the vaguely defined Sinkiang-Kashmir boundary", created condition for the evolution of the China-Pakistan boundary line. It was on October 23, 1959 that Pakistan publicly stated that 483 km. (300 mile) undefined boundary line between Sinkiang and the part of Kashmir under Pakistan control, required to be settled and defined. Pakistan mildly accused China of illegally occupying certain areas of Pakistan.

It is necessary to provide a brief account of the physiography of the region. The greater part of the region is snowcapped with curvo-linear mountain range which have orthogonal structure. The Karakoram Range extending from the Hunza in the northwest to the Shyok in the east for a total distance of more than 400 km., is known as the shining crest of the earth. Almost the entire crest is covered with perpetual snow with a number of giant glaciers crawling slowly down the slope. Some of the glaciers seem to be the largest outside the polar areas. K[2], Mt. Godwin Austen (8611 m), is the highest peak of the Karakoram Range. There are at least half a dozen peaks in the Karakoram region exceeding 7500 m in elevation: Borad Peak (8056 m), Muztagh Tower (7259 m), Gasherbrum I (above 8000 m), Gasherbrum II (8068 m),

Rakaposhi (7788 m), Disteghil Sar (7885 m) and Triver (7788 m). Among the notable glaciers, the Hispar and the Batura glaciers are important. They are 58 to 61 km. long, the former drain into the Indus and the latter discharge through the Hunza. Other important glaciers are the Biafo and the Baltoro glaciers, about 60 km. long which drain into the Shigar, a tributary of the Indus. The Siachen glacier, 72 km. long, discharges into the Nubra. Similarly the Chogolunguva and Rimo glaciers fall into the Shigar and the upper Shyok respectively. The important mountain passes of the Karakoram Range are Hispar Pass (5352 m), Muztagh Pass (5700 m), Sia La, Bilatard, Marpoha (5611 m), and Saser La (5300 m). The Karakoram Range is the main hydrographic divide of the region, separating the basins of the Indus and the Qara Qash and the Yarkand rivers.[18]

Jones[19] (1945) distinguished four stages of boundary evolution - allocation, delimitation, demarcation and administration. Allocation refers to the political decision on the distribution of territory; delimitation involves the selection of possible geographical coordinates for the specific boundary site; demarcation involves the process of marking of the boundary on the ground and administration relates to the provision for supervising the maintenance of the boundary. The evolution of the China-Pakistan boundary undoubtedly followed the four distinct stages of boundary evolution and that gave it a stable character. The first attempt in this regard was made on March 1961 when Pakistan sent a formal note to China which the latter reciprocated after a year and suggested a provisional agreement pending the settlement of the Kashmir dispute. Negotiations for the allocation of the territory formally began on October 12, 1962 and at the end of 1962 and on February 22, 1963 a joint Committee announced complete agreement on the delimitation of the geographical coordinates and the alignment of the boundary. The boundary agreement was signed in Peking on March 2, 1963 and the text was also released in Karachi the same day. It came into force with immediate effect and provided for a joint demarcation commission to conduct a survey of the boundary area on the ground, to fix boundary pillars at jointly agreed points to facilitate the delineation of the boundary line on jointly-prepared maps.[20]

According to the article (2) of the agreement the boundary commences from the northwestern extremity of Pakistan occupied Kashmir at height 5630 m (a peak which is at 74°34′E and 37°03′N) and runs eastward and then southeastward strictly along the main watershed between the tributaries of the Tashkurgan river of the Tarim river system on the one hand and the tributaries of the Hunza river of the Indus river system on the other hand passing through the Kilik Daban, the Minitake Pass, the Kharchanai (reference on Chinese map only), the Mutsjilga Daban (again on Chinese map only) and the Parpik Pass and reaches the Khunjerab Pass. The alignment continues to follow the main watershed till it leaves the main watershed to follow the crest of a spur lying in southeasterly direction which is the hydrographic divide between the Akjilga river on the one hand and the Taghumbash (Oprang) river and the Koliman SU (Oprang Jilga) on the other hand and then runs across the principal thalweg of the Kohiman Su to reach its confluence with the Elechin river.

From the confluence of the aforesaid two rivers, the boundary line ascends the crest of the corresponding spur and runs along it, passing through height of 6520m till it joins the Karakoram range main watershed at a peak which is approximately at 75°57′E longitude and 36°03′ N latitude. The boundary then follows the main Karakoram watershed passing through the east Muztagh Pass, the top of the Chogri Peak(K^2), the top of the Gasherbrum II (8068 m), the Indrakol Pass and the top of the Teram Kankri Pass and reaches its southeastern extremity at the Karakoram Pass (Fig 20.1). Lamb[21] was of the opinion that the 1963 boundary agreement, in fact, formalised the arrangement decided upon in 1927, which in turn represented the state of affairs obtaining since the end of the nineteenth century.

The boundary agreement, thus achieved, gave China a control over 5309 sq. km. (2050 sq. miles) but China agreed to withdraw her frontier forces and administration from 1942 sq. km. (750 square miles). The major post-alignment geographical consequence was the construction of a Sinkiang-Gilgit link road. The Chinese side had completed the construction of the road north of the Mintaka Pass in 1968 and on the Kashmir side the road between Gilgit and Pasu was completed in 1972 and a new jeepable road from Pasu to Mintaka Pass was also constructed. Thus Sinkiang came to be linked with Kashmir which gave China a direct access to Rawalpindi. The Sinkiang-Gilgit road in fact has brought China on the coast of the Arabian sea vis-a-vis the Indian Ocean. The alignment has also placed India in an unfavourable balance of power situation in South Asia.

It is apparent from the above analysis that the process of delimitation across the mountainous region does not involve complication because the geographical co-ordinates usually followed in mapping are prominent on the maps and with ease they are marked upon. Normally, the main watershed and the crest are probable criteria usually followed in the delimitation. Mountain boundaries are the most stable bound

FIG. 20.1:

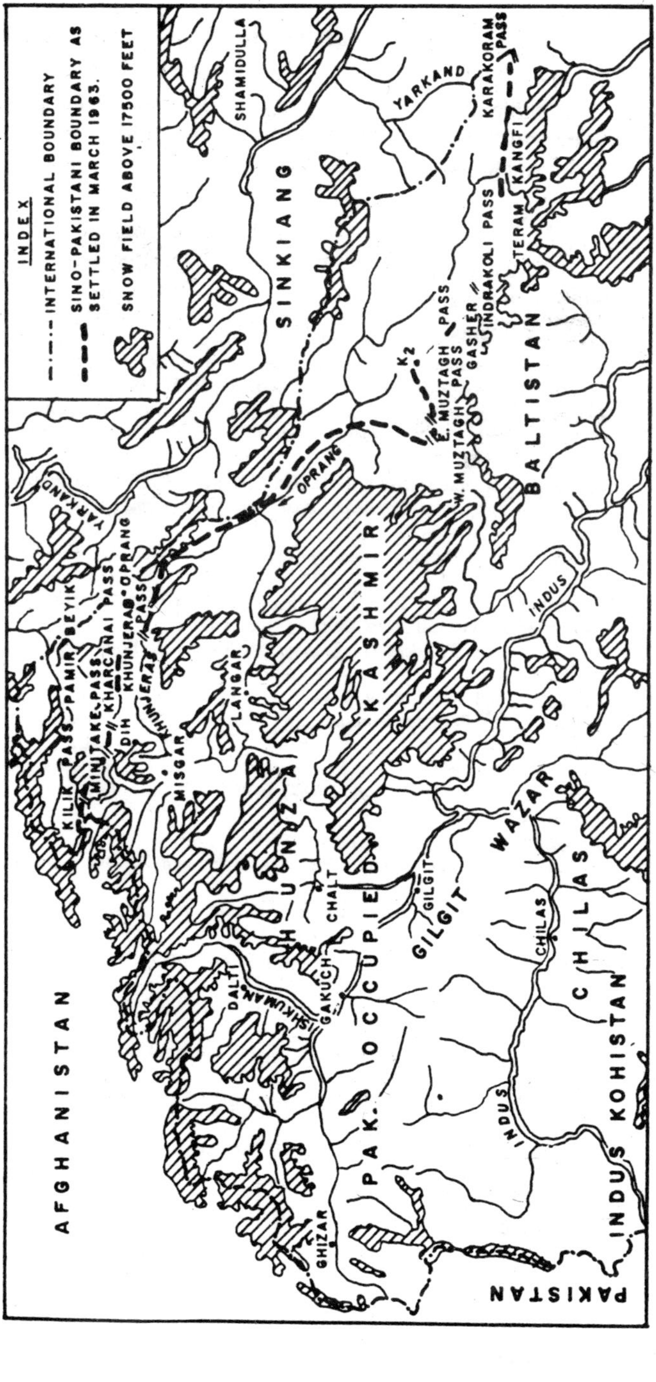

Sketch Map

aries because they show no fluctuation in their normal disposition. However, they possess immense strategic significance. The China-Pakistan boundary which has come out of an agreement, follows the main Karakoram watershed except for the Sokh Bulaq. Will it prove to be one of the stable mountain boundaries in South Asia?

REFERENCES

1. Kristof, L.D.K.: The Nature of Frontiers and Boundaries, *Annals of the Association of American Geographers*, Vol. 49, (1969), pp. 269-282.
2. Jones, S.B.: Boundary Concepts in the Setting of Place and Time, *Annals of the Association of American Geographers*, Vol. 49, (1959), pp.247-251.
3. Adhikari, S.: *Kautilya's Arthasastra: A Politico-Geographical Interpretation*, M.A. Dissertation, (1971), Department of Geography, Patna University, Patna, pp. 102-8.
4. Reynolds, D.R. and McNulty, M.L.: On the Analysis of Political Boundaries on barriers: A Perceptual Approach, *East Lakes Geographers*, Vol. 4, (1968), p. 26.
5. Prescott, J.R.V.: *Political Geography*, Methuen & Co. Ltd., London. (1972), p. 56.
6 Valkenburg, S.V. and Stotz, C.L.: *Elements of Political Geography*, Prentice Hall of India (Pvt.) Ltd., New Delhi. (1963), p. 86.
7. Pounds, N.J.G.: *Political Geography*, McGraw Hill Book Co., New York. (1972), p. 86.
8. Velkenburg and Stotz, *op. cit.* p. 89.
9. Holdich, T.H.: *Political Frontiers and Boundary Making*, Macmillan & Co., London. (1916), p. 146-7.
10. Weigert, W.H. and *et al.*: *Principles of Political Geography*, Appleton-Century-Crofts Inc., New York. (1957), p. 96.
11. Pounds, N.J.G., *op. cit.*, p. 87.
12. Weigert, W.H., and *et al.*; *op. cit.*; pp. 96-97.
13. Spykman, N.J.: "Geographic Objectives in Foreign Policies", *American Pol. Sci. Rev.* No. 33, (1939), pp. 401-2.
14. Prescott, J.R.V.: *The Geography of Frontiers and Boundaries*, Hutchinson University Library, London. (1967), p. 57.
15. Lamb, A.: 'The Sino-Pakistani Boundary Agreement of 2nd March, 1973, *Australian Outlook*, Vol. 18, (1964), No. 13.
16. Janaki, V.A.: *Some Aspects of Political Geography of India*, M.S. University of Baroda Press, Baroda. (1977).
17. Woodman, D.; *Himalayan Frontiers*, Barrie and Rockcliff, London. (1969), p. 30.
18. Singh, R.L. (ed.): *India: A Regional Geography*, National Geographical Society of India, Varanasi. (1971), pp. 355-357.
19. Jones, S.B.: *Boundary Making: A Handbook for Statesman*, Washington. (1945).
20. Woodman, D., *op. cit.*, p. 307.
21. Lamb, A., *op. cit.*

TWENTY-ONE

Ram Nandan P. Sinha

Tribal Boundary Concepts: A Case Study in a Garo Village (India)

THE investigations into the boundary concepts prevalent in tribal cultures have been both inadequate and inconclusive. It has commonly been assumed that primitive societies under their 'tribal' political systems have no concept of linear boundaries, but only of boundary zones or frontiers. As Ratzel put it, "Not lines but the position are the essentials for this concept.[1] Brigham while propounding a system of boundary evolution employed a three-fold division – tribal, transitional and ideal – in which he envisaged the tribal boundaries as primitive, and having a zonal quality, which made them frontiers rather than boundaries.[2] Nicholson also agreed with the ideas of Brigham so far as the tribal stage of the boundary evolution is concerned.[3] Jones while agreeing that "primitive men have primitive ideas about boundaries"[4] cited some exceptions as brought forward by the studies of the tribal societies and their polity by Forde,[5] Lowie,[6] Sharp,[7] Pospisil[8] and Barton[9] which go to prove that some tribal societies under varying environmental conditions have clear cut internal and external boundaries. Jones, however, failed to give any such example from India and he dismissed India in two small paragraphs while reviewing some Asian boundary concepts and practices.

The present paper attempts to investigate into the boundary concepts prevalent among the Garo tribe of India. To test the validity of the prevalent belief among political geographers, a village that may meet a variety of requirements for detailed investigation has been selected for the case study. Its external and internal boundaries have been identified, the significance of elements used to define the boundaries have been interpreted, the nature of power conflict, kinship-territory interaction, legal sanctions etc. have also been investigated to understand the forces responsible for the present boundary. An attempt is also made to see how far the Garo concept of boundary is at variance with those understood by earlier researchers. The necessary policy implications of the study have also been indicated.

Certain assumptions and criteria for choice of a suitable case for study were kept in mind. A village with long history is likely to inherit its concept of boundary from primitive past. Also more than one settlement has the likelihood of some inherited boundary to divide land ownership between settlements inherited by different clans or subclans. The various types of agricultural practices again have the possibility of different types of boundaries to define ownership of land of different utility and value. Local enquiry from responsible village elders was made to collect the necessary information.

Village Darugiri (inset in Fig. 21.1) is in Garo Hill District of Meghalaya State in north-eastern India. The general terrain of Shillong Plateau is hilly with numerous streams draining into the Brahmaputra River, but the village has some lowlands along the river Daru and its tributaries Taling, Sitoli, Dangdik and Mandechiring.

Garo hills (and the village) is inhabited by Garo tribe known for its matrilineal society in which women, not men, inherit the property of the family headed and ruled by the mother. Tribal customary laws prevail over the locally little known Indian Penal Code. A village council composed of responsible village elders enforce discipline through the village customary laws. Modern education and Christianity, the significant signs of modernisation, have not brought about much change into the tribal life style of the villages.

Darugiri is one of the former two hundred and odd independent village kingdoms into which the Garo Hills were divided before the incoming of the colonial administration in the later half of the nineteenth century. These village kingdoms were at perpetual war with their neighbours till the last quarter of the nineteenth century when the colonial government could exercise effective control over the area. Even then, the British Government activities were confined to maintenance of law and order without disturbing or interfering with the tribal customs and life style.

Boundary Evolution

In the process of colonisation of these hills there might have been "no-man's land" between the 'domains' of the different village kingdoms.

Later with the stabilisation of this process and territorial expansion of various village kingdoms the frontier zones might have been reduced to sharp clear cut boundary lines as a result of balancing of forces from either side. No written evidence is available to prove this type of boundary evolution in this tract, but this much is quite known that the village kingdoms were at perpetual war with each other. On this account it may be envisaged that the village boundaries were determined as a result of power conflict and hence were power political in content.

FIG. 21.1:

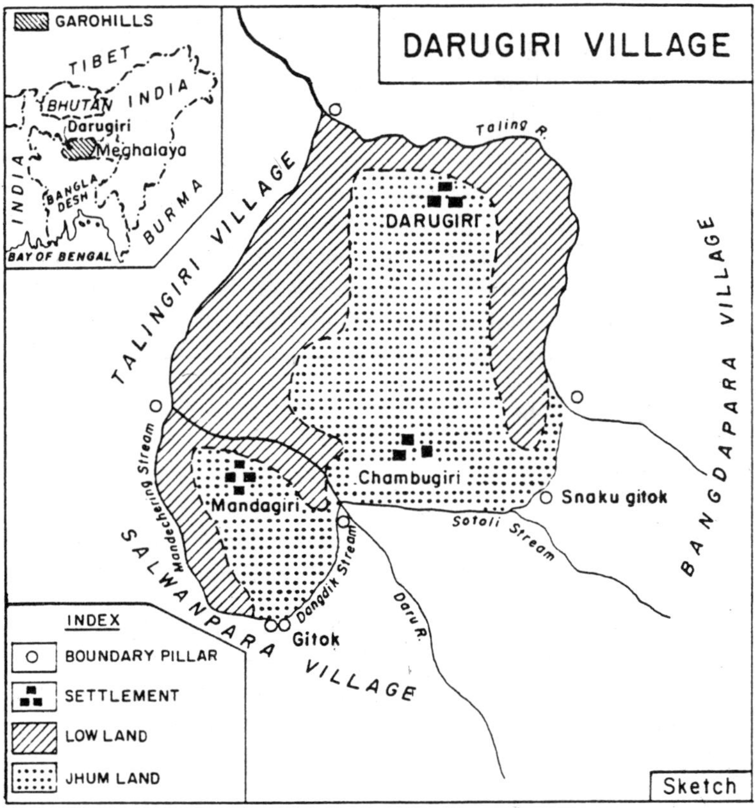

With the introduction of British rule the inter-village warfare came to a close and the boundaries were stabilised. The village boundaries which we now see are almost the same as they existed before the British came. By tracing the boundaries about the villages and enquiring about the ideas of the villagers about them we can come to a conclusion about the boundary concepts and practices of the Garos.

The village elders recall that the present boundary is in existence since the beginning of the present century. They do not know if it has ever changed. The village-elders' ignorance of any change indicates that there may not have been any change in the boundary during at least three generations before the present century (thirty years being considered as a generation's span). Normally, all important events are passed down in stories and anecdotes to the succeeding generations. Any significant change in the boundary should have been remembered in this manner and would have been alive in oral tradition. However, it is logical to believe that the increased pressure of population evident from the satellite growth of Mandagiri and Chambugiri settlements, deep tribal love for land, and warfare between the neighbouring villages must have necessitated clarity in demarcation of inter-village boundaries. This is how the "no-man's land" between the villages might have been reduced, in the distant past, to the present sharp lines. Therefore it is logical to believe that the boundary of Darugiri has gone through the process or evolution from vague "no-man's land" to the present well defined lines.

External Boundary

The external boundary of Darugiri follows all along the lines of natural features, especially the rivers and streams. Taling river separates Darugiri from Talingiri village in the north and east. The river Daru after serving as its western boundary for about two-thirds of the village's western flank, turns south-eastward leaving quite a big chunk of territory across it in the south-west. This north-western portion is bounded by two streams Mandechiring and Dangdik, the tributaries of the Daru, till they almost meet headward near a pass (Gitok, in local language). The south-eastern flank is bounded by another tributary of the Daru, Sitoli, a branch of which bifurcates northward to approach the upper reaches of the Taling river. The point, where the tributary of the Sitoli takes a northward turn, is marked by a col where stands a 'snaku' tree (hence the name of the pass Snaku Gitok). Thus all around the village the boundary follows the Daru river and its tributary streams, and at two places it is marked by passes. This clearly demonstrates the principle of natural boundaries as practiced by the Garos. This tribal principle is worth noting in context of Pound's belief that the doctrine of natural boundaries was a product of the Age of Reason and nationalism in France.[10]

Boundary Markers

Besides the natural boundary features, the villagers adopted or erected some boundary markers as well. Mention has been made of the Snaku Gitok, the pass, at the south-east corner of the village. Two Snaku trees have been planted on either side of boundary, one each by the either village. Similarly, two trees have been placed side by side at the pass between the headwaters of the Dangdik and Mandechiring streams in the south. Adoption of trees as boundary markers has been in vogue in almost whole of north-eastern region of India where forest is an essential constituent of the natural landscape. This is evident from the old copper-plate inscription of the time of the Ahom King, Ratnapal (1016). While describing a boundary along the Brahmaputra river in his kingdom, it says:

"(Its) boundaries (are as follows): on the east, the Calmali trees, on the big dike; on the south-east, the Calmali tree on the steep bank (of the river Brahmaputra)....."[11]

But in case of this village the boundary markers – the trees – are invariably reenforced by a girdle of pieces of rocks or boulders or stone-pillars. Here trees of both sides stand shoulder to shoulder leaving almost no space between them, but sometimes they may stand three to fifteen feet apart thus leaving a forest-covered "no-man's land" between the village boundaries. No cutting of trees is allowed within this zone. The defaulters will have to pay a fine or Rs. 50 to 100. The same fine is imposed for removal of boundary markers.

Besides these tree-cum-stone girdles, there are four stone pillars marking the boundary of the village. Two things are worth noting as regards the placing of these stone pillars. One is that they are placed near the confluence of the streams or where the streams seem to meet headwards; and the other that they are deliberately placed on the other side of the rivers, thus including the whole of the water course within the territorial jurisdiction of this village to the detriment and disadvantage of the village on the other side. The latter feature is an indication of the earlier power political concept put into practice by the inhabitants of this village. The alignment, choice of boundary markers, and placing of these markers are significant from more than one point of view. The villagers have made good use of natural features - rivers, trees, and passes for easy identification of their boundary. At the same time, they have not accepted them as final markers of boundary. The addition of stone-girdle and stone pillars, and interposition of buffer zones suggest that the villagers have taken great care in defining and reinforcing their boundary. This clearly indicates the importance the Garos attach to their boundary. Greater the care in defining (delimitation) and actual placing (demarcation), more specific and sharper will be the boundary. This emphasis on clear demarcation takes the Garo concept of boundary away from the "zonal qualities" of boundary as suggested by Ratzel.

Often three to fifteen feet forest covered no-man's-land between the village boundaries may at first glance suggest that the Garos use zones rather than lines to define their boundaries. But actually they make two parallel lines one for each neighbour to be maintained with individual care allowing the intervening vegetation to grow high and emphasise limits of the territories on either side. This minimises the possibility of border violations, as responsibilities can be easily determined from the cutting or felling on the either side.

Legal Aspect

Such an efficient workable solution is not possible unilaterally. The neighbours must agree to recognise the limits and preserve them with regulations of their own (fine of Rs. 50 to 100). This practice is in keeping with the concept of contractual boundary.

The village boundaries may sometimes change in keeping with the concept of contractual boundary. According to the Garo customary laws the Akhing land belongs to the *nokma* or the headmen by virtue of his being the husband of the head of the clan inhabiting the village (*Akhing*). If a village-clan owes any amount to another or the same clan of a different village and is not able to pay it back, it may instead give a portion of the village land, thus bringing about a change in the original Akhing boundary.

These tribal boundaries are not defined in any document hence they may lack any legal sanction in the modern sense of the term (as Brigham intends), but they are, no doubt, clearly understood according to the Garo Hill District Council regulations and definitely conform to the "Jural law", one of the three types of laws determining the limits of states as defined by Kristof.[12]

The strength of the customary laws flows from kinship-territory interaction. Here in this case kinship and territory, the two major principles of territorial organisation, are cooperative rather than competitive. Darugiri is inhabited by a Sangma clan. The main and the original settlement is inhabited by this clan which owns the Akhing land. But some land was allotted to the Manda people, a sub-clan of the Sangmas, in the trans-Daru region of the *Akhing*, and a new settlement – Mandagiri-was founded. Usually no land ownership is granted to any other clan though they may be allowed to settle and cultivate on an initial payment of some fee to the *nokma.* Thus the kin unit seems to be stronger than the territorial unit as we saw earlier that the territorial bounds may change whereas kin units have no tendency to break.

Internal Boundaries

Darugiri, Chambugiri and Mandagiri are three settlements in the village but there is no internal boundaries separating their territorial jurisdictions. Mandagiri residents do not have private ownership over the land but have the privilege to cultivate and live. Chambugiri is an overspill of Sangma clan from the growing Darugiri, the principal settlement. As such Darugiri and Chambugiri have joint ownership of the village land under the administrative authority of the village head (Nokma) at Darugiri. But sometimes a Garo village (Akhing) may be subdivided into a number of villages, again with distinct linear boundaries along natural features — streams or ridges.

Darugiri has no such internal boundaries. But it has got some boundaries demarcating the subdivisions of agricultural lands. The entire *Jhumland* (area of shifting cultivation) is divided into seven blocks, each block corresponding with one year of seven year jhuming cycle. These Jhum blocks are known as *Arings*. The *Aring* left under forest is known as *Ajiri*; the clearing being cultivated for the first year is known as *Aba* which is parcelled into as many plots as the number of families in the village (Akhing). The clearing being cultivated for the second year is known as *Abreng*. All these plots under the cultivation of each family are distinctly demarcated with the help of tree-stumps, tree-trunks felled in the clearing, clumps of bushes, or such other markings. However, these markings and subdivisions are not permanent. They are identified and recognised for the two-year period of cultivation after which they lose significance, when the land is abandoned for wild growth. When again the same land comes under cultivation in the next Jhum cycle, a new set of plots is demarcated. As such, the families do not get the same plots of land they had in the last cycle though their position in relation to other plots may remain the same. Thus, in demarcation of plots of *Jhum lands*, position is important as it is related to the quality of land. The lesser the gradient, more convenient the land for cultivation. Nevertheless, the boundaries are sharply defined, though they are temporary, valid only for the current Jhum-cycle.

In contrast, the plots under permanent cultivation in the valley bottoms have permanent position of dykes that are also useful in holding water and reducing run-off and consequent soil erosion.

In the vicinity of residences, the homestead lands devoted to kitchen gardening, frequently have bamboo, reed or cane fences to demarcate the property and to protect the greenery from let-loose grazing animals.

Thus the tribal village boundaries in the Garo Hills are well marked by natural as well as man-made features. They have evolved from the former forested "no-man's land" to sharp, clear cut lines demarcated by stone-girdles, trees and stone-pillars. They present evidences of the power political boundary concept in their earlier stages ending with the contractual boundary concept in the recent past.[13]

Policy Implications

As Garos and Darugiri move further into transitional stage towards modernity, the primitive tribal cultural values and practices will be challenged by the new generation. Tribal customary laws will not be acceptable to the youth who will seek justice from civil court under the State government. If the Government is to discharge these duties equitably, there is the need to understand the primitive concepts and practices of its people. The Garo boundary practices raise serious questions for the government. Should they accept the Nokma's ownership of village land and his right to transfer it to repay debts? Can the neighbouring villages be denied the use of the river because in the distant past powerful Darugiri people annexed it within their village boundary? Can the Mandagiri residents be denied the ownership of the land they have been cultivating for generations? The purpose here is not to answer these questions but to raise them to show how knotty and complicated are the traditional practices. Their resolution will need far greater indepth understanding. Social scientists, Jurists, public administrators all need to study the practices of Garos to help them resolve the conflicts inherent in their march towards modernity.

Acknowledgement

The author is indebted to Mr. Shrikant N.P. Sinha, formerly Asstt. Town Planner (Nagaland), presently with the County Planning Organisation, Media, Pennsylvania, U.S.A., for his critical review and valuable suggestions, and to the Indian Council of Social Science Research, New Delhi, for financial support to carry out the field work.

REFERENCES

1. Friedrich Ratzel quoted by Stephen B. Jones in 'Boundary Concepts in the Setting of Place and Time', *Annals. Assn. of American Geog.*, XLIX No. 3 (1959), p.241.
2. A.P. Brigham; "Principles in the delimitation of boundaries", *Geog. Rev. 7*, (1917) pp. 201 - 19.
3. N.L. Nicholson; the Boundaries of Canada, its provinces and territories, *Dept. of Mines and Technical Surveys, Geographical Branch, Memoir 2*, Ottawa, p. 116.
4. *op. cit.* p. 241.
5. C. Daryll Forde; *Habitat, Economy and Society, Geographical Introduction to Ethnology*, (1934) p.145.
6. Robert H.Lowie; *Social Organization*, (1948), p. 139.
7. R. Lauriston Sharp; "People Without Politics", Systems of Political Control and Bureaucracy in Human Societies. *Proceedings, American Ethnological Society*, Seatle, (1958), pp. 3-4.
8. Leopold Pospisil; *Kapauku Papuans and Their Law*, New Haven; Yale University Publications in Anthropology, (1958), No. 54, pp. 96-97.
9. R.P. Barton; *The Kalingas: Their Institutions and Custom Law*, University of Chicago Press, (1949).
10. Cited by Jones *op. cit.*
11. E. A. Gait; *A History of Assam* (1906), p. 368.
12. Ladis D. Kristof, "The Nature of Frontiers and Boundaries", *Annals Assn. American Geographers* XLIX, No. 3 (1969), p. 272.
13. Most of the material for this paper has been collected with the kind help of Shri Noho B. Sangma of Darugiri village. As no maps are available he also drew a sketch map for the village, on which basis the accompanying map has been prepared.

PART – IX

CARTOGRAPHY

TWENTY-TWO

S.P. Das Gupta

Rural Settlement Mapping in India

THE urgent need for evolving a viable national strategy for development of rural settlements is being keenly felt by all planners and social thinkers in India. With the advent of new technologies and under conditions of rapid social and economic changes the traditional patterns of Indian rural settlement are undergoing great metamorphosis. It is, therefore, essential that the quality of life and the existing morphology of some 576,000 villages which give shelter to 502 million rural population (1981) should be properly assessed and understood so as to plan in a better way the social well-being of the country. For proper environmental planning in India, it is of utmost importance to know how our villages are spread over different parts of the country. It goes without saying, for example, that the pattern of infrastructural development in dispersely settled rural areas would have to be vastly different from what should be in areas of more close knit network of villages. The rural development planning strategy would obviously have to be flexible enough in keeping with the distribution pattern of various types of rural settlements. For this purpose the immediate requirement is to correctly identify the different types of rural settlements in India and map them at a sufficiently large scale so as to delineate the broad regional variations in the country.

Such a cartographic effort would help Indian planners to formulate the national planning policy frame for rural development and locate rural growth centres and market centres in an integrated manner with a view to bringing the various services within the reach of each village.

Primarily, the rural settlements in India, as elsewhere in the world, can be broadly classified into two broad types: (i) clustered and (ii) dispersed, depending upon the distribution of the individual dwelling units constituting a village. Despite the high density of population in greater part of the country, there are vast tracts in several regions where rural settlements are of totally dispersed character such as in the coastal plains of Kerala, the higher slopes in the Himalayas, the pioneer fringe of the Sundarbans, and in the remote forest tracts of the Peninsular India. But in greater parts of the Indo-Gangetic plains and rich arable tracts of the coastal and plateau areas, the villages tend to be more of clustered type and lying fairly close to each other. In their layouts, the clustered rural settlements usually assume various types of ground plans depending upon the controlling physical set-up. There are thousands of villages, especially riverine and on coastal plains, which tend to grow in a linear fashion strung along some natural lineaments like a ridge or along cultural straight-edges such as a road or a canal. Often the social conditions and community structure play important roles in the makeup of the village ground plan in many traditional areas where each social group may have a separate hamlet or locality of its own within the territorial format of a village. In many areas such community-based hamlets cluster around a central nuclear core inhabited by the richer or elite groups of the village. The rural settlements planners will have to take all these and various other social patterns of settlements into due consideration for policy framing purposes.

The traditional house-types of Indian villages show a surprisingly great variety, depending upon the climatic diversity and the local sources of construction materials. With introduction of modern technological aids and under changing social circumstances, there is a need to modify the human dwelling styles in rural India with a view to providing safer and better shelters to the villagers. Today under various pressing circumstances, a large number of villages had to be set up in areas where natural environment is harsh or hazardous. The setting and design for human shelters and village layouts in such hazardous areas have to be avoided if possible and planned out properly so as to be in keeping with the prevailing physical environment.

Some of the traditional patterns of rural settlements designed after the principles laid down in the Indian Silpa Shastras may not be in tune with the needs of the day. So far, the problem of rural shelter design and physical settlement planning has not attracted much of attention of our architectural planners and designers. As a result, during the recent past thousands of new rural settlements have come up in such a fashion as to expose themselves to severe environmental hazards, both natural and man-made. For example, durng the 'fifties and sixties', thousands of villages had to be shifted in India from areas submerged by coming up of new reservoirs created by dammed rivers. These villagers had to move upstream or downstream or away from the stream, often facing unfamiliar environment unsuitable for human settlement. The new villages which sprang up around the lower reaches of the Damodar river, for example, are now severely exposed to floods caused by sudden discharge of water released from the upstream reservoirs during heavy rains. Paucity of living space has often driven people to take shelter on unfavourable slopes of upland forest areas liable to landslides, erosion and strong winds such as in the Himalayas, Dandakaranya and coastal areas of India. Many modern innovations, either in agriculture or industry, have resulted in introduction of new chemical compounds, insects, pests and other pollutants which are going into the ecosystem creating instability in the social fabric of Indian rural communities. New planning strategy for rural development and settlement location in the country must have to take stock of the future technological growth pattern into consideration.

The UN Conference on the Human Environment held at Stockholm in 1972 and the follow-up International Habitat Conference held at Vancouver in 1976 emphasized the urgent need for preservation and enhancement of the environment and called upon different nations to give high priority to the planning for human settlements in order to achieve the social well-being in all the countries on the globe. It also emerged therefrom that research should be initiated on several priority areas on such aspects as theories, policies and methods of comprehensive rural settlements and on the environmental socio-economic indicators of the quality of human settlements, particularly in terms of the desirable occupancy standards and residential densities.

In the rapidly changing environment of today, as in India, it is felt that there is an urgent necessity to identify the varied patterns of rural settlements as prevailing in the country so that such an analysis could be useful for social planners. It was, therefore, thought appropriate that the National Atlas and Thematic Mapping Organisation should take up to project for mapping the variegated patterns of the rural settlement in the country. Thus with a view to depicting the distribution of major types of villages on a map, it was found expedient to take a small grid square measuring 5 minutes of latitude and longitude as the basic areal unit for study of patterns of rural settlements. India is covered by some 45,000 grids of this size (75 km² on an average). The existing pattern of the rural settlement and the average spacing between villages falling in each of these 45,000 areal units were determined by study and interpretation of over 8,000 large scale maps (1:50,000). Wherever necessary, air photographs (1:60,000) were consulted and field observations carried out.

For this purpose, rural settlements have been classified into four broad types, namely, (i) compact, (ii) semicompact, (iii) hamleted and (iv) dispersed in accordance with the relative closeness or dispersal of the rural habitations in villages. The clustering type of rural dwellings were first identified at 1:50,000 scale. The information thus obtained for all the 45,000 grids of the country were then plotted on the corresponding appropriate location at scale 1:1,000,000 which was eventually reduced to 1:6,000,000 for final reproduction.

Similarly, spacing of villages has been determined by the total number (n) of villages falling in each grid and striking the average distance (d) from the relation, $d = \sqrt{A/n}$ where A is the area of the grid square and n is the number of villages in each. The spacing parameter has been grouped into six classes, namely: (i) less than 1 km., (ii) 1 to 2 km., (iii) 2 to 3 km., (iv) 3 to 4 km., (v) 4 to 6 km. and (vi) more than 6 km. Thus a map showing the spacing of rural settlements has been prepared at scale 1:6,000,000 on the basis of information plotted for all the 45,000 grids.

Eventually the two aspects, one relating to the patterns of clustering of rural settlements and the other indicating spacing of villages, have been integrated on one larger scale map showing the following 13 types of village clustering patterns at 1:2,000,000 scale:

(i)	Compact villages less than	2 km. apart
(ii)	" " " "	2-4 km. apart
(iii)	" " " "	more than 4 km. apart
(iv)	Semicompact villages less than	2 km. apart
(v)	" " " "	2-4 km. apart
(vi)	" " " "	more than 4 km. apart
(vii)	Hamleted villages less then	2 km. apart
(viii)	" " " "	2-4 km. apart
(ix)	" " " "	more than 4 km. apart
(x)	Dispersed villages less than	2 km. apart
(xi)	" " " "	2-4 km. apart
(xii)	" " " "	more than 4 km. apart
(xiii)	Sparsely settled areas	more than 4 km. apart

These maps show how there has been sporadic clustering of compact villages in the east coastal belt, Deccan plateau upland, north Bihar Plain, plains of Punjab, Haryana, western Uttar Pradesh, Rajasthan and Gujarat. Dispersed villages and sparsely settled areas are widely scattered throughout the country from the Himalayas to the Kerala coastal belt and from western Rajasthan to Arunachal Pradesh. It is also seen that the villages in the Punjab plain, Gangetic plain, Assam valley, Orissa coast, Thanjavur delta, Cauvery basin, Kerala coastal plain and Mysore plateau recur within every two kilometres. There are, in fact, pockets in south Bihar and eastern Uttar Pradesh where villages lie even closer than one kilometre from each other. On an average, as one goes up the Ganga, the distance between villages increases from one kilometre and a half in West Bengal to about two kilometres in Punjab. Conversely, in the Great Himalayas of Ladakh, Himachal Pradesh, Uttar Pradesh, Sikkim and Arunachal Pradesh, the villages are few and far between (6 to 25 km. apart). Similarly, in the deserts of Western Rajasthan, hills of Eastern India, forest belts of the Peninsular India, the villages are usually spaced at a distance of more than 6 kilometres.

Such maps prepared by the National Atlas and Thematic Mapping Organisation now offer a synoptic view of the whole of India and indicate the areas where the attention of planners and social thinkers should have to be focussed for planning for a better rural habitation in the country. The requirement, for example, for connecting road network in sparsely settled rural areas would have to be different from what would be needed in the densely settled areas. Similarly, while planning for new village layout the existing clustering pattern of habitations as brought out on the maps would have to be taken into consideration. These maps, therefore, can be used as effective tools in evolving appropriate strategies for rural settlement planning in different parts of the country.

Research Publications of Prof. (Mrs.) V. A. Janaki

Books

1. *The Geography of Padra Town*, M. S. University of Baroda Press, 1962.
2. *Transport and the Changing Patterns of Population and Land Utilisation in Waghodia Taluka*, M. S. U. of Baroda Press, 1965.
3. *Functional Classification of Towns in Gujarat*, M. S. U. of Baroda Press, 1966.
4. *Some Aspects of the Population Patterns in the Different Functional Groups of Towns in Gujarat*, M. S. U. of Baroda Press, 1967.
5. *Gujarat as the Arabs knew it*, M. S. U. Baroda Press, 1969.
6. *Vanadha-Chalamli : A Study in Rural Dynamics with a note on Ancient Village Patterns*, M. S. U. of Baroda Press, 1970.
7. *Kandla, the North West Gateway of India*, M. S. U. of Baroda Press, 1973.
8. *Some Aspects of the Historical Geography of Surat*, M. S. U. of Baroda Press, 1974.
9. *Some Aspects of the Political Geography of India*, M. S. U. of Baroda Press, 1977.
10. *The Commerce of Cambay from Early Times to the 19th Century*, M. S. Univerisity, 1978
11. *Economic Geography : Factors Influencing the Location of Economic Activity*, Concept Publishing Company, New Delhi. 1985

Papers

1. Geographical basis for the distribution and pattern of Rural Settlements in Kerala., *M. S. University Journal*, Vol. 2, Oct. 1953.
2. Functional Classification of Urban Settlements in Kerala, *M. S. U. Jour.*, Vol. 3, No. 2, 1954.
3. Rainfall Rhythm and Rice Cultivation in Kerala, Abstract; Proceedings of the 44th Session of the Indian Science Congress.
4. Historical Development of Settlements in Kerala, *M. S. U. Jour.*, Vol. 2, 1957.
5. Urban Influence and the changing face of a Gujarat Village, *M S. U. Jour.*, Vol. X, No. 3, 1961.
6. Tributary Area of Baroda, *M. S. U. Jour.*, Vol. X, No. 3, 1962.
7. The Physical features of Bhavnagar Dist., *Dist. Gazetteers of Gujarat*, 1965-66.
8. 27 articles on the Districts, Talukas and Towns of Gujarat and Madhya Pradesh in the *Encyclopaedia Britannica*, London, 1966-67.
9. Physical Features of Jamnagar Dist., *Dist. Gazetteers of Gujarat*, 1966-67.
10. Physical Features of Gujarat; Souvenir Volume, 66th Session of the Indian National Congress, Bhavnagar, 1966.
11. Maps and National Development, *Indian Journal of Geography*, Vol. I, Jan. 1966.
12. The Geography of the Northern Frontier of India, *M. S. U., Faculty of Science Magazine*, 1962-63.
13. Careers for Geographers, *M. S. U., Faculty of Science Magazine*, 1962-63.
14. Political Geography of the Malay Archipelago, *M. S. U., Faculty of Science Magazine*, 1963-64.
15. Indo-China : a study in Political Geography, *M. S. U., Faculty of Science Magazine*, 1964-65.
16. Geography in World Politics, M. S. U., *Faculty of Science Magazine*, 1965-66
17. The Gulf of Aqaba, *M. S. U., Faculty of Science Magazine*, 1966-67.
18. What is wrong with our Education?, *M. S. U., Faculty of Science Magazine*, 1966-67.
19. Crisis in the Middle East, *M. S. U., Faculty of Science*

Magazine, 1967-68

20. Czechoslovakian Puzzle, *M. S. U., Faculty of Science Magazine*, 1968-69.
21. Imperialism - Then and Now., *M. S. U., Faculty of Science Magazine*, 1969-70.
22. Old Theories and New Trends, *M. S. U., Faculty of Science Magazine*, 1970-71.
23. The Agony of Bangla Desh, *M. S. U., Faculty of Science Magazine*, 1971-72.
24. Indian Ocean Politics, *M. S. U., Faculty of Science Magazine*, 1974-75.
25. Sea Power and the Law of the Sea, *M. S. U., Faculty of Science Magazine*, 1975-76.
26. The Geographic Method : A Reappraisal, *M. S. U., Faculty of Science Magazine (Hermanitied)* 1981.
27. Location of the Textile Industry in India and its Trade in the 17th Century with Special Reference to Gujarat, *M. S. U., Faculty of Science Magazine*, 1986.

Ph.D. Guidance

1. Urban Geogrphy of Kapadvanj by J.K. Parmar.
2. Commerce of Broach upto 1815 by B.R. Mishra, 1982.

Index

Accessibility, 166,168
Adhikari, Sudeepta, xxiv, 303
Administrative factors, 152-53
Afghanistan, 297
Age-sex composition, 133-34
Agglomeration, 101, 113
Agricultural economy, 123; productivity, 5, 135
Ahatas, 19
Ahmedabad, conceptual framework, 223; crimes in, 226-27; functional areas, 224-25; muslim population, 228; social attributes of, 223-24
Air-borne dust, 9
Air pollution, 6-7; control, 22-23; geographical analysis, 9
Ajmer, 123
Ajmersharief, 216
Akbar, 257
Akola, 46, 47; zones of road system, 187-94
Alaska, 238
Allahabad, 267
Allied activities, 113
Amravati, 46, 47
Ankara, 66; population distribution of, 66; unplanned city, 74
Ankara Master Plan Bureau (AMPB), 69
Arab/Islamic urban development, 28-29
Aravalli range, 123-25
Argentina, xviii
Arthasastra, 304
Arunachal Pradesh, 329
Aurangabad, 60
Aurangzeb, 260
Ayodhya, 253, 254, 260
Ayub Khan, 308

Bahlol Lodi, 257
Balutedars, 106
Bangladesh, 213, 299
Baroda, Maharaja Sayajirao University, xvii
Berry, B.J.L., 68
Bhakra-Nangal irrigation, 125, 218
Bharatvarsha, geographical boundary of, 293-95
Bhiwandi, 49,58
Bhole, A.S., xxii, 131
Bihar, 329
Bikaner, 124
Bi-weekly vegetable market, 96
Bladen, Welford A., xxi, 27
Bokaro coalfield, xxi, 83, 85
Bombay, 45; industrial urban growth, 50,54
Bombay-Port Complex, 281,284
Boscoff, A., 172
Boundary markers, 317-18; evolution of, 314
Brahmaputra valley, 212, 317
British colonial rule, 66
Brush, John, 65, 74 207
Bucklin, L.P., 164
Budhana, 46, 47

Cadwallader, M., 164
California, xxiii; jadeite possible source of, 243-46
Canada, 242
Canal irrigation, 124
Carpathian mountains, 305
Carthaginian settlement, 27
Cash crops, 113
Central places, growth of, 187, 268-69; functions, 267
Chandragupta Maurya, 297
Channel network, 187

Chatterjee, S.P., 208
China-Pakistan Boundary, xxiv, 303, 307-309
Chotanagpur plateau, 95
Christallar, W., 163
Christian missionary activity, 208
Clark, Colin, 67
Clark, John R., xxi, 65
Clark, W.A.V., 166
Clustered rural settlements, 326
Coal-seel belt, 100
Coast-wise shipping, 285
Colledge, R.G., 166
Conceptual factors, 153-54
Constraints, 109, 164
Consumers, frequency of visit, 176-77; intermarket visit, 178-79; travel patterns, factors of, 163, 169
Convenience shopping centre, 154
Correlation Coefficient, 167
Correlation matrix, 136-39
Crimes, Gategories of, 221-24; spatial pattern, xxiii, 225-26
Critical densities, natural logarithims, 76
Cultural factors, xxiii, 49, 154
Custom duties, 284
Cyrenaica, 28

Dalai Lama, 308
Damodar Valley, 83
Darugiri, external boundary, 316-17
Das Gupta, S.P., xxiv, 325
Datye, V.S., xxii, 105
Davis, Kingsley, 208
Delhi - Agra muslim core areas, 211-215
Delhi Development Authority, 152, 155, 156
Delhi, repid growth of, 155
Density Gradient Model, 67, 73-74
Devgun, Satish, 208, 212, 213
Diddee, Jaymala, xxii, 105
Dolmus, 77
Drinking water, 89
Dual economy, 65
Dutt, Ashok K., xxiii, 207, 208, 212, 213
Dutta, Gauri, 194

East India Company, 261
East Indian Railway, 263
Economic exploitation, 84; factors, 152
Environmental planning, 325; pollution, 6; population, xxi
Escalation, 52
Exploitation, 84, 116

Fagerlund, B.G., 179
Fa Hian, 253, 254
Firoz Shah Tughlak, 256
First World War, 99, 268
Free Market, 74, 77
Forde, C. Daryll, 313

Ganganagar, 124, 126, 127
Ganga water, characteristics of, 4, 10-11, 15
Garbage, characteristics of, 17-18; management of, 23
Garden houses, 78
Garner, B., 157
Garo customary laws, 314, 318
Garo Hill District Council, 319
Gaya, data and methodology, 199-200; industrial composition, 199-200
Geographical factors, 123-29
Ghaziabad, 269, 270
Gosal, Gurdev, 208
Gravity models, 164
Greed belt, 83
Great desert area, 129
Green revolution technology, 80
Groth pole, 188, 190
Guhagar laluka, 138, 139 142
Gujarat, 329
Gunwadi, 106

Hamlet, growth characteristics of, 105, 112-14; repercussion of, 118-19; occupational structure of, 116-17; social morphology, 115-16; trends population diffusion of, 118
Harshavardhana, 254
Haryana, 329
Hastinapur, 295
Hess, C.F., 174
Highway strip services centre, 85
Hill, P., 179

Hilly tehsil categories of, 107-8
Hirt, Howard F., xxii, 151
Hiuen Tsang, 253, 254
Hodder, B.W., 180
Huff, D.L., 164
Hypothesis, 166, 167

Index of diversity, 210
Indian Penal Code, 314
Industrial economy, 204; environment, 226; landscape, 131; pollution, 22; revolution, 96; segregation, 203
Industries, types of, 5
Infrastructural facilities, 132
Inter-hamlet migration, 115
International Habitat Conference, 327
Intra-urban mobility, 157-170

Jadeite, genesis of, 241-43; varieties of, 235-38
Jahangir, 259
Jain, N.G., 187
Jain community, 216
Jaipur, 124
Jaisalmer, 127
Jalgaon, 46, 47
Jamshedpur, 95
Jamuna, 4
Janaki, V.A., xvii, xviii, xix, 307
Janapadas, 296
Japan, 242
Jhuggie-Jhonpree, 155
Jodhpur, 124
Jonassan, C.T., 174
Jones, S.B., 309
Junnar tehsil, 107, 109

Kabar traders, 167, 180
Kang, Darshan S., xxiii, 235
Kanpur, 261; business structure of, 158: environment improving, 22-23; housing problems, 19-20; miseropolis, 3; new industrialization, 5; occupational structure, 171-72; population of, 5-6; solid waste disposal in, 13; water pollution, 9-10
Kanyakumari, 293, 297
Karan, P.P., xxi, 27
Kashmir problem, 304, 307, 308
Kaul, Arun, xxii, 123
Kayastha, S.L., 3
Keles, Rusen, 76
Kirloskar wadi, 106
Kuju urban sprawl, 86-87, 90
Kulkarni, K.M., xxii, 221
Kumar, A., 85
Kumar, Suman, 199
Kumra, V.K., xxi, 3
Kurukshetra, 295

Lakshmanan, T.R., 164
Lamb, A., 307, 310
Land under cultivation, proportion of, 139-40
Landuse degradation, 83
Latham, R.F., 69
Lentz, Peggy A., 69
Libya, city size distribution, 38-39; urbanization and spatial development, 27-28, 30-31
Literacy, 135-36
Lloyed, E.F., 168
Lorenz Curve, 210
Lowie, Robert H., 313
Luni river, 126

Mahabharata, xxiv, 293, 294
Mahalle (neighbourhood), 70-72
Maharana Pratap Singh, 214
Maharashtra, physical and cultural aspects of, 44; rural settlements in, 105; urban population, distribution of, 47-48; urban system of, 43-64
Maharashtra Industrial Development Corporation (MIDC), 62
Majumdar, D.N., 172
Malshe, P.T., xxi, 43
Maria Renee, Cura, xxiii, xix
Maritime activities, 279, 283 ; policy, xxiii
Market, hierarchy of, 169 ; geography, xxii
Mason, Alfred Bishop, 237
Master Plan, 153
Mc Kim, W., 179
Meru mountain, 297

Meso American Jadeits, 236-38, 246-47
Meso-Umland of Bombay, 55
Methodology, 158-59
Middle American cultural artifacts, 235-38
Misallate, Abdalla, xxi, 27
Mlechchhas, 296
Modern industries, triggering growth of, 46
Modern industrial centres, 43, 54
Modern show cases, 65
Mountain boundaries, spatial characteristics of, 304-5
Mukerji, A.B., 208
Multi-functional urban magnet, 45
Multiple trips, 165
Murdie, R.A., 163, 168
Muslim dominated Pakistan, 214
Muslim dominated Western Kashmir, 212

Nagapatnam, 277
Nagpur, 46, 47
National Atlas and Thematic Mapping Organization, 327
National urban system, 43
Natural environment, 21, 326
Naval rivalry, 279
Nephrite, 238, 241
New capital phenomenon, 66
Newling, Bruce E., 69
New Zealand, 238
Nicholson, N.L., 313
Noble, Allen G., xxiii, 207
Noise Control Act, 19
Noise pollution, problems of, 17-19
Non-agricultural occupations, 145-46

Oglewadi, 106
Ottoman Turks, 30
Orient Jadeite hypothesis, 293
Outmigration, xxii, 142-43, impact of, 131-40

Pahl, R.E., 174
Pakistan, 214, 299, 308; muslims predomination, 208
Pakistan occupied Kashmir, 309
Peak Value Intersection (PVI), 72
Periodic market, characteristics of, 157-60, 163-66
Petro-chemical industries, 45
Pillsbury, Richard, 20
Planned obsolescence programme, 83
Planned shopping centres, problem of, 151-52
Polynomical curve, 68
Policy implications, 320
Pondicherry, 278
Pondu water, characteristics of, 13-14
Population density changes, 65
Poona, industrialization in, 107
Ports, functional variables of, 284-85, 291-92; impediments of, 286-287; locational spacing of, 286; regional classifications, 278, 284-85
Portuguese, rivalries of, 281-82
Public sector material supply system, 204
Punjab, 208, 212, 214, 329
Puranas, 297-98

Qara Qash, 309

Rajasthan, 329; canal irrigation, 129; climatic factors, 125; industrial function, 128; population by religion; 214; religious diversity, 208
Ramayana, xxiv, 293, 294
Ramoshi, 106
Ranchi, cultural landscape, 99; evolution of, 95-98; growth urban complex, 97; historical phases, 97-100; multiplying functions, 98; projected urban profile of, 102
Rank-size distribution, 32-33, 38
Rapid urbanization, 66
Ratzel, Friedrich, 313
Ress, Philip H., 69
Regional distribution, 54
Regional development, problem in, 86
Religious diversity pattern, 207-220
Road system, comparative analysis, xxiii, 193-95
Rourkela, 95
Rural areas, physical factors, 107-108; dwellings, 328; environment, 31
Rural settlement, clusters of, 125; con-

centration of, 124, 128; distribution of, 123; types of, 325-26; traditional pattern of, 326; mapping, 325
Rural-urban migration, 19
Rustan, G., 164, 166

Salt lakes, 127
Sawant, S.B., xxii, 131
Scatterisation, 87
Scott, P., 158
Second World War, 65, 99
Segregation, industry measurement of, 201-202
Settlement system, instability of, 56
Sewage water collects, 89
Sex-selective outmigration, 136-37
Shahjahan, 259
Sharma, R.N.P., 95
Sharp, R.L., 313
Shekhawati region, 125
Shivaji, maritime activities, 277-90
Shopping trips, 157, 164-65, 171
Sikandar Lodi, 257
Sikh-dominated Punjab, 207
Sikh refugees, 216
Sikhism, confinement, 208
Singh, D.P., 95
Singh, O.P., xxiii, 251
Singh, U.P., 83
Sinha, Ram Nandan P., 315
Slow growing centres, 270
Slum localities, types of, 19
Social environment, 222
Socio-economic factors, impact of, 110
Soil pollution, 21
Solid waste disposal, 13
South Delhi, planning and retailing in, 151-55
South Konkan, population characteristics of, 131-24, 143-44; urbanization of, 136
Spate, O.H.K., 216
Srivastava, R.C., xxii, 157,158
Stockholm, 327
Strahler, N., 188
Stream order method, 188
Subarbanization, 76
Suryavanshi, Bhagwansingh, xxiii, 293

Tamaskar, B.G., xxiii, 277
Tanjore, 277
Tibeto-Indian Boundary, 306
Temporal synchronization, 175-76
Temporal travel pattern, 159,176
Thar desert, 126
Third Five Year Plan, 100
Tocharians, 296
Topological matrix, 170
Towns, industrial bases of, 268-69
Trajectories, 56
Transportation facilities, 84; network, 131; system, 7
Travel patterns, 158, 163-64
Tribal boundary concepts, 313-20
Tribal customary laws, 320
Tribal political system, 313
Tripoli, 27, 32, 38
Trips, categories, 157
Turkey, industrial growth in, 66, 73

Uddiyana, 296
Ukwa, U.I., 176
Ulhasnagar, 49, 58
U.N. Conference on the Human Environment, 327
Underwood, F.W., 180
Unemployment, 5, 66
Unplanned, population of, 72-73
Uparmal, 124
Urban centres, classwise distribution of, 51
Urban central places, origin and evolution of, 251-52
Urban environment, appraisal of, 3-22
Urban settlements, location of, 124, 128
Urban sprawl, 83-90; characteristics of, 84-86
Urban systems, nature of changes in, 46-49; processes of change, 45-47
Urbanization, balance growth of, 62; values of, 48
Uttar Pradesh, 251, 329; early British period, 262-63; early medieval period, 255-56; Mughal period, 257-58; population growth, 268; post-revolution period, 265-66; pre-British period, 260-61; pre-historic period,

253-64; pre-muslim transitional period, 255

Value system, 172
Variables, 56
Varnasankaras, 296
Village clustring pattern, 328
Vishnupurana, 298
Voncouver, 327

Wadis, growth of, 105, 109
Wagholi, 112
Waste water, 13
Water pollution, 9-10
Webber, M.M., 172
Weekly markets, 85
Wheeler, P.T., 158
Wilkinson, Captain, 96
Wilson, Paul B., xxiii, 235
Winter pollution, 79
Working population, proportion of, 134-35
Wyoming, 238

Yeates, M.H., 69, 157
Yodar, H.S., 241
Yuill, R.S., 175

Zelinsky, Wilbur, 207
Zilla Parishad, 107
Zipfs' rank size rule, xxi, 38
Zoming regulations, 153-54
Zonal qualities, 318
Zuwaylah, 28